PLACE IN RETURN BOX to remove this checkout from your record.
TO AVOID FINES return on or before date due.

DATE DUE	DATE DUE	DATE DUE

Reform of the Taxation of Mergers, Acquisitions, and LBOs

Reform of the Taxation of Mergers, Acquisitions, and LBOs

Samuel C. Thompson, Jr.

CAROLINA
ACADEMIC
PRESS

700 KENT ST.
DURHAM, NC
27701

To my father, Samuel C. Thompson, Sr.
Going strong at 82

ISBN: 0-89089-534-1
Library of Congress Card Number: 92-76163

Carolina Academic Press
700 Kent Street
Durham, North Carolina 27701
919-489-7486   FAX 919-493-5668

Printed in the United States of America

Contents

· ·

Part 3   LBOs and Related Transactions

Table of Cases

· ·

Preface

· ·

This book urges Congress to amend the Internal Revenue Code (the "Code") to rationalize the treatment of taxable and tax-free corporate acquisitions and to adopt a sensible limitation on the use of debt in leveraged buyouts ("LBOs") and related transactions. Thus, this book addresses two of the major policy issues presented by the current structure of the federal income taxation of corporations.

Part 1, which consists of chapters 1 through 3, sets the stage for the policy prescriptions proposed here. Chapter 1 provides an introduction to the substantial literature on this topic, and chapter 2 discusses the current treatment of taxable and tax-free corporate acquisitions, mergers, and LBOs. Chapter 3 presents a background discussion to the policy issues addressed here.

Part 2, which consists of chapters 4 through 9, proposes a rationalization of the general merger and acquisition provisions of the Code. Chapter 4 deals with tax-free acquisitive reorganizations, which are transactions in which an acquiring corporation acquires the stock or assets of a target corporation in exchange for stock of the acquiring corporation. This chapter proposes, *inter alia*, that uniform rules regarding the continuity of interest doctrine be adopted for all forms of acquisitive reorganizations.

Chapters 5 through 7 deal with various aspects of taxable acquisitions, with chapter 5 proposing a carryover basis rule for certain taxable asset acquisitions, chapter 6 proposing an exception to the recognition rule for goodwill in certain taxable acquisitions, and chapter 7 proposing a mandatory Section 338 election in certain stock acquisitions. The adoption of the proposals in these three chapters would provide for neutrality between taxable asset and taxable stock acquisitions.

Chapter 8 proposes rules that would prevent the misallocation of purchase price in both taxable and tax-free corporate acquisitions. Chapter 9, the final chapter in Part 2, illustrates the above rules in the context of several prototype acquisitions. Appendix B contains suggested amendments to the Code needed to effectuate the changes proposed in Part 2.

Part 3, which addresses LBOs and related transactions, consists of chapters 10 through 14. Chapter 10 discusses the treatment of LBOs and other equity conversion transactions under current law, and chapter 11 surveys various proposals dealing with such transactions. Chapter 12, which is the heart of Part 3, proposes a limitation on the deduction for interest in certain LBO and equity conversion transactions involving publicly-held corporations. For the reasons outlined in chapter 12, these interest limitation rules would not apply to acquisitions of closely-held corporations and to acquisitions of divisions and subsidiaries of publicly-held corporations.

The rules proposed in chapter 12 are illustrated in chapter 13 in the context of several prototype LBO and leveraged recapitalization transactions. Chapter 14, the last chapter in Part 3, examines whether the proposals contained in chapter 12 withstand scrutiny under various arguments in favor of a continuation of the present rules regarding the deduction of interest in LBO and other equity conversion transactions. Appendix C contains suggested amendments to the Code needed to effectuate the LBO changes proposed in Part 3.

Part 4 consists of chapters 15 and 16. Chapter 15 examines the impact on the proposals set out in this book of various prototypes for integrating the corporate and personal income taxes recently advanced by both the Treasury Department and the American Law Institute. As is demonstrated in chapter 15, the general merger and acquisition proposals contained in Part 2 are consistent with each of these integration prototypes. Also, the LBO proposals contained in Part 3 are consistent with three of the four integration prototypes addressed by the Treasury and the one prototype proposed by the American Law Institute. The LBO proposals would not be needed, however, under the Treasury's comprehensive business income tax ("CBIT") integration prototype.

Chapter 16 provides concluding remarks and discusses the neutrality of the proposals made here. Appendix A provides in tabular form a demonstration of this neutrality.

Acknowledgments

. . . .

This book is built on over twenty years of experience in studying, teaching, practicing, and writing about the taxation of mergers, acquisitions, and LBOs. Many of my teachers, colleagues, and students have helped enrich my thinking about this topic.

My interest in this topic had its genesis in my days as a student in Professor Bernard Wolfman's course on Corporate Taxation at the University of Pennsylvania Law School in the fall of 1970. There I was first introduced to the *General Utilities* case and to the continuity of interest doctrine, two concepts that are dealt with extensively in this book. I will forever be indebted to Professor Wolfman for igniting my interest in this subject.

My interest was nurtured by my exposure to some of the practical aspects of the taxation of mergers and acquisitions while at Davis Polk & Wardwell in New York City. While there, I also continued to study this topic in the Graduate Tax Program at the NYU Law School, where I took Professor Jim Eustice's course on Corporate Reorganizations.

My interest accelerated in my days as an Assistant Professor at the Northwestern University School of Law, where I taught a heavy dose of corporate tax. This development continued when I served as an Attorney-Advisor in the U.S. Treasury's Office of Tax Policy and had the opportunity to work on a variety of corporate tax issues.

After Treasury, I was fortunate to continue my work in this area as a Professor at the University of Virginia School of Law. There I taught several courses dealing with various aspects of the taxation of mergers and acquisitions, and in 1979, I published a casebook entitled *Federal Income Taxation of Domestic and Foreign Business Transactions*, which deals in part with this topic.

I left Virginia to "practice what I teach" as the partner-in-charge of the Tax Division of the law firm of Schiff Hardin & Waite in Chicago. For nine years my practice principally involved mergers, acquisitions, LBOs, and related transactions. During this time, I also wrote, with three of my partners, a treatise (*Federal Taxation of Business Enterprises*) which has several chapters dealing with mergers, acquisitions, and LBOs. Also, while at Schiff Hardin, I taught a course entitled Tax Aspects of Mergers and Acquisitions as an adjunct professor at the University of Chicago School of Law and the IIT Chicago-Kent College of Law.

To be better able to reflect on policy issues in taxation and to work on projects like this, I left the full-time practice at Schiff Hardin in 1990 and became a Professor of Law at the UCLA School of Law, where I continue to teach Tax Aspects of Mergers and Acquisitions.

Hopefully these varied experiences in studying, teaching, practicing, and writing about this subject have permitted me to present here valuable policy proposals that Congress will enact.

I owe a great deal of debt to Jeffrey Sheffield of Kirkland & Ellis in Chicago for his insightful comments on a prior draft of this book. Diana L. Wollman, a recent graduate of UCLA and one of the finest students I ever had, also read the entire manuscript and gave me many helpful suggestions. I greatly appreciate the comments I received on prior drafts from Bill Klein and Mike Asimow, my tax colleagues here at UCLA School of Law, and from the other members of the Southern California Tax Policy Discussion Group, particularly Ellen Aprill of the Loyola School of Law and Ed McCaffery of the University of Southern California School of Law. Also thanks to Martin Lipton and UCLA Business Professor Fred Weston for their comments.

Chapter 15, which deals with the Treasury's and American Law Institute's recent integration proposals, was prepared shortly after the publication of these studies. I am particularly indebted to the following for their valuable and timely comments on a draft of chapter 15: Anne Alstott, formerly Treasury, Tax Legislative Counsel's Office; Professor Jennifer J. S. Brooks, International Program, Harvard; Professor Daniel I. Halperin, Georgetown Law School; Jeffrey Sheffield; Professor Alvin C. Warren, Jr., Harvard Law School; Diana L. Wollman; and the members of the Southern California Tax Discussion Group.

I received substantial help on this project from my two research assistants, Byron W. Cooper and Daniel Bosis, who will graduate from the UCLA School of Law in May, 1993. Of course, I am fully responsible for any errors and for the views expressed.

My appreciation also goes to Dean Susan Prager of the UCLA School of Law for providing me with the research assistance needed to complete this project. Further, I want to thank those members of the secretarial staff here at UCLA School of Law who were helpful at the various stages of the project, including Margaret Kiever and Jean-Paul Dervaux, and especially Veronica Wilson, who provided invaluable services.

My thanks also goes to Mayapriya Long and the excellent staff at Carolina Academic Press for their helpful and professional assistance in the preparation of this book.

Finally, thanks to my parents, Sam and Emmitt Thompson, for their unswerving love, encouragement, and good judgment.

Samuel C. Thompson, Jr.

Part 1
Introduction
and Current Rules

CHAPTER 1

· · · · · · · · · ·

Introduction

The Debate

The debate over the proper tax treatment of mergers, acquisitions, and leveraged buyouts (LBOs) is unrelenting. For example, a 1938 article opened with the following words: "With federal tax reform the issue of the hour," the "problems" with the merger and acquisition provisions of the Internal Revenue Code "move into sharp focus."[1] The focus continues to be sharp as illustrated in a 1989 study by the American Law Institute (ALI 1989 Study).[2] This study, which builds on a prior report by the ALI (ALI 1982 Study),[3] sets forth comprehensive proposals for dealing with taxable and

---

1. Milton Sandberg, *The Income Tax Subsidy to "Reorganizations,"* 38 Colum. L. Rev. 98 (1938). All references to the Internal Revenue Code [hereinafter cited as "Code" or "I.R.C."] are to the Internal Revenue Code of 1986 or one of its predecessors. All references to Arabic numbered sections (*e.g.*, Section 338) are to sections of the Code, unless otherwise indicated.

2. The American Law Institute, Federal Income Tax Project, Reporter's Study Draft (June 1, 1989) (William D. Andrews Reporter) [hereinafter cited as *"ALI 1989 Study"*]. This study draft does not represent the position of the ALI.

3. The American Law Institute, Federal Income Tax Project, Subchapter C (William D. Andrews Reporter) (1982) [hereinafter cited as *"ALI 1982 Study"*]. Many of the suggestions contained in the ALI 1982 Study, including the suggested repeal of the *General Utilities* doctrine, are reflected in a 1985 report of the staff of the Senate Finance Committee. *See* Staff of the Senate Committee on Finance, 99th Cong., 1st Sess., Report on Subchapter C Revision Act of 1985 (Comm. Print 1985) [hereinafter cited as "1985 SFC Proposals"]. These proposals are discussed briefly in chapter 3, p. 47. For a description and critique of these 1985 proposals *see* Samuel C. Thompson, Jr. *Suggested Alternative Approach to the Senate Finance Committee Staff's 1985 Proposals for Revising the Merger and Acquisition Provisions*, 5 Va. Tax. Rev. 599 (1986) [hereinafter cited as "Thompson, *Suggested Alternative Approach*"]. For an argument that the proposals contained in this 1985 report (and

tax-free acquisitions of C corporations,[4] LBOs involving C corporations, and redemptions of stock by C corporations.

In the past Congress has listened to the ALI. For example, in the Tax Equity and Fiscal Responsibility Act of 1982,[5] Congress followed a suggestion made in the ALI 1982 Study and enacted Section 338. This section, which permits the elective step-up in the basis of a target's assets after a stock acquisition, replaced former Section 334(b)(2), which provided a basis step-up after a stock acquisition only if the target was liquidated.

Thus, under Section 338 an acquiring corporation that purchases at least 80 percent of the stock of a target corporation may elect to treat the stock acquisition as if the transaction were an asset acquisition. As a consequence of the election, the target is treated as if it had sold and immediately repurchased its assets. The target, therefore, has a taxable gain on the deemed sale and takes a fresh, fair market value (stepped-up) tax basis for its assets. As a result of the stepped-up basis, the target has higher depreciation and other deductions, but at a cost of taxation on the deemed sale. Prior to the enactment of Section 338, the target had to be liquidated in order to get a basis step-up.

Also, in the Tax Reform Act of 1986,[6] Congress followed a recommendation in the ALI 1982 Study and repealed the *General Utilities*[7] doctrine. This doctrine allowed a corporation to avoid tax on a liquidating sale or distribution.[8] Under the *General Utilities* doctrine, it was generally possible

---

perforce the proposals contained in the ALI 1982 Study and carried over to the ALI 1989 Study) should be enacted, *see* John R. McGowan, *Subchapter C Reform of Mergers and Acquisitions After General Utilities: Now What is Congress Waiting For?* 24 Akron Law Rev. 129 (1990) [hereinafter cited as "McGowan, *Subchapter C Reform of Mergers and Acquisitions After General Utilities*"].

4. C corporations are regular corporations that are subject to a tax under Section 11 of the Code. The maximum rate under Section 11 is presently 34 percent. The shareholders of C corporations are subject to tax on dividends from C corporations. Thus, one level of tax applies to C corporations, and a second level of tax applies to the shareholders. S corporations are generally not subject to taxation; the shareholders are taxed on the income and deduct the losses. Thus, there is only one level of tax. An S corporation cannot have more than 35 shareholders, and all of the shareholders must be individuals or certain trusts or estates. *See* I.R.C. § 1361. Except where noted otherwise, this book does not deal with the treatment of S corporations.

5. Tax Equity and Fiscal Responsibility Act of 1982, Pub. L. No. 97–248, 96 Stat. 324 (1982).

6. Tax Reform Act of 1986, Pub. L. No. 99–514, 100 Stat. 2085 (1986) [hereinafter cited as "TRA 1986"].

7. *General Util. & Oper. Co. v. Helvering*, 296 U.S. 200 (1935).

8. *See, e.g.*, House Comm. on Ways and Means, 86th Cong., 1st Sess., *An Ap-*

for a target corporation to sell all of its assets to an acquiring corporation and avoid tax on the gain as long as the proceeds of the sale were distributed to the target's shareholders as a liquidating distribution.[9] The shareholders were taxed on the proceeds at capital gains rates.[10] Thus, under the *General Utilities* doctrine, there generally was only one level of tax on a liquidating sale by a corporation. As a result of the repeal of the *General Utilities* doctrine by the TRA 1986, both a corporate and shareholder level tax apply in this type of transaction.

In the TRA 1986, Congress also followed a suggestion made in the ALI 1982 Study and amended Section 382, which deals with the utilization of net operating losses after an acquisition.[11] Section 382 is best illustrated by an example:

Target corporation (TC) has $200K of net operating losses (NOLs) that are available to be carried over and utilized to reduce future taxable income of TC. Acquiring corporation (AC) purchases all of the stock of TC for $500K. Under Section 382, after the acquisition of TC's stock by AC, TC's NOLs can be utilized in any tax year after the acquisition only in an amount equal to the long term tax-exempt rate, say 8 percent, times the purchase price of TC's stock ($500K). TC's $200K of NOLs, therefore, can only be utilized to the extent of $40K (8 percent of $500K) in each taxable year after the acquisition. Thus, Section 382 limits the deductibility of a target's NOL carryover after the acquisition of the target.

The TRA 1986 did not, however, adopt proposals contained in the ALI 1982 Study for the repeal of the acquisitive reorganization provisions of the Code and the adoption of a much more liberal approach to the taxation of mergers and acquisitions. The acquisitive reorganization provisions[12] provide for tax-free treatment at both the corporate and shareholder levels in certain mergers, stock acquisitions, and asset acquisitions in which a significant portion (and in some cases all) of the consideration is stock of the acquiring corporation or of its parent corporation. There are three basic types of acquisitive reorganizations:

---

proach to Subchapter C, 3 Tax Revision Compendium 1619 (Comm. Print 1959) (Brown).

9. Former I.R.C. § 337 (1986).

10. *See* I.R.C. §§ 331 and 1201 (1991).

11. This article does not deal with Section 382 or any other provisions dealing with net operating losses and related issues.

12. I.R.C. §§ 368 and 354 to 362 (1991).

1. The merger, pursuant to state law, of the target into the acquiring corporation, with the target's shareholders receiving stock of the acquiring corporation in exchange for their target stock.

2. The acquisition by the acquiring corporation from the target's shareholders of their stock solely in exchange for voting stock of the acquiring corporation; and

3. The acquisition by the acquiring corporation of the target's assets solely in exchange for voting stock of the acquiring corporation.

The requirement under the reorganization provisions that stock of the acquiring corporation be used as the consideration in the acquisition of the target is referred to as the "continuity of interest" requirement. Thus, to qualify as a reorganization, the target's shareholders must have a "continuity of interest" in the target's assets through a stock interest in the acquiring corporation. Acquisitive reorganizations are explored further in chapter 2.

Under the approach taken in the ALI 1982 Study and carried over in the ALI 1989 Study, if there is an acquisition of the target and the shareholders of the target swap their stock in the target for stock in the acquiring corporation the exchange is tax-free. Such tax-free treatment is not limited (as under present law) to transactions in which a substantial portion of the consideration consists of stock of the acquiring corporation. Thus, the ALI approach would repeal the continuity of interest requirement of present law and replace this concept with what amounts to a "like kind exchange" approach for swaps of stock in a target for stock in an acquiring corporation.

Under the present like kind exchange provision (Section 1031), property (not including stock) used in business or for investment may be swapped tax-free for property of a like kind. Thus, if a taxpayer swaps an old crane used in its business for a new crane to be used in its business, the gain inherent in the old crane is not subject to tax.

The economic substance of the ALI proposal is to amend Section 1031 to permit certain stock (*i.e.*, stock of a target corporation) to be swapped tax-free for stock of a like kind (*i.e.*, stock of the acquiring corporation). Thus, the ALI proposal for target shareholder treatment is referred to here as a like kind exchange approach.

In addition to the like kind exchange approach, the ALI 1989 Study contains many other proposed revisions to the taxation of mergers and acquisitions,[13] including a proposal to explicitly allow what the ALI refers to as the "clean mirror" transaction.[14] As explained more fully in chapter 3, mirror transactions permit a corporation to dispose of part of its assets with

---

13. *See* chapter 3, p. 41 and p. 47.
14. *See* chapter 3, p. 42.

only a shareholder level tax. Congress, deciding that mirrors erode the corporate tax base and are inconsistent with the repeal of the *General Utilities* doctrine, has shut down all forms of mirrors. The ALI's "clean mirror" proposal would reverse this sound congressional judgement.

Although the TRA 1986 stopped short of adopting all of the ALI's proposed changes, in the TRA 1986 Congress directed the Treasury Department to conduct a study of various proposals to reform the corporate provisions of the Code.[15] The ALI's 1989 Study was at least partially designed to influence the Treasury's study.

The Treasury study was to be submitted to Congress by January 1, 1988. On April 9, 1987, the Treasury published an outline (Treasury Subchapter C Outline) of the issues to be addressed in the study.[16] The study was not, however, completed on time, and in the Revenue Reconciliation Act of 1990, Congress delayed the due date of the study to January 1, 1992.[17]

At the time of the enactment of the TRA 1986 it appeared that the Treasury's Subchapter C study would focus on a comprehensive analysis of the merger and acquisition provisions, and this expectation is reflected in the breadth of the issues set forth in the Treasury Subchapter C Outline. The public concern with the recent (but now abating) wave of LBOs, however, deflected both the Treasury and the Congress from a comprehensive look at the merger and acquisition provisions generally and toward a hard look at LBOs, which are just one type of corporate acquisition transaction.

As an example of the concern in Congress with LBOs, in the Budget Reconciliation Bill of 1987,[18] the House Ways and Means Committee included provisions that would have imposed a heavy tax cost on hostile takeovers and would have restricted the deduction for interest in non-hostile stock acquisitions.[19] Although these provisions were not enacted, the 1987 Act adopted restrictions on mirror transactions[20] and on greenmail payments,[21]

---

15. *See* § 634 of TRA 1986, *supra* note 6.

16. Treasury Department News Release B–942, April 9, 1987 [hereinafter cited as *"Treasury Subchapter C Outline"*].

17. Section 11831(a)(3) of the Revenue Reconciliation Act of 1990, Pub. L. No. 101–508, 104 Stat. 1388 (1990) [hereinafter cited as "RRA 1990"].

18. Budget Reconciliation Bill of 1987, H.R. 3545, 100th Cong., 1st Sess. (1987). This bill is discussed further in chapter 11, p. 154.

19. *See* chapter 11, p. 154.

20. Mirror transactions are discussed in chapter 3, p. 42. *See also*, Samuel C. Thompson, Jr., Paul R. Wysocki, Robert R. Pluth and Catherine A. Jacobson, *Federal Taxation of Business Enterprises* vol. 2, ch. 14, § 14:17 (Callaghan, 1989, supplemented quarterly) [hereinafter cited as *"Federal Taxation of Business Enterprises"*].

21. *Id.* at vol. 1, ch. 11, § 11:17. Greenmail is a practice in which a hostile acquiring corporation purchases some of the stock of a target on the open market and then encourages the target to buy its stock from the acquiring corporation at more than

both of which originated in the House Bill. Also, the Revenue Reconciliation Act of 1989[22] enacted several provisions that limit to a degree certain of the benefits of LBO transactions, including a limitation on the carryback of net operating losses that arise because of postacquisition interest expense.[23]

Congressional hearings[24] on the LBO issue have produced many different ideas for dealing with this issue,[25] but no consensus has yet emerged. In reporting on the hearings on LBOs before the House Commerce Subcommittee on Telecommunications and Finance, one reporter says that the hearings "produced the following conclusion: No conclusion can be reached on LBOs."[26]

Many of the proposals for dealing with LBOs have involved suggestions for curtailing the deduction for interest payments made on debt issued in LBO transactions;[27] others have proposed the opposite approach of a deduction for dividends on equity,[28] in other words, integrating the corporate

---

the market price. Thus, the acquiror is said to have "greenmailed" the target into making the purchase at an above the market price.

22. Revenue Reconciliation Act of 1989, Pub. L. No. 101–239, 103 Stat. 406 (1989).

23. *See* J. Roger Mentz, et. al., *Leveraged Buyouts: A Washington Perspective of 1989 Legislation and Prospects for 1990*, 46 Tax Notes 1047 (Feb. 26, 1990).

24. Tax Policy Aspects of Mergers and Acquisitions, Hearings before the House Committee on Ways and Means, 101st Cong., 1st Sess. (1989); Hearings on LBOs before the House Commerce Subcommittee on Telecommunications and Finance, 101st Cong., 1st Sess. (1989); Leveraged Buyouts and Corporate Debt, Hearings before the Senate Committee on Finance, 101st Cong., 1st Sess. (1988); Tax Aspects of Acquisitions and Mergers, Hearings before the Subcommittee on Oversight and Subcommittee on Select Revenue Measures of the House Committee on Ways and Means, 99th Cong., 1st Sess. (1985).

25. *See, e.g.*, Staff of the Joint Committee on Taxation, *Federal Income Tax Aspects of Corporate Financial Structures*, Prepared for Hearing before Senate Finance Committee (Jan. 18, 1989) [hereinafter cited as *"Joint Committee LBO Study"*]; House Ways and Means Committee Press Release Announcing Further Hearings on LBOs and Outlining Tax Options for Curbing Such Transactions, 43 Tax Notes 349 (1989) [hereinafter cited as *"House Ways and Means' LBO Options"*]; Statement of Acting Assisting Treasury Secretary, John Wilkins, at Hearings on Leverage Buyouts Before House Ways and Means Committee, May 16, 1989 [hereinafter cited as *"Treasury LBO Testimony"*].

26. Pat Jones, *Energy and Commerce Takes Turn Looking at LBOs*, 43 Tax Notes 1065 (May 29, 1989).

27. *ALI 1989 Study, supra* note 2, at part I.

28. *See, e.g.*, Michael J. Graetz, *The Tax Aspects of Leverage Buyouts and Other Corporate Financial Restructuring Transactions*, 42 Tax Notes 721 (1989) [hereinafter

and individual taxes. Various tax professionals have argued for a corporate integration solution.[29] Also, the ALI has issued a Reporter's study draft on integration (ALI Reporter's 1992 Integration Draft).[30]

Thus, the debate concerning LBOs has led to a debate concerning integration. In many LBO transactions the use of debt has been so extensive and the interest deduction so large that the corporate tax has been eliminated. In view of this *de facto* integration of the corporate and individual taxes, it seems anomalous that the Congressional response to this obvious problem with LBOs would be to adopt *de jure* integration.

Although at the time of enactment of the TRA 1986 it was anticipated that the Treasury study would comprehensively address mergers, acquisitions and LBOs, the Treasury's study,[31] which was released on January 6, 1992, only addresses the topic of integration. In his letter transmitting the Treasury 1992 Integration Study to Congress, the Assistant Secretary of Treasury for Tax Policy says that Congress's directive to the Treasury in 1986 was "quite broad" and that the Treasury concluded that

> . . . a comprehensive study of the issues presented by integration of the corporate and individual income tax would address fundamental questions concerning how the corporate income tax might be restructured to reduce tax distortions of important corporate financial decisions and to achieve a more efficient system.

---

cited as "Graetz, *Tax Aspects of LBOs*"]. *See also*, Alvin C. Warren, Jr., *Recent Corporate Restructuring and the Corporate Tax System*, 42 Tax Notes 715 (1989) [hereinafter cited as "Warren, *Recent Corporate Restructuring*"]. For earlier arguments in favor of integration *see* Charles McClure, *Must Corporate Income Be Taxed Twice?* (1979) and Alvin C. Warren, Jr., *The Relation and Integration of Individual and Corporate Income Taxes*, 94 Harv. L. Rev. 717 (1981). The ALI 1989 Study proposed allowing a deduction for dividends on new contributed equity. *See ALI 1989 Study*, *supra* note 2.

29. *See, e.g.*, John K. McNulty, *Reform of The Individual Income Tax By Integration of the Corporate Income Tax*, 46 Tax Notes 1445 (1990); Scott A. Taylor, *Corporate Integration in the Federal Income Tax: Lessons from the Past and a Proposal for the Future*, 10 Va. Tax Rev. 237 (1990). *See, generally*, Willard B. Taylor and M. Bernard Aidinoff, *Approaches to Debt: Is Integration the Answer?* 67 Taxes 931 (Dec. 1989).

30. The American Law Institute, Federal Income Tax Project, Tax Advisory Group Draft No. 21, Reporter's Study Draft (William D. Andrews and Alvin C. Warren, Jr., Reporters) (March 2, 1992) [hereinafter cited as "*ALI Reporter's 1992 Integration Draft*"]. This study draft does not represent the position of the ALI.

31. The Treasury's study is entitled "*Treasury Department Report, Integration of the Individual and Corporate Tax Systems, Taxing Business Income Once*, (January 6, 1992) [hereinafter cited as "*Treasury 1992 Integration Study*"].

He goes on to say that an examination of integration should "precede consideration of other, less fundamental, approaches to corporate income tax reform."[32]

The Treasury 1992 Integration Study, which is examined in chapter 15, addresses only one aspect of the merger and acquisition puzzle: the treatment of LBOs. This is also true for the ALI Reporter's 1992 Integration Draft, which is also examined in chapter 15. As will be seen in chapter 15, under two of the methods of integration discussed in the Treasury 1992 Integration Study, one of which is the Treasury's preferred method, there would continue to be a tax incentive for engaging in LBOs and similar transactions. Also, depending on the circumstances, such an incentive may also exist under the ALI's proposal.

The concern with LBOs should not be used as the reason for moving in the direction of integration. In the words of Professor Kwall, the case for integration is "uncertain."[33] The problem with overly leveraged LBOs and similar transactions can be addressed directly as proposed here.

In summary, the debate concerning the proper tax treatment of mergers and acquisitions continues[34] today and is likely to increase in intensity in coming years. It is the purpose of this book to persuade Congress to enact the comprehensive proposals offered here.[35]

---

32. *See* Letters from Kenneth W. Gideon, Assistant Secretary (Tax Policy) to the Honorable Dan Rostenkowski, Chairman Committee on Ways and Means, US House of Representatives and the Honorable Lloyd Bentson, Chairman Committee on Finance, US Senate, dated January 6, 1992 [hereinafter cited as "*Gideon Integration Letter*"].

33. *See* Jeffrey L. Kwall, *The Uncertain Case Against the Double Taxation of Corporate Income*, 68 N.C. Law Rev. 613 (1990) [hereinafter cited as "Kwall, *The Uncertain Case*"]. *See also*, Report of a speech given by the then Chief of Staff of the Joint Committee of Taxation, Pearlman, in which he said it is unrealistic to expect that any corporate integration effort would result in repeal of the corporate tax. Daily Tax Report, G–3 (November 11, 1990).

34. Some of the early income tax cases involved the proper tax treatment of mergers and acquisitions, *see, e.g. Marr v. United States*, 268 U.S. 536 (1925).

35. Several articles address one or more of the issues raised in the ALI 1989 Study. For a debate over the ALI's carryover basis proposal and the related issue of whether there should be a mandatory Section 338 election, *see* George K. Yin, *A Carryover Basis Asset Acquisition Regime?: A Few Words of Caution*, 37 Tax Notes 415 (1987) [hereinafter cited as "Yin, *Carryover Basis Asset Acquisitions*"]; David F. Shores, *Section 338—Do We Need a Change? A Response to Professor Yin*, 37 Tax Notes 939 (1987); George K. Yin, *Yin Responds to Shores on Corporate Stock and Asset Acquisitions*, 37 Tax Notes 1279 (1987); Jasper L. Cummings, Jr., *More on the Yin-Shores Debate Over Carryover Basis Asset Acquisitions*, 38 Tax Notes 293 (1988); Martin D. Ginsburg, et al., *Reexamining Subchapter C: An Overview and Some Modest*

The Approach and Relationship to Integration

This book calls for a comprehensive revision of the merger, acquisition, and LBO provisions of the Code within the context of the present classical system in which C corporations are subject to one level of tax and shareholders another.

As demonstrated in chapter 15, even if an integrated system of taxation were adopted, the proposals in part 2 governing mergers and acquisitions, which deal generally with the classification of an acquisition as taxable or

<hr/>

Proposals to Stimulate Debate, in *Corporate Tax Reform, A Report of the Invitational Conference on Subchapter C*, American Bar Association Section of Taxation, New York State Bar Association Tax Section 39 (1988) [hereinafter cited as "Ginsburg et al., *A Modest Proposal*." This book is hereinafter referred to as "*Invitational Conference*"].

For a proposal for mandatory corporate level tax on the change of control of a corporation, *see* James B. Lewis, *A Proposal for a Corporate Level Tax on Major Stock Sales*, 37 Tax Notes 1041 (1987) [hereinafter cited as "Lewis, *Corporate Level Tax*"].

For a proposal for mandatory carryover basis of the target's assets in all acquisitions, *see* Glen E. Coven, *Taxing Corporate Acquisitions: A Proposal for Mandatory Uniform Rules*, 44 Tax L. Rev. 145 (1989) [hereinafter cited as "Coven, *Mandatory Uniform Rules*"].

For a proposal for mandatory taxation at both the corporate and shareholder levels in all acquisitions, *see* David J. Shakow, *Whither, "C"!*, 45 Tax L. Rev. 177 (1990) [hereinafter cited as "Shakow, *Whither, "C"!*"].

For an extension of the proposal contained in the ALI 1989 Study for a corporate level tax on corporate distributions, *see* George K. Yin, *A Proposed Tax on Corporate Distributions*, 67 Taxes 962 (Dec. 1989) and George K. Yin, *A Different Approach to the Taxation of Corporate Distributions: Theory and Implementation of a Uniform Corporate-Level Distribution Tax* 78 Georgetown Law J. 1837 (1990).

See, generally, McGowan, *Subchapter C Reform of Mergers and Acquisitions After General Utilities, supra* note 3; Paul B. Stephan III, *Disaggregation and Subchapter C Rethinking Corporate Tax Reform*, 76 Va. L. Rev. 655 (1990); Bernard Wolfman, *Whither "C"?*, 38 Tax Notes 1269 (1988); Bernard Wolfman, *Subchapter C and the 100th Congress*, 33 Tax Notes 669 (1986); Peter L. Faber, *The Search for Consistency in Corporate Acquisitions*, 13 J. Corp. Tax 187 (1986); Eric M. Zolt, *Corporate Taxation After the Tax Reform Act of 1986: A State of Disequilibrium*, 66 N.C.L. Rev. 839 (1988).

Among other things, this book proposes (1) the retention of the reorganization provisions (*see* chapter 4), (2) the adoption of an elective carryover basis regime for certain taxable acquisitions of a target's assets (*see* chapter 5), (3) a limited mandatory Section 338 election for certain stock acquisitions (*see* chapter 7), and (4) substantial limitations on the deductibility of interest in LBOs and other equity conversion transactions (*see* chapter 12).

tax-free, would still have vitality.[36] Even in a fully integrated system (which exists today with S corporations)[37] Congress would have to determine the proper treatment (taxable or nontaxable) of the various parties to an acquisition.[38] Also, depending on the type of integration proposal enacted, the proposals in part 3 relating to LBOs and similar transactions might have continuing vitality.[39]

In any event, the enactment of an integrated system would likely have a serious adverse revenue effect, and therefore, it is unlikely that such a system will be enacted soon. The current debate over integration is not a reason for Congress to delay addressing the present problems with the taxation of mergers, acquisitions, and LBOs. Congress should act on the proposals contained in this book now.

Structure of this Book

This book is divided into four parts. Part 1, contains this introductory chapter and chapter 2, which summarizes the current provisions governing (1) acquisitive reorganizations, (2) taxable acquisitions, and (3) LBOs and related transactions. Part 2 consists of chapters 3 through 9 and deals with mergers and acquisitions generally. Part 3 consists of chapters 10 through 14 and addresses LBOs and related transactions. Part 4 consists of chapter 15, which explores the impact of the Treasury and ALI integration prototypes on the proposals made in this book, and chapter 16, which provides summary remarks.

Part 2: Mergers and Acquisitions

Part 2 sets out an alternative approach to the portion of the ALI 1989 Study that deals with the tax treatment (basically taxable or tax-free) of the

---

36. *See* chapter 15, p. 232.

37. For a discussion of the tax treatment of S corporations that participate in taxable and tax-free acquisitions, *see Federal Taxation of Business Enterprises, supra* note 20, chs. 38 and 50. Although this book does not deal specifically with S corporations, the principles discussed here (with appropriate modifications where necessary) should apply also to S corporations.

38. This issue of the proper scope of recognition treatment would be eliminated only in a system where gains and losses are taxed whether or not realized. For such a proposal *see* David A. Shakow, *Taxation Without Realization: A Proposal for Accrual Taxation*, 134 U. Pa. L. Rev. 1111 (1986). *See also* Jeff Strand, *Periodicity and Accretion Taxation: Norms and Implementation* 99 Yale L. J. 1817 (1990) and Mary L. Fellows, *A Comprehensive Attack on Tax Deferral*, 88 Mich. L. Rev. 722 (1990). An integrated system would not require taxation of unrealized gains and losses.

39. *See* chapter 15, p. 236. Professor Warren has made this point. *See* Warren, *Recent Corporate Restructuring, supra* note 28, at 720.

parties to an acquisitive transaction. Specific proposals are made here for revising the provisions of the Code dealing with acquisitive reorganizations and taxable acquisitions.

This book rejects the ALI's suggestion that the reorganization concept be repealed and replaced with what is, in essence, a "like kind exchange" approach[40] at the shareholder level and an express codification of the mirror transaction[41] at the corporate level. Part 2 accepts, although in a more limited form, the ALI's suggestion for elective carryover basis treatment of the target's assets in certain asset acquisitions. Under this carryover basis regime, a target does not have taxable gain on the disposition of its assets, and the acquiring corporation takes as its basis for those assets the target's old basis for the assets (*i.e.*, takes a carryover basis). Thus, the price of tax-free treatment to the target is a carryover basis for the assets in the hands of the acquiring corporation.

Five basic tax policy questions are addressed in part 2. First, should Congress adopt the ALI's suggestion that the shareholder level consequences in a corporate acquisition be separated from the corporate level consequences? That is, should (as the ALI has proposed) the acquisitive reorganization concept be eliminated? In this connection, should the continuity of interest doctrine be eliminated, retained, or strengthened? Also, should the "substantially all" concept apply uniformly to all forms of acquisitive reorganizations? Under the "substantially all" concept, which applies to four of the seven forms of acquisitive reorganizations, the acquiring corporation must acquire "substantially all" of the target's assets to qualify the acquisition as a reorganization. With uniformity, tax-free treatment would be available only in an acquisitive transaction in which substantially all of the target's assets are either acquired in an asset reorganization, or held by the target after the acquisition of the target in a stock reorganization.

Second, should a carryover basis rule be provided for taxable asset acquisitions? With the repeal of *General Utilities*, a very heavy tax burden applies when a target sells its assets and then distributes the proceeds to its shareholders in liquidation. Both the target and its shareholders are fully taxed on such transactions. This high tax cost effectively eliminates the use of taxable asset acquisitions, even though such transactions serve a useful business purpose. A carryover basis rule would allow the target to escape taxation on such transactions, but the acquiring corporation would take the target's basis for the assets (*i.e.*, a carryover basis) and not a fair market value basis. There would only be a shareholder level tax.

---

40. The like kind exchange approach is briefly summarized above. *See* p. 6.
41. The mirror transaction is discussed in chapter 2, p. 34 and chapter 3, p. 42.

Third, should there be an exception to the repeal of the *General Utilities* doctrine for taxable acquisitions involving the liquidating sale or distribution of goodwill in which the parties do not choose the carryover basis rule discussed above. If an exception for goodwill applied, the target would be taxable on the liquidating sale of all of its assets, except goodwill and other non-amortizable intangibles. The target's shareholders would be fully taxed on the receipt of the liquidating proceeds. Also, should this elective non-recognition treatment apply even if Congress provides an amortization deduction for goodwill, as is currently proposed?[42]

Fourth, assuming the adoption of a carryover basis election for a limited class of taxable asset acquisitions, should parity in the treatment of taxable stock acquisitions be adopted? Parity could be obtained by imposing mandatory target level taxation (*i.e.*, a mandatory 338 election) for a stock acquisition that could not have been structured as a carryover basis asset acquisition. Under this rule, in certain circumstances a target would automatically be deemed to have sold its assets after an acquisition of the target's stock.

Fifth, what needs to be done in order to curtail the mischaracterization of purchase price as deductible payments in both acquisitive reorganizations and taxable acquisitions? With the current small capital gains preference, taxpayers have been allocating significant portions of what is in economic reality purchase price of stock to deductible payments, such as covenants not to compete. This is a clear abuse and needs to be stopped.

Chapter 3 provides a more comprehensive discussion of the background of these five policy issues.

Chapter 4 sets out proposals regarding reorganizations, which encompass various types of tax-free acquisitions. These proposals are premised on the judgment that the central themes of the reorganization provisions reflect correct tax policy:

> An exception to the general recognition (*i.e.*, taxation) rule of Section 1001 should apply at the corporate and shareholder levels for corporate acquisitions in which for a good business purpose the acquiring corporation acquires the target's historic assets and a significant portion of the consideration received by the target's historic shareholders is stock of the acquiring corporation.

Thus, the position taken in chapter 4 is that the business purpose, continuity of business enterprise, and continuity of interest doctrines of present law are consistent with proper tax policy. If the spirit of these doctrines is satisfied in a corporate acquisition, the transaction is not analogous to a

---

42. *See* chapter 6, p. 112.

sale or taxable exchange because the target's shareholders have a continuing interest in the historic assets of the target through their ownership of stock of the acquiring corporation. Consequently, it is appropriate in such cases to provide nonrecognition treatment for both the target corporation and its shareholders. This position is directly contrary to that taken in the ALI 1989 Study.

If the reorganization concept is reformed as proposed here, there would be uniformity in the application of both (1) the continuity of interest requirement, and (2) the substantially all requirement. Under present law, the continuity of interest requirement differs for the various types of reorganizations, and the substantially all requirement applies only in the stock for asset reorganization[43] and in the forward and reverse subsidiary merger reorganizations.[44] Consequently, under the proposals here there would be consistency in the treatment of acquisitive reorganizations, manipulation would be prevented, and the operation of these provisions would be reflective of the underlying policy rationale.[45]

In striving for consistency, chapter 4 attempts to eliminate many of the needless traps in the reorganization provisions, such as the *Bausch & Lomb* doctrine,[46] and to codify those principles in the case law and rulings that are consistent with the fundamental concept of a reorganization, such as the *McDonalds*[47] decision.

No significant changes are suggested here to Sections 354 to 362, which govern the tax treatment of the parties to a reorganization.[48] Under Section 354, a shareholder of a target corporation acquired in a reorganization receives tax-free treatment upon the swap of her target stock for stock of the

---

43. I.R.C. § 368(a)(1)(C).

44. I.R.C. § 368(a)(2)(D) and (E).

45. The proposed changes build on and expand upon proposals made in a prior article. *See* Thompson, *Suggested Alternative Approach, supra* note 3.

The proposals here go much further than proposed amendments to Section 368 which were proposed by the ABA Tax Section. *See* ABA Comm. on Corporate Stockholder Relationships, *Tax Section Recommendation No. 1981–5, To Amend the Internal Revenue Code of 1954 to Simplify, Redefine and Make Uniform the Various Forms of Acquisitive Corporate Reorganizations,* 34 Tax Law 1386 (1981) [hereinafter cited as "ABA Reorganization Recommendations"].

46. *Bausch & Lomb Optical Co. v. Commissioner,* 267 F.2d 75 (2d Cir. 1959); *see* chapter 4, p. 79.

47. *McDonalds Restaurants of Illinois, Inc. v. Commissioner,* 688 F.2d 520 (7th Cir. 1982); *see* chapter 4, p. 76.

48. These provisions are discussed in chapter 2, p. 38. There is one slight modification to Section 358 to eliminate the substituted basis rule that currently applies to the acquiring corporation in a stock for stock (B) reorganization under Section 358. *See* chapter 4, p. 68.

acquiring corporation, and under Section 358, the shareholder takes as her basis for the stock of the acquiring corporation received the basis for her stock of the target exchanged. Similar rules apply upon the exchange of securities (*i.e.*, long term debt instruments) of the target for securities of the acquiring corporation.

Under Section 361, the target generally does not recognize gain or loss in a reorganization, and under Section 362 the acquiring corporation takes as its basis for the target's stock or assets acquired the transferor's basis for the stock or assets. If in addition to receiving stock of the acquiring corporation, a target's shareholder receives nonstock consideration (*i.e.*, boot), then under Section 356 any gain realized by the shareholder is taxed to the extent of the fair market value of the boot. The taxable gain is capital gain, unless the transaction has the effect of a dividend. In *Clark v. Commissioner*,[49] the Supreme Court adopted the approach in *Wright v. United States*[50] for determining whether the receipt of boot by the target's shareholders has the effect of a dividend under Section 356(a)(2). The *Clark* decision is correct from a tax policy perspective;[51] therefore, this book does not propose to amend Section 356(a)(2).[52]

The proposals made here regarding taxable acquisitions are contained in chapters 5, 6, and 7 and arise out of the repeal by the TRA 1986 of the *General Utilities* doctrine. As a result of the repeal of this doctrine, a target corporation is fully taxed on the liquidating sale or distribution of its assets. Also, the target's shareholders are taxed under general principles upon receipt of the liquidation proceeds. Thus, today there is a double level of tax on liquidating sales; prior to the repeal of the *General Utilities* doctrine, only a tax at the shareholder level generally applied.

Chapter 5 would eliminate the current barrier to taxable asset acquisitions of stand-alone target corporations by providing for carryover basis treatment for a taxable acquisition of the assets of a nonsubsidiary target. With carryover basis treatment, the target would not be subject to tax and the acquiring corporation would take the target's assets with the target's

---

49. *Clark v. Commissioner*, 489 U.S. 726 (1989).

50. *Wright v. United States*, 482 F.2d 600 (8th Cir. 1973) (in determining whether boot received in a reorganization has the effect of a dividend, hypothesize that stock of the acquiring corporation was received in lieu of the boot and immediately after the reorganization such hypothetical stock was redeemed by the acquiring corporation in a transaction governed by Section 302).

51. This author has previously proposed the adoption of the *Wright* approach. *See* Thompson, *Suggested Alternative Approach*, *supra* note 3, at 647.

52. Although the ALI 1989 Study would repeal the reorganization definition and replace the concept with a qualified acquisition concept, the ALI 1989 Study would not make significant changes to Sections 354 to 362 and would codify the *Wright* decision.

basis (*i.e.*, a carryover basis). The target's shareholders would be taxed upon receipt of the liquidating proceeds. Thus, there would be only one level of tax.

This carryover basis treatment would be available only if the acquisition would have qualified as an acquisitive reorganization under the proposals contained in chapter 4, but for the failure to satisfy the continuity of interest requirement.[53] Thus, carryover basis treatment would be allowed only if the acquiring corporation acquires substantially all of the target's historic assets. This carryover basis proposal provides a limited exception to the repeal of the *General Utilities* doctrine. This basic concept of a carryover basis for taxable acquisitions was first introduced in the ALI 1982 Study and is also present in the ALI 1989 Study, although different from that proposed here.

Chapter 6 proposes tax-free treatment in a liquidating sale by a nonsubsidiary target corporation of goodwill and going concern value. This exception would apply only if the parties do not treat the transaction under the carryover basis rule set forth in chapter 5. A special rule would apply if Congress enacts currently proposed legislation that would provide an amortization deduction for goodwill and going concern value.[54] As is the case for carryover basis treatment, this nonrecognition rule for goodwill would be available only if the transaction would have qualified for acquisitive reorganization treatment under the proposals contained in chapter 4, but for the failure to satisfy the continuity of interest requirement. Thus, this exception to the repeal of the *General Utilities* doctrine is available only if the acquiring corporation acquires "substantially all" of the target's historic assets. This proposal is similar to a proposal contained in the ALI 1989 Study. The circumstances in which nonrecognition is available, however, are more limited under the proposal here. Also, the ALI would require the acquiring corporation to take a carryover basis for goodwill acquired in a nonrecognition transaction, but under the proposal here the purchaser would take a cost basis.[55]

The carryover basis rule in chapter 5 and the goodwill nonrecognition rule in chapter 6 are mutually exclusive. Thus, in any liquidating taxable sale of substantially all of a target's historic assets, the parties would have two options: (1) a carryover basis acquisition in which the target is not subject to tax and the acquiring corporation takes a carryover basis for the target's assets; or (2) taxable treatment for the target, except for goodwill and

---

53. This proposal is similar to, but more limited than, one made by Professor Yin. *See* Yin, *Carryover Basis Asset Acquisitions, supra* note 35.

54. *See* chapter 6, p. 112.

55. The reasons for rejecting the ALI's carryover basis rule are set forth in chapter 6, p. 110.

other non-amortizable intangibles. In both cases, the target's shareholders would be taxed upon receipt of the liquidating proceeds.

Chapter 7 provides a rule requiring mandatory target level taxation (*i.e.*, a mandatory Section 338 election) for certain stock purchases in which the target's assets could not have been acquired in a carryover basis asset acquisition. The effect of this mandatory Section 338 election is to treat the target as if it had sold and repurchased its assets in a taxable transaction. This mandatory Section 338 election applies if, at the time of the acquisition of at least 80 percent of the target's stock by an acquiring corporation, the target does not hold substantially all of its historic assets. The purpose of this provision is to prevent the use of a stock acquisition for the purpose of acquiring only a portion of the target's assets in a carryover basis transaction. The carryover basis proposal and the mandatory Section 338 proposal should provide neutrality in the treatment of taxable stock and asset acquisitions.

Chapter 8 proposes the adoption of a statutory limit on the amount of consideration that can be allocated to a covenant not to compete or similar deductible item. This provision applies in both taxable acquisitions and acquisitive reorganizations. This provision will curtail the misallocation of purchase price.

Chapter 9, the last chapter in part 2, illustrates the application of the proposed reforms in the context of a variety of prototype acquisition transactions.

As demonstrated in the chart contained in appendix A, and as discussed further in the last chapter, the adoption of the rules proposed in part 2 would eliminate the inconsistencies under present law in the treatment of the various forms of acquisitive reorganizations and would provide for a parity in treatment of taxable stock and asset acquisitions. Thus, these proposals satisfy the neutrality principle of tax policy:[56] similar transactions should be taxed similarly.

Part 3: LBOs and Related Transactions

Part 3 of this book sets out an alternative to the portions of the ALI 1989 Study dealing with LBOs and related transactions. Thus, the proposals here are offered as alternatives to the ALI's proposals for (1) a minimum tax on distributions, and (2) an absolute prohibition on the deduction for interest on debt issued in an equity conversion transaction.

---

56. *Cf.* Richard A. Musgrave and Peggy B. Musgrave, *Public Finance in Theory and Practice* 216 (4th ed. 1989) (setting out the requirement of a good tax structure) [hereinafter cited as "Musgrave and Musgrave, *Public Finance*"]. The Treasury 1992 Integration Study, *supra* note 31, at 12–14, indicates that neutrality is a goal of integration.

For the reasons discussed below, this book suggests changes in the tax rules governing the deduction of interest in LBOs and related transactions involving publicly held corporations; no changes are suggested for such transactions involving privately held firms and divisions and subsidiaries of publicly held firms.

This book is not motivated by a belief that LBOs are bad for the economy and should be discouraged or penalized. An underlying theme of this book is that although LBOs and related transactions are on balance good for the economy in that they move assets into the hands of those who can put those assets to their highest and best use, the deduction for interest under the present tax system has resulted in excessively leveraged LBOs and related transactions involving publicly held corporations. The excessive leverage is inconsistent with sound tax policy because such leverage erodes the corporate tax base and has a great potential for being economically harmful. This harm results because such transactions (1) increase bankruptcy risk above acceptable levels,[57] and (2) put an unacceptable damper on expenditures for investment and research and development, thereby reducing opportunities to exploit value maximizing strategies. If the suggestions made here were to be adopted, there would be a prudent level of equity in these transactions, the bankruptcy risk would be reduced, and the equity base would give the firm greater opportunities to invest, conduct R & D, and grow.

Although concerns with excessive leverage can arise in a variety of contexts, it appears that the principal concern is with excessively leveraged LBOs and related transactions involving publicly held corporations. Although similar problems can exist with acquisitions of privately held corporations and acquisitions of divisions and subsidiaries of publicly held corporations, the current concern with LBOs arose out of acquisitions of publicly held firms. Also, there does not appear to be a problem with the issuance of debt for the purpose of internal corporate expansion by the purchase of bricks and mortar. For this reason, the proposals contained in part 3 would merely eliminate the tax incentive for excessively leveraged acquisitions and related transactions of publicly held corporations.

Chapter 10 discusses the current treatment of LBOs and related transactions under the Code. Chapter 11 outlines the policy concerns that have been expressed about such transactions and discusses proposals for altering the tax treatment of such transactions that have been made both by the ALI 1989 Study and by others.

Chapter 12 sets out the proposal here for the denial of the deductibility of interest in certain equity conversion transactions involving publicly held

---

57. *See, e.g., Treasury 1992 Integration Study, supra* note 31, at vii., and *ALI Reporter's 1992 Integration Draft, supra* note 30, at 2–3.

corporations. The proposals here would get at the core of the problem of LBOs and other equity conversion transactions of publicly held corporations by disallowing the deduction for interest on the following debt issued by such corporations: (1) debt issued as a dividend; (2) debt issued for the purpose of directly or indirectly paying an extraordinary dividend or making an extraordinary redemption, such as a leveraged recapitalization; and (3) all junk debt and any excessive nonjunk debt issued for the purpose of acquiring either control stock or substantially all the assets of a publicly held corporation.[58] Thus, the rules here would apply to both LBOs and various types of leveraged recapitalizations involving publicly held corporations.

Junk debt includes, for example, zero coupon bonds and payment in kind bonds issued in the acquisition of a publicly held corporation. Also, under the junk debt rule, interest above a stated level on straight junk debt is not deductible; there is no effect on the interest below the stated level. The excessive debt rule prevents the use of excessive debt in LBOs involving publicly held corporations.

The rule regarding junk debt applies to tax-free reorganizations[59] as well as to taxable acquisitions. There could not be excessive debt in a reorganization, and therefore, the excessive debt rule has no application to reorganizations. The rules disallowing interest on debt issued as a dividend, in a redemption, or in a leveraged recapitalization are designed to eliminate a needless tax incentive for excessive leveraging and to prevent a corporation from avoiding the effect of the disallowance rule that applies in acquisition transactions.

Chapter 13 illustrates the operation of the LBO and leveraged recapitalization rules. Chapter 14, the final chapter in part 3, examines whether the proposals made in chapter 12 can withstand attack from what appears to be the most comprehensive argument to date in favor of continuation of the present tax treatment of LBOs and related transactions. This chapter examines much of the extensive finance literature dealing with LBOs and related transactions.

Some readers may ask why the proposals in part 3 relating to LBOs should be enacted in view of the recently changed landscape of merger and acquisition deals. Many of the mergers and acquisitions of public corporations today involve "strategic" transactions involving mergers of viable enterprises in which stock is the merger consideration.[60] These transactions,

---

58. *See* chapter 12.

59. Part 2 suggests retention of the acquisitive reorganization concept in a radically modified form.

60. *See, e.g.*, proposed merger of Chemical Banking Corp. and Manufacturers Hanover Corp., reported in Wall Street Journal, July 16, 1991, at 1, col. 6.

which are the subject of the proposals in part 2, differ significantly from highly leveraged financial transactions in which the acquiror is an LBO company with few, if any, operating assets. Also, because of the decline in the junk bond market, it is likely that any leveraged acquisition done today will have more equity than was present in many of such acquisitions completed in the mid-1980s.

Although there has been both a decrease in the number of highly leveraged acquisitions of publicly held firms and an increase in the amount of equity in the transactions that are completed, this does not mean that the day of the overly leveraged transaction will not return. Rather than waiting for such a possible return and the attendant increases in bankruptcy risk,[61] it would be prudent for Congress to adopt the LBO proposals now.

Part 4: Impact of Integration and Conclusion

Part 4 consists of chapters 15 and 16. Chapter 15 examines both the Treasury 1992 Integration Study and the ALI Reporter's 1992 Integration Draft. The purpose of chapter 15 is to determine the impact the various integration prototypes contained in these studies would have on the merger and acquisition proposals contained in part 2 and the LBO proposals contained in part 3.

As demonstrated in chapter 15, the possibility of a future integrated system is no reason to delay enacting the proposals contained in parts 2 and 3.

Chapter 16 sets out the conclusion and demonstrates the neutrality of the proposals in parts 2 and 3.

Implementation

This is a call for legislative action. To assist in an analysis and evaluation of these proposals, proposed statutory language is provided in appendices B, C, and D. All of the changes regarding mergers and acquisitions in part 2 are implemented by amendments to Section 368, which defines the term "reorganization."[62] (*See* appendix B.)

---

61. One of the reasons given in the Treasury 1992 Integration Study for moving to an integrated system is to encourage the "adoption of capital structures less vulnerable to instability in times of economic downturn." *Treasury 1992 Integration Study, supra* note 31, at vii.

62. The reasons all the amendments are to Section 368 are as follows:

    (1) the amendments regarding carryover basis treatment and the nonrecognition rule for goodwill apply only in asset acquisitions that would qualify as acquisitive reorganizations but for the failure to satisfy the continuity of interest doctrine, and

    (2) the provision regarding the curtailment of misallocation of purchase price applies to both taxable acquisitions and acquisitive reorganizations.

The amendments regarding acquisitive reorganizations are principally contained in Proposed Sections 368(a)(1), (2), and (4),[63] and the amendments relating to taxable acquisitions are provided in Proposed Section 368(a)(5). (*See* appendix B.)

The proposals in part 3 for disallowing the deduction for interest on debt issued in dividend and redemption transactions are implemented by amendments to Section 163, which are contained in appendix C. The proposals for disallowing interest on certain acquisition indebtedness are implemented by amendments to Section 279, which are contained in appendix D. The amendments to Section 279 would put teeth into this toothless provision.

Brief commentary on each amendment with references to the text is provided in the appendices. The applicable amendment is also set forth in the notes to the relevant discussion in the text.

Revenue Effect

Although a revenue analysis of the impact of these proposals is not undertaken here, a few observations can be made about such effects. First, it would appear that the adoption of the provisions in part 2 would be revenue positive because, *inter alia*, the requirements for qualifying for tax-free reorganization treatment would be raised and much of the tax gamesmanship in the acquisition process would be eliminated. Looked at in isolation, the proposals for limited carryover basis treatment for certain taxable asset acquisitions (*see* chapter 5) may produce a revenue loss.[64] Compelling economic reasons exist, however, for allowing such transactions, especially for closely held corporations. Also, any revenue loss from the adoption of this provision should be more than offset by the revenue gains from the adoption of other provisions. Further, although it may appear counterintuitive, nonrecognition for a target corporation on the disposition of goodwill appears to be revenue positive.[65]

Although the revenue effect of the adoption of these rules is likely to be positive, it would appear that the adoption of the ALI's like kind exchange and clean mirror approaches could have a significant adverse revenue effect.[66]

---

63. No changes are made to the investment company provisions, Section 368(a)(2)(F), or title II bankruptcy provisions, Section 368(a)(3).

64. *See* chapter 5, p. 97. It is not certain this provision would result in a revenue loss; it has the same economic effect as a taxable stock acquisition without a Section 338 election to step-up the basis of assets.

65. This point is discussed in chapter 6, p. 108.

66. At the Invitational Conference, Mr. Pearlman said: "I had the feeling, albeit

Also, the adoption of the provisions proposed here should not contribute to an increase in general merger and acquisition activity. Further, the provisions would eliminate many tax driven devices, such as the tax-free treatment that was accorded the Chairman of MCA, Inc. in the otherwise taxable acquisition of MCA by Matsushita Electrical Industrial Co., Ltd.[67]

Simplicity

Although the rules proposed here are not the paradigm of simplicity, neither the proposals in the ALI 1989 Study nor the rules of current law are simple. In this regard, Ron Pearlman, the former Assistant Secretary of Treasury for Tax Policy and the former Chief of Staff of the Joint Committee on Taxation, thinks it would be a mistake to assume it is possible to write simple rules to govern the taxation of complicated corporate transactions.[68] Specifically, Mr. Pearlman said:

> I submit it would be dishonest to attempt to sell the American Law Institute [1982] proposals, the Senate Finance Staff Report [see note 3], or Professor Ginsburg's modest proposals [see note 35] as mere technical changes to the corporate tax system appropriate of a staff/ private sector collegial effort.
>
> Nor, in my opinion, should fundamental corporate tax reform be sold as simplification. In my October, 1983 appearance [as the Assistant Secretary of Treasury for Tax Policy] before the Senate Finance Committee on the subject of corporate tax reform following issuance of the Finance Committee Staff's preliminary report, I said:
>
> > We think it a bit dangerous . . . to sell these . . . proposals as simplification. Corporate transactions by their nature are com-

---

not based on fact, that corporate-level electivity, a major feature of both the American Law Institute and Finance Staff proposals, would bring more flexibility to the acquisition planning process, and thereby likely increase the level of merger and acquisition activity." *Invitational Conference, supra* note 35, at 35. The corporate level electivity in the proposals here (*see* chapter 5) is much more limited than that contained in either the SFC 1985 Proposals (*see* Thompson, *Suggested Alternative Approach, supra* note 3, at 647–59) or the ALI 1989 Study. Further, as pointed out above, there is a good economic justification for the rule proposed here and the overall revenue effect should be positive.

67. *See* chapter 4, p. 85 for a description of this transaction and of the proposal here to prohibit such transactions.

68. Pearlman, *The Political Environment of Corporate Tax Reform,* in *Invitational Conference, supra* note 35, at 34.

plex, and they will continue to remain complex, we suspect. We would guess that, ultimately, the rules governing those transactions will be complex. . . .

My views have not changed.[69]

Although the rules proposed here are not simple, they are less susceptible to abuse, more consistent, and more rational than the present rules. Also, the adoption of these rules should not add significantly to the complexity in the Code.

Summary

In evaluating these proposals, Congress should not be concerned that the proposals would deplete the tax revenues, unleash tax driven mergers and acquisitions, or significantly increase the complexity of the Code.

The adoption of the proposals contained in part 2 would rationalize the treatment of strategic type acquisitions in which a real acquiring corporation (like Chemical Bank) acquires a real target (like Manufactures Hanover Bank).

The adoption of the proposals contained in part 3 would make it more likely that there would be an adequate equity base in LBOs and other financially driven transactions. The adoption of all of the proposals contained here would lead to a more sensible structure for taxing mergers, acquisitions, and LBOs.[70]

---

69. *Id.*

70. This book deals only with the tax treatment of mergers and acquisitions involving domestic subchapter C corporations. It does not deal with (1) S corporations or other special types of corporations, (2) net operating losses and related issues, (3) foreign issues, or (4) collateral issues, such as the golden parachute and the greenmail rules.

· ·

CHAPTER 2

Current Treatment of Taxable Acquisitions, LBOs, and Tax-Free Acquisitive Reorganizations

Corporate acquisitions of stand-alone (*i.e.*, nonsubsidiary) target corporations fall into two broad categories: (1) taxable acquisitions, and (2) tax-free acquisitive reorganizations under Section 368.[1] Within each of these broad categories there can be either taxable or tax-free mergers, stock acquisitions, or asset acquisitions. Leveraged buyouts (LBOs) are taxable stock or asset acquisitions in which a substantial part of the consideration paid in the transaction is either debt or cash raised through the issuance of debt. Thus, LBOs are a subset of taxable acquisitions.

The principal distinguishing feature between a taxable acquisition and a tax-free acquisitive reorganization is the consideration paid by the acquiring corporation. The consideration paid in a taxable acquisition generally consists of cash or debt instruments of the acquiring corporation or a combination of the two. Also, in certain cases, stock may be used in taxable acquisitions. If a substantial portion (and in certain cases all) of the consideration paid by the acquiring corporation consists of its stock or stock of its parent corporation, the acquisition may (assuming certain other conditions are satisfied) qualify as a tax-free acquisitive reorganization.

The taxable sale by a corporation of part of its assets, such as a division, does not present significant tax policy issues and for that reason is not discussed here.[2] The taxable sale of the stock or assets of a subsidiary is dis-

---

1. For a more detailed discussion of this topic *see Federal Taxation of Business Enterprises, supra* chapter 1, note 20, vol. 3, at chs. 28–35 (taxable acquisition and LBOs) and chs. 41–48 (reorganizations).

2. As pointed out in chapter 3, p. 42, the proposal in the ALI 1989 Study for elective carryover basis on the sale of part of a corporation's assets is rejected here.

cussed further below; however, no changes in the present treatment of such transactions are recommended. Thus, this book focuses principally on the tax treatment of the acquisition of the stock or of substantially all of the assets of a target corporation that is not a subsidiary of another corporation. Such targets are sometimes referred to here as stand-alone targets.

The taxable stock acquisitions considered here involve the acquisition of at least 80 percent of the stock of the target as determined under Section 1504(a)(2) so that the transaction constitutes a qualified stock purchase within the meaning of Section 338(d)(3).

The various forms of taxable acquisitions, LBOs, and acquisitive reorganizations are discussed below. Finally, a partially taxable and partially nontaxable form of stock acquisition which employs a Section 351 incorporation transaction is discussed at p. 39.

Summary of Taxable Acquisitions and LBOs

Current law has three basic patterns of taxable acquisitions of stand-alone target corporations:

1. *Taxable Asset Acquisition.* In this first pattern, the acquiring corporation purchases for cash or debt instruments the target's assets, followed by the liquidation of the target (*i.e.*, an asset acquisition). This transaction may also be effectuated by merging, pursuant to state law, the target into the acquiring corporation. In a merger, the target's assets and liabilities are automatically transferred to the acquiring corporation, and the target's shareholders receive the merger consideration (*e.g.*, cash or debt instruments) in exchange for their target stock. The target's shareholders are required to cash in their stock or dissent and have their shares appraised. Also, the target may merge into a subsidiary of the acquiring corporation; this is generally referred to as a taxable forward triangular (or subsidiary) merger. Both of these mergers are treated as a taxable purchase of the target's assets followed by the liquidation of the target. Taxable forward triangular mergers are discussed further below.[3] These types of mergers can also be structured as tax-free reorganizations.[4]

2. *Taxable Stock Acquisition.* In this second pattern, the acquiring corporation purchases for cash or debt instruments the target's stock. After the acquisition the acquiring corporation may make an election under Section 338 to treat the stock acquisition as if there had been a purchase of the target's assets. If the Section 338 election is made, the target is treated as if it sold and immediately repurchased its assets. The stock acquisition can be

---

3. *See* p. 29.
4. *See* p. 36.

effectuated by a taxable reverse triangular (or subsidiary) merger. In this transaction, the acquiring corporation forms a shell subsidiary, and the shell merges into the target, with the following results: (1) the target's shareholders receive cash or debt instruments for their shares, and (2) the target becomes a subsidiary of the acquiror. Although the taxable reverse triangular merger is treated as a stock acquisition, the taxable forward triangular merger is treated as an asset acquisition. The taxable reverse triangular merger is discussed further below.[5] A reverse triangular merger can also be structured as a tax-free reorganization.

3. *Taxable Liquidation.* The third pattern involves the liquidation of the target followed by a sale of the target's assets by its shareholders. This third pattern is used much less often than the first two.

Treatment of Target's Shareholders in a Taxable Acquisition

The treatment of the target's shareholders is the same in each of these transactions. The shareholders have capital gain: (1) on the receipt of the sales proceeds upon the liquidation of the target after a direct sale of the target's assets, or after a taxable forward merger of the target into the acquiring corporation or its subsidiary; (2) on the sale of their stock in either a stock purchase or a taxable reverse subsidiary merger; and (3) on the receipt of the target's assets in liquidation in anticipation of sale.

If the target's stock is nontradable and the target's shareholders receive nontradable debt instruments of the acquiror, such instruments may qualify for installment sale treatment under Section 453.[6] If this section applies, the target's shareholders have nonrecognition until actual cash payments are received.[7] In a liquidation prior to sale, the target's shareholders take a fair market value basis for the target's assets;[8] assuming no post-liquidation appreciation in value, no gain or loss results from the sale of the assets to the acquiror.

---

5. *See* p. 29.

6. Section 453 does not apply to a sale of tradable stock (*see* I.R.C. § 453(k)(2)(A) (1991)) or to the receipt of a debt instrument that is tradable or payable on demand (*see* I.R.C. § 453(f)(3) and (4) (1991)).

7. The selling shareholder's basis of the installment obligation is not stepped up on death. *See* I.R.C. § 691(a)(4) (1991). Thus, once a target's shareholder sells his or her stock for an installment obligation, the gain inherent in the obligation will be recognized at some point. On the other hand, in the case of the receipt by a target shareholder of stock of an acquiring corporation in a tax-free acquisitive reorganization, the basis of the stock is stepped up (or down) on the death of the shareholder. *See* I.R.C. § 1014 (1991). Thus, death wipes out potential taxable gain.

8. I.R.C. § 334(a) (1991).

Except for the proposal in chapter 9 to prevent misallocations of purchase price, this book does not suggest any changes in the treatment of the target's shareholders in a taxable acquisition.

Treatment of Target Corporation in a Taxable Acquisition

Stand-Alone (nonsubsidiary) Target Corporation

As a result of the repeal of the *General Utilities* doctrine by the Tax Reform Act of 1986 (TRA 1986), the target has recognition treatment on the direct sale of its assets and on the disposition of its assets in a taxable forward merger into the acquiring corporation or a subsidiary of the acquiring corporation. Also, the target recognizes gain (and in some cases loss) under Section 336 upon the distribution of its assets in liquidation. The target has nonrecognition upon the purchase of its stock, unless the acquiror elects under Section 338 to treat the transaction as an asset acquisition. If a Section 338 election is made, the target has full recognition of gains and losses and takes a cost basis for its assets.

As a result of the repeal of the *General Utilities* doctrine, an acquisition of a nonsubsidiary target corporation with appreciated assets generally is structured as a stock acquisition without a Section 338 election, thereby avoiding the corporate level tax. The present value of the tax benefits to the acquiring corporation from a step-up in basis of the target's assets does not offset the detriment associated with an immediate tax paid by the target corporation.[9]

An exception to this general rule applies if the target has net operating losses or credits that can be utilized to offset the corporate level tax that is otherwise due in an asset acquisition or a stock acquisition followed by a Section 338 election.[10]

The maximum potential double tax from an asset sale or Section 338 election is approximately 52 percent, illustrated as follows:

Assume that target corporation has assets with a fair market value of $1 million and with a zero tax basis. The target has no net operating losses or tax credits. The target has a sole shareholder who has a zero basis for her stock. If the target's assets are sold for $1 million, the target incurs a tax

---

9. This point is extensively developed in Coven, *Mandatory Uniform Rules, supra* chapter 1, note 35, at 159–64.

10. If a Section 338 election is made there is no limitation on the amount of the target's net operating losses and unused credits that can be utilized to offset the gain recognized by the target as a result of the election. *See* I.R.C. §§ 382(h)(1)(C) and 383 (1991). *See, generally* Coven, *Mandatory Uniform Rules, supra* note 14, at 162–164.

liability under Section 11 of $340,000 on the sale and has $660,000 of after-tax proceeds. The target distributes the after-tax proceeds to its sole shareholder, who incurs a 28 percent tax equal to $184,800. Thus, the total corporate and shareholder level taxes equals $524,800, or approximately 52 percent.

———————

Prior to the TRA 1986, the maximum tax on an asset sale or stock sale with a Section 338 election was 20 percent, assuming the target had no appreciated land or equipment or other recapture assets that would produce ordinary income on sale. Under the law then in effect, Section 337 provided nonrecognition treatment (assuming no recapture items) on the sale of the target's assets or upon a Section 338 election, and the maximum capital gains rate on shareholders was 20 percent.[11]

Because of the increase in the tax rate on asset sales from as little as 20 percent prior to the TRA 1986 to 52 percent after, the repeal of the *General Utilities* doctrine has practically eliminated taxable asset sales and taxable forward mergers by nonsubsidiary target corporations that do not have net operating losses or other credits available to shelter the corporate level tax. Thus, the overwhelming number of taxable acquisitions of nonsubsidiary target corporations are structured as stock acquisitions without Section 338 elections. This is so even though there may be good business reasons for structuring the acquisition as an asset acquisition. For example, the acquiring corporation may only want to acquire certain of the target's assets and assume certain of its liabilities. This is possible in an asset acquisition. In a stock acquisition, however, the target continues to hold all of its assets and liabilities.

Chapters 5 and 6 contain proposals (relating to carryover basis treatment and to nonrecognition on a disposition of goodwill) that would reduce the tax cost associated with certain taxable asset acquisitions, thereby permitting those transactions to again be utilized. The proposal in chapter 5 would permit the acquisition of a target's assets to be completed as a carryover basis transaction in which the target has nonrecognition treatment and the acquiring corporation takes a carryover basis for the target's assets. The proposal in chapter 6 would apply if the parties in a taxable assets acquisition do not elect carryover basis treatment. In such cases, the target is not taxed on the sale of its goodwill and other nonamortizable intangibles.

Reverse and Forward Subsidiary (Triangular) Mergers

Reverse Subsidiary Mergers. If the stock of a publicly held corporation is being acquired, the acquisition can be structured as a taxable reverse subsidiary merger. In this transaction, an acquiring parent first forms a new

———————

11. *See* Former I.R.C. § 1202 (1985).

wholly-owned subsidiary (acquiring sub) and transfers the merger consideration to acquiring sub. Acquiring sub then merges into the target with the following consequences: (1) the target survives the merger, (2) the target's shareholders receive the purchase price to be paid (cash or debt investments) for their target shares which are canceled, and (3) the acquiring parent's shares in the acquiring sub are converted into shares of target so that target becomes a wholly-owned subsidiary of acquiring parent. This transaction may be diagramed as in figure 1.

The Internal Revenue Service treats this transaction as a purchase by the acquiring parent of the target's stock.[12] The target has nonrecognition treatment unless the acquiring parent makes a Section 338 election. The target's shareholders are taxed. The acquiring sub has no tax consequences. Thus, the reverse subsidiary merger produces the same tax results as a direct stock purchase.

The principal business advantage of the reverse subsidiary merger is that it allows the acquiring parent to acquire in one transaction all of the stock of the target without the target's shareholders having the right to retain their shares. Shareholders may, pursuant to the applicable state business corporation law, dissent from the transaction and be cashed out at the appraised value of their shares.

Virtually every taxable acquisition of a publicly held corporation is effectuated with a reverse subsidiary merger. In stock acquisitions of closely held corporations, the reverse subsidiary merger may also be used to force recalcitrant shareholders of the target to sell their stock.

If the consideration paid in a reverse subsidiary merger constitutes voting stock of the acquiror, the transition may constitute a tax-free reorganization.[13] Thus, a reverse subsidiary merger may be either taxable or tax-free.

Forward Subsidiary Mergers.   In a taxable forward subsidiary merger, an acquiring parent forms a new, wholly-owned subsidiary (acquiring sub) and transfers the merger consideration to acquiring sub. The target then merges into the acquiring sub with the acquiring sub surviving. The target's shareholders receive the merger consideration. A forward subsidiary merger may be diagramed as in figure 2.

This transaction is treated as a sale by the target of its assets followed by a liquidating distribution of the merger consideration by the target to its shareholders.[14] Both the target and its shareholders are taxed on the transaction, but the acquiring sub has nonrecognition treatment.

---

12. Rev. Rul. 90–95, 1990–2 C.B. 67; Rev. Rul. 67–448, 1967–2 C.B. 144.

13. I.R.C. § 368 (a)(2)(E) (1991). *See* p. 38.

14. *See, e.g.,* Rev. Rul. 69–6, 1969–1 C.B. 104 and *West Shore Fuels, Inc. v. United States,* 598 F.2d 1236 (2d Cir. 1979).

Figure 1. Reverse Subsidiary Triangular Merger

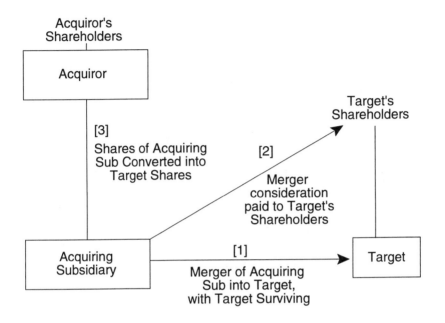

WHEN THE DUST SETTLES

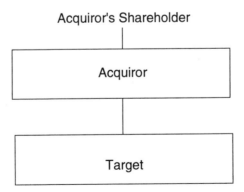

Figure 2. Forward Subsidiary Triangular Merger

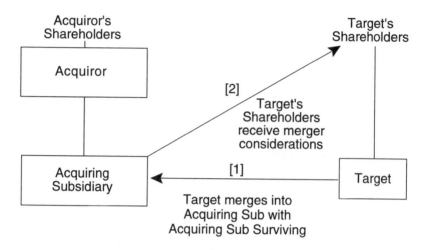

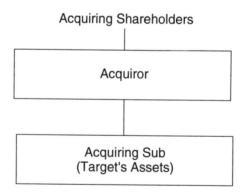

WHEN THE DUST SETTLES

Generally a taxable forward merger is not used because as a result of the repeal of the *General Utilities* doctrine the target has complete recognition of gain.

This artificial distinction between taxable forward and reverse subsidiary mergers would largely be eliminated if the proposal for carryover basis treatment in chapter 5 is adopted.

If the consideration paid in the acquisition of the target is stock of the acquiror, the transaction may qualify as a reorganization.[15] Thus, the forward subsidiary merger may be either taxable or tax-free.

Acquisition of Target that is a Subsidiary

The acquisition of a subsidiary corporation that is a member of a consolidated group generally is structured as either (1) a direct asset acquisition, or (2) a stock acquisition with a Section 338(h)(10) election. If a Section 338(h)(10) election is made, the transaction is treated as an asset sale by the target with the gain or loss being reported in the consolidated return of the selling parent corporation. Only one level of tax applies on the sale of the assets of the subsidiary target, because under Section 332, the parent has no tax upon receipt of the deemed liquidating proceeds.

It generally is prudent to file a Section 338(h)(10) election in a stock acquisition of a subsidiary. If, however, the parent's basis for the subsidiary's stock is substantially higher than the subsidiary's basis for its assets, the transaction generally is structured as a stock sale without a Section 338 election. In these situations, the parent's taxable gain on the sale of the stock is less than it would be with either an asset sale or a stock sale with a Section 338(h)(10) election.

In view of the enactment of Section 1503(e) by the 1987 Act, in many cases there is likely to be little difference between the basis to the parent for the subsidiary's stock and the basis for the subsidiary's assets. Section 1503(e), overrides the decision in *Woods Investment*,[16] which, in essence, held that under the consolidated return regulations a parent corporation could have an inappropriately high basis in the stock of a subsidiary. Section 1503(e) eliminates this distortion by providing that prior to the sale of stock of a subsidiary, the parent's basis for the subsidiary's stock is redetermined without regard to certain limits in computing earnings and profits. For a subsidiary that was not previously acquired in a taxable stock acquisition, this provision causes the parent's basis for the subsidiary's stock to approximate the subsidiary's basis for its assets. Thus, the parent is likely to have the same gain or loss on sale of the subsidiary's stock as it would have on a sale of the subsidiary's assets. Thus, Section 1503(e) makes it more

---

15. I.R.C. § 368(a)(2)(D) (1991). *See* p. 36.

16. *Woods Investment Co. v. Commissioner*, 85 T.C. 274 (1985).

likely that a Section 338(h)(10) election will be filed on the sale of the stock of a subsidiary.

The rules governing taxable dispositions of subsidiaries are basically sound. These rules are not addressed further here, except to make the point that the ALI's proposal for break-up dispositions[17] should be rejected.

Summary of Treatment of Target Corporation

In summary, an acquisition of a nonsubsidiary target corporation that does not have net operating losses or credits generally is structured as a stock acquisition without a Section 338 election. The stock acquisition may be effectuated either as a direct purchase by the acquiring corporation of the target's stock or as a taxable reverse subsidiary merger. An acquisition of a subsidiary target corporation is generally structured as either an asset acquisition or a stock acquisition with a Section 338(h)(10) election to treat the transaction as an asset sale.

Anti-mirror Subsidiary Provisions

As pointed out in chapter 3, the mirror subsidiary technique can no longer be used to accomplish a tax-free break-up of a target corporation after a stock purchase. The anti-mirror legislation and regulations reach the correct policy result, and therefore, the proposal in the ALI 1989 Study regarding break-up dispositions, which would reinstate the mirror, should be rejected.

Treatment of the Acquiror in a Taxable Acquisition

In a taxable asset acquisition, the acquiring corporation takes a cost basis for the target's assets. None of the target's tax attributes such as net operating losses come over to the acquiror. In a taxable stock acquisition the acquiror takes a cost basis for the target's stock. After a stock acquisition there is no change in the target's basis for its assets and all of the target's tax attributes, such as net operating losses continue, subject to the limitations of Sections 382 and 383.[18] If the acquiror makes a Section 338 election, the target has complete recognition treatment and takes a cost basis for its assets. In a Section 338 election, all of the target's tax attributes disappear; net operating losses may, however, be utilized to offset gain recognized.[19]

The tax treatment of the acquiror in taxable acquisitions is basically sound; however, the proposals contained in chapters 5 and 6 (relating to carryover basis treatment and to nonrecognition on a disposition of goodwill) affect both the target and the acquiring corporation.

---

17. See chapter 3, p. 42.

18. Sections 382 and 383 are beyond the scope of this book; however, the basic elements of Section 382 are illustrated in chapter 1, p. 5.

19. I.R.C. § 382(h)(1)(C) (1991).

Treatment of LBOs

LBOs are taxable acquisitions in which a substantial portion of the consideration is either debt or is raised by the issuance of debt. In many LBOs, such as KKR's acquisition of RJR Nabisco, Inc., the acquisition vehicle is a shell corporation that is formed by a venture capitalist for the sole purpose of effectuating the acquisition. The shell issues debt needed to complete the transaction. LBOs are generally structured as stock acquisitions (or reverse subsidiary mergers which are treated as stock acquisitions) for the same reason that other taxable acquisitions are so structured: to prevent the recognition of gain at the target corporate level. A major issue in any LBO is whether the debt is treated as debt for federal income tax purposes. Another issue is whether the interest on debt that is treated as debt for federal income tax purposes is disallowed under (1) Section 279, which disallows the interest deduction on certain convertible and subordinated acquisition indebtedness, or (2) Section 163(i), which disallows the interest deduction on certain high yield discount obligations.

Chapter 10 discusses in greater detail the equity conversion feature that exists with LBOs and the concerns with LBOs.[20]

Summary of Acquisitive Reorganizations

In an acquisitive reorganization, a substantial portion of the consideration paid in the acquisition of the target is stock of the acquiror. These transactions are defined as "reorganizations" and are set forth in Section 368 of the Code. To qualify as a reorganization there must be a continuity of interest[21] (i.e., the target's shareholders must receive a stock interest in the acquiror), a continuity of business enterprise[22] (i.e., the business previously conducted by the target must be continued), and a business purpose (as distinguished from a pure tax avoidance motive).[23]

---

20. Part 3 deals generally with LBOs and other equity conversion transactions.

21. Reorganizations under Section 368(a)(1)(B) and (C) and the reverse triangular reorganization under Section 368(a)(2)(E) have statutorily mandated continuity-of-interest requirements. In addition, courts also have imposed a nonstatutory continuity of interest requirement for all Section 368(a) reorganizations. See, e.g., Helvering v. Minnesota Tea Co., 296 U.S. 378, 385 (1935) (stock interest received must be "definite and material" and a substantial part of the value of the thing transferred). The present continuity of interest requirement and the proposed revisions in that requirement are set forth in chapter 4, pp. 53, 59, and p. 74.

22. See Treas. Reg. § 1.368–1(d) (1980). The continuity of enterprise requirement and its suggested retention are discussed in chapter 4, p. 53, and p. 91.

23. See, e.g., Treas. Reg. § 1.368–1(b) (1980); Gregory v. Helvering, 293 U.S. 465 (1935). The business purpose requirement and its suggested retention is discussed in chapter 4, p. 53.

In an acquisitive reorganization, the target's shareholders receive nonrecognition treatment on the exchange of their target stock or securities for stock or securities of the acquiror.[24] If the target's shareholders receive other property (*i.e.*, boot) they recognize gain to the extent of the boot,[25] and the gain is treated as a dividend if the transaction has the "effect of the distribution of a dividend."[26] The target and the acquiror generally have nonrecognition treatment,[27] with the acquiror taking a carryover basis in the target's assets.[28]

There are seven basic forms of acquisitive reorganizations: (1) four reorganizations in which the assets of the target are acquired (asset reorganizations), and (2) three reorganizations in which the stock of the target is acquired (stock reorganizations). The stock or assets acquired in any of the above seven reorganizations may be pushed down to a subsidiary (over and down reorganizations).

Asset Reorganizations

In the four asset reorganizations, the assets of the target corporation are acquired either by the acquiring corporation or by a subsidiary of the acquiring corporation. The following are the asset reorganizations:

Direct Merger Under Section 368(a)(1)(A). The target merges into the acquiror.[29] Although the statute does not set forth a requirement that the consideration paid be stock of the acquiring corporation, courts have held that there is such a requirement (*i.e.*, a continuity of interest requirement).[30] The Service's current ruling policy is that to satisfy the continuity of interest requirement in a direct merger at least 50 percent of the consideration paid must be stock of the acquiror.[31]

Forward Triangular Merger Under Section 368(a)(2)(D). The target merges into a subsidiary (acquiring subsidiary) that is a wholly owned (or at least an 80 percent owned) subsidiary of the acquiring parent. Under the Service's ruling policy, at least 50 percent of the consideration paid must consist of stock of the acquiring parent. The acquiring subsidiary must ac-

24. I.R.C. § 354(a) (1991).
25. I.R.C. § 356(a)(1) (1991).
26. I.R.C. § 356(a)(2); *Clark v. Commissioner*, 489 U.S. 726 (1989).
27. I.R.C. §§ 361, 1032 (1991).
28. I.R.C. § 362 (1991).
29. I.R.C. § 368(a)(1)(A) (1991).
30. *See, e.g.*, *Helvering v. Minnesota Tea Co.*, 296 U.S. 378 (1935).
31. *See* Rev. Proc. 77–37, § 3.02, 1977–2 C.B. 568. This is only ruling policy and does not necessarily set the limits of the law. One court held that the continuity of interest requirement is satisfied where stock of the acquiring corporation was only 25 percent of the consideration paid. *See Miller v. Commissioner*, 84 F.2d 415 (6th Cir. 1936).

quire "substantially all" of the target's assets.[32] This transaction is the same as the taxable forward subsidiary merger diagramed on page 32, except at least 50 percent of the merger consideration must be stock of the acquiring parent.

Direct Acquisition of Target's Assets Under Section 368(a)(1)(C). The acquiror acquires "substantially all" of the target's assets in exchange for voting stock of the acquiror.[33] The acquiror may assume liabilities of the target.[34] Subject to the "boot relaxation rule," the acquiror can pay consideration other than its stock. Under this rule, the amount of money or other property (including the assumption of liabilities) that can be paid by the acquiror is limited to 20 percent of the value of the target's assets.[35] The target must, pursuant to the plan of reorganization, distribute the stock, securities and other property it receives, as well as its other properties.[36]

Triangular Acquisition of Target's Assets Under Section 368(a)(1)(C). A wholly-owned (or at least an 80 percent owned) subsidiary of an acquiring parent acquires "substantially all" of the target's assets in exchange for voting stock of the acquiring parent.[37]

Stock Reorganizations

There are three types of reorganizations in which the stock of the target corporation is acquired by either the acquiring corporation or one of its subsidiaries:

Direct Stock-for-Stock Acquisition Under Section 368(a)(1)(B). The acquiror acquires "control" of the target (*i.e.*, at least 80 percent of the target's stock) in exchange "solely" for voting stock of the acquiror.[38] The acquiring corporation is not required to receive at least 80 percent of the stock in the transaction; the acquiring corporation only needs to hold at least 80 percent after the transaction. Thus, "creeping" stock for stock reorganizations are allowed as long as pre-reorganization stock of the target held by the acquiring corporation has been held for a significant period before the reorganization.[39]

---

32. I.R.C. § 368(a)(2)(D) (1991). The forward subsidiary merger has the same continuity of interest requirement as the direct merger. *See* Treas. Reg. § 1.368–2(b)(2) (1985); Rev. Proc. 77–37, § 3.02, 1977–2 C.B. 568. Stock of the acquiring subsidiary cannot be issued to the target's shareholders.

33. I.R.C. § 368(a)(1)(C) (1991).

34. *Id.*

35. I.R.C. § 368(a)(2)(B) (1991).

36. I.R.C. § 368(a)(2)(G) (1991).

37. This is also a "C" reorganization under I.R.C. § 368(a)(1)(C) (1991) (parenthetical clause). The requirements for this type of reorganization are essentially the same as those for a direct acquisition of the target's assets.

38. I.R.C. § 368(a)(1)(B) (1991).

39. Treas. Reg. § 1.368–2(b)(2) (1985).

Triangular Stock-for-Stock Acquisition Under Section 368(a)(1)(B). A wholly-owned (or at least an 80 percent owned) subsidiary of an acquiring parent acquires "control" of the target in exchange "solely" for voting stock of the acquiring parent.[40]

Reverse Triangular Merger Under Section 368(a)(2)(E). A wholly-owned (or at least an 80 percent owned) subsidiary (acquiring subsidiary) of an acquiring parent merges into the target. In the merger, the acquiring parent acquires "control" of the target (*i.e.*, at least 80 percent of the target's stock) in exchange for voting stock of the acquiring parent; the target thus becomes a subsidiary of the acquiring parent. The acquiring corporation must actually receive at least 80 percent of the target's stock in the transaction.[41] Thus, "creeping" reverse triangular mergers are severely limited. The target must continue to hold substantially all of its assets.[42] This transaction is the same as the taxable reverse subsidiary merger diagramed on page 31, except at least 80 percent of the target's stock must be exchanged for voting stock of the acquiring parent.

Over and Down Reorganizations Under Section 368(a)(2)(C)

Finally, after any of the seven reorganizations discussed above, the target's stock or assets, as the case may be, may be pushed down to a subsidiary.[43] This type of transaction is generally referred to as an "over and down."

Summary of Treatment of Parties to a Reorganization

If an acquisition of a target by an acquiror or an acquiring subsidiary satisfies any of the seven forms of acquisitive reorganizations, the following tax treatment results to the parties to the transaction. The target's shareholders have nonrecognition treatment, except to the extent they receive nonstock consideration (*i.e.*, boot). Gain realized is recognized to the extent of the boot. The recognized gain may be a dividend if the transaction has the effect of a dividend. The target has nonrecognition treatment. The acquiror and any acquiring subsidiary have nonrecognition treatment and take a carryover basis for the target's stock or assets, as the case may be.

---

40. *See id.* (parenthetical clause). This is another form of a "B" reorganization. Consequently, the requirements for this type of acquisition are virtually the same as those for the direct stock for stock acquisition.

41. Treas. Reg. § 1.368–2 (j)(3)(i) (1985).

42. I.R.C. § 368(a)(2)(E) (1991). The target also must hold substantially all of the assets of the aquiring subsidiary, other than the merger consideration.

43. I.R.C. § 368(a)(2)(C) (1991).

Chapter 4 proposes amendments to the reorganization definition to provide for uniform treatment of all forms of stock and asset reorganizations. Only minor changes are suggested in the treatment of the parties to a reorganization.

Combination Stock Acquisitions and Tax-Free Section 351 Contributions

If an acquisition of a target is being planned and a minority of the target shareholders (say 20 percent) desire tax-free treatment and a majority (say 80 percent) prefer to receive cash, the transaction will not qualify as a tax-free reorganization. To address this problem, a transaction could be structured in which the acquiring corporation first forms a new corporation (Newco) to which it transfers cash in exchange for new common stock. Simultaneously with this transfer by the acquiring corporation, the shareholders of target who desire tax-free treatment contribute their target stock in exchange for stock (probably preferred stock) of Newco. This transaction is treated as a tax-free incorporation transaction under Section 351. In the second step of the transaction, Newco either purchases directly (or purchases indirectly in a taxable reverse subsidiary merger)[44] the stock of target held by the shareholders of target who desire to sell for cash. After the dust settles, acquiror controls all of the common stock of Newco, which owns all of the stock of target, and the shareholders of target desiring tax-free treatment own preferred stock of Newco.

The Service has ruled that this type of transaction will not be viewed as a failed reorganization and that the Section 351 portion of the transaction will be respected.[45] Chapter 4, p. 85 denies this type of acquisitive transaction the benefit of Section 351 by testing the transaction under the reorganization provisions.

---

44. Rev. Rul. 67–448, 1967–2 C.B. 144. See the diagram of a reverse subsidiary merger on p. 31.

45. Rev. Rul. 84–71, 1984–1 C.B. 106.

CHAPTER 3

. . . .

Background to Policy Issues Involved in Mergers and Acquisitions

This chapter discusses the background of the issues addressed in this book relating generally to mergers and acquisitions. The background to the issues involving LBOs and similar transactions is addressed in chapters 10 and 11.

The principal reference point for this discussion is the ALI 1989 Study,[1] which sets out comprehensive proposals for the reform of the merger and acquisition provisions. Discussed first is the ALI's proposed treatment of the target and acquiror in an acquisitive transaction. The discussion then turns to the ALI's proposed like kind exchange approach for the treatment of the target's shareholders.

Next, this chapter sets forth other approaches that have been suggested for the treatment of a target in an acquisition. Finally, it addresses the problems of the misallocation of purchase price in both taxable and tax-free acquisitions. The ALI's proposed treatment for LBOs and other equity conversion transactions is discussed in chapter 11.

ALI's Approach to the Treatment of the Target and Acquiror in an Acquisition

Carryover Basis Rule

Both the ALI 1982 Study[2] and the ALI 1989 study[3] suggest that the acquisitive reorganization concept be removed from the Code and that the

---

1. *ALI 1989 Study, supra* chapter 1, note 2.
2. *ALI 1982 Study, supra* chapter 1, note 3. For a description of these proposals

treatment of the target corporation in an acquisition transaction be decoupled from the treatment of the target's shareholders. The ALI's like kind approach to the treatment of the target's shareholders is addressed in the next section.[4] This section focuses on the treatment of the target and the acquiror, including the ALI's clean mirror approach.[5]

Under the ALI proposal, the acquiring corporation and the target may elect, in both stock and asset acquisitions, to treat the transaction in one of the following ways. First, they can elect carryover basis treatment. With this election, the target has nonrecognition in both a stock acquisition and an asset acquisition. In a stock acquisition, no change in the basis of the target's assets occurs, and in an asset acquisition, the acquiring corporation takes the target's assets with a carryover basis (*i.e.*, the target's basis). Second, the parties can elect cost basis treatment. With a cost basis, the target has recognition treatment in both a stock and an asset acquisition, except in certain situations with respect to goodwill. In a stock acquisition, the target takes a fair market value basis for its assets, except for nonrecognized goodwill, and in an asset acquisition, the acquiring corporation takes a cost basis for the target's assets, except for nonrecognized goodwill.

Although the proposal made here retains the reorganization concept,[6] it is suggested here that (1) an elective carryover basis regime apply for certain taxable asset acquisitions,[7] and (2) the target have nonrecognition on the disposition of goodwill in certain taxable asset acquisitions.[8] The ALI has made similar proposals; however, the circumstances in which these rules would apply under the proposals here are much more limited than the circumstances in which they would apply under the ALI 1989 Study. This point is developed further in chapters 5 and 6.

Break-Up Dispositions: Adoption of a "Clean Mirror" Approach

At the corporate level, the ALI would extend its carryover basis rationale to the point of allowing what the proposals refer to as break-up disposi-

---

when they were in draft form, *see* Renato Beghe, *The American Law Institute Subchapter C Study: Acquisitions and Distributions*, 33 Tax Law. 743 (1980); *See also*, Bernard Wolfman, *Continuity of Interest and The American Law Institute*, 57 Taxes 840 (1979) [hereinafter cited as "Wolfman, *Continuity of Interest*"].

3. *ALI 1989 Study, supra* chapter 1, note 2, at part II, proposal 15.

4. *See* p. 46.

5. *See* p. 42.

6. *See* chapter 4.

7. *See* chapter 5.

8. *See* chapter 6.

tions,[9] which would explicitly allow mirror transactions. Mirror transactions became visible after the repeal of the *General Utilities* doctrine in 1986.[10] The Congressional response to the mirror and related transactions provides guidance on the current policy issues involving taxable acquisitions and the ALI's proposal to allow break-up dispositions. For this reason, both the mirror and the Congressional responses are examined briefly here.

A typical mirror transaction involved the acquisition by an acquiring parent corporation of stock of a target corporation that had some assets the acquiring parent did not need. The acquiring parent, therefore, structured the acquisition to allow the parent to dispose of the unwanted assets without taxable gain. Prior to the acquisition, the parent would form two subsidiaries and transfer the consideration to be paid to the subsidiaries. One of the subsidiaries would be given consideration equal to the value of the unwanted assets, and the second subsidiary would be given consideration equal to the value of the wanted assets. The subsidiaries would then purchase the stock of the target corporation in the same proportions as the consideration held. The target would then liquidate distributing the wanted assets to one subsidiary and the unwanted assets to the other. Under the stock aggregation rules of the consolidated return regulations,[11] the liquidation was treated as if the target liquidated into its parent in a nontaxable liquidation under Section 332.

If the aggregation principle applied after the repeal of the *General Utilities* doctrine, the target corporation would have nonrecognition treatment on the liquidation under current Section 337. After the liquidation the parent would then sell the stock of the subsidiary that held the unwanted assets. No gain or loss would be recognized on such sale because the sale proceeds would equal the parent's basis in the stock of that subsidiary.

Prior to the Revenue Act of 1987 (1987 Act),[12] it was uncertain whether the Treasury would promulgate regulations under its general regulatory authority under Section 337(d) to repeal the stock aggregation rules of the

---

9. *ALI 1989 Study*, *supra* chapter 1, note 2, at part V, proposals 12 and 13.

10. For general background discussion of the mirror transaction, *see Federal Taxation of Business Enterprises*, *supra* chapter 1 note 20, at § 14:17. *See also* Samuel C. Thompson, Jr., *A Review of the Provisions of the Tax Reform Act of 1986 Relating to Corporate Acquisitions*, 33 Tax Notes, 399, 401 (1986); Lee A. Sheppard, *Room Full Of Mirrors, Enforcing General Utilities Repeal*, 33 Tax Notes 281 (1986); Eric M. Zolt, *The General Utilities Doctrine: Examining the Scope of Repeal*, 65 Taxes 819 (1987).

11. Treas. Reg. § 1.1504–34 (1966).

12. The Revenue Act of 1987, Pub. L. No. 100–203, 101 Stat. 1330–382 (1987) [hereinafter cited as the "1987 Act"].

consolidated return regulations as they apply under Section 337. Repeal would have denied nonrecognition treatment under current Section 337 upon the liquidation of the target corporation in a typical mirror transaction.

Before the Treasury addressed the issue, Congress acted. In the 1987 Act Congress eliminated the possibility of a mirror transaction by providing for nonrecognition to a corporation under Section 337 only for distributions to an actual 80 percent parent corporation.[13]

In addition to the mirror transaction, taxpayers developed other transactions which arguably avoided the repeal of the *General Utilities* doctrine. One such transaction was known as the "Son of Mirrors." The Service announced that the investment adjustment provisions of the consolidated return regulations would be amended to prohibit this transaction,[14] and the Treasury has published regulations that effectively shut down the Son of Mirrors and related transactions.[15] Two other transactions involved (1) the application of Section 304 to a sale by one controlled subsidiary of stock of a lower-tiered subsidiary to a sister-controlled subsidiary,[16] and (2) the use of a tax-free spin off under Section 355 in connection with a taxable stock acquisition.[17] These variants of mirrors have been eliminated by (1) the 1987 Act, which added Section 304(b)(4) and amended Section 355(b)(2)(D),[18] and (2) the Revenue Reconciliation Act of 1990, which added Section 355(d).[19]

The basic policy decision reflected in the anti-mirror regulations and legislation is that after the acquisition by an acquiring corporation, the tax law should not allow the disposition of a portion of target's assets without a corporate level tax. This is so even though (1) there is a carryover basis for the assets, and (2) the target's old shareholders are subject to tax. This legislative decision protects the integrity of the corporate tax and, therefore, should not be reversed.

---

13. I.R.C. § 337(c) (1991).

14. Notice 87–14, 1987–1 C.B. 445. *See, generally,* Lee A. Sheppard, *The Prodigal Son of Mirror,* 34 Tax Notes 444 (1987).

15. Treas. Reg. § 1.337-(d) (1991); Treas. Reg. § 1.1502–20 (1991). *See Federal Taxation of Business Enterprises, supra* chapter 1, note 20, at § 14:17.

16. *See* Lawrence M. Axelrod, *Section 304, Excess Loss Accounts and Other Consolidated Return Gallimaufry,* 36 Tax Notes 729 (1987).

17. *See, e.g.,* Karla W. Simon and Daniel L. Simmons, *The Future of Section 355,* 40 Tax Notes 291 (1988).

18. *See* Richard H. Nicholls, *1987 Tax Provisions Affecting Corporate Acquisitions & Dispositions,* 39 Tax Notes 637 (1988).

19. RRA 1990, *supra* chapter 1, note 17.

The legislative decision on mirrors is directly contrary to the ALI's proposals regarding break-up dispositions.[20] Under the break-up disposition proposal, corporations would have no gain or loss upon a sale of stock of a subsidiary if the sales proceeds are distributed to the shareholders in liquidation or otherwise.[21] Thus, if a parent corporation sold all of the stock of its wholly-owned subsidiary and distributed the proceeds to the parent's shareholders, the parent would not be subject to tax on the transaction.[22] There would only be a shareholder level tax, and the subsidiary would keep its basis for its assets, unless a Section 338 election was filed. This transaction produces results similar to the mirror transaction (that is, a carryover basis on the disposition of part of the target's assets and a shareholder level tax).

In the context of break-up dispositions, the ALI 1989 Study would explicitly allow the result of a mirror transaction by providing that after the acquisition of a target corporation, the basis of the stock of any prior or newly formed subsidiary of the target is stepped-up to reflect its allocable portion of the purchase price paid for the target's stock.[23] Thus, after the acquisition, the stock of any of the target's subsidiaries could be sold without recognition of gain and the purchaser would hold the stock of the purchased subsidiary that had a carryover basis for its assets.[24] Of course, the basis could be stepped-up with a Section 338 election, but such an election would only rarely be made. In the words of the ALI 1989 Study, the proposal would make it feasible to achieve the results of a "clean mirror" acquisition without the necessity of organizing mirrors.[25]

The ALI's carryover basis rule which is discussed above, in combination with its break-up disposition rule would lead to unlimited deferral of the corporate tax on the nonordinary course disposition of assets. Under these two rules, it is likely that virtually every such disposition would be made tax-free with a carryover basis for the assets. The break-up disposition rule would be used on a sale of part of the assets, and the carryover basis rule would be used on the sale of all of the assets. The only exception would be situations in which the selling corporation had net operating losses that could offset taxable gain.

Congress was correct in adopting the anti-mirror legislation because unbounded deferral is fundamentally inconsistent with the concept of a cor-

---

20. *See ALI 1989 Study, supra* chapter 1, note 2, at part II, proposals nos. 12 and 13, pp. 114–31.

21. *ALI 1989 Study, supra* chapter 1, note 2, at proposal 12, p. 115.

22. *See ALI 1989 Study, supra* chapter 1, note 2, at proposal 12.

23. *ALI 1989 Study, supra* chapter 1, note 2, at proposal 13(c) pp. 126, 129–30.

24. *ALI 1989 Study, supra* chapter 1, note 2, at 129–30.

25. *ALI 1989 Study, supra* chapter 1, note 2, at 124.

porate tax. For the same reasons, Congress should not adopt the ALI's break-up disposition proposal. Any break-up or other sales of a corporation's assets or stock should be subject to immediate tax (except, as is demonstrated below, with respect to certain goodwill).[26] This rule is consistent with the repeal of the *General Utilities* doctrine.

For the above reasons, the possible repeal of the anti-mirror legislation or the possibility of adopting the break-up disposition rule suggested by the ALI are not addressed further here.

Treatment of Target's Goodwill

The ALI 1989 Study also proposes that even in a cost basis acquisition the parties be allowed to elect carryover basis treatment for goodwill, going concern value, and other nonamortizable intangibles.[27] Such a proposal was contained in the original ALI proposals.[28] Further, the Treasury's Subchapter C Outline calls for the review of possible exceptions to the repeal of the *General Utilities* doctrine for assets such as goodwill and subsidiary stock.[29] Thus, it can be expected that the treatment of goodwill will be one of the continuing policy issues. This issue is addressed here, both under the assumption that the cost of goodwill continues to be nondeductible for tax purposes and under the assumption that proposed legislation making such cost deductible will be enacted.[30]

ALI's Proposals for the Treatment of the Target's Shareholders

In repealing the reorganization concept, the ALI proposals would automatically repeal the business purpose,[31] continuity of business enterprise,[32] and continuity of interest[33] doctrines. Thus, the ALI would allow any shareholder of a target corporation to swap tax-free his or her stock in the target for stock of the acquiring corporation (or a controlled subsidiary),

---

26. *See* chapter 6.

27. *See ALI 1989 Study, supra* chapter 1, note 2, at part II, proposal no. 14., p. 132.

28. *ALI 1982 Study, supra* chapter 1, note 2, at proposal C-2, p. 120. *See also,* Stephen B. Land, *Unallocated Premium in Corporate Acquisitions Under the American Law Institute Subchapter C Proposals,* 34 Tax Law. 341 (1981), and Ginsburg, et al., *A Modest Proposal, supra* chapter 1, note 35.

29. *Treasury Subchapter C Outline, supra* chapter 1, note 16.

30. *See* chapter 6.

31. *See, e.g.,* Treas. Reg. § 1.368–1(b) (1980).

32. *See, e.g.,* Treas. Reg. § 1.368–1(d) (1980).

33. *See, e.g.,* Treas. Reg. § 1.368–1 (1980) and –2 (1985).

without respect to the amount of stock consideration used in the acquisition.[34] This rule would essentially extend the like kind exchange provision, Section 1031, to swaps of stock of a target corporation for stock of an acquiring corporation. It would not, however, give nonrecognition treatment to swaps of stock outside of the acquisition context.

Under the ALI proposals, a shareholder of a target corporation would receive tax-free treatment on the swap of stock in the target for stock in the acquiring corporation even though (1) no business purpose exists for the transaction, (2) the acquiring corporation does not acquire any of the target's historic assets but rather acquires, for example, solely cash realized by the target from the sale of its assets to a third party (*i.e.*, there is no continuity of business enterprise), and (3) the stock of the acquiring corporation is merely a *de minimis* portion of the consideration paid in the transaction (*i.e.*, there is no continuity of interest).[35] Consequently, the business purpose, continuity of interest, and business enterprise doctrines, which have been the bedrocks of the reorganization provisions since their enactment in 1918,[36] are rejected by the ALI.

Many of the ALI proposals are reflected in a 1985 report by the staff of the Senate Finance Committee ("1985 SFC Staff"),[37] which proposed the replacement of the reorganization concept with the concept of "qualified stock acquisitions" and "qualified asset acquisitions" (*i.e.*, "qualified acquisitions").[38]

The 1985 SFC staff is correct in observing that, as presently structured, the reorganization provisions "lack consistency" and are "subject to manipulation."[39] And, the ALI 1989 Study is also correct in saying that the "matter of qualifying as a reorganization is exceedingly complicated . . . with an apparently senseless variety of different criteria applicable to different forms of acquisitions."[40] Both the 1985 SFC Staff and the ALI are wrong, however, in concluding that because of the present defects, the reorganization concept needs to be abandoned and replaced with rules which would explicitly allow taxpayers to accomplish almost any result in the context of a corporate merger or acquisition. Rather than abandoning the reorganiza-

---

34. *ALI 1989 Study*, *supra* chapter 1, note 2, at part II, proposal 15.

35. *See* Wolfman, *Continuity of Interest*, *supra* note 2.

36. Revenue Act of 1918, Pub. L. No. 65–254, § 202, 40 Stat. 1057, 1060 (1919).

37. *1985 SFC Proposals supra* chapter 1, note 3. The *1985 SFC Proposals* are discussed and critiqued in Thompson, *Suggested Alternative Approach*, *supra* chapter 1, note 3.

38. For a discussion of the *1985 SFC Proposals* regarding qualified acquisitions, *see* Thompson, *Suggested Alternative Approach*, *supra* chapter 1, note 3.

39. *1985 SFC Proposals*, *supra* chapter 1, note 3, at 37.

40. *ALI 1989 Study*, *supra* chapter 1, note 2, at 113.

tion concept, the provision should be reformed to eliminate the inconsistencies and to prevent manipulation;[41] this is the approach taken here.[42]

Other Recent Suggested Approaches for the Treatment of the Target and Its Shareholders

There have been other suggested approaches for taxation at both the target corporate level and the target shareholder level.

Some have suggested adoption of a mandatory Section 338 election for any stock acquisitions covered by that section.[43] Under these proposals, mandatory corporate level recognition would be required upon the acquisition of at least 80 percent of the stock of a target corporation. Also, in its Budget Reconciliation Bill of 1987,[44] the House Ways and Means Committee proposed to make the Section 338 election mandatory in the case of hostile stock acquisitions. This provision was not enacted.[45] Along similar lines Professor Lewis' proposal for "uniform corporate level recognition" would impose a corporate level tax whenever there is an acquisition of at least 50 percent of the stock of a corporation.[46]

In an even more radical proposal, Professor Shakow has suggested that upon a change in control of a corporation, a tax be imposed at both the corporate and the shareholder levels.[47] Even non-selling shareholders

---

41. Professor Ginsburg, a strong proponent of the ALI and *1985 SFC Proposals*, is wrong in concluding that since he can accomplish "anything" with the current reorganization provisions, they should be scrapped and replaced with the *1985 SFC Proposals*. *See* Martin D. Ginsburg, *Panel Discussion*, 5 Va. Tax. Rev. 689, 695 (1986) [hereinafter cited as "*Panel Discussion*"]. Apparently, Professor Ginsburg is principally referring to the manipulation of the continuity of interest doctrine which is possible under current law. That type of manipulation should not be possible under the suggested reforms to the reorganization provisions proposed here.

42. *See* chapter 4.

43. *See* Yin, *Carryover Basis Asset Acquisitions*, *supra* chapter 1, note 35. *See also*, H.R. 2995, 100th Cong., lst Sess. (1987), *Federal Income Tax Aspects of Mergers and Acquisitions*, Hearing Before the Subcomm. on Oversight and the Subcomm. on Select Revenue Measures of the House Committee of Ways and Means, 99th Cong., lst Sess., 155–56 (1985) (David Brockway, Chief of Staff of Joint Committee, Statement that mandatory Section 338 election would provide greater neutrality in corporate acquisitions and cut back the number of such acquisitions).

44. Budget Reconciliation Bill of 1987, H.R. 3545, 100th Cong., lst Sess. (1987).

45. For a detailed discussion of this and other provisions in that bill *see* chapter 11, p. 154.

46. Lewis, *Corporate Level Tax*, *supra* chapter 1, note 35.

47. Shakow, *Whither, "C"!*, *supra* chapter 1, note 32.

would be subject to tax. Under this proposal, control would be determined under the principles that apply under Section 382. That section provides a limitation on the use of a corporation's net operating losses after a change of at least 50 percent in the ownership of the stock of the corporation.

Professor Coven has gone in the opposite direction by proposing a mandatory carryover basis for the target's assets in all acquisitions, both taxable and nontaxable.[48]

Thus, while both Professors Shakow and Coven reject the ALI's proposal for explicit elective cost or carryover basis treatment at the target level, their proposals go in opposite directions. Professor Shakow proposes mandatory taxation of the target with a cost basis for the assets; Professor Coven proposes mandatory nonrecognition treatment for the target and a carryover basis for its assets. Professor Shakow also proposes full taxation at the target shareholder level, whereas Professor Coven would apparently retain the present scheme for taxing shareholders who participate in a reorganization.

With the repeal of the *General Utilities* doctrine, the maximum potential tax rate in a corporate acquisition involving both a corporate and shareholder level tax is approximately 52 percent.[49] In view of the current maximum effective rates of 31 percent for individuals and 34 percent for corporations, it would be patently unfair to mandate such a high rate of tax on every taxable stock acquisition; therefore, Congress should not adopt general mandatory corporate level tax in stock acquisitions. There should, however, be parity in the treatment of (1) stock purchases in which the target keeps a carryover basis for its assets, and (2) taxable asset acquisitions in which carryover basis treatment is available under the proposals here.[50] This parity is accomplished here by a limited form of mandatory Section 338 election. The mandatory election applies when prior to a stock acquisition the target has, in contemplation of the stock purchase, disposed of a substantial portion of the assets.[51]

Mischaracterization of Purchase Price

Another issue is the growing amount of mischaracterization of purchase price in corporate acquisitions. Congress will certainly have to address this issue in a more direct way than it did with the reporting requirements of Section 1060, which were enacted by the Tax Reform Act of 1986 (TRA 1986) and amended by the RRA 1990.[52]

---

48. Coven, *Mandatory Uniform Rules, supra* chapter 1, note 32.
49. The derivation of the 52 percent rate is set forth in chapter 2, p. 28.
50. *See* chapter 5.
51. *See* chapter 7.
52. RRA 1990, *supra* chapter 1, note 17.

Section 1060 requires the parties to an asset acquisition to allocate the purchase price among the assets in accordance with the principles in Section 338(b)(5) and to report the allocations to the IRS. Section 338(b)(5) and Temp. Treas. Reg. § 1.338(b)-2T require that the value of goodwill and similar intangibles be determined under the residual method. Under this method, all other assets are first valued, and any of the purchase price remaining after allocation to all other assets is allocated to goodwill and similar intangibles.

As a result of an amendment to Section 1060 made by the RRA 1990 any shareholder of a target who owns 10 percent or more of the stock of a target and who in connection with the sale of such stock enters into an employment agreement, a covenant not to compete or a similar arrangement is required (along with the purchaser) to report such payments to the IRS.

The purpose of the reports required under Section 1060 is to permit the Service to police misallocations of purchase price.[53]

Prior to the repeal of the capital gains preference by the TRA 1986, in many cases a tension existed between the selling party and the purchasing party on the allocation of purchase price. Sellers preferred to have purchase price allocated to capital assets, and purchasers preferred to have purchase price allocated to depreciable or amortizable items such as covenants not to compete. After the TRA 1986, except with respect to basis recovery, a selling shareholder was completely indifferent between receiving additional purchase price for stock, or a payment for a covenant not to compete, or similar arrangement. Consequently, in many post-1986 transactions, a built-in incentive exists for the parties to an acquisition to allocate an unreasonable portion of the purchase price to deductible payments like covenants not to compete.

As a result of the adoption by the RRA 1990 of a 28 percent maximum individual rate for capital gains and a 31 percent maximum rate for ordinary income, some tension now exists between sellers and purchasers. In view of the mere 3 percentage point differential, however, the tension is not significant. Consequently, in many taxable transactions being structured today, the parties are mischaracterizing purchase price as payments for covenants not to compete or similar arrangements which purportedly give rise to deductions to the purchaser. These types of arrangements lead to an erosion of the tax base and must be curtailed. This issue, which can also arise in tax-free acquisitive reorganizations, is addressed here.[54]

Action needs to be taken on this problem even if a significant capital gains preference is restored because the tax tension between buyer and seller is often not enough of a policeman against abusive misallocations.

---

53. See, generally, Federal Taxation of Business Enterprises, supra chapter 1, note 20, at § 35:09.

54. See chapter 8.

Part 2
Mergers and
Acquisitions

CHAPTER 4

. . . .

Proposed Changes to the Reorganization Definition

This chapter discusses the changes proposed here to the reorganization concept, and chapters 5 through 8 deal with the proposed changes relating to taxable acquisitions. All of these changes are illustrated in chapter 9.

The first section sets forth the basic policy reasons for retaining the reorganization concept and the continuity of interest, continuity of business enterprise, and business purpose doctrines. These doctrines must be satisfied in order to qualify as a reorganization. Next, the reasons for making the continuity of interest doctrine uniform for all forms of reorganizations are set forth, and an argument is made for the adoption of a uniform "substantially all" requirement for all forms of reorganizations.

The chapter then (1) explores the proposed structure of the reorganization provisions, (2) discusses the implementation of the proposed uniform continuity of interest requirement, and (3) sets forth the proposed rules for implementing the uniform "substantially all" requirement. The final three sections deal, respectively, with (1) incorporations prior to reorganizations, (2) direct dispositions of subsidiaries in acquisitive reorganizations followed by the distribution of the stock received, and (3) a consistency requirement for reorganizations.

Retention of the Reorganization Concept and the Continuity of Interest, Continuity of Business Enterprise, and Business Purpose Doctrines

General Rule of Recognition and Exceptions for Continuing Interest

It is a fundamental principle of the federal income tax law that, except in certain specified circumstances, a taxpayer is taxed upon a swap of one piece of property for another.[1] Thus, if a taxpayer holds stock in GM and swaps that stock for stock in IBM, the transaction is taxable. This is a sensible rule because otherwise a taxpayer who held GM stock and wanted to sell and invest the after-tax proceeds in IBM could avoid the tax by arranging to swap his or her GM stock for IBM stock. The general rule that swaps of property are taxable prevents an erosion of the tax base.

There are many exceptions to the general rule that swaps or exchanges are taxable.[2] An underlying theme runs through most of these exceptions to the general recognition rule: *Nonrecognition is appropriate where the taxpayer continues to have an interest in the property exchanged.*

This concept is best seen in the context of Sections 721 and 351. Section 721 provides for nonrecognition treatment upon the transfer of property to a partnership in exchange for a partnership interest, and Section 351 provides for nonrecognition treatment for the transferors of property to a corporation in exchange for stock of such corporation amounting to control (*i.e.*, at least 80 percent).[3] In both cases, the transferors continue to have an interest in the property transferred through their ownership of interests in the entity.

The continuing interest, however, can be attenuated with both partnerships and corporations. For example, a person can transfer property to a partnership in exchange for any size partnership interest (say, one percent) and still receive tax-free treatment under Section 721. Also, as long as a transferor is a member of a control group (*i.e.*, a group of persons who transfer property to a corporation in exchange for in the aggregate at least 80 percent of the corporation's stock), the transferor receives tax-free treatment under Section 351 without respect to the amount of stock received by that person (say, one percent). Thus, under both the partnership and corporate provisions, the continuing interest of the contributing owner can be small. Nonrecognition is provided, however, only if there is a continuing equity interest.

In the case of contributions to both partnerships and corporations, the entity generally takes a carryover basis for the property received[4] (*i.e*, the property is "transferred basis property" as defined in Section 7701(a)(43)),

---

1. *See* I.R.C. § 1001 (1991).

2. *See, e.g.*, I.R.C. §§ 1031 to 1042, 721 (1991) (relating to transfers of property to partnerships in exchange for partnership interests), 351 (relating to transfers to corporations in exchange for stock), and 354 (relating to an exchange of stock in a party to a reorganization).

3. I.R.C. §§ 351(a) and 368(c) (1991).

4. I.R.C. §§ 723 (1991) (in the case of partnerships) and 362(a) (in the case of corporations).

and the transferors generally take a substituted basis for the interests received[5] (*i.e.*, the property is "exchanged basis property" as defined in Section 7701(a)(44)).

In addition to the continuing interest of the transferors, the organization of partnerships and corporations are economically desirable transactions that should not be discouraged by the imposition of a tax. It is sound tax policy to provide for nonrecognition treatment in such organization transactions in which the contributors receive no property other than a partnership interest or stock.

The idea of a continuing interest is also the underlying rationale of Section 1031, the like kind exchange provision. Under Section 1031(a), nonrecognition treatment applies if property held for productive use in a trade or business or for investment (not including such items as inventory, stocks, securities and partnership interests) is exchanged for property of a "like kind" to be held in the productive use in a trade or business or for investment. The taxpayer takes a substituted basis for the property received.[6]

The purpose of Section 1031 is to allow a taxpayer to swap one item of business property, such as an old machine, for another item of business property of a like kind, such as a new machine, without incurring a tax on the gain inherent in the old machine. The gain is deferred until the sale of the new machine.

In explaining the exception to the recognition rule for like kind exchanges, the House Report to the Revenue Act of 1924[7] says that the provision results in a "postponement of tax until the gain is realized by a pure sale or by such an exchange as amounts to a pure sale."[8] Nonrecognition treatment is available only if the taxpayer continues to use the new item of property in its business or holds it for investment.[9] Thus, although there is not a continuing interest in the property disposed of there is a continuing use of like kind property in business. It is economically desirable for businesses to upgrade plant and equipment, and it is appropriate for such transactions to be free of tax under the like kind exchange provision.

Corporate acquisitions in which the target's shareholders receive stock of the acquiring corporation are also transactions in which the target's shareholders continue to participate in the assets transferred.

---

5. I.R.C. §§ 722 (1991) (in the case of partnerships) and 358 (in the case of corporations).

6. I.R.C. § 1031(d) (1991).

7. The Revenue Act of 1924, Pub. L. No. 68–176, 43 Stat. 253 (1924).

8. H.R. Rep. No. 179, 68th Cong., 1st Sess. (1924), 1939–1 C.B. (part 2) 241, 253 (1939).

9. Rev. Rul. 75–292, 1975–2 C.B. 333.

Economic Desirability of Equity

Corporate acquisitions in which a substantial part of the consideration paid is stock of the acquiring corporation are more economically desirable than transactions in which an acquisition is financed substantially with debt, such as junk bonds. It appears that no one has ever expressed a concern about the use of too much equity in acquisitions. On the other hand, many have expressed concerns about the use of too much debt. The problem with overly leveraged acquisitions has been well documented[10] and is addressed in part 3. It is sound tax policy, therefore, to encourage, through nonrecognition treatment, the use of substantial amounts of equity in corporate acquisitions.

Thus, a properly designed reorganization concept can act as a carrot to induce the parties to structure acquisitions with substantial amounts of equity so that the selling shareholders can qualify for tax-free treatment.

Desirability of a Relative Size Limitation

Few would argue that a tax should be imposed on a merger of two corporations of substantially equal size in which the shareholders of the target receive only stock of the acquiring corporation. In such mergers, the target's shareholders have a substantial continuing interest in the target's assets, and the value of the stock of the acquiring corporation received is significantly affected by the value of the target's assets. On the other hand, a strong argument can be made for taxing the merger of the local Corner Grocery Store, Inc. into a large corporate conglomerate in exchange for stock of the conglomerate. The shareholders of the Grocery Store do not have a significant continuing interest in the assets transferred.[11]

The House version of the bill that became the 1954 Code contained a relative size limitation that would have extended tax-free treatment only to mergers or acquisitions involving corporations of the same relative size.[12] This provision did not become law, however, and the current reorganization provision does not have a size limitation concept. The ALI 1982 Study concludes that there are strong reasons for not adopting a relative size limitation standard,[13] but the study sets out a relative size limitation rule that would operate on the receipt of marketable stock.[14]

---

10. Peter C. Canellos, *The Over-Leveraged Acquisition*, 39 Tax Law. 91 (1985).

11. For a discussion of the merits of a relative size limitation, *see* Thompson, *Suggested Alternative Approach, supra* chapter 1, note 3, at 630–31. Portions of the following text and notes are adapted from that discussion.

12. *See* § 359(a)(1), H.R. Rep. No. 1337, 83d Cong., 2d Sess., A133 (1954). The relative size rule that was contained in the 1954 House bill would have denied reorganization treatment to any transaction in which the acquiror was more than four times larger than the target.

13. *ALI 1982 Study, supra* chapter 1, note 3, at 159–63.

14. *Id.*, at 182–87. Basically, the rule set out in the ALI 1982 Study would extend

In arguing against a relative size limitation, Professor Blum makes the point that such a limitation would deny the shareholders of small closely held corporations, many of whom may be advanced in age, the ability to participate in tax-free reorganizations with large publicly-held corporations, whereas shareholders of large publicly-held corporations could do so.[15] That type of bias against small business, he argues, would be politically unpalatable. Also, he further argues that as long as there is a step-up in the basis at death provision in the Code,[16] it is sound policy to give an aged owner of a small closely held corporation the opportunity to have his corporation acquired in a tax-free acquisition.

Powerful arguments can be made on both sides of this issue.[17] The conclusion reached here is that there should be no relative size limitation for the following reasons. First, it is sound economic policy to preserve equity investments, and the adoption of a relative size limitation would likely re-

---

14. *Id.*, at 182–87. Basically, the rule set out in the ALI 1982 Study would extend nonrecognition treatment to marketable stock received in a qualified acquisition only if the target's shareholders receive, as a result of the acquisition, a proportionate common stock interest in the acquiring corporation equal to at least one-fifth of their proportionate interest in the target prior to the acquisition. Thus, if a target had one shareholder and the target were acquired in a qualified acquisition in exchange for marketable stock, in order to receive nonrecognition treatment the target's shareholder would have to receive at least 20 percent of the common stock of the acquiring corporation. Thus, this restriction would make it practically impossible for an acquiring corporation that had common stock which was worth more than five times the common stock of the target to acquire the target in a tax-free exchange in which the consideration paid was marketable stock. The concept of limiting nonrecognition treatment where marketable stock is involved was proposed in a more drastic form by Professor Hellerstein who argued that nonrecognition treatment should not be available in any reorganization transaction where the target's shareholders receive "stock traded on an exchange or in the over-the-counter market if an adequate market exists for the sale of the stock received." Jerome R. Hellerstein, *Mergers, Taxes, and Realism*, 71 Harv. L. Rev. 254, 284 (1957).

15. *See* Walter J. Blum, *Corporate Acquisitions Under the Income Tax: Another Approach*, 50 Taxes 85 (1972). In arguing against a relative size limitation Professor Blum says: "Would anyone advocate that we adopt a broad policy of encouraging the union of two equal size companies but not two firms of radically different sizes." *Id.* at 100.

16. I.R.C. § 1014 (1991).

17. For a suggestion that the amount of boot that can be paid in a reorganization be a function of the relative sizes of the two corporations, *see* Thompson, *Suggested Alternative Approach*, *supra* chapter 1, note 3, at 641–42. For the reasons cited in the text and because of the complexity this provision would add, this proposal is not suggested here.

sult in a substantial reduction in the use of equity as the consideration in acquisitions of targets that did not satisfy the relative size test.

Second, the potential of a tax-free sale of a small corporation to a large corporation in exchange for stock in a reorganization enhances economic efficiency. The reorganization provisions eliminate what could otherwise be a substantial tax barrier to desirable acquisitions. Since there must be a business purpose to qualify as a reorganization, such transactions are likely to move assets into the hands of those who are better able to manage those assets. For example, under the current provisions, the aged controlling shareholder of a small corporation can use the acquisitive reorganization provisions to transfer his or her corporation to new management without a tax cost. If the tax-free reorganization route were not available, many such shareholders would hold onto their stock until death. Their heirs would then receive a stepped-up basis for the stock under Section 1014 and could sell the stock without tax. Thus, a relative size limitation would lead many owners of small corporations to hold on to those firms long past the point at which the firms should be disposed of.

Third, just as there is no size restriction upon the transfer of property on the organization of partnerships and corporations, there should be no size restriction for reorganizations among corporations. A continuing interest is present in each of these transactions and each transaction is economically desirable.

Summary

In summary, nonrecognition treatment should be available in a corporate acquisition in which the target's shareholders receive stock of the acquiring corporation in exchange for a substantial portion of their stock in the target corporation. In other words, the basic continuity of interest requirement should continue to apply to acquisitive reorganizations. The concept should, however, be modified as proposed below.[18] Also, reorganization treatment should be available only for those transactions in which the continuity of business enterprise[19] and the business purpose[20] doctrines are satisfied. These doctrines help to distinguish true reorganizations from liquidations or other nonreorganization transactions. Further, for the reasons set out below, the "substantially all" concept, with certain modifications, should be extended to all forms of acquisitive reorganizations.[21]

---

18. *See* pp. 59 and 74.

19. Treas. Reg. § 1.368–1(d) (1980). *See* chapter 4, p. 91.

20. *See, e.g., Gregory v. Helvering*, 293 U.S. 465 (1935); Treas. Reg. § 1.368–2(g) (1985).

21. *See* pp. 62 and 87.

The ALI's proposal for the repeal of the reorganization concept runs counter to sound tax policy and would erode the tax base by needlessly expanding the number of tax-free transactions. The core of the ALI's proposals is that if there is a corporate acquisition, the like kind exchange provision of Section 1031 should apply to any shareholder of the target corporation who swaps stock in the target for stock in the acquiror. The ALI proposal would, in essence, expand the nonrecognition treatment available under Section 1031 at a time when Congress has taken measures (and has considered others) to restrict the availability of nonrecognition treatment under that section.[22]

If the continuity of interest doctrine were repealed as proposed in the ALI 1989 Study, a proliferation of transactions like the one in *Kass*[23] would result. In *Kass* most of the target's shareholders were paid in cash and only a small percentage received stock of the acquiring corporation (5 percent in the case of Mrs. Kass). The court in *Kass* correctly held that the transaction did not qualify as a reorganization because of a failure to satisfy the continuity of interest doctrine. Under the approach taken in the ALI 1989 Study, shareholders like Mrs. Kass who receive stock in such transactions would qualify for nonrecognition treatment. This kind of expansion of nonrecognition treatment would erode the income tax base and could have a substantial adverse revenue effect.

A Uniform Standard of Continuity of Interest Should Be Adopted[24]

The many dimensions of the continuity of interest requirement and the implementation of the proposed rules are discussed later in this chapter. The broad guiding principles to be followed in formulating the proposed rules are set out here.

No tax policy justification exists for the disparate treatment of continuity of interest in the various forms of acquisitive reorganization. There is no principled reason for allowing:

---

22. Congress amended Section 1031 in the Tax Reform Act of 1984, Pub. L. No. 98–369, § 77(a), 98 Stat. 494, 595 (1984), to make it clear that a swap of a partnership interest does not qualify for Section 1031 treatment. The House Ways and Means Committee has considered restricting the availability of Section 1031 to defer the gain from swaps of real estate to $100,000 a year. *See* Omnibus Budget Reconciliation Act of 1987, H.R. 3545, § 10105 (1987). This provision was not enacted as part of the Revenue Act of 1987.

23. *Kass v. Commissioner*, 60 T.C. 218 (1973), aff'd 491 F.2d 749 (3d Cir. 1974) (*per curiam*).

24. This section is based in part on Thompson, *Suggested Alternative Approach*, *supra* chapter 1, note 3, at 625.

(1) Fifty percent (or possibly less) nonstock consideration (*i.e.*, boot) in both a direct merger of a target into an acquiror under Section 368(a)(1)(A)[25] and a forward triangular merger of a target into a subsidiary of the acquiror under Section 368(a)(2)(D),[26]

(2) Twenty percent boot both in a reverse triangular merger of a subsidiary of the acquiror into a target under Section 368(a)(2)(E)[27] and a direct or triangular acquisition of the assets of a target for stock of the acquiror under Section 368(a)(1)(C),[28] and

(3) No boot in a direct or triangular acquisition of the stock of a target in exchange for stock of an acquiror under Section 368(a)(1)(B).[29]

Similarly, there is no justification for allowing nonvoting common or preferred[30] stock to qualify for continuity of interest purposes both in a direct merger under Section 368(a)(1)(A) and in a forward subsidiary merger under Section 368(a)(2)(D), but requiring voting stock for continuity of interest purposes in each of (1) a stock for stock acquisition under Section 368(a)(1)(B), (2) a stock for asset acquisition under Section 368(a)(1)(C), and (3) a reverse subsidiary merger under Section 368(a)(2)(E).

The following five principles should guide the structure of a sensible and rational continuity of interest rule.

First, there is no reason why the stock that qualifies for continuity purposes has to be stock of the acquiring corporation or of its parent. There is no policy justification for prohibiting the use of the stock of a grandparent or great grandparent corporation. These transactions are referred to here as grandparent type reorganizations, as distinguished from triangular reorganizations. Indeed, it should be possible to satisfy the continuity of interest requirement with the stock of any corporation that is in direct or indirect 80 percent control (an "acquiring parent") of the acquiring corporation.[31]

---

25. *See* chapter 2, p. 36 for a description of a direct merger under Section 368(a)(1)(A).

26. *See* chapter 2, p. 36 for a description of a forward triangular merger under Section 368(a)(2)(D).

27. *See* chapter 2, p. 38 for a description of the reverse triangular merger under Section 368(a)(2)(E).

28. *See* chapter 2, p. 37 for a description of the direct and triangular acquisition of the target's assets under Section 368(a)(1)(C).

29. *See* chapter 2, p. 37 for a description of the direct and triangular stock-for-stock acquisition under Section 368(a)(1)(B).

30. *See John A. Nelson Co. v. Helvering*, 296 U.S. 374 (1935).

31. The ALI also takes this approach in its like kind exchange concept. *See ALI 1989 Study, supra* chapter 1, note 2, at 136.

Second, except as noted below, the continuity of interest requirement should be satisfied only with underlying voting common stock of the acquiring corporation or an acquiring parent. This requirement would ensure that the target's shareholders have a real continuing interest that is the same type of interest they had in the target.

This underlying voting stock requirement is consistent with the financial accounting requirement for reporting a corporate acquisition as a pooling rather than as a purchase. In a pooling the financial statements of the acquiror and target are combined as if they had always been together. In a purchase the target's assets and liabilities are accounted for as if they had been purchased by the acquiror. Pooling of interest applies only if the acquiring corporation issues "common stock with rights identical to those of the majority of its outstanding voting common stock in exchange for . . . [90 percent] of the voting common stock interest of the [target]."[32]

Third, although there is no scientific way to determine the minimum continuity requirement, the guiding principle should be that a substantial portion of the consideration paid must constitute underlying common stock of the acquiring corporation or its direct or indirect parent. One reason for not requiring that all of the consideration be stock is that there should be some flexibility in planning the transaction. It would appear that 20 percent leeway is reasonable. This is the amount of leeway allowed in the reverse subsidiary merger under Section 368(a)(1)(E), which is used quite frequently, such as, for example, in Time's original agreement with Warner Bros.[33] and in Bristol Meyers' acquisition of Squibb.[34] Thus, the conclusion here is that in order to satisfy the continuity of interest requirement in each type of acquisitive reorganization 80 percent of the consideration paid must constitute underlying voting common stock of the acquiring corporation or of a direct or indirect acquiring parent.

This rule liberalizes both the present stock for stock (B) reorganization, which does not allow any boot, and the present direct and triangular (C) reorganizations, which only rarely allow for up to 20 percent boot. The rule significantly tightens the continuity of interest requirement that applies to the straight merger under Section 368(a)(1)(A) and to the forward subsidiary merger under Section 368(a)(2)(D).

Fourth, the continuity of interest rule should not be subject to manipulation by use of such devices as (1) a reverse acquisition[35] in which the real

32. Accounting Principles Board Opinion No. 16 ¶ 476.

33. Time Inc. and Warner Bros., Inc. Joint Proxy Statement (May 22, 1989).

34. Bristol Meyers and Squibb Joint Proxy Statement (Oct. 3, 1989).

35. *See* p. 83. The reverse acquisition is not the same as a reverse subsidiary merger. *See* chapter 2, pp. 29 and 38 for a discussion of the reverse subsidiary merger.

target acts nominally as the acquiring corporation, or (2) a Section 351 incorporation transaction that is part of a larger acquisition.[36]

Fifth, there should be a codification of the other aspects of the continuity of interest requirement, including the rules regarding (1) who must receive the stock of the acquiring corporation (*i.e.*, the target's historic shareholders),[37] (2) how long such stock must be held,[38] (3) the impact of the continuity of interest requirement in creeping acquisitions,[39] and (4) the redeployment of assets after a reorganization.[40]

The revenue effect of these changes should be positive. The revenue gains would principally come from (1) the tightening of the continuity of interest requirement for the direct merger under Section 368(a)(1)(A) and the forward subsidiary merger under Section 368(a)(2)(D), and (2) the prevention of manipulation. These gains should far exceed any revenue loss resulting from the liberalization of the continuity of interest requirement for the stock for stock reorganization under Section 368(a)(1)(B) and the stock for asset reorganization under Section 368(a)(1)(C). Merger reorganizations are much more utilized than stock for stock or stock for asset reorganizations, and the direct merger and the forward subsidiary mergers are particularly popular because they have the most liberal continuity of interest requirement, that is, 50 percent. Consequently, it would appear that many future direct mergers and forward subsidiary mergers would be adversely affected by the enhanced continuity requirements. On the other hand, a much smaller number of future stock for stock or stock for asset reorganizations should benefit from the liberalization of the continuity of interest requirement.

The uniform continuity of interest requirement proposed here is implemented in the sections beginning on p. 74.

A Uniform "Substantially All" Test with Exceptions for Spin Offs

Under the present statute, a "substantially all" test applies to the stock-for-asset reorganization under Section 368(a)(1)(C) and to the forward and reverse subsidiary mergers under Sections 368(a)(2)(D) and (E). Under this test, the acquiring corporation must acquire substantially all of the target's assets to qualify the transaction as a reorganization. The substan-

---

36. *See* p. 85.
37. *See* p. 76.
38. *See* p. 76.
39. *See* p. 79.
40. *See* p. 82.

tially all test does not apply to the direct merger under Section 368(a) (1)(A) or to the direct or triangular stock for stock reorganization under Section 368(a)(1)(B).

The "substantially all" test was initially adopted as part of the original (C) reorganization.[41] The purpose of the test was to ensure that a stock for asset reorganization resembled a merger reorganization transaction. The test was also adopted as part of the forward and reverse triangular reorganizations when those provisions were added to the Code in 1968 and 1971, respectively.[42]

The "substantially all" test prevents a strip down of the target corporation's assets prior to disposition of the target in a tax-free reorganization under these forms of reorganization.[43] In a strip down transaction, prior to an acquisitive reorganization, the target disposes of assets that the acquiring corporation does not want. A tax-free distribution of stock of a subsidiary under Section 355 is one possible kind of strip down transaction. The interface between Section 355 distributions and the "substantially all" test is explored in the next section.

Section 355, Elkhorn Coal, and Morris Trust

Under Section 355, a corporation (Distributing Corporation) may make a tax-free distribution to its shareholders of the stock of a subsidiary corporation (Controlled Corporation).[44] The distribution is tax-free to the Distributing Corporation, the Controlled Corporation, and the shareholders of the Distributing Corporation.

The Controlled Corporation may be either a preexisting subsidiary or a newly organized recipient of business assets from the Distributing Corporation in a transaction that also qualifies as a (D) reorganization under Section 368(a)(1)(D). As a practical matter, the Distributing Corporation must distribute all of the stock of the Controlled Corporation.[45]

The stock of the Controlled Corporation may be distributed either pro rata (a spin off) or in redemption of part of the stock of the Distributing Corporation (a split off). Also, the stock of two or more Controlled Corporations may be distributed in liquidation of the Distributing Corpora-

---

41. Section 202(b)(2) of the Revenue Act of 1921, P.L. 98, 42 Stat. 227 (1921).

42. Pub. L. No. 90–621, 82 Stat. 1310 (1968); Pub. L. No. 91–691, 84 Stat. 2074 (1971).

43. *See, e.g., Helvering v. Elkhorn Coal Co.*, 95 F.2d 732 (4th Cir. 1938), *cert. denied*, 305 U.S. 605 (1938).

44. For a discussion of Section 355 and the (D) reorganization *see Federal Taxation of Business Enterprises, supra* chapter 1, note 20, ch. 44.

45. I.R.C. § 355(a)(1)(D) (1991) (permits retention of stock of Controlled Corporation in only limited circumstances).

tion (a split up). These three types of Section 355 distributions are referred to here as "spin off type transactions."

There are many requirements for qualifying for tax-free treatment under Section 355, including the following:

1. There must be a business purpose for the transaction.[46]

2. There must be a continuity of interest.[47]

3. The transaction cannot be used as a device for the distribution of earnings and profits.[48]

4. Both the Distributing Corporation and each Controlled Corporation must own assets that constitute a business that was actively conducted by either the Distributing Corporation or the Controlled Corporation for a period of five years before the distribution.[49]

The "substantially all" test that applies to direct and triangular stock for asset reorganizations under Section 368(a)(1)(C) and to forward and reverse subsidiary mergers under Sections 368(a)(2)(D) and (E) eliminates (as a practical matter) the use of these forms of acquisitive reorganizations after a spin off type transaction. This result follows from the Fourth Circuit's decision in *Helvering v. Elkhorn Coal Co.*[50] *Elkhorn Coal* involved a spin off prior to the acquisition of the balance of the distributing corporation's assets in a purported stock for asset (C) reorganization. The Fourth Circuit held that the purported (C) reorganization did not satisfy the substantially all test because of the prior spin off.

Elkhorn Coal has come to stand for the proposition that in determining if the "substantially all" test is satisfied any pre-reorganization strip down of the target's assets must be taken into account. The Service reflects the principle of *Elkhorn Coal* in its ruling guidelines on the meaning of substantially all:

> All payments to dissenters and all redemptions and distributions (except for regular, normal distributions) made by the corporation immediately preceding the transfer and which are part of the plan of reorganization will be considered as assets held by the corporation immediately prior to the transfer.[51]

In the forms of reorganizations that have a "substantially all" requirement (*i.e.*, the direct and triangular (C) and the forward and reverse trian-

---

46. Treas. Reg. § 1.355–2(b) (1989).

47. Treas. Reg. § 1.355–2(c) (1989).

48. I.R.C. § 355(a)(1)(B) (1991).

49. I.R.C. § 355(b) (1991).

50. *Helvering v. Elkhorn Coal Co.*, 95 F.2d 732 (4th Cir. 1938), *cert. denied*, 305 U.S. 605 (1938).

51. Rev. Proc. 77–37, 1977–2 C.B. 568, § 3.01.

gular mergers), it is not possible (as a practical matter) to have the reorganization preceded by either a tax-free spin off under Section 355 or any significant taxable disposition of unwanted assets.

On the other hand, for those forms of reorganization that do not have a "substantially all" requirement (*i.e.*, the direct (A) merger and the direct and triangular stock for stock (B) reorganizations), a spin off type transaction may be effectuated prior to such a reorganization. Also, except for the requirement that the continuity of business enterprise test[52] be satisfied, there is, in general, no prohibition against taxable strip-downs in the form of sales, dividends, and redemptions prior to such reorganizations.[53]

The original authority allowing a pre-reorganization spin off is *Commissioner v. Morris Trust*.[54] There the Fourth Circuit was faced with a situation in which an acquiring corporation was legally prohibited from acquiring certain assets of the target corporation. The target, therefore, disposed of the unwanted assets by first contributing the unwanted assets to a newly formed Controlled Corporation and then by distributing the stock of the Controlled Corporation to the target's shareholders in a transaction that satisfied all the conditions for tax-free treatment under Section 355. Finally, the acquiring corporation acquired the stripped down target in a transaction that was intended to be a tax-free merger of the target into the acquiring corporation under Section 368(a)(1)(A).

The Service's position was that since the distribution of the stock of the Controlled Corporation was a preliminary step to the merger, the distribution did not qualify under Section 355.

The *Morris Trust* court rejected this position and held that the spin off qualified under Section 355, and the subsequent merger qualified as a reorganization under Section 368(a)(1)(A). In published rulings the Service has accepted *Morris Trust*[55] and variants of the *Morris Trust* transaction, including spin offs followed by stock for stock (B) reorganizations.[56] In one

---

52. Treas. Reg. § 1.368–1(d) (1980).

53. With respect to a Section 368(a)(1)(B) reorganization, *see* Rev. Rul. 70–172, 1970–1 C.B. 77 (dividend before a "B"); Rev. Rul. 68–285, 1968–1 C.B. 147 (redemptions of dissenting shareholders before a "B"). *Compare* Rev. Rul. 75–360, 1975–2 C.B. 110 (redemptions by target of stock of its shareholder prior to a purported "B" with proceeds of short-term bank loan that was repaid by acquiring corporation immediately after the purported "B" violates the solely for voting stock requirement), with *McDonald v. Commissioner*, 52 T.C. 82 (1969) (to the contrary).

54. *Commissioner v. Morris Trust*, 367 F.2d 794 (4th Cir. 1966).

55. Rev. Rul. 68–603, 1968–2 C.B. 148.

56. *See, e.g.*, Rev. Rul. 72–530, 1972–2 C.B. 212 (spin off of Controlled Corporation followed by merger of target into Distributing Corporation qualifies both under Section 355 and as a reorganization); Rev. Rul. 75–406, 1975–2 C.B. 125 (spin off of Controlled Corporation followed by merger of Controlled Corporation

published ruling, however, the Service held on technical grounds that a Controlled Corporation could not be acquired immediately after the spin off in a (B) reorganization.[57] The position in *Morris Trust* is now reflected in the regulations.[58]

As a policy matter, the *Morris Trust* decision is correct. The shareholders of a corporation should not be prohibited from causing their corporation to engage in a Section 355 distribution prior to an acquisitive reorganization involving either or both the Distributing Corporation and the Controlled Corporation. Section 355 has its own internal restrictions and limitations to ensure that the distribution is not used for tax avoidance purposes; those limitations are sufficient.

Further, if Section 355 treatment prior to an acquisitive reorganization is denied, then shareholders would be penalized for choosing to operate under one corporate umbrella as opposed to two or more. Moreover, there is no step-up in basis of the assets at the corporate level in either the spin off or in the subsequent acquisitive reorganization;[59] the shareholders of both the distributing corporation and the target receive nonrecognition treatment[60] and a substituted basis[61] for the stock received. There is merely a deferral of the gain at both the corporate and shareholder levels in both the spin off and the acquisitive reorganization.

Thus, there are sound policy reasons behind Section 355,[62] and those reasons are not undermined if after the distribution one or more of the sibling corporations participates in an acquisitive reorganization.

---

into acquiring corporation qualifies both under Section 355 and as a reorganization); Rev. Rul. 76–527, 1976–2 C.B. 103 (spin off of Controlled Corporation followed by acquisition by such corporation of target in a merger qualifies both under Section 355 and as a reorganization); Rev. Rul. 70–434, 1970–2 C.B. 83 (spin off of Controlled Corporation followed by disposition of Distributing Corporation in a purported (B) qualifies both under Section 355 and as a reorganization); Rev. Rul. 78–251, 1978–1 C.B. 89 (essentially same as Rev. Rul. 70–434 but with Distributing Corporation paying dissenters, qualifies under Section 355 and as a reorganization).

57. Rev. Rul. 70–225, 1970–1 C.B. 80 (spin off of Controlled Corporation followed by disposition of Controlled Corporation in a purported (B) reorganization does *not* qualify as either a Section 355 distribution or as a reorganization because the shareholder of Distributing Corporation is not in control of the Controlled Corporation after the distribution). In view of the proposals made here this provision should be overridden in the regulations.

58. Treas. Reg. § 1.355–2(b) (1989).

59. I.R.C. §§ 362(a) and 362(b) (1991).

60. I.R.C. §§ 354, 355 (1991).

61. I.R.C. § 358 (1991).

62. Karla W. Simon & Daniel L. Simmons, *The Future of Section 355*, 40 Tax

Finally, Section 355 has been amended to prevent its use as a device for effectuating a surrogate mirror transaction.[63]

The "Substantially All" Proposal

In analyzing whether the "substantially all" test should be retained, it is desirable to focus separately on the application of the test in the case of tax-free spin offs and in the context of sales, dividends, and redemptions. Tax-free spin offs under Section 355 which precede an acquisitive reorganization do not give rise to any potential abuse for the reasons outlined in the previous section. Also, since both the spin off and the acquisitive reorganization involve tax-free transactions, there is a fundamental consistency in those transactions. For this reason, the "substantially all" test should not be a barrier to an acquisitive reorganization that occurs after a tax-free spin off under Section 355. The proposal contained on pages 88–90 would, therefore, explicitly allow such transactions.

On the other hand, a taxable disposition of assets prior to an acquisitive reorganization is fundamentally inconsistent with the concept of a reorganization. No principled reason exists for allowing a target corporation to sell off a substantial part of its assets, distribute the proceeds, and then do a tax-free reorganization for the balance of its assets.[64]

It is inherent in the concept of a reorganization that there is a continuation of the target's business enterprise. For the reorganizations to which the "substantially all" test applies, the test ensures the integrity of the continuation of the business concept. No justifiable reason exists for having the test apply to some reorganizations and not to others. The substantially all test should be extended to all forms of acquisitive reorganizations; an exception, however, should apply for Section 355 distributions that occur prior to an acquisitive reorganization. Even with this exception, there will

---

Notes 291, 300 (1988) (reaching the conclusion that Section 355 is basically sound).

63. I.R.C. §§ 355(b)(2)(D) and 355(d) (1991). *See* chapter 3, p. 42.

64. It seems that Congress has not addressed the distinction between Section 355 strip downs and taxable strip downs. In adopting the "substantially all" test for the (C) in 1921 Congress explicitly negated the use of the taxable sale followed by a tax-free stock for asset (C) reorganization. Since the Congressional intent was to make the (C) like the merger, Congress must have been of the view that a taxable strip down would not have been permitted in the merger reorganization under the predecessor of Section 368(a)(1)(A). On the other hand, at the time of the enactment of the initial predecessor of the (C) in 1921, Congress could not have had a view on the merits of a tax-free spin off followed by either a merger reorganization or a stock for asset reorganization because the initial provision allowing tax-free spin offs was not added to the law until 1924. *See* § 203(b)(1)(B) of the Revenue Act of 1924, 43 Stat. 253 (1924).

be a continuation of the business enterprise because upon the acquisition of the Distributing Corporation or the Controlled Corporation after the spin off under Section 355 both the Distributing Corporation and the Controlled Corporation must actively conduct a trade or business that has operated for at least 5 years before the distribution.

It appears that taxpayers have not encountered significant problems in satisfying the "substantially all" test because two of the most common forms of acquisitive reorganizations are the forward and reverse subsidiary mergers, both of which have a "substantially all" requirement. Thus, the extension of the test to all forms of reorganizations should not substantially increase complexity.

The revenue effect of this proposal should be positive. A revenue gain should come from the tightening of the direct merger and the stock for stock (B) reorganizations by the addition of a "substantially all" test. This gain should offset any revenue loss from the liberalization of the substantially all test to allow tax-free spin offs under Section 355 in the direct and triangular (C) reorganizations and in the forward and reverse subsidiary mergers.

The uniform "substantially all" test proposed here is implemented on pages 68 and 87.

Proposed Structure of Acquisitive Reorganizations

Restructuring the Forms of Reorganization Under Section 368: Retention of Sections 354 through 362

The following approach is taken in implementing the uniform continuity of interest requirement and the uniform "substantially all" requirement discussed above. The changes are implemented by amendments to Section 368. The specific amendments are set out in the notes to the applicable text, and the complete revised Section 368 is set out in appendix B, with commentary. Later sections discuss the proposed structure of the definition of the term reorganization as it relates to mergers, stock acquisitions, and asset acquisitions. Pages 74–87 discuss various aspects of the uniform continuity of interest requirement. Pages 87–91 address the implementation of the uniform "substantially all" requirement, and pages 92–95 deal with incorporations prior to reorganizations, direct dispositions of subsidiaries in acquisitive reorganizations and a consistency requirement for reorganizations.

Except for one minor change to Section 362 to eliminate the carryover basis rule that currently applies to the acquiring corporation in a stock for stock reorganization under Section 368(a)(1)(B), no changes are proposed to Section 354 through Section 362, which deal with the treatment of the various parties to a reorganization. Under the current Section 362 carryover basis rule, in a (B) reorganization the acquiring corporation takes as its basis for the target's stock the basis of the target's shareholders in that stock. This rule would be changed to a net basis rule.[65]

Thus, the parties to a reorganization would receive the following treatment under the proposals here. The shareholders of the target would have (1) nonrecognition under Section 354 upon receipt of stock of the acquiring corporation, and (2) recognition treatment under Section 356 upon the receipt of boot. The boot may be treated as a dividend under Section 356(a)(2) as that provision has been interpreted by the Supreme Court in *Clark v. Commissioner*.[66] The substituted basis rule of Section 358 would apply to the target's shareholders; they would, therefore, take as the basis for the stock in the acquiring corporation received in the reorganization the basis for their stock in the target adjusted for any boot received. Similar rules would apply under Sections 354, 356, and 358 upon the exchange by the target's securityholders (*i.e.*, long-term debtholders) of their securities for securities of the acquiring corporation.

Under Section 361, the target would have nonrecognition upon the receipt and distribution of the consideration received in the reorganization. Under Section 362, in an asset acquisition, the acquiring corporation would take a carryover basis for the target's assets. In a stock acquisition, Section 362 would be amended to give the acquiring corporation a net basis for the target's stock under the principles in Prop. Reg. § 1.358–6.[67]

In triangular and grandparent type reorganizations, the principles of Prop. Reg. § 1.1032–2[68] would apply to give the acquiring subsidiary non-

---

65. Prop. Treas. Reg. § 1.358–6 provides that in the case of a triangular (C) stock for asset reorganization, a triangular Section 368(a)(2)(D) forward subsidiary merger reorganization and a triangular Section 368(a)(2)(E) reverse subsidiary merger reorganization (but not a triangular (B) stock for asset reorganization), the acquiring parent takes a net basis for the stock of the acquiring subsidiary or target, as the case may be. A net basis is in essence the basis of the target's assets minus the target's liabilities. The purpose of the net basis rule is to approximate the basis the acquiring parent would have if the acquiring parent had acquired the target's assets and liabilities directly and then transferred the assets and liabilities to a subsidiary of the acquiring parent. In such case, the acquiring parent's basis under Section 358 for the subsidiary's stock should be the same as a net basis. The net basis does not apply to the triangular (B), because under Section 362 the acquiring subsidiary takes a carryover basis for the target's stock and, therefore, the acquiring parent is given a carryover basis for the stock of the acquiring subsidiary. This net basis is discussed further in chapter 4, p. 72.

66. *Clark v. Commissioner*, 489 U.S. 726, (1989). *See* chapter 2, p. 36.

67. This net basis is discussed further on p. 72.

68. Prop. Treas. Reg. § 1.1032–2 provides that an acquiring subsidiary does not

recognition treatment upon issuance of stock of the parent or grandparent. Also, the net basis rules of Prop. Reg. § 1.358–6 would apply to such reorganizations. Under these rules, the parent or grandparent would take a net basis for the stock of the acquiring subsidiary (and any intermediate corporations). Section 355, which deals with spin off transactions, would be retained in its present form.

Definition of "Target," "Acquiring Corporation," and "Acquiring Parent"

The first change to the reorganization definition is the addition of definitions for (1) "target corporation" in Proposed Section 368(a)(4)(A),[69] (2) "acquiring corporation" in Proposed Section 368(a)(4)(B),[70] and (3) "acquiring parent" in Proposed Section 368(a)(4)(C).[71] The acquiring parent is any corporation that has direct or indirect 80 percent control of the acquiring corporation. Thus, in a reorganization involving just two corporations, the "acquiring corporation" is the corporation that acquires in a transaction defined in Section 368(a)(1)(A), (B), or (C) either (1) substantially all of the historic assets of the "target corporation," or (2) at least 80 percent control of the stock of the "target corporation." Definitions are provided below for "substantially all" and "historic assets." As indicated below, the acquiring corporation may redeploy the target's assets or stock after the reorganization.[72] The definition of "acquiring parent" is structured to allow not only triangular reorganizations in which a first tier sub-

---

recognize gain or loss when it issues the stock of the parent in a triangular reorganization.

69. Proposed Section 368(a)(4)(A).
TARGET CORPORATION—The term "target corporation" means the corporation whose stock or assets are acquired in a transaction described in paragraph (1)(A), (1)(B) or (1)(C).

70. Proposed Section 368(a)(4)(B).
ACQUIRING CORPORATION—The term "acquiring corporation" means the corporation which as a result of a transaction described in paragraph (1)(A), (1)(B) or (1)(C) acquires either substantially all of the historic assets of the target corporation or controls (as defined in subsection (c)) the target corporation. In the case of a consolidation under paragraph (1)(A), the acquiring corporation is the consolidated corporation whose shareholders own the greatest percentage of the stock of the resulting corporation.

71. Proposed Section 368(a)(4)(C).
ACQUIRING PARENT—The term "acquiring parent" means a corporation that is in direct or indirect control, within the meaning of subsection (c), of the acquiring corporation. In determining whether the indirect control test is met the attribution rule of section 318(a)(2)(C) shall apply (substituting 80 percent for 50 percent as used therein).

72. See chapter 4, p. 90.

sidiary is the acquiring corporation as under present law, but also to allow a second or lower tier controlled acquiring corporation to utilize the stock of its grandparent or of one of its great- or higher tier grandparents in a reorganization. As long as the acquiring corporation is controlled by the direct or indirect parent whose stock is used in the reorganization, there is no policy reason for restricting the use of triangular or grandparent type reorganizations. Thus, this rule completely overrules the *Groman* and *Bashford* doctrines,[73] which prohibit the use of triangular reorganizations, except where specifically permitted by the Code.

Unifying Definition of Merger, Stock for Stock, and Stock for Asset Reorganizations

The definitions of (1) a merger in present Section 368(a)(1)(A), (2) a stock for stock acquisition in present Section 368(a)(1)(B), and (3) a stock for asset acquisition in present Section 368(a)(1)(C), are amended so that each of these provisions encompasses direct, triangular, and grandparent type[74] reorganizations in which both the continuity of interest requirement and the "substantially all" test are satisfied. Each of these forms is taken up separately below.

The (A) Merger Reorganization

Proposed Section 368(a)(1)(A)[75] encompasses not only direct mergers under the present Section 368(a)(1)(A),[76] but also (1) the present forward

---

73. *Groman v. Commissioner*, 302 U.S. 82 (1937); *Helvering v. Bashford*, 302 U.S. 454 (1938).

74. Section 1032 or the regulations thereunder will have to be amended to provide nonrecognition for an acquiring corporation upon the issuance of the stock of an indirect parent in a grandparent reorganization. *See, e.g.*, Prop. Treas. Reg. § 1.1032–2, relating to nonrecognition for an acquiring corporation upon issuance of its parent's stock in a triangular reorganization. Also, basis rules similar to those in Prop. Treas. Reg. § 1.358–6, relating to triangular reorganizations, will have to be adopted for grandparent type reorganizations.

75. Proposed Section 368(a)(1)(A). . . . [T]he term "reorganization" means . . . a statutory merger or consolidation in which:

(i) the acquiring corporation (as defined in paragraph(4)(B)) acquires (aa) substantially all (as defined in paragraph (4)(G)) of the historic assets (as defined in paragraph (4)(H)) of the target corporation (as defined in paragraph (4)(A)), or (bb) control (as defined in subsection (c)) of the target corporation (whether or not the acquiring corporation had control immediately before the acquisition) and the target corporation holds substantially all of its historic assets; and

(ii) the historic shareholders (as defined in paragraph (4)(F)) of the target corporation receive in exchange for their stock in the target corporation stock of the acquiring corporation (or stock of any acquiring parent (as defined in paragraph (4)(C)) which stock satisfies the continuity of interest requirement (as defined in paragraph (4)(E)).

76. *See* chapter 2, p. 36 for a description of the current (A) reorganization.

subsidiary merger under Section 368(a)(2)(D),[77] (2) the reverse subsidiary merger under Section 368(a)(2)(E),[78] and (3) all forms of grandparent type merger reorganizations. Grandparent type mergers include, for example, the merger of a target into a third-tier wholly-owned subsidiary of an acquiring parent with the target's shareholders receiving stock of the acquiring parent. In each of these forms, the "substantially all" test (*see* Proposed Section 368(a)(1)(A)(i)(aa)), and the continuity of interest requirement (*see* Proposed Section 368(a)(1)(A)(ii)) must be satisfied. These tests are discussed further below.

Because of the parenthetical clause "(whether or not the acquiring corporation had control immediately before the acquisition)" in Proposed Section 368(a)(1)(A)(i)(bb), there is no prohibition, as under the current Section 368(a)(2)(E),[79] against creeping reverse subsidiary mergers. Under the current Section 368(a)(2)(E), the acquiring corporation must acquire 80 percent control of the target in the reverse subsidiary merger. Consequently, if the acquiring corporation holds more than 20 percent of the target's stock, the transaction cannot qualify as a reverse subsidiary merger. Because of the parenthetical clause in Proposed Section 368(a)(1)(A)(i)(bb), a transaction may qualify as a reverse subsidiary merger even if the acquiring corporation owns more than 20 percent of the stock of the target immediately before the acquisition. This is the same standard that applies under the current and Proposed (B). This standard is discussed further below in the section beginning on page 79, which addresses creeping acquisitions.

The (B) Stock for Stock Reorganization

Proposed Section 368(a)(1)(B)[80] encompasses direct, triangular, and grandparent type stock for stock reorganizations, and thus replaces the cur-

---

77. *See* chapter 2, p. 36 for a description of the current forward triangular merger under Section 368(a)(2)(D).

78. *See* chapter 2, p. 38 for a description of the current reverse triangular merger under Section 368 (a)(2)(E).

79. Treas. Reg. § 1.368–2(j)(3)(i) (1985). *See* chapter 2, p. 38.

80. Proposed Section 368(a)(1)(B). . . . [T]he term "reorganization" means . . . a stock acquisition in which:

(i) the acquiring corporation acquires control (within the meaning of subsection (c)) of the target corporation (whether or not the acquiring corporation had control immediately before the acquisition);

(ii) after the acquisition the target corporation holds substantially all of its historic assets; and

(iii) the historic shareholders of the target corporation receive in exchange for their stock in the target corporation stock of the acquiring corporation (or stock of any acquiring parent) which stock satisfies the continuity of interest requirement.

rent stock for stock (B) reorganization.[81] Pursuant to Proposed Section 368(a)(1)(B)(i), the acquiring corporation must acquire at least 80 percent control, within the meaning of present Section 368(c), of the target. Also, pursuant to Proposed Section 368(a)(1)(B)(iii), the 80 percent continuity of interest requirement specified below must be satisfied.

Although there is some overlap between the 80 percent control test in Proposed Sections 368(a)(1)(A) and (B) and the continuity of interest requirement (*see* p. 79), the control test continues to serve a function, particularly in creeping acquisitions; the test is, therefore, retained. Section 368(c) is amended, however, to permit the Treasury to issue regulations that eliminate or modify the control test in a manner consistent with the continuity of interest requirement.[82]

Under Proposed Section 368(a)(1)(B)(ii), the target must hold substantially all of its assets after the acquisition. As discussed on page 79, creeping stock acquisitions are allowed as under current law.[83]

In a direct, triangular, or grandparent type stock for stock (B) reorganization, the basis to the acquiring corporation of the stock of the target is to be the net basis for the target's assets under principles similar to those in Prop. Treas. Reg. § 1.358–6.[84] Thus, the Section 362 carryover basis rule (*i.e.*, the acquiring corporation takes the basis of the target's shareholders as its basis for the target's stock), which applies to the current direct and triangular (B) reorganizations, is replaced by the net basis rule of Prop. Treas. Reg. § 1.358–6. The net basis rule currently applies to the stock of the acquiring subsidiary in (1) the triangular (C) stock for asset reorganization, and (2) the triangular merger reorganizations under Sections 368(a)(2)(D) and (a)(2)(E). The net basis is, in essence, the basis of the target's assets over the target's liabilities. This change could be implemented by simply excepting the Proposed (B) reorganizations from the carryover basis rule of Section 362 and imposing instead a net basis concept as determined in regulations.[85]

---

81. *See* chapter 2, pp. 37 and 38 for a description of the current direct and triangular stock for stock (B) reorganization.

82. Section 368(c).
CONTROL DEFINED—For purposes of part I (other than Section 304), part II, this part, and part V, the term "control" means the ownership of stock possessing at least 80 percent of the total combined voting power of all classes of stock entitled to vote and at least 80 percent of the total number of shares of all other classes of stock of the corporation. *Pursuant to regulations, this requirement may be eliminated or modified to make it consistent with the continuity of interest requirement of section 368(a)(4)(E).*

83. Treas. Reg. § 1.368–2(c) (1985).

84. *See* note 65, *supra*.

85. *See* note 67, *supra*.

The (C) Stock for Asset Reorganization

Proposed Section 368(a)(1)(C)[86] encompasses direct, triangular, and grandparent type stock for asset reorganizations, and thus replaces the current stock for asset (C) reorganizations.[87] To qualify under this provision, the transaction must satisfy the continuity of interest requirement (*see* Proposed Section 368(a)(1)(C)(ii)), the "substantially all" test (*see* Proposed Section 368(a)(1)(C)(i)), and the liquidation requirement of current law (*see* Proposed Section 368(a)(1)(C)(iii)). As discussed on page 79, there is no prohibition as under current law against creeping stock for asset acquisitions. Thus, the *Bausch & Lomb* doctrine[88] is overridden.

Summary of Changes to the (A), (B), and (C)

The structural changes here are not great, and they build on current law. The largest structural change is that Proposed Section 368(a)(1)(A) deals with all types of mergers, thus eliminating Sections 368(a)(2)(D) and (E) which deal, respectively, with forward and reverse subsidiary mergers. Proposed Sections 368(a)(1)(B) and (C) deal respectively with stock for stock and stock for asset reorganizations, just as the present Sections 368(a) (1)(B) and (C) deal with such reorganizations. The principal substantive changes are the adoption for each form of reorganization of a uniform substantially all the historic assets test and a uniform continuity of interest test. These uniform requirements are discussed below.[89]

These various forms of acquisitive reorganizations are illustrated in chapter 9. The balance of this chapter elaborates on the continuity of interest requirement, the "substantially all" requirement, and other aspects of the reorganization concept.

Implementation of the Continuity of Interest Requirement

There are several dimensions to the continuity of interest requirement. The first dimension concerns the amount and character of stock of either

---

86. Proposed Section 368(a)(1)(C). . . . [T]he term "reorganization" means . . . an asset acquisition in which:

(i) the acquiring corporation acquires substantially all of the historic assets of the target corporation;

(ii) the historic shareholders of the target corporation receive in exchange for the stock in the target corporation stock of the acquiring corporation (or stock of any acquiring parent) which stock satisfies the continuity of interest requirement; and

(iii) the target corporation satisfies the distribution requirement as provided in paragraph (2)(G).

87. *See* chapter 2, p. 37 for a description of the current direct and triangular C reorganizations.

88. *Bausch & Lomb Optical Co. v. Commissioner*, 267 F.2d 75 (2d Cir. 1954), *cert. denied*, 361 U.S. 835 (1959). *See also*, Rev. Rul. 54–396, 1954–2 C.B. 147.

89. *See* p. 74 (continuity of interest) and p. 87 (substantially all).

the acquiring corporation or the acquiring parent or grandparent that must be paid in the transaction (*see* page 76). As noted above, the judgment here is that at least 80 percent of the consideration paid must be in underlying voting common stock of either the acquiring corporation or a direct or indirect acquiring parent. This rule applies the 80 percent voting stock requirement currently applicable to the reverse subsidiary merger under Section 368(a)(2)(E) to all forms of reorganization. Also, the rule overrides the case law that permits the continuity of interest requirement to be satisfied with stock that is not underlying voting common stock, such as nonvoting preferred.[90]

The second dimension concerns the shareholders who must receive the required stock consideration and whether prereorganization shifts in ownership are taken into account. The judgment here is that the historic shareholders must receive the required consideration (*see* p. 76). This is a codification of current law.

The third dimension concerns the length of time the historic shareholders must retain the stock received in the reorganization (*see* p. 76). The judgment here is that at the time of the reorganization the historic shareholders must have unrestricted rights to hold, and must not intend to dispose of, shares that satisfy the continuity of interest requirement. This is essentially a codification of current law.

There are many other dimensions to the continuity of interest requirement:

1. The operation of the continuity of interest requirement when the acquiring corporation owns stock of the target prior to the reorganization, that is the so-called creeping acquisition problem (*see* p. 79);

2. The limitations placed by the continuity of interest doctrine on the redeployment of assets by the acquiring corporation after a reorganization, that is, the *Groman* and *Bashford* problem (*see* p. 82);

3. The possible avoidance of the continuity of interest requirement by having a small target corporation acquire a large acquiring corporation, that is, the reverse acquisition problem (*see* p. 83);

4. The possible avoidance of the continuity of interest requirement by structuring an acquisition as a Section 351 incorporation rather than as a reorganization, that is, the 351 reorganization overlap problem (*see* p. 85);

5. The impact of the continuity of interest requirement in transactions in which shareholders of the target corporation own 50 percent of the stock of an acquiring corporation that acquires the assets of the target corporation, that is, the nondivisive (D) problem (*see* p. 86); and

6. The impact of the continuity of interest requirement (and also the step transaction doctrine) in a transaction in which a shareholder transfers as-

---

90. *John A. Nelson Co. v. Helvering*, 296 U.S. 374 (1935).

sets to a target corporation immediately before and in contemplation of the acquisition of the target in a reorganization (*see* p. 92).

The 80 percent Continuity Requirement, Historic Shareholders, and Holding Period

The basic continuity of interest requirement is set forth in Proposed Section 368(a)(4)(E).[91] The requirement that 80 percent of each class of stock of the target corporation be exchanged for underlying voting common stock of the acquiring corporation or of the direct or indirect acquiring parent should eliminate questions of value. Thus, there is an 80 percent continuity of interest requirement for each class of the target's stock. (*See* Proposed Section 368(a)(4)(E)(i).)

Pursuant to Proposed Section 368(a)(4)(E)(i)(II), the Treasury is authorized pursuant to regulations to permit stock of the target that is not underlying voting stock to be acquired in exchange for stock with substantially similar features of either the acquiring corporation or a direct or indirect acquiring parent. This rule does not apply to target stock issued in contemplation of the reorganization. Thus, for example, if a target corporation has common stock and preferred stock outstanding and the preferred was not issued in contemplation of the planned reorganization, the acquiring corporation would be able to satisfy the continuity of interest requirement with respect to the target's preferred stock by issuing preferred stock of the acquiring corporation with substantially similar features in exchange for 80 percent of the target's preferred.

Also, pursuant to the second sentence of Proposed Section 368(a)(4)(E), (i) the Treasury is authorized to promulgate regulations overriding

---

91. Proposed Section 368(a)(4)(E).
CONTINUITY OF INTEREST REQUIREMENT—
(i) Basic 80% Requirement. The continuity of interest requirement for transactions described in paragraphs (1)(A), (1)(B) or (1)(C) is satisfied if as a result of the transaction the historic shareholders of the target corporation in the aggregate receive (and hold as specified below) in exchange for at least 80% of each class of stock of the target corporation either (I) stock of the acquiring corporation or stock of an acquiring parent, as the case may be, representing the underlying voting common stock of the acquiring corporation or the acquiring parent; or (II) pursuant to regulations, stock of the acquiring corporation or stock of the acquiring parent, as the case may be, with substantially similar terms to, or with greater equity features than, the stock of the target corporation surrendered. Pursuant to regulations, the class of stock requirement may be waived where it is otherwise clear that at least 80% of the consideration paid is the underlying voting stock of the acquiring corporation or of the acquiring parent.
(ii) The Holding Requirement. The historic shareholders are deemed to hold the requisite amount of stock of the acquiring corporation or acquiring parent provided such stock is received with unrestricted rights of ownership and without any preconceived plan or agreement for disposing of such requisite amount of stock.

the class-by-class requirement if it is clear that 80 percent of the consideration paid for the fair market value of all of the target's stock is underlying voting common stock of the acquiring corporation. Thus, for example, assume that publicly held target has outstanding common stock with a value of $90 million and preferred with a value of $10 million. The 80 percent continuity test could be satisfied by having the acquiring corporation issue $80 million of its underlying voting common stock in exchange for $80 million of the target's voting common stock. The $10 million balance of the target's common and the $10 million of the target's preferred could be acquired for cash.

The principle of *McDonald's Restaurants of Illinois, Inc. v. Commissioner* is adopted.[92] This decision holds that the continuity of interest requirement is not satisfied if the target shareholders intend at the time of the reorganization to dispose of the stock of the acquiring corporation. This concept is reflected in Proposed Section 368(a)(4)(E)(ii). Under this provision the historic shareholders must have unrestricted rights of ownership in and must not have a plan to dispose of the minimum amount of stock needed to satisfy the continuity of interest requirement (*i.e.*, 80 percent). Thus, the requirement in Rev. Rul. 66–23[93] that the target's shareholders have unrestricted rights for at least five years is rejected; there must be unlimited unrestricted rights. If more than 80 percent of the consideration is underlying voting stock of the acquiring corporation, the historic shareholders may have a prior agreement to dispose of the amount in excess of 80 percent.

The continuity of interest requirement has to be satisfied with respect to the historic shareholders of the target corporation. This follows the principle of *Superior Coach of Florida, Inc. v. Commissioner*.[94] In determining the historic shareholders, prereorganization sales by the target's shareholders are disregarded except for sales to, or arranged by, the acquiring corporation or any corporation or person controlled by or in direct or indirect control of the acquiring corporation. Thus, the Service's position in Rev. Rul. 85–138[95] is codified. Under this rule, the continuity of interest requirement could be satisfied even if arbitrageurs buy a substantial portion of the target's stock in contemplation of a reorganization. Arbitrageurs would be considered historic shareholders as long as they are not acting on behalf of the acquiror.

This prereorganization shift concept is reflected in the definition of historic shareholders in Proposed Section 368(a)(4)(F)(i).[96] In determining

---

92. *McDonald's Restaurants of Illinois, Inc. v. Commissioner* 688 F.2d 520 (7th Cir. 1982).

93. Rev. Rul. 66–23, 1966–1 C.B. 67.

94. *Superior Coach of Florida, Inc. v. Commissioner* 80 T.C. 895 (1983).

95. Rev. Rul. 85–138, 1985–2 C.B. 122.

96. Proposed Section 368(a)(4)(F)(i) Historic Shareholder, Basic Rule.

the number of shares held by historic shareholders, any shares of the target corporation redeemed prior to an intended reorganization are treated as outstanding and held by historic shareholders, provided such redemption is pursuant to a plan arranged by the acquiring corporation or a related party. Thus, any such redemption amounts would be treated as boot paid in the transaction. This principle is reflected in Proposed Section 368(a)(4) (F)(ii)[97] and, in essence, codifies the Service's position.[98]

Under the amendments to the definition of party to reorganization in Proposed Section 368(b),[99] if the continuity of interest requirement is satisfied with respect to the stock of the acquiring parent, then nonrecognition treatment is accorded under Sections 354 and 361 upon receipt of stock of the acquiring corporation. The reverse is not true, however.

Under these rules, the continuity of interest requirement for each form of reorganization is satisfied if (1) at least 80 percent of the consideration

---

The term "historic shareholders" means the shareholders of each class of stock of the target corporation who have not acquired their shares pursuant to a plan or arrangement negotiated or agreed upon with the acquiring corporation (or a related party) prior to the transaction intended to qualify under paragraph (1)(A), (1)(B) or (1)(C).

97. Proposed Section 368(a)(4)(F)(ii) Historic Shareholders . . . Redemptions, etc.

For purposes of determining the total number of shares held by historic shareholders, any shares redeemed pursuant to a plan or arrangement negotiated or agreed upon with the acquiring corporation (or related party) prior to the transaction intended to qualify under paragraph (1)(A), (1)(B) or (1)(C) shall be treated as outstanding and held by historic shareholders.

98. See Rev. Proc. 77–37, 1977–2 C.B. 568. See also, Rev. Rul. 75–360, 1975–2 C.B. 110 (redemption by target prior to a purported (B) breaks the (B) where acquiring corporation provides the funds).

99. Proposed Section 368(b).

PARTY TO A REORGANIZATION—For purposes of this part, the term "a party to a reorganization" includes:

(1) a corporation resulting from a reorganization, and
(2) both corporations, in the case of a reorganization resulting from the acquisition by one corporation of stock or properties of another.

In the case of a reorganization qualifying under paragraph (1)(A), (1)(B) or (1)(C) of subsection (a), if the stock exchanged for the stock or properties is stock of an acquiring parent (as defined in subsection (a)(4)(C)), and such stock satisfies the continuity of interest requirement, the term "a party to a reorganization" includes the acquiring parent. In the case of a reorganization qualifying under paragraph (1)(A), (1)(B), (1)(C) or (1)(G) of subsection (a) by reason of paragraph (2)(C) of subsection (a), the term "a party to a reorganization" includes the corporation controlling directly or indirectly the corporation to which the acquired assets or stock are transferred.

received by the target's historic shareholders constitutes voting common stock of the acquiring corporation or of the acquiring parent, and (2) the historic shareholders have the unrestricted right to hold and intend to hold such stock at the time of the reorganization.

Impact of Continuity of Interest and Bausch & Lomb on Pre-reorganization Stock Ownership by the Acquiring Corporation

Pursuant to Proposed Section 368(a)(4)(F)(iv),[100] the acquiring corporation may, pursuant to regulations, be treated as a historic shareholder of the target with respect to the stock of the target held by the acquiring corporation prior to the contemplation of the proposed reorganization. Under this provision, in an asset reorganization under Proposed Section 368(a)(1)(A) or (C), the acquiring corporation is treated as receiving, in exchange for target stock held by it, stock of the acquiring corporation or of the acquiring parent with an equivalent value. As pointed out below, this rule overrides the *Bausch & Lomb* doctrine. These provisions treat such pre-reorganization ownership of the target's stock as counting toward satisfaction of the continuity of interest requirement of Proposed Section 368(a)(4)(E).

Thus, for example, if the acquiring corporation is a historic shareholder of the target with respect to 30 percent of the target's only class of stock, the continuity of interest requirement is satisfied if in a transaction under Proposed Section 368(a)(1)(A), (B), or (C) the acquiring corporation issues its stock to the other shareholders for an additional 50 percent of the target's stock. Consequently, there would be a reorganization under Proposed Section 368(a)(1)(A) if the target were to merge into the acquiring corporation, with the target's other shareholders receiving, pursuant to the merger, stock of the acquiring corporation in exchange for 50 percent of the outstanding stock of the acquiring corporation and cash or other consideration for the 20 percent balance. This transaction would also qualify under Proposed Section 368(a)(1)(A) if it were structured as a reverse or forward subsidiary merger. In such a transaction, the shareholders of the

---

100. Proposed Section 368(a)(4)(F)(iv) Historic Shareholders.... Bausch & Lomb Override.

Pursuant to regulations, an acquiring corporation (or related party) that owns stock of a target corporation, which stock was acquired prior to the contemplation of the reorganization, may be considered as a historic shareholder for purposes of determining whether the continuity of interest requirement is satisfied. In such case, the acquiring corporation (or related party) shall for purposes of determining whether an asset reorganization under paragraph (1)(A) or (1)(C) satisfies the continuity of interest requirement of paragraph (4)(E) be treated as receiving in exchange for such stock of the target corporation, stock of the acquiring corporation or the acquiring parent of an equivalent value.

target, other than the acquiring corporation, could receive (1) voting common stock of the acquiring parent in exchange for their common stock amounting to 50 percent of the outstanding stock, and (2) cash in exchange for the balance of their common stock. In a forward subsidiary merger, the target's stock held by the acquiring corporation would be canceled.

This rule codifies what is apparently the Service's internal position on the application of the continuity of interest requirement in direct merger reorganizations under Section 368(a)(1)(A) in which the acquiring corporation has a prereorganization stock interest in the target corporation.[101]

This transaction, however, cannot be effectuated as a reverse subsidiary merger under the present Section 368(a)(2)(E); under that provision at least 80 percent of the stock of the target must be acquired in the reorganization.[102] Thus, under present law, if the acquiring corporation has a greater than 20 percent prereorganization stock ownership interest in the target, it is not possible for the acquiring corporation to complete a creeping acquisition of the balance of the target's stock with a reverse subsidiary merger reorganization. This senseless impediment is eliminated under the proposed rules.

Further, there would be a stock for stock reorganization under Proposed Section 368(a)(1)(B) if an acquiring corporation that has a 30 percent preexisting stock interest in the target, acquired at least 50 percent of the target's stock from the other shareholders in exchange for stock of the acquiring corporation. In such case, both the 80 percent control test and the 80 percent continuity requirement are met for the Proposed (B). This is essentially a codification of current law.[103]

Finally, in a stock for asset reorganization under Proposed Section 368(a)(1)(C), the acquiring corporation could acquire substantially all of the target's assets in exchange for consideration consisting of (1) the cancellation of the acquiring corporation's 30 percent stock interest in the target, (2) stock of the acquiring corporation in an amount equal to the value of 50 percent of the target's outstanding stock, and (3) cash or other consideration for the 20 percent balance of the target's stock. Thus, on the liquidation of the target pursuant to the requirement in present Section 368(a)(2)(G), the shareholders of the target other than the acquiring corporation would receive (1) stock of the acquiring corporation in exchange for 50 percent of the outstanding stock of the target, and (2) cash or other consideration in exchange for the balance of their shares. This transaction would not qualify as a reorganization under the present Section 368(a)

---

101. GCM 39404 (April 15, 1982).
102. Treas. Reg. § 1.368–2(j)(3)(i) (1985).
103. Treas. Reg. § 1.368–2(c) (1985).

(1)(C) because of the doctrine set down in *Bausch & Lomb Co. v. Commissioner.*[104]

In *Bausch & Lomb*, the acquiring corporation owned approximately 79 percent of the stock of the target prior to the contemplation of the reorganization. In a transaction intended to qualify as a (C) reorganization, the acquiring corporation acquired in exchange solely for its voting stock all of the assets and liabilities of the target corporation. The target was then liquidated. In this liquidation the target distributed 21 percent of the stock it held in the acquiring corporation to the minority shareholders in exchange for their target stock, and the target distributed the 79 percent balance of the stock it held in the acquiring corporation to the acquiring corporation in exchange for its target stock. The court held that the transaction did not qualify as a reorganization because the consideration paid by the acquiring corporation was not solely its voting stock but rather was a combination of 21 percent of its voting stock and 79 percent of the stock of the target that was given up on the liquidation of the target. Thus, the court ignored the issuance by the acquiring corporation of the 79 percent of its stock which it received on the liquidation of the target corporation.

Proposed Section 368(a)(4)(F)(iv)[105] overrides the decision in *Bausch & Lomb* in the following manner. An acquiring corporation that holds a prereorganization stock interest in the target is treated as a historic shareholder of the target and in that capacity receives in the reorganization a constructive exchange of its target shares for shares of the acquiring corporation. Thus, under the Proposed (C), the acquiring corporation is not treated as receiving in exchange for its target stock a liquidating distribution of target's assets, which was the result in *Bausch & Lomb*. The acquiring corporation is, instead, treated as receiving from the target in a liquidating distribution stock of the acquiring corporation with a value equal to the value of the target stock actually owned by the acquiring corporation.

Thus, this rule adopts the taxpayer's position in *Bausch & Lomb* and thereby eliminates one of the obscure traps for the unwary. The arbitrariness of this trap can vividly be illustrated by considering two alternative ways the acquiring corporation may acquire the target's assets. First, as the court in *Bausch & Lomb* pointed out, if the target had merged into the acquiring corporation (rather than having its assets acquired for stock), the transactions would have qualified as a reorganization under the predecessor of the present Section 368(a)(1)(A). Second, the Service has issued a ruling to the effect that the *Bausch & Lomb* problem can be eliminated by the

---

104. *Bausch & Lomb Optical Co. v. Commissioner*, 267 F.2d 75 (2d Cir. 1959). *See also*, Rev. Rul. 54–396, 1954–2 C.B. 147.

105. *See* note 100, *supra*.

use of a triangular (C) reorganization.[106] Thus, if, instead of acquiring the target's assets directly, the acquiring corporation forms a subsidiary that uses stock of the acquiring corporation in acquiring substantially all of the assets of the target, which is then liquidated, the transaction qualifies as a triangular C reorganization. This is so even though on liquidation of the target 79 percent of the stock of the acquiring corporation held by the target is distributed to the acquiring corporation.

If the acquiring corporation (or related party) is a historic shareholder with respect to at least 80 percent of the target's stock, then no additional stock consideration is required to be issued in order for an acquisition of the target to qualify under the Proposed (A), (B), or (C). The transaction may also qualify as a tax-free liquidation under Section 332, in which case that provision takes precedence over the reorganization provisions.[107]

In creeping acquisitions the above rules (1) follow the model of the treatment of such acquisitions under the current (B) reorganization, without a solely for voting stock requirement, (2) clarify the law under the current (A),[108] (3) overrule the doctrine of *Bausch & Lomb* under the current (C), and (4) provide for uniform treatment of the acquiring corporation's prereorganization ownership in the target in all forms of reorganization. Thus, under these proposed rules, a creeping acquisition would qualify as a reorganization under all direct, triangular, and grandparent type mergers, stock for stock, and stock for asset reorganizations, provided the following two requirements are satisfied. First, the 80 percent continuity of interest requirement (counting in each case the acquiring corporation's prereorganization stock ownership in the target toward the 80 percent) is met. Second, the "substantially all" requirement is satisfied. Creeping acquisitions are illustrated in chapter 9.

Impact of Continuity of Interest on Push Up and Push Down of Assets After an Acquisitive Reorganization

There should generally be no prohibition against the redeployment of the target's stock or assets within the affiliated group of which the acquiring corporation is a member. This rule should apply, however, only if the target's shareholders have a continuing interest in the target's assets. This continuing interest would be realized if the acquiring parent or grandparent corporation owned a stock interest in the corporation, or corporations, that holds the target's stock or assets. Such redeployments are permitted, pursuant to regulations, by a proposed amendment to Section 368(a)(2)(C).[109] This rule expands the present statutory override to the *Groman*

---

106. Rev. Rul. 57–278, 1957–1 C.B. 124.
107. *See* I.R.C. § 332(b) (1991).
108. *See, e.g.*, GCM 39404, April 15, 1982.
109. Proposed Section 368(a)(2)(C).

and *Bashford*[110] doctrine. This doctrine, which has been partially overridden in the triangular reorganization provisions, provides that the continuity of interest test is not satisfied if the target's assets are held by a subsidiary of the acquiring corporation. This amendment, which also has an effect on the "substantially all" test, is discussed further in the section beginning on page 90.

Impact of Continuity of Interest in Reverse Acquisitions[111]

The continuity of interest test of present law focuses on the consideration paid for the target's shares. Assume, for example, the parties are planning a transaction in which 80 percent of the target's shareholders are going to be cashed out and 20 percent are going to receive stock in the acquiring corporation. For the following reasons, the transaction cannot qualify under any of the present forms of reorganization. Because of a failure to satisfy the solely for voting stock requirement, the transaction cannot qualify as (1) a direct or triangular stock for stock (B), (2) a direct or triangular stock for asset (C), or (3) a reverse subsidiary merger. Also, the transaction cannot qualify as a direct (A) merger or a forward subsidiary merger because of a failure to satisfy the 50 percent continuity guideline.[112] Even though this is just a guideline and does not set the limits of the law, the lowest a court has gone in finding that the continuity requirement is satisfied is 25 percent stock consideration.[113] The 20 percent stock consideration almost certainly would not satisfy the continuity requirement for either a direct merger or a forward triangular merger.

On the other hand, assume that the structure of the transaction is reversed with the real acquiring corporation merging into the target. In such transaction, the shareholders of the acquiring corporation receive stock of the target corporation in exchange for their stock, and 80 percent of the

---

TRANSFERS OF ASSETS OR STOCK TO SUBSIDIARIES IN CERTAIN PARAGRAPH (1)(A), (1)(B), (1)(C) and (1)(G) CASES—A transaction otherwise qualifying under paragraph (1)(A), (1)(B) or (1)(C) shall not be disqualified by reason of the fact that part or all of the assets or stock which were acquired in the transaction are transferred, pursuant to regulations, by the acquiring corporation to another corporation that is in the same affiliated group, as defined in section 1504(a), as the acquiring corporation. A similar rule shall apply to a transaction otherwise qualifying under paragraph (1)(G) where the requirements of subparagraphs (A) and (B) of Section 354(b)(1) are met with respect to the acquisition of assets.

110. *Groman v. Commissioner*, 302 U.S. 82 (1937) and *Helvering v. Bashford*, 302 U.S. 454 (1938).

111. This section is based in part on Thompson, *Suggested Alternative Approach*, chapter 1 *supra* note 3, at 637.

112. Rev. Proc. 77–37, 1977–2 C.B. 568.

113. *Miller v. Commissioner*, 84 F.2d 415 (6th Cir. 1936).

target's shareholders are redeemed for cash and the 20 percent balance continue to own their shares. Since the real target is the surviving corporation, the transaction presumably qualifies as a direct merger under Section 368(a)(1)(A); the continuity of interest test is satisfied.[114] Thus, as Professor Wolfman points out, if in the transaction in *Kass*[115] the merger had gone the other way, Mrs. Kass would not have been subjected to tax.[116]

Professor Wolfman's observation is not a justification for repealing the continuity of interest doctrine; it is, however, a strong argument for preventing abuse of the doctrine through reverse acquisitions in which the real acquiring corporation is disguised as the target and the real target is disguised as the acquiror.

A reverse acquisition concept is not new. It applies under the consolidated return regulations for determining the common parent[117] and was included in the 1985 SFC Proposals for determining which party to a qualified acquisition is the target and which the acquiror.[118]

A reverse acquisition provision should be added to the present reorganization provision to prevent the avoidance of the continuity of interest requirement. Proposed Section 368(a)(4)(D)[119] is such a provision. Under this provision, if as a result of an acquisitive reorganization, the shareholders of the target corporation have 50 percent control, within the meaning of Section 304(c), of the acquiring corporation, then the nominal target is treated as the acquiring corporation and the nominal acquiring corporation is treated as the target. The Treasury by regulations will address situations in which shareholders of both the target and acquiring corporation are in control.

---

114. Also the acquisition could be effectuated as a Section 351 transaction. *See* p. 85.

115. *Kass v. Commissioner*, 60 T.C. 219 (1973).

116. *Panel Discussion*, *supra* chapter 3, note 41, at 697.

117. Treas. Reg. §§ 1.1502–1(f)(3) and–75(d)(3) (1972). The reverse acquisition concept is different from the reverse subsidiary merger which is discussed in chapter 2, pp. 29 and 38.

118. *1985 SFC Proposals*, *supra* chapter 1, note 3, at § 366(e).

119. Proposed Section 368(a)(4)(D).
REVERSE ACQUISITION—If as a result of a transaction described in paragraph (1)(A), (1)(B) or (1)(C) the shareholders of the target corporation have control (within the meaning of Section 304(c)) of the acquiring corporation or the acquiring parent, then for purposes of determining whether the transaction qualifies under paragraph (1)(A), (1)(B) or (1)(C), the nominal target corporation shall be treated as the acquiring corporation and the nominal acquiring corporation or acquiring parent shall be treated as the target corporation. The Treasury by regulations shall deal with situations in which both the target corporation's shareholders and the acquiring corporation's shareholders are in control of the acquiring corporation.

Impact of Continuity of Interest in Overlaps Between Reorganizations and Section 351 Transactions[120]

Section 351 may be used to give nonrecognition treatment to shareholders of a target corporation in an acquisition transaction that does not qualify as a reorganization under current law. For example, the acquiring corporation and a minority shareholder of the target (*e.g.*, a 15 percent shareholder) form a new corporation with the acquiring corporation contributing cash and the minority shareholder contributing target stock. The acquiring corporation receives all of the common stock of the new corporation and the minority shareholder all of the preferred. The transaction on its face qualifies under Section 351 and the minority shareholder receives nonrecognition treatment. The new corporation then purchases for cash the 85 percent balance of the stock of the target. As a result, the acquiring corporation has acquired all of the common equity in the target for 85 percent cash and 15 percent stock. The minority target shareholder has received nonrecognition treatment, and the majority target shareholders have a taxable transaction. Further, the new corporation could make a Section 338 election and step-up the basis of the target's assets.

This type of transaction was utilized by Japan's Matsushita in its acquisition of MCA Inc. in 1990.[121] Matsushita formed a new Delaware Corporation, Holding. In simultaneous transactions, Matsushita transferred cash to Holding in exchange for common stock, and Lou Wasserman, the Chairman of MCA, transferred to Holding his common stock in MCA in exchange for preferred stock in Holding. This transaction qualified for nonrecognition treatment to Wasserman under Section 351. Acquisition Sub, a wholly-owned subsidiary of Holding, then made a tender offer for the balance of the common stock of MCA. Finally, the shares of MCA that were not tendered were acquired in a reverse subsidiary merger. This last transaction was treated as a purchase of the stock of MCA.[122]

The Service has been around in a circle on this type of transaction. First, in a private letter ruling involving National Starch the Service ruled that the transaction qualifies under Section 351.[123] The Service then issued two revenue rulings denying Section 351 treatment.[124] Finally, reversing its field

---

120. This section is based in part on Thompson, *Suggested Alternative Approach*, *supra* chapter 1, note 3, at 633.

121. *See* Offer to Purchase Common Shares of MCA Inc. by Matsushita Acquisition Corp., a wholly-owned subsidiary of Matsushita Electric Industrial Co., Ltd., Nov. 30, 1990.

122. *See* chapter 2, p. 29.

123. *See* Pvt. Ltr. Rul. 7839060 (June 28, 1978).

124. *See* Rev. Rul. 80–284, 1980–2 C.B. 117; Rev. Rul. 80–285, 1980–2 C.B. 119. *See* chapter 2, p. 39.

again, the Service withdrew its two published rulings and held in another revenue ruling that Section 351 applies.[125]

There is no principled reason why taxpayers should be able to use Section 351 as an end run around the continuity of interest doctrine. Certainly the purpose behind Section 351 is not to facilitate tax-free treatment to some of a target's shareholders in an otherwise taxable acquisition of the target's stock. Rather, the purpose of Section 351 is to facilitate the organization of corporations to carry on business operations. No such purpose exists when Section 351 is used solely to give a shareholder in the position of Mr. Wasserman tax-free treatment in an otherwise taxable acquisition.

For these reasons, Proposed Section 368(a)(4)(N)[126] provides that any transaction that, pursuant to regulations, fits the pattern of an acquisitive reorganization does not qualify under Section 351. Thus, Section 351 could no longer be used to accomplish the result reached by Mr. Wasserman in the MCA acquisition. This provision, like the reverse acquisition rule, protects the integrity of the reorganization provisions.[127]

Impact of Continuity of Interest in Nondivisive D Reorganizations

A nondivisive (D) reorganization under Sections 368(a)(1)(D) and 354(b) occurs if one or more shareholders of a target corporation own directly or indirectly 50 percent or more of the stock of a corporation that acquires the target's assets.[128] The purpose of the provision is to treat a purported sale of assets between commonly controlled corporations as a reorganization.

Thus, for example, the statute literally applies if (1) a target sells its assets to an acquiring corporation for cash, and (2) the acquiring corporation is controlled by a one percent shareholder of the target. Consequently, the acquiror is treated as acquiring the target's assets with a carryover basis under Section 362(a), and the target has nonrecognition under Section 361. The cash distributed to shareholders of the target other than those who are also shareholders of the acquiror produces capital gain or loss; cash distributed

---

125. Rev. Rul. 84–71, 1984–1 C.B. 106.

126. Proposed Section 368(a)(4)(N).
PRECEDENCE OF SECTION 368 OVER SECTION 351—Any transaction that, pursuant to regulations, fits the pattern of a reorganization under paragraph (1)(A), (1)(B) and (1)(C) may not qualify under Section 351.

127. In his proposal to repeal the reorganization provisions and to impose tax at both the corporate and shareholder levels in the case of an acquisition, Professor Shakow also proposes to amend Section 351 to deny nonrecognition treatment for the types of transactions covered by Rev. Rul. 84–71, 1984–1 C.B. 106. Shakow, *Whither, "C"!, supra* note 35, at 196–201.

128. I R.C. § 368(a)(2)(H) (1991).

to the continuing shareholders may be treated as a dividend under Section 356(a)(2).

It is uncertain under current law whether and how the continuity of interest doctrine applies in this type of transaction. As a matter of policy, the transaction should be treated as a reorganization only if shareholders of the target corporation who own 50 percent of the stock of the target also own 50 percent of the stock of the acquiring corporation. A clause to this effect is proposed, to be added to Section 368(a)(2)(H).[129]

Implementation of Uniform Substantially All Requirement Overriding Elkhorn Coal and Relationship to Continuity of Business Enterprise Requirement

Uniform Substantially All Standard and Historic Assets

The uniform "substantially all" requirement which is proposed earlier in this chapter is implemented in Proposed Sections 368(a)(1)(A), (B), and (C). These provisions contain a requirement that the "substantially all" test be satisfied.[130] Thus, in each form of reorganization (whether stock or asset, direct, triangular, or grandparent type) substantially all of the target's assets must be either acquired in the transaction or held by the target after the transaction. Proposed Section 368(a)(4)(G)[131] codifies the Service's 90 percent/70 percent ruling guideline for determining whether the substantially all test is satisfied.[132] Under this guideline substantially all means 90 percent of the target's net assets and 70 percent of its gross assets.

The "substantially all" requirement proposed here applies to the corporation's historic assets. These assets are defined in Proposed Section

---

129. Proposed Section 368(a)(2)(H).
SPECIAL RULE FOR DETERMINING WHETHER CERTAIN TRANSACTIONS ARE QUALIFIED UNDER PARAGRAPH (1)(D).—In the case of any transaction with respect to which the requirements of subparagraphs (A) and (B) of Section 354(b)(1) are met, for purposes of determining whether such transaction qualifies under subparagraph (D) of paragraph (1), the term "control" has the meaning given to such term by Section 304(c), *and the transaction shall so qualify only if the shareholder or shareholders of the transferor corporation who are in such control of the transferee corporation were also in control, within the meaning of Section 304(c), of the transferor corporation immediately before the transaction.*

130. *See* p. 68.

131. Proposed Section 368(a)(4)(G).
SUBSTANTIALLY ALL OF THE HISTORIC ASSETS—The term "substantially all of the historic assets" means at least 90% of the fair market value of the net historic assets and 70% of the fair market value of the gross historic assets.

132. Rev. Proc. 77–37, 1977–2 C.B. 568.

368(a)(4) (H)(i)[133] to mean all assets held prior to the contemplation of the acquisitive reorganization. Thus, under this definition a target corporation could not, pursuant to an arrangement with the acquiring corporation, sell a significant portion of its assets for cash and then have the balance of its assets plus the cash acquired in an acquisitive reorganization. Such a transaction is fundamentally inconsistent with the concept of a reorganization. The Service, however, has blessed this type of transaction in a recent ruling under Section 368(a)(1)(C).[134]

Exception for Tax-Free Spin Offs Under Section 355

The section beginning on page 59 explains that an exception would apply to the uniform "substantially all" test for pre-reorganization tax-free spin off type transactions under Section 355, but the "substantially all" test should block pre-reorganization taxable strip down transactions. Thus, it is proposed here to:

1. Override for all forms of acquisitive reorganizations the *Elkhorn Coal*[135] doctrine (which prevented a strip down prior to a stock for asset (C) reorganization because of the "substantially all" requirement) as that concept applies to prereorganization spin offs,

2. Codify the *Elkorn Coal* doctrine as it applies to prereorganization taxable strip downs, and

3. Codify for all forms of acquisitive reorganizations the *Morris Trust*[136] doctrine (which allowed a target to spin off a sub prior to the acquisition of the target in an (A) merger reorganization).

As pointed out in the section beginning on page 59, there is no principled reason why after a Section 355 distribution it should be possible, as under present law, to effectuate a direct merger under Section 368(a)(1)(A) or a direct or triangular (B) reorganization under Section 368(a)(1)(B) but not (because of the "substantially all" test) a direct or triangular (C) under the present Section 368(a)(1)(C) or a forward or reverse subsidiary merger under Sections 368(a)(2)(D) and (E). As a policy matter, all forms of acquisitive reorganizations should be allowed after a Section 355 distribution. For that reason, the *Elkhorn Coal* doctrine as it applies to prereorganization spin off type transactions under Section 355 (but not to taxable strip down transactions) is overridden and the *Morris Trust* doctrine is cod-

---

133. Proposed Section 368(a)(4)(H).
HISTORIC ASSETS—

(i) General Rule. The term "historic assets" means all assets that were held prior to the contemplation of a transaction described in paragraph (1)(A), (1)(B) or (1)(C).

134. Rev. Rul. 88–48, 1988–1 C.B. 117 (target which, pursuant to an overall plan, sold half of its assets for cash could have balance of assets plus cash acquired in a (C) reorganization).

135. *See* p. 63.

136. *See* p. 63.

ified, in the following manner. Nothing in Proposed Section 368(a)(1)(A), (B), or (C) prohibits the use of a Section 355 distribution before a reorganization. The *Morris Trust* principle, therefore, is inherent in these proposals.

Although under the proposals here, a substantially all of the historic assets requirement applies to each form of acquisitive reorganization, the definition of historic assets is structured in such a way as to allow a prior Section 355 distribution in an *Elkhorn Coal* type transaction.

Under Proposed Section 368(a)(4)(H)(ii),[137] in determining if a Distributing Corporation in a Section 355 transaction satisfies the substantially all test, historic assets do not include either the stock of a Controlled Corporation or assets held by such corporation. Thus, the distribution of the stock of the Controlled Corporation has no effect in determining if the Distributing Corporation satisfies the "substantially all" test. Also, under this provision the historic assets of the Controlled Corporation include the assets held by it immediately before the distribution. Consequently, the decision in *Elkorn Coal* as it applies to prereorganization Section 355 spin off type transactions is overridden, both for the Distributing Corporation and the Controlled Corporation, in all forms of acquisitive reorganizations.

Under Proposed Section 368(a)(4)(H)(ii), the target corporation could, for example, distribute the stock of a subsidiary in a Section 355 distribution prior to an acquisitive reorganization without causing the acquisition to fail to satisfy the "substantially all" test. Also, under this definition, the Controlled Corporation in a Section 355 spin off type transaction could be acquired in an acquisitive reorganization, without failing the substantially all test. Thus, the *Morris Trust* principle is extended to all forms of acquisitive reorganizations. On the other hand, any disposition by a target of any of its assets, including the stock of a subsidiary, in a taxable distribution or sale prior to the reorganization would be taken into account in determining whether the "substantially all" test is satisfied.

A tax-free Section 355 distribution, which is essentially a reorganization of a single corporation, is compatible with a tax-free acquisitive reorganization. The same is not true of a taxable disposition.

Thus, as a result of Proposed Section 368(a)(4)(H)(ii), after a Section 355 distribution, the Distributing Corporation and the Controlled Corporation can be acquired in a tax-free direct, triangular, or grandparent

---

137. Proposed Section 368(a)(4)(H)(ii).
HISTORIC ASSETS—
   (ii) Exception for Section 355 Distributions. In the case of a distribution governed by Section 355, the historic assets of the distributing corporation do not include either the stock of any controlled corporation or the assets contributed to such controlled corporation, and the historic assets of the controlled corporation include the assets held by it immediately before the distribution.

type (1) merger reorganization under Proposed Section 368(a)(1)(A), (2) stock for stock reorganization under Proposed Section 368(a)(1)(B), or (3) stock for asset reorganization under Proposed Section 368(a)(1)(C).

Finally, in view of the adoption of this rule, which makes a spin off type transaction compatible with an acquisitive reorganization, it is also proposed on page 93 to permit this type of transaction to be effectuated directly between the Distributing Corporation and the acquiring corporation. Under this approach, provided all the requirements (other than the distribution requirement) of Section 355 are satisfied (*e.g.*, business purpose, continuity of interest, and active trade or business), the Distributing Corporation could dispose of the stock of the Controlled Corporation (or the Controlled Corporation could dispose of its assets) in a tax-free acquisitive reorganization, and the Distributing Corporation could then make a tax-free distribution to its shareholders of the stock of the acquiring corporation received in the acquisitive reorganization.

Exception for Section 351 Transfers

Proposed Section 368(a)(4)(H)(iii) provides a special rule for determining historic assets after the transfer of assets to a corporation in a tax-free exchange under Section 351. This provision is discussed later in this chapter.

Push Up and Down of Assets After an Acquisition

The current "substantially all" test has the effect of preventing an acquiring corporation from transferring, after an acquisitive reorganization, a substantial portion of the target's assets to the parent of the acquiring corporation. Such a transfer would cause the acquiring corporation to fail to hold substantially all of the target's assets.[138] On the other hand, under Section 368(a)(2)(C) neither the "substantially all" test nor the continuity of interest test are violated by reason of a transfer by the acquiring corporation of the target's stock or assets to a controlled subsidiary of the acquiring corporation. The purpose of this provision was to overrule the holdings in the *Groman* and *Bashford* cases.[139]

There is no reason for prohibiting an acquiring corporation from redeploying the target's stock or assets within the affiliated group of which the acquiring corporation is a member as long as those assets are under the control of the acquiring corporation or the acquiring parent. For that reason there is a proposed amendment to Section 368(a)(2)(C)[140] to allow,

---

138. *See* Philip C. Cook & John L. Coalson, Jr., *The "Substantially All of the Properties" Requirement in Triangular Reorganizations: A Current Review*, 35 Tax Law. 303 (1982).

139. *Groman v. Commissioner*, 302 U.S. 82 (1937) and *Helvering v. Bashford*, 302 U.S. 454 (1938).

140. *See* note 109, *supra*.

pursuant to regulations, an acquiring corporation to push up or push down the target's assets or stock to any corporation that is in the same affiliated group, determined under Section 1504(a), as the acquiring corporation. It is contemplated that the regulations will allow a push up or push down only where the target's shareholders have a continuing interest in substantially all of the target's assets.[141] For example, in a forward triangular merger under Proposed Section 368(a)(1)(A), the acquiring corporation would be permitted to push up the target's assets to the acquiring parent. The acquiring parent would not, however, be permitted to push up those assets to its parent (assuming it had one) because in that case the target's shareholders would not have any continuing interest in the target's assets through stock ownership in the acquiring parent.

Retention of Continuity of Business Enterprise Requirement

In order to qualify as an acquisitive reorganization under present law the transaction must satisfy the continuity of business enterprise requirement.[142] Under this requirement, after an acquisitive reorganization the acquiring corporation must either (1) continue the target's historic business or (2) use a significant portion of the target's assets in a business.[143]

The inclusion of a "substantially all" test for all forms of acquisitive reorganizations should eliminate pressure on the continuity of business enterprise doctrine. This doctrine, however, serves the useful purpose of preventing potential devices for circumventing the purposes behind the "substantially all" test and, therefore, should be retained. Proposed Section 368(a)(4)(M)[144] codifies the continuity of business enterprise requirement as provided in regulations.

Incorporations Prior to Acquisitive Reorganizations[145]

If a sole proprietor incorporates her business for the purpose of having the newly formed corporation acquired in a tax-free acquisitive reorgani-

---

141. Because of the repeal of the *General Utilities* doctrine, a push up of assets will be a taxable transaction; however, if consolidated returns are filed, gain or loss on the transaction would be deferred. *See* Treas. Reg. § 1.1502–13 and –14 (1988).

142. Treas. Reg. § 1.368–1(d) (1980).

143. Treas. Reg. § 1.368–1(d)(2) (1980).

144. Proposed Section 368(a)(4)(M).
CONTINUITY OF BUSINESS ENTERPRISE—In order to qualify as a reorganization under paragraph (1)(A), (1)(B) or (1)(C), the transaction must satisfy the continuity of business enterprise requirement as specified in regulations. Such regulations shall provide when and under what circumstances the continuity of business enterprise doctrine is satisfied in situations in which, pursuant to Section 368(a)(4)(H), historic assets are acquired by a corporation in a transaction governed by Section 351.

145. This discussion is based in part on Thompson, *Suggested Alternative Approach, supra* chapter 1, note 3, at 632.

zation, the Service will likely take the position that the transaction is a taxable acquisition by the acquiring corporation of the assets of the sole proprietor. Thus, the Service will ignore the Section 351 tax-free incorporation.[146] Similarly, if a corporation that operates several different divisions transfers one of its divisions to a new subsidiary for the purpose of having the subsidiary acquired in an acquisitive reorganization, the Service will likely treat the transaction as a taxable acquisition of the division. Thus, only old and cold target corporations may participate in acquisitive reorganizations.

This puts an unnecessary premium on the form in which a business is operated. Proposed Section 368(a)(4)(O)[147] eliminates this problem. This section provides that a Section 351 transfer to a corporation of the assets and liabilities of an active trade or business as defined in Section 355(b)(2) (without regard to the five year requirement) is not disqualified under such section merely because the transferee corporation is acquired in an acquisitive reorganization.

Also, under the definition of historic assets in Proposed Section 368(a)(4) (H)(iii),[148] such term includes assets contributed to a target corporation in a transaction qualifying under Section 351, provided (1) the assets constituted an active trade or business in the hands of the transferor, and (2) such assets were not acquired by the transferor in contemplation of the transaction. Thus, the "substantially all" test of Proposed Section 368(a) (4)(G)[149] will be satisfied as long as substantially all of the contributed assets are acquired in the reorganization.

In addition, under the definition of historic shareholders in Proposed Section 368(a)(4)(F)(iii),[150] such term includes the owners of any shares

---

146. *See, e.g.*, Rev. Rul. 70–140, 1970–1 C.B. 73; *West Coast Marketing Corp. v. Commissioner*, 46 T.C. 32 (1966).

147. Proposed Section 368(a)(4)(O).
SECTION 351 INCORPORATIONS PRIOR TO ACQUISITIVE REORGANIZATIONS—A transaction otherwise qualifying under Section 351 shall not fail to qualify under such section solely because after the transfer the transferee corporation is acquired in an acquisitive reorganization. This provision applies only to the transfer of assets that constitute an active trade or business, within the meaning of Section 355(b)(2), without regard to the five year period provided therein.

148. Proposed Section 368(a)(4)(H)(iii).
HISTORIC ASSETS—
(iii) Exception for Section 351 Transfers. Historic assets shall include assets contributed to a target corporation in a transaction qualifying under Section 351 provided such assets constituted an active trade or business, within the meaning of Section 355(b)(2), in the hands of the transferor (or transferors) and such assets were not acquired by such transferor (or transferors) in contemplation of the transaction.

149. *See* p. 87.
150. Proposed Section 368(a)(4)(F)(iii) Historic Shareholders . . . Effect of

received in exchange for the transfer of property to a corporation in a transaction governed by Section 351, provided such property constitutes historic assets of a trade or business that was actively conducted by the contributing shareholders. Thus, the incorporators of a new business are treated as historic shareholders.

As a result of these amendments, a sole proprietor may incorporate her proprietorship, or a partnership may incorporate its assets, or a corporation may incorporate a division, and then cause the newly formed corporation to be acquired in an acquisitive reorganization. Proposed Section 368(a)(4)(O) specifically permits the incorporation of an active trade or business before an acquisitive reorganization, and because of the definitions of historic assets and historic shareholders in Proposed Sections 368(a)(4)(H) and (a)(4)(F), respectively, the "substantially all" test and the continuity of interest test are satisfied in the subsequent reorganization.

If the enactment of this provision would result in a significant revenue loss, the provision could be eliminated without doing damage to the other proposals in chapter 4.

Disposition of Subsidiaries That Could Have Qualified Under Both Section 355 and the Acquisitive Reorganization Provisions

The policy decision has been made to allow a spin off of a Controlled Corporation under Section 355 to be followed by an acquisition of either the Distributing Corporation or the Controlled Corporation in an acquisitive reorganization.[151] The question addressed here is: Should the Distributing Corporation be able to dispose of a Controlled Corporation in a reorganization and then make a tax-free distribution of the stock of the acquiring corporation?[152] The economic effect of this transaction is the same as in the spin off of a Controlled Corporation followed by the acquisition of the Controlled Corporation in an acquisitive reorganization.[153]

Incorporations.
Historic shareholders shall include the owners of any shares received in exchange for the transfer of property to a corporation in a transaction governed by Section 351, provided such property constitutes the historic assets (as defined in subparagraph (H) below) of a trade or business that was actively conducted by such contributing shareholder or shareholders.

151. See p. 62 and p. 88.

152. See the discussion of spin offs followed by acquisitive reorganizations in chapter 4, p. 62 and p. 88.

153. This transaction is different from the break-up acquisition which is proposed in the ALI 1989 Study. As explained in chapter 3, the break-up acquisition produces the same results as a "mirror" transaction, which Congress overruled in the 1987 Act. See also, ALI 1982 Study, supra chapter 1, note 3, at 92–101.

Consequently, since the spin off is going to be allowed, no reason exists for disallowing the more direct route of reaching the same end result.

Proposed Section 368(a)(4)(I)[154] gives tax-free treatment in the direct acquisition. It provides that in a disposition of a controlled subsidiary in an acquisitive reorganization (1) the distribution by the parent corporation of the stock, securities, and other property received is governed by the nonrecognition provisions of Section 361, and (2) the shareholders of the parent corporation are treated in accordance with the provisions of Sections 355 and 356 upon receipt of the stock, securities, and other property. Thus, if the only consideration paid is stock of the acquiring corporation, the transaction would be tax-free to both the parent corporation and its shareholders.

Proposed Section 368(a)(4)(J)[155] and (K)[156] provide definitions for the terms "controlled subsidiary" and "parent corporation" for purposes of this special distribution rule.

This tax-free treatment is available only if the transaction would have qualified under both Section 355 and the acquisitive reorganization provisions if (1) the parent corporation had distributed to its shareholders the stock of the controlled subsidiary, and (2) such shareholders had independently decided to enter into the acquisitive reorganization.[157] Also, the par-

---

154. Proposed Section 368(a)(4)(I).
SPECIAL DISTRIBUTION RULE FOR SUBSIDIARY REORGANIZATION THAT COULD HAVE QUALIFIED UNDER SECTION 355—If in a reorganization described in paragraph (1)(A), (1)(B) or (1)(C) the target corporation is a controlled subsidiary (as defined in subparagraph (J)) and the parent corporation (as defined in subparagraph (K)) distributes all of the consideration received in the reorganization to one or more of its shareholders and security holders, then Section 361 shall apply to the parent corporation with respect to the distribution and Section 355 or 356 shall apply to the shareholders and security holders of the parent corporation with respect to the receipt of the consideration, provided that the transaction would have qualified under Section 355 and paragraph (1)(A), (1)(B) or (1)(C) if the transaction had been structured first as a distribution by the controlling parent of the stock and securities of the controlled subsidiary to one or more of shareholders and security holders of the common parent and after such distribution the acquiring corporation had acquired the stock or assets of the controlled subsidiary, pursuant to the independent decision of the shareholders of such subsidiary.
155. Proposed Section 368(a)(4)(J).
CONTROLLED SUBSIDIARY—The term "controlled subsidiary" means a corporation, the stock of which is controlled within the meaning of subsection (c) by the parent corporation, as defined in subparagraph (K).
156. Proposed Section 368(a)(4)(K).
PARENT CORPORATION—The term "parent corporation" means a corporation that is in control within the meaning of subsection (c) of a controlled subsidiary.
157. Proposed § 368(a)(4)(I). Section 381, relating to carryover of tax attri-

ent must distribute all of the consideration received in the acquisitive reorganization.

This provision may be illustrated as follows. Assume a parent corporation has conducted an active trade or business for at least five years, and the parent owns stock of a controlled subsidiary that also has conducted an active trade or business for five years. The parent may cause the controlled subsidiary to be acquired in an acquisitive reorganization. The parent could then distribute to its shareholders the stock of the acquiring corporation. In this transaction, the parent corporation (1) has nonrecognition under Section 354 upon receipt of stock from the acquiring corporation, and (2) has nonrecognition under Section 361 on the distribution of such stock to its shareholders. The shareholders have nonrecognition treatment under Section 355 upon receipt of stock of the acquiring corporation. The same result would follow if the controlled subsidiary were newly organized.

The result is the same as if the parent had first distributed the stock of the controlled subsidiary to the shareholders and the shareholders had then caused the controlled subsidiary to be acquired in an acquisitive reorganization.

If the enactment of this provision would result in a significant revenue loss, the provision could be eliminated without doing damage to the other proposals in chapter 4.

Consistency Requirement

Section 338 and regulations thereunder contain an elaborate set of consistency requirements. These requirements are designed to prevent the acquisition of a part of the assets of a target corporation (or assets of an affiliated group of which the target is a member) in a cost basis transaction, and the related acquisition of the target's stock without making a Section 338 election for the stock.[158] The underlying theory is that it is inconsistent for an acquiring corporation to acquire from a target corporation or its affiliated group some assets with a cost basis and other assets with a carryover basis.

This principle is sound and should apply in the context of acquisitive reorganizations. Proposed Section 368(a)(4)(L)[159] grants to the Service the

---

butes, does not apply to this transaction, just as it does not apply to a Section 355 spinoff. Treas. Reg. § 1.381(a)-1(b)(3) (1975). However, Section 312(h), relating to an allocation of earnings and profits in a Section 355 transaction should be amended to apply to this type of transaction.

158. These consistency rules are not discussed here. *See Federal Taxation of Business Enterprises, supra* chapter 1, note 20, vol. 2, at §§ 32:10 to 32:15.

159. Proposed Section 368(a)(4)(L).
CONSISTENCY REQUIREMENT—Pursuant to regulations, any assets acquired by the acquiring corporation, or any member of an affiliated group of corporations,

authority to write regulations dealing with situations in which the acquiring corporation, or any member of its controlled group, acquires assets from the target corporation within the 12 month period prior to an acquisitive reorganization involving the target. Any such assets are to be treated as if they had been acquired in the reorganization. As a consequence, the acquiring corporation would take a carryover basis for such assets and the target may not recognize gain on the sale.[160]

Demonstration of Neutrality of the Reorganization Proposal

The adoption of the above rules would eliminate the inconsistencies that currently exist in the different forms of acquisitive reorganizations and would thereby promote neutrality. This neutrality is illustrated in the examples in chapter 9 and is demonstrated in the chart in appendix A. In horizontal row [A] of the chart, both the continuity of interest and the substantially all test are satisfied. Consequently, as indicated by the vertical columns, for all forms of stock and asset acquisitions (1) the transaction qualifies as a reorganization, and (2) the tax treatment of the particular parties to the transaction is the same.

Appendix A is discussed further in the *Conclusion*, chapter 16.

---

within the meaning of Section 1504, of which the acquiring corporation is a member, from the target corporation within the 12 month period prior to a reorganization described in paragraph (1)(A), (1)(B) or (1)(C) shall be considered to have been acquired in the reorganization.

160. The Service has recently liberalized the consistency regulations under § 338. *See* Prop Reg. § 1.338–4.

CHAPTER 5

. . . .

Proposed Adoption of Carryover Basis Rule for Certain Taxable Asset Acquisitions

The Tax Reform Act of 1986 (TRA 1986) repealed the *General Utilities* doctrine, and the Revenue Reconciliation Act of 1990 (RRA 1990) adopted a maximum 28 percent rate on the long-term capital gains of individuals. As a result of these two legislative actions, a maximum rate of tax of approximately 52 percent applies to the following transactions: (1) the taxable sale of the assets of a stand-alone target corporation followed by the distribution of the sales proceeds to its shareholders in liquidation (*i.e.*, a taxable asset acquisition), and (2) the taxable purchase by an acquiring corporation of a target's stock followed by a Section 338 election to treat the target as if it had sold and repurchased its asset (*i.e.*, a taxable stock acquisition with a Section 338 election).[1]

The approximate 52 percent rate arises because in both transactions a shareholder level capital gains tax applies at a rate of 28 percent for individuals and a corporate level tax applies at a rate of 34 percent.[2] Prior to the repeal of the *General Utilities* doctrine by the TRA 1986, only a shareholder level tax at a maximum 20 percent rate applied to these transactions, except to the extent the corporation had recapture gain, such as recapture of depreciation under Section 1245. Thus, prior to 1986, if the target had no recapture gain, a maximum tax rate of 20 percent applied both to a taxable asset acquisition and to a taxable stock acquisition in which a Section 338 election was made.

As a result of this double tax, it is unlikely under current law that a stand-alone target corporation will sell its assets in a taxable asset acquisition or

---

1. *See* chapter 2, p. 28.

2. The computation of this 52 percent rate is set forth in chapter 2, p. 28. These are maximum individual and corporate rates.

that a Section 338 election will be made after a purchase of a target's stock, unless the target has net operating losses that offset the taxable gain. Thus, most acquisitions of stand-alone target corporations are structured as stock purchases without a Section 338 election, thus avoiding the corporate level tax.

In addition to curtailing the use of a straight taxable purchase of the target's assets, this high tax cost has also curtailed the use of the taxable forward merger transaction in which a target merges into the acquiring corporation or a subsidiary of the acquiring corporation (*i.e.*, a forward triangular merger), with the target's shareholders receiving cash or debt instruments.[3] There are many good business reasons for structuring a transaction as a direct purchase of the target's assets or as a taxable forward merger. For example, the acquiring corporation may want to avoid assuming certain of the target corporation's liabilities through the use of a taxable purchase of assets, or the acquiring corporation may desire to have the target's assets transferred by operation of law in a taxable forward merger.

This tax impediment to transactions that can serve a bona fide business purpose presents the question whether taxpayers should be able to elect carryover basis treatment for taxable asset acquisitions and taxable forward mergers. Under a carryover basis regime, the target corporation would not recognize gain or loss on the transfer of its assets, and the acquiring corporation would take a carryover basis for such assets. The target's shareholders, however, recognize gain or loss under Section 331 upon receipt of the liquidating proceeds. Thus, the transaction is the economic equivalent of a stock purchase without a Section 338 election.

As indicated in chapter 3, the ALI 1989 Study contains a proposal for a carryover basis election for both taxable and nontaxable acquisitions. This ALI proposal is for carryover basis treatment where an acquiring corporation acquires substantially all the assets of a target, with substantially all being measured at the time of the acquisition.[4] The ALI 1989 Study would, therefore, allow a target to dispose of part of its assets in a strip down transaction and then do a final carryover basis disposition of its remaining assets. Also, under the ALI's break-up disposition proposal,[5] the strip down sales could be effectuated without a corporate level tax as long as the target dis-

---

3. Such a merger is treated as a sale of assets and not as a reorganization. *See, e.g.*, *West Shore Fuel, Inc. v. United States*, 598 F.2d 1236 (2nd Cir. 1979). While the forward taxable merger (with the target being the disappearing corporation) is treated as a purchase of assets, the reverse subsidiary merger (with the target surviving) is treated as a purchase of the target's stock. *See* Rev. Rul. 90–95, 1990–2 C.B. 67. See both the discussion and diagram of forward and reverse subsidiary mergers in chapter 2, p. 29.

4. *See ALI 1989 Study, supra* chapter 1, note 2.

5. *See* chapter 3, p. 42.

tributed the sales proceeds to its shareholders. The ALI refers to this break-up disposition rule as a "clean mirror" approach.[6] Adoption of the break-up disposition rule would overturn the decision recently made by Congress that mirror transactions are fundamentally inconsistent with the corporate tax and, therefore, should be prohibited.

The adoption of both the ALI's break-up disposition rule and the ALIs carryover basis rule would effectively repeal the corporate tax on non-ordinary sales of corporate assets. Thus, the conclusion reached here is that both of these rules should be rejected.[7]

In view of the proposal in chapter 4 to retain the reorganization concept, the basic policy question addressed here is: *Assuming the reorganization concept is retained, should there nevertheless be an elective carryover basis for taxable asset acquisitions, and if so, what should be the scope and content of the election?*

As pointed out by Professor Yin,[8] some have argued for elective carryover basis treatment for the sale of any of the target corporation's assets. This is known as the pencil-by-pencil approach. The ALIs break-up disposition rule does not go quite this far. At the other end of the carryover basis spectrum, Professor Coven has argued for mandatory carryover basis treatment.[9] Taking a middle of the road position that is similar to the proposal contained in the ALI 1989 Study, Professor Yin has proposed that carryover basis elective treatment be allowed under the following circumstances. First, the election would be available only where there is an acquisition of substantially all of the assets of a stand-alone (*i.e.*, nonsubsidiary) target corporation. Second, the "substantially all" test would be applied at the time of the acquisition and, therefore, distributions in anticipation of an acquisition would not be taken into account. Third, the election would not be allowed where there are multiple corporate buyers, except where the last buyer acquires substantially all of the target's assets. Fourth, the target would have to liquidate. Finally, there would be a consistency requirement so that the acquiring corporation could not acquire some assets with a cost basis and some assets with a carryover basis.[10]

Also, Treasury's Subchapter C Outline lists elective carryover basis treatment as one of the topics to be considered.[11]

Going in the opposite direction, Professor Shakow has argued for complete taxation at both the target and shareholder levels in acquisition transactions.[12]

---

6. *See Id.*

7. *See Id.*

8. *See* Yin, *Carryover Basis Asset Acquisitions, supra* chapter 1, note 35.

9. *See* Coven, *Mandatory Uniform Rules, supra* chapter 1, note 35.

10. Yin, *Carryover Basis Asset Acquisitions, supra* chapter 1, note 35, at 420–23.

11. *Treasury Subchapter C Outline, supra* chapter 1, note 16, at II.B.4.b.

12. *See* Shakow, *Whither, "C"!, supra* chapter 1, note 35.

Carryover Basis Proposal

There are good business reasons for structuring taxable asset acquisitions, and consequently, there should be a carryover basis regime that reduces the tax barrier to such acquisitions. Professor Yin's proposal is used as the base line for structuring the proposal here. Professor Yin is correct in concluding that there should not be a pencil-by-pencil approach to carryover basis treatment. Such an approach is inconsistent with the anti-mirror legislation in the 1987 Act.[13]

Professor Yin is also correct in concluding that carryover basis treatment should be available only where an acquiring corporation acquires substantially all of the target's assets. Both Professor Yin and the ALI 1989 Study are wrong, however, in concluding that "substantially all" should be determined at the time of the acquisition, thereby permitting a sale of part of a target's assets to one party followed by a carryover basis acquisition of the balance of the target's assets by a second party. The carryover basis concept is embodied in the reorganization provisions, and it seems logical and prudent to make carryover basis treatment for taxable asset acquisitions available only in those cases in which a transaction would qualify as an acquisitive reorganization, but for the failure to satisfy the continuity of interest requirement. Thus, carryover basis treatment should be available only if the acquiring corporation acquires substantially all of the target corporation's historic assets, thereby preventing a potential simultaneous taxable and carryover basis disposition of the target's assets.

Further, Professor Yin is correct in concluding that carryover basis treatment should be available only for acquisitions of stand-alone target corporations and that there ought to be a consistency rule for carryover basis acquisitions. Since it is likely that the parties in a taxable asset acquisition would desire carryover basis treatment, it would be wise to provide explicitly for such treatment in acquisitions unless the parties elect otherwise. Thus, rather than adopting Professor Yin's proposal for elective carryover basis treatment, there should be elective taxable treatment. This is the same as the rule that applies to stock acquisitions.

Proposed Section 368(a)(5)(A)[14] effectuates the above principles. This section provides that if a taxable asset acquisition of a noncontrolled cor-

---

13. *See* chapter 3, p. 42.

14. Proposed Section 368(a)(5)(A).
CARRYOVER BASIS FOR NON-QUALIFIED ASSET REORGANIZATION—
If an asset acquisition of a noncontrolled corporation, as defined in paragraph (5)(B), would have qualified as a reorganization under paragraph (1)(A) or (1)(C) but for the fact that the continuity of interest requirement of paragraph (4)(E) is not satisfied, then unless a taxable election is made pursuant to paragraph (5)(D),

poration (*i.e.*, a stand-alone target) would have qualified as a merger reorganization under Proposed Section 368(a)(1)(A) (*i.e.*, a forward subsidiary merger) or as a stock for asset reorganization under Proposed Section 368(a)(1)(C) but for the fact that the continuity of interest requirement is not satisfied, then unless the parties elect otherwise, the transaction is treated as follows. First, the target corporation is treated as having disposed of its assets in a nonrecognition transaction described in current Section 361. This section gives nonrecognition treatment to a target that participates in a reorganization. Second, the target takes a fair market value basis for any property received. Third, the target receives nonrecognition treatment upon the distribution of the proceeds in accordance with the rules under current Section 361(b). This rule applies to a target in a reorganization. Fourth, the acquiring corporation's basis for the target's assets is determined under the carryover basis rules of current Section 362(b). This rule also applies to the acquiring corporation in a reorganization.

Since the transaction is not a reorganization, the target's shareholders have recognition treatment upon receipt of the proceeds.

Section 381, which provides for the carryover of tax attributes other than basis (such as net operating losses) in certain asset reorganizations, is applicable to the transaction.[15] Therefore, the target's tax attributes specified in Section 381 pass over to the acquiring corporation. This result is sensible because the substantially all test is satisfied. Also, this ensures parity in the treatment of (1) carryover basis asset acquisitions, and (2) stock acquisitions in which the Section 338 election is not made. There is no change in a target's attributes after a stock acquisition, unless a Section 338 election is filed, and there should be no change in a target's attributes after a carryover basis asset acquisition. Of course, Sections 382 and 383 would apply to limit the use of the target's net operating loss carryovers and similar attributes, but this is also true in a stock acquisition.

Since the acquiror's basis for the target's assets, including stock of acquired subsidiaries, is determined under Section 362, there is no purchase of the stock of such subsidiaries for purposes of Section 338.[16] Consequently, the acquiring corporation cannot make a Section 338 election with respect to any subsidiaries that are acquired from the target in the asset acquisition. Both the assets acquired from the target and the assets held by any acquired subsidiaries have a carryover basis.

(i) the noncontrolled corporation shall be deemed to have disposed of its assets in a transaction described in Section 361, and (ii) the acquiring corporation's basis for the assets of the noncontrolled corporation shall be determined under Section 362(b).

15. A technical amendment to Section 381 will reflect this point.

16. I.R.C. § 338(h)(3) (1991).

The term noncontrolled corporation is defined in Proposed Section 368(a)(5)(B)[17] to mean a corporation, other than a common parent, that is not a member of an affiliated group. Pursuant to regulations, such term may include a subsidiary of a stand-alone target that is itself a party to the same transaction. This rule is similar to the rule under former Section 337(c)(3). Under former Section 337, which codified the *General Utilities* rule for sales followed by liquidating distributions, a target corporation that adopted a plan of liquidation, sold its assets and liquidated, all within one year, was not subject to tax on the sale, except with respect to recapture items. Former Section 337 (c)(3) allowed a subsidiary to also sell its assets under Section 337 provided the parent corporation was a stand-alone corporation that was also selling its assets in a Section 337 sale. Under the rule proposed here, if the stand-alone target sells its assets in a carryover basis transaction, a subsidiary may also sell its assets to the same party in a carryover basis transaction.

The parties may elect under Proposed Section 368(a)(5)(D)[18] to have the transaction treated as a taxable acquisition. If this election is made, then under Proposed Section 368(a)(5)(E)(i),[19] the target corporation (subject to the exception for goodwill discussed in chapter 6) is subject to tax and the acquiring corporation takes a cost basis for the target's assets.

In the case of a merger, the taxable election is made by the acquiring corporation, and in the case of a taxable purchase, the election is made jointly by both parties. A consistency rule applies to carryover basis acquisitions under Proposed Section 368(a)(5)(C).[20] This rule prevents an acquiring

---

17. Proposed Section 368(a)(5)(B).
NONCONTROLLED CORPORATION—The term "noncontrolled corporation" means a corporation that is not a member (other than as a common parent corporation) of an affiliated group within the meaning of section 1504(a). However, pursuant to regulations, such term includes a member of an affiliated group of which a noncontrolled corporation that is the common parent of such group is a party to a transaction described in paragraph (5)(A).
18. Proposed Section 368(a)(5)(D).
TAXABLE ELECTION—Pursuant to regulations, a taxable election for a nonqualified asset acquisition under paragraph (5)(A) is made by the acquiring corporation in a transaction meeting the pattern described in paragraph (1)(A) and by the acquiring corporation and the noncontrolled corporation in a transaction meeting the pattern described in paragraph (1)(C).
19. Proposed Section 368(a)(5)(E)(i).
EFFECT OF TAXABLE ELECTION. . . . General Rule.
If a taxable election is made, the noncontrolled corporation, as defined in paragraph (5)(B), shall be treated as having sold its assets in a taxable transaction and the acquiring corporation shall be treated as having acquired such assets in a taxable acquisition.
20. Proposed Section 368(a)(5)(C).

corporation from acquiring some of the target's assets with a cost basis and some with a carryover basis.

This proposal does not change the treatment of nonreorganization reverse subsidiary mergers; these transactions continue to be treated as stock acquisitions.[21]

This proposal would allow most taxable asset acquisitions, such as sales of substantially all the assets of closely held corporations, to be completed on a carryover basis, unless the parties elected taxable treatment. Because of the substantially all test, this approach may be viewed by some as quite restrictive. However, since carryover basis treatment for taxable asset acquisitions is a departure from the general rule of recognition treatment, strong policy reasons exists for making such a regime available only in the most limited circumstances.

The carryover basis proposal conceptually may be viewed as relief from the repeal of the *General Utilities* doctrine as manifested in former Section 337. That section gave a target corporation nonrecognition treatment (except for recapture items) on the sale of its assets pursuant to a plan of liquidation effectuated within a twelve-month period. Under former Section 337, a target was not required to sell substantially all of its assets to one person.[22] As a practical matter, however, most transactions under former Section 337 appear to have involved such sales. Thus, the carryover basis treatment proposed here applies to the garden variety sale and liquidation under former Section 337. The rule proposed here, however, produces results that are radically different from the results under former Section 337. Under this proposal, the acquiring corporation takes a carryover basis for the target's assets, whereas under former Section 337, the acquiring corporation took a fair market value basis.

Finally, the adoption of this proposal will eliminate the artificial distinction under present law between (1) taxable forward triangular mergers in which the target merges into a subsidiary of the acquiring corporation, and (2) taxable reverse triangular mergers in which a subsidiary of the acquiring corporation merges into the target. The taxable forward triangular merger

---

CONSISTENCY REQUIREMENT—Pursuant to regulations, any asset acquired by the acquiring corporation or any member of an affiliated group of corporations, within the meaning of section 1504(a), of which the acquiring corporation is a member, from the target corporation within the 12 month period prior to the carryover basis transaction described in paragraph (5)(A) shall be considered to have been acquired in such a carryover basis transaction.

21. Rev. Rul. 90–95, 1990–2 C.B. 67. *See* chapter 2, p. 29.

22. In order to qualify for nonrecognition treatment on the sale of inventory, the inventory had to be sold in a bulk sale transaction to one purchaser. Former I.R.C. § 337(b)(2) (1985).

is treated as a sale of the target's assets,[23] and the taxable reverse triangular merger is treated as an acquisition of the target's stock for which a Section 338 election may be made.[24] If the parties inadvertently slip up and effectuate a forward subsidiary merger there is automatically both a corporate and shareholder level tax, whereas if the reverse subsidiary merger is utilized there is only a shareholder level tax unless a Section 338 election is made (which will generally not be the case).

Under the proposal here, the nonreorganization reverse subsidiary merger continues to be treated as a stock acquisition, and there is no corporate level tax, unless a Section 338 election is made or unless the mandatory Section 338 election provided in chapter 7 applies. On the other hand, under the carryover basis rule of Proposed Section 368(a)(5)(A), a taxable forward triangular merger in which substantially all of the target's assets are acquired results in tax at the shareholder level but nonrecognition and carryover basis treatment at the corporate level, unless the taxable election is made. Thus, the adoption of this rule will provide for parity of treatment between taxable forward triangular mergers and taxable reverse triangular mergers.[25]

Finally, under this carryover basis rule, S corporations that were previously C corporations would be exempt from the built-in gains tax that applies under Section 1374.

Demonstration of Neutrality of the Carryover Basis Rule

As illustrated in the examples in chapter 9 and as demonstrated in the chart in appendix A, the adoption of this proposal (together with the proposals contained in chapters 6 and 7) would promote neutrality in the treatment of taxable stock and asset acquisitions. The carryover basis rule proposed here only applies to transactions that satisfy the substantially all test but not the continuity of interest test and for which the taxable asset election is not made. Also, as indicated in chapter 7, a mandatory Section 338 election applies to a taxable stock acquisition if the substantially all test is not satisfied. If the substantially all test is satisfied, however, the target corporation keeps a carryover basis for its assets after such a stock acquisition, unless a Section 338 election is made.

---

23. *See, e.g.*, *West Shore Fuel, Inc. v. United States*, 598 F.2d 1236 (2d Cir. 1979). *See* chapter 2, p. 29.

24. *See, e.g.*, Rev. Rul. 90–95, 1990–2 C.B. 67. *See* chapter 2, p. 29.

25. Also, taxable direct mergers of the target into the acquiring corporation are given carryover basis treatment, unless the parties elect otherwise.

In row [B] on the horizontal axis of the appendix A chart, the continuity of interest test is not satisfied but the substantially all test is satisfied. Also, neither the taxable asset election nor the Section 338 election is made. Consequently, as indicated on the vertical axis, the treatment to the parties (*i.e.*, acquiring corporation, target, and target's shareholders) to the transaction is the same in both stock or asset acquisitions.

Appendix A is discussed further in the *Conclusion*, chapter 16.

CHAPTER 6

. . . .

Proposed Exception from Recognition for Goodwill

Under the original ALI 1982 Study, in cost basis taxable acquisitions, the parties could elect carryover basis treatment for goodwill and other non-amortizable intangibles (hereafter collectively referred to as goodwill.)[1] This proposal is also contained in the ALI 1989 Study,[2] and a similar non-recognition proposal for goodwill is set forth in the second section of this chapter. The principal purpose of the proposal set out here is to reduce the high tax cost presently associated with asset acquisitions and, thereby, increase the number of circumstances in which taxpayers can structure a taxable acquisition as a sale of the target's assets. Thus, this proposal, like the carryover basis proposal contained in chapter 5, is designed to mitigate the current tax impediment to asset acquisitions.

Under the ALI's carryover basis proposal, the target corporation has no gain or loss on the disposition of goodwill, and the acquiring corporation takes the target's basis in the goodwill. For example, if a target has a zero basis in its goodwill and an acquiring corporation purchases the target's assets in a taxable acquisition for which a carryover basis is not elected, the parties can nevertheless elect carryover basis treatment for the goodwill. As a consequence, the acquiring corporation takes a zero basis for the goodwill and the target does not recognize gain on the transfer of the goodwill.

The ALI proposal is based on the theory that since under current law neither the target nor the acquiring corporation can amortize (*i.e.*, deduct

---

1. See *ALI 1982 Study, supra* chapter 1, note 3, at 120–33. *See, generally*, Land, *Unallocated Premium in Corporate Acquisitions Under the American Law Institute Subchapter C Proposals*, 34 Tax Law. 341 (1981). For a suggestion that there be an exception to the repeal of the *General Utilities* doctrine for goodwill and land and buildings used in the active conduct of a trade or business, *see* Thompson, *Suggested Alternative Approach, supra* chapter 1, note 3, at 669–74.

2. See *ALI 1989 Study, supra* chapter 1, note 2, at 108.

for tax purposes) the cost of goodwill, it is not necessary from a policy perspective to impose a tax on the sale of goodwill, as long as the purchaser takes a carryover basis. Under both the ALI's proposal and the proposal set forth here, nonrecognition would not be available for intangibles that give rise to a deduction in the acquiror's hands. Thus, the proposals discussed here would not apply to intangibles the cost of which are deductible under general principles. Also, the proposal here would not apply to any intangibles, including goodwill and going concern value, that would be deductible if Section 197, which is contained in the Tax Fairness and Economic Growth Bill of 1992,[3] is enacted into law. As explained later, if, however, the acquiring corporation elects not to amortize the cost of any goodwill or going concern value that becomes amortizable upon enactment of Section 197, then the nonrecognition treatment provided here for goodwill and going concern value would continue to apply.

One of the principal reasons Congress repealed the *General Utilities* doctrine in the TRA 1986 was to enhance revenues,[4] and it can be expected that Congress will be reluctant to provide an exception for goodwill if the exception would give rise to a large revenue loss.

Although it might seem counter intuitive, it would appear that the adoption of an exception for goodwill would give rise to increased revenues. This conclusion is reached through the following logic:

First, as indicated in chapter 2, because of the high tax rate on taxable asset acquisitions of stand-alone targets, taxpayers are avoiding these acquisitions. Taxable asset acquisitions are generally used only if the target corporation has substantial net operating losses or other tax credits that can offset the gain. Thus, the preferred form of taxable acquisition is a stock acquisition without a Section 338 election. The election, however, may be made if the target has net operating losses.[5] Therefore, with the repeal of the *General Utilities* doctrine, few acquisitions are completed in which the basis of the target's assets is stepped-up. With an exception for goodwill, more taxable asset acquisitions would occur, because the tax liability on the target corporation would be reduced.

As demonstrated by the following example, nonrecognition treatment for goodwill would have the effect of accelerating the collection of reve-

---

3. Tax Fairness and Economic Growth Bill of 1992, H.R. No. 4287, 102nd Cong., 2nd Sess. § 4501 (1992) [hereinafter cited as "1992 House Bill"]. This bill was passed by Congress but was vetoed on March 20, 1992 by the President.

4. *See, e.g.*, Staff of the Joint Comm. on Int. Rev. Tax, General Explanation of the Tax Reform Act of 1986, at 354 (1987).

5. The Section 382 limitation on the utilization of net operating losses does not apply to gain recognized as a result of a Section 338 election. I.R.C. § 382(h)(1)(C) (1991).

nues; the Treasury would collect more tax from selling target corporations at the cost of reduced tax revenues in the same amount in the future from acquiring corporations. Assume that a target corporation has assets with a value of $100K and a basis of 0. Assume also that $50K of the value is attributable to goodwill and the other $50K is attributable to property that is depreciable under the ACRS system over five years. Assume further that the target's assets are expected to generate $10K of income in each of the next 5 years. Because of the high cost of a double tax under the current regime, the target does not sell its assets in a taxable asset acquisition. The acquiring corporation, instead, acquires the target's stock and does not make a Section 338 election. As a consequence, in each of the five years after the acquisition, the target's assets earn $10K and a tax of $3.4K is imposed on those earnings.

On the other hand, assume that if there were a goodwill exception to the repeal of the *General Utilities* doctrine, the target would sell its assets to the acquiring corporation for $100K. Because of the exception for goodwill, only $50K of the target's gain would be subject to tax, thereby giving rise to a tax liability of $17K. The basis for the target's depreciable assets in the hands of the acquiring corporation would be $50K. Assuming straight line depreciation over the next five years, there would be 0 taxable income from the target's assets in each of those years because the depreciation would offset the $10K of income.

Thus, with an exception for goodwill, the Treasury collects $17K from the target in the year of the sale and nothing from the acquiring corporation for the five years after the sale. On the other hand, without an exception for goodwill, the Treasury collects nothing from the target upon the purchase by the acquiring corporation of the target's stock because a Section 338 election is not made, but the Treasury collects a total tax of $17K (*i.e.*, $3.4K a year x 5) from the target over the first five years after the acquisition. Since a $1 today is worth more than $1 tomorrow, the Treasury collects more revenue with an exception for goodwill.

An exception to the recognition rule for goodwill is a departure from the normal concept of an income tax and should, therefore, be available only in limited circumstances. It seems appropriate to allow the exception in the same kinds of transactions to which the carryover basis rule in chapter 5 applies. That provision, which also is a departure from income tax norms, is narrowly crafted.

Thus, the exception for goodwill should be available only for transactions that could have qualified as reorganizations, but for the failure to satisfy the continuity of interest requirement. The exception would, therefore, be unavailable unless the substantially all test is satisfied.

The adoption of the proposed exception for goodwill does not mean that taxpayers will necessarily elect this method for nonreorganization asset acquisitions over the carryover basis method set forth in chapter 5. The tax cost of a taxable asset acquisition, even with a goodwill exception, is quite high. For that reason, it can be expected that in most nonreorganization asset acquisitions the parties will elect carryover basis treatment. There will be, however, cases in which the parties will have good business reasons for structuring a taxable asset acquisition with an exception for goodwill, and there is no reason to deny taxpayers this flexibility. Also, a target may have losses that can shelter the taxable gain. There is no good reason for denying the use of real losses against real gains.

Goodwill Proposal

Assuming No Amortization Deduction for Goodwill and Going Concern Value

This section discusses the proposed exception to recognition for goodwill and going concern value (hereinafter sometimes referred to as goodwill) assuming that no amortization deduction is allowed for goodwill. Later, this chapter discusses the modification to this proposal that would be needed if Congress were to enact Section 197 of the Tax Fairness and Economic Growth Bill of 1992, which would specifically provide for an amortization deduction for purchased goodwill, going concern value, and other intangibles.

There should be an exception to the repeal of the *General Utilities* doctrine for goodwill, and the acquiring corporation should not have to take a carryover basis for goodwill as proposed by the ALI. If the acquiring corporation is required to take a carryover basis, a penalty would be imposed on the acquiring corporation if it later disposed of the goodwill in a taxable asset acquisition in which the carryover basis election was not made. No such penalty is needed; apparently no abuse would result from allowing the acquiring corporation to take a cost basis for goodwill.

Thus, there should be a blanket exception for the disposition of goodwill in taxable asset acquisitions and in Section 338 transactions of a noncontrolled corporation (*i.e.*, a stand-alone target). The exception should apply, however, only if the transaction would otherwise have qualified as an acquisitive reorganization, but for the failure to satisfy the continuity of interest requirement.

Proposed Section 368(a)(5)(E)(ii)[6] accomplishes the above result in a taxable asset acquisition of a stand-alone target for which the taxable elec-

---

6. Proposed Section 368(a)(5)(E)
EFFECT OF A TAXABLE ELECTION: TREATMENT OF GOODWILL—
(i) General Rule. If a taxable election is made, the noncontrolled corporation, as defined in paragraph (5)(B), shall be treated as having sold its assets in a taxable

tion is made under Proposed Section 368(a)(5)(E)(i). Proposed Section 368(a)(5)(E)(ii) provides that if an asset acquisition would have qualified for carryover basis treatment under the rules discussed in chapter 5, then the target corporation (and, pursuant to regulations, any subsidiary) has nonrecognition with respect to the disposition of goodwill and other non-amortizable intangibles. This nonrecognition treatment is available, however, only if a proper allocation agreement is entered into and the acquiring corporation agrees to treat the purchase price as non-amortizable premium.

By limiting the nonrecognition treatment to asset acquisitions from stand-alone corporations, this nonrecognition rule is consistent with former Section 337. This section provided nonrecognition treatment on the sale of assets of a stand-alone corporation. Former Section 337 did not apply to a sale of assets of a subsidiary, unless such a sale was part of a larger liquidation of the subsidiary's stand-alone parent corporation. The same result is reached here through the definition of noncontrolled corporation in Proposed Section 368(a)(5)(B).[7]

Proposed Section 368(a)(5)(F)[8] applies if a Section 338 election is made for a stock acquisition which, but for the failure of the continuity of interest

---

transaction and the acquiring corporation shall be treated as having acquired such assets in a taxable acquisition.

(ii) Exception for Goodwill. If the transaction could have qualified for carryover basis treatment under section 368(a)(5)(A) in the absence of a taxable election, the noncontrolled corporation shall not recognize gain with respect to its sale or exchange of goodwill or similar nonamortizable intangibles, provided that, pursuant to regulations, the noncontrolled corporation and acquiring corporation enter into an allocation agreement with respect to all transferred assets and the acquiring corporation agrees not to deduct under section 162 or otherwise any amounts allocated to goodwill or other nonamortizable intangibles. Pursuant to regulations, such nonrecognition treatment for goodwill shall also apply to any corporation that is a member of the noncontrolled corporation's affiliated group of corporations, as defined in section 1504(a).

7. Proposed Section 368(a)(5)(B)
NONCONTROLLED CORPORATION—The term "noncontrolled corporation" means a corporation that is not a member (other than as a common parent corporation) of an affiliated group within the meaning of section 1504(a). However, pursuant to regulations, such term includes a member of an affiliated group of which a noncontrolled corporation that is the common parent of such group is a party to a transaction described in paragraph (5)(A).

8. Proposed Section 368(a)(5)(F)
EFFECT ON GOODWILL OF SECTION 338 ELECTION AFTER AN OTHERWISE QUALIFYING STOCK REORGANIZATION—If a stock acquisition of a noncontrolled corporation (as defined in paragraph (5)(B)) would have qualified under paragraph (1)(A) or (1)(B) but for the fact that the continuity of interest requirement is not satisfied, and the acquiring corporation makes a section 338

requirement, would have qualified as a reorganization under Proposed Section 368(a)(1)(A) (reverse subsidiary merger) or Proposed Section 368(a)(1)(B) (stock for stock acquisitions). Under this provision, the target (or pursuant to regulations any subsidiary of the target) does not recognize gain with respect to goodwill or similar nonamortizable intangibles, provided the parties agree not to take any deductions with respect to the goodwill or other intangible. Thus, there is parity of treatment of goodwill in both taxable asset and taxable stock acquisitions.

Finally, pursuant to Proposed Section 368(a)(5)(G),[9] the Secretary is authorized to provide nonrecognition treatment for certain liquidating distributions of goodwill.

Assuming Amortization Deduction for Cost of Goodwill and Going Concern Value

This section discusses the modifications to the above nonrecognition rule that should be made if Congress enacts a provision like Section 197, which is contained in the Tax Fairness and Economic Growth Bill of 1992.[10]

Under Section 197, taxpayers would be allowed to amortize the cost of any "amortizable section 197 intangible" ratably over a 14-year period.[11] A "section 197 intangible" is defined very broadly to mean, among other things, (1) goodwill, (2) going concern value, (3) certain patents, (4) know how, (5) customer based intangibles, and (6) covenants not to compete and similar arrangements entered into in connection with an acquisition of an interest in a trade or business.[12] Thus, the term "section 197 intangible" includes certain intangibles the cost of which is amortizable under current law, such as the cost of certain customer based intangibles and covenants

---

election with respect to the noncontrolled corporation, the noncontrolled corporation (and, pursuant to regulations, any member of its affiliated group, within the meaning of section 1504(a)) shall not recognize gain with respect to the deemed sale under section 338(a) by it of goodwill or similar nonamortizable intangible provided that, pursuant to regulations, both the acquiring corporation and the noncontrolled corporation agree not to deduct under section 162, or otherwise, any amounts allocable to goodwill or other nonamortizable intangible.

9. Proposed Section 368(a)(5)(G)
TREATMENT OF GOODWILL IN CERTAIN LIQUIDATING DISTRIBU-
TIONS—The Secretary is authorized, pursuant to regulations, to provide for non-recognition treatment upon the liquidating distribution of goodwill and similar items. Such nonrecognition treatment shall be consistent with the purposes of paragraphs (5)(E) and (5)(F).

10. § 4501 of 1992 House Bill, *supra* note 3.
11. Proposed I.R.C. § 197(a).
12. Proposed I.R.C. § 197(d)(1).

not to compete, as well as intangibles the cost of which is not amortizable under current law, such as the cost of goodwill and going concern value. The Report to the 1992 House Bill explains that the 14 year amortization period for all Section 197 intangibles was selected so that the provision would be "revenue neutral over the next five fiscal years."[13]

An "amortizable section 197 intangible" is defined as a Section 197 intangible that is acquired by the taxpayer after the date of enactment of Section 197 and that is held in connection with the conduct of a trade or business.[14]

If enacted, Section 197 would apply in both taxable asset acquisitions and taxable stock acquisitions for which a Section 338 election is made.[15] Thus, in each of these transactions, the cost of goodwill, going concern value, and any other Section 197 intangible would be amortizable over a 14-year period.

There would be good reasons for adopting the basic nonrecognition rule for goodwill set forth above even if proposed Section 197 is enacted. Although the cost of virtually all intangibles, including goodwill and going concern value, would be deductible if Section 197 were enacted, the enactment of that section will not substantially mitigate the current tax impediment to the use of the asset acquisition form. Even with the enactment of Section 197, the parties to a taxable acquisition are likely to continue to utilize the stock acquisition without a Section 338 election. Thus, the reasons for adopting an exception to recognition for goodwill would continue to apply even with the adoption of Section 197.

Thus, if this, or any similar provision is enacted the basic nonrecognition rule of Proposed Section 368(a)(5)(E)(ii) should continue to apply with the following modifications. First, the target should qualify for nonrecognition treatment only for goodwill and going concern value which is not an "amortizable section 197 intangible" to the target. Thus, only self created goodwill and going concern value and any other nonamortizable goodwill and going concern value held by the target should be eligible for nonrecognition treatment. If the target has amortized the goodwill or going concern value, then the target should be fully taxable on any gain from the disposition of such assets.

Second, no other "section 197 intangible," such as certain patents, and customer based intangibles should qualify for nonrecognition treatment. Most such other "section 197 intangibles" are amortizable under current law, at least under certain circumstances, and therefore, the basic rationale for nonrecognition treatment does not apply to such items.

---

13. H. Rept. WMCP 102–35, 102 Cong., 2d Sess., 217 (1992) [hereinafter cited as "1992 House Report"].

14. Proposed I.R.C. § 197(c)(1).

15. 1992 House Report, *supra* note 13, at 231–32.

Third, the acquiring corporation would have to elect not to take the amortization deductions otherwise allowable under Section 197 for the goodwill and going concern value purchased from the target.

To effectuate these changes, the first sentence of Proposed Section 368(a)(5)(E)(ii)[16] would be revised to read as follows:

> (ii) Exception for Goodwill and Going Concern Value. If the transaction could have qualified for carryover basis treatment under section 368(a)(5)(A) in the absence of a taxable election, the noncontrolled corporation shall not recognize gain with respect to the sale or exchange of goodwill or going concern value specified in section 197(d)(1)(A) and (B), provided (aa) the acquiring corporation elects, pursuant to regulations, not to take the amortization deduction allowed in section 197, or otherwise, for the cost of such goodwill and going concern value, (bb) the noncontrolled corporation establishes pursuant to regulations, that it has not taken an amortization deduction under section 197 or otherwise with respect to such goodwill and going concern value, and (cc) the noncontrolled corporation and the acquiring corporation enter into an allocation agreement with respect to the transferred assets.

Under this provision, the target has nonrecognition on the sale of its nonamortizable goodwill and going concern value, provided the acquiring corporation gives up its right to amortize the cost of such goodwill and going concern value.

Similar amendments would be made to (1) Proposed Section 368(a)(5)(F),[17] which provides for nonrecognition treatment for goodwill in a Section 338 election, and (2) Proposed Section 368(a)(5)(G),[18] which provides for nonrecognition treatment for goodwill that is distributed in a liquidation.

Demonstration of Neutrality of Goodwill Exception

As illustrated in the examples in chapter 9 and as demonstrated in the chart in appendix A, the adoption of this proposal (together with the proposals contained in chapters 5 and 7) would promote neutrality in the treatment of nonreorganization stock and asset acquisitions.

---

16. *See* Proposed Section 368(a)(5)(E)(ii), *supra* note 6 and appendix B.
17. *See* Proposed Section 368(a)(5)(F), *supra* note 8 and appendix B.
18. *See* Proposed Section 368(a)(5)(G), *supra* note 9 and appendix B.

The exception to recognition for goodwill applies only to those nonreorganization stock and asset acquisitions that satisfy the substantially all test and for which the taxable asset election or Section 338 election is made. Thus, this rule has no effect if the carryover basis rule applies. If the substantially all test is not satisfied in a nonreorganization asset acquisition, there is complete recognition. If this test is not satisfied in a nonreorganization stock acquisition, then the mandatory Section 338 election provided for in chapter 7 applies, and there is complete recognition, even for goodwill.

In row [C] on the horizontal axis of the appendix A chart, the continuity of interest test is not satisfied, but the substantially all test is satisfied. Further, in an asset acquisition the taxable asset election is made, and in a stock acquisition the Section 338 election is made. Consequently, as indicated on the vertical axis, the treatment of the parties (*i.e.*, the target's shareholders, the target, and the acquiring corporation) to the transaction is the same in both stock and asset acquisitions.

Appendix A is further discussed in the *Conclusion*, chapter 16.

CHAPTER 7

Proposed Mandatory Section 338 Election in Stock Purchases that could not Qualify for Carryover Basis Treatment for Asset Acquisitions

A carryover basis asset acquisition under Proposed Section 368(a)(5)(A)[1] is analogous to a stock purchase under current law in which a Section 338 election is not made. In both transactions, the target's shareholders have taxable treatment, and the target's assets have a carryover basis. In a stock acquisition, the acquiring corporation holds the stock of the target, which continues to hold its assets with no change in basis. In a carryover basis asset acquisition, the acquiring corporation in a direct asset acquisition (*i.e.*, purchase by the acquiring corporation of the target's assets) and the subsidiary of the acquiring corporation (the acquiring sub) in a triangular asset acquisition (*i.e.*, purchase by the acquiring sub of the target's assets), hold the target's assets with a carryover basis.

The direct asset acquisition may be effectuated by a taxable forward merger of the target into the acquiring corporation, and the taxable triangular asset acquisition may be effectuated by a taxable forward triangular merger of the target into the acquiring sub.[2]

Under the rules proposed here, the following four taxable stock and asset acquisitions produce essentially the same results: (1) the taxable stock acquisition; (2) the taxable reverse triangular merger, which is treated as a stock acquisition; (3) the taxable triangular asset acquisition (*i.e.*, purchase

---

1. *See* chapter 5, note 14.
2. *See* chapter 2, p. 29.

by acquiring sub of target's assets); and (4) the taxable forward triangular merger. In each of these acquisitions, the acquiring corporation has a fair market value basis for the stock of the corporation that holds the target's assets (that is, the target in a stock acquisition and in a reverse triangular merger and the acquiring sub in both a triangular asset acquisition and a forward triangular merger). Also, assuming that neither a Section 338 election nor a taxable election under Proposed Section 368(a)(5)(D) is made, in each of these transactions, the target's assets have a carryover basis in the hands of the corporation that holds the assets (*i.e.*, the target in both a stock acquisition and a reverse triangular merger and the acquiring sub in both a triangular asset acquisition and a forward triangular merger).

The form of the direct asset acquisition and direct forward merger differ slightly from the form of the above four transactions. In each of these four transactions, the target's assets are held in a subsidiary of the acquiring corporation, whereas in the direct asset acquisition and the direct forward merger the acquiring corporation holds the target's assets.

The carryover basis treatment under Proposed Section 368(a)(5)(A) for all forms of asset acquisitions, including taxable forward triangular mergers, is available only if the acquiring corporation acquires "substantially all" of the target's assets. Under current law, no such requirement exists for carryover basis treatment in a taxable purchase of a target's stock, including the acquisition of the target in a taxable reverse triangular merger. Consequently, the question arises whether a "substantially all" requirement should be a condition for carryover basis treatment in a stock acquisition?[3]

The carryover basis treatment provided in Proposed Section 368(a)(5)(A) prevents a target corporation from entering into an arrangement with an acquiring corporation pursuant to which the target sells a significant portion of its assets and then enters into a carryover basis transfer of the balance of its assets to the acquiring corporation. Should a similar rule apply to a sale by a target of part of its assets followed by a purchase of the target's stock by an acquiring corporation?

As indicated in the discussion in chapter 5, it is a sensible policy to permit carryover basis treatment only for acquisitions of stand-alone targets that would otherwise qualify for reorganization treatment were it not for the failure to satisfy the continuity of interest requirement. For the same reason, carryover basis treatment should be available in a stock acquisition of a stand-alone target only if the transaction could have qualified as a reorganization but for the failure to satisfy the continuity of interest requirement.

---

3. Professor Yin discusses generally the discontinuity between taxable stock and asset acquisitions. *See* Yin, *Carryover Basis Asset Acquisitions, supra* chapter 1, note 35.

This policy rule can be accomplished by imposing a mandatory Section 338 election in any stock acquisition that would not have qualified as an acquisitive reorganization because of the failure to satisfy the "substantially all" requirement. In any such acquisition, the mandatory Section 338 election treats the target as if it had sold and then reacquired its assets in a taxable acquisition. Such a rule provides for parity in the treatment of taxable stock acquisitions and taxable asset acquisitions: *Carryover basis treatment applies to both types of transactions provided the substantially all test is satisfied, and if that test is not satisfied, then in both types of transactions the target corporation is subject to taxation and there is a step-up in basis for its assets.*

Limited Mandatory Section 338 Proposal

The principles discussed above are implemented in Proposed Section 368(a)(5)(I).[4] This section applies if the stock of a stand-alone target corporation is acquired in a qualified stock purchase, as defined in Section 338(d)(3) (*i.e.*, an acquisition by purchase of at least 80 percent of the target's stock), and the following condition is satisfied: *The stock purchase does not qualify as an acquisitive reorganization because of a failure to satisfy the substantially all requirement, without regard to whether the continuity of interest requirement is satisfied.* Thus, this provision applies if, for example, an acquiring corporation purchases for cash or stock or any other consideration at least 80 percent of the stock of a target corporation and at the time of the acquisition the target does not hold substantially all of its assets as defined in Proposed Section 368(a)(4)(G).

If Proposed Section 368(a)(5)(I) applies, then the purchasing corporation is treated as having made an election under Section 338(g). As a consequence of the election, the stand-alone target corporation is treated as having sold its assets and takes a fair market value basis for the assets. There is recognition with respect to goodwill; the exception in Proposed Section 368(a)(5)(F)[5] does not apply because the transaction could not have qual-

---

4. Proposed Section 368(a)(5)(I).
MANDATORY SECTION 338 ELECTION FOR STOCK ACQUISITIONS WHEN TARGET DOES NOT HOLD SUBSTANTIALLY ALL OF ITS ASSETS—If the stock of a noncontrolled corporation, as defined in paragraph (5)(B), is acquired in a qualified stock purchase, as defined in section 338(d), and such purchase did not qualify under paragraph (1)(A) or (1)(B) because the substantially all requirement of paragraph (4)(G) is not satisfied (without regard to whether the continuity of interest requirement of paragraph (4)(E) is satisfied), then the purchasing corporation, as defined in section 338(d)(1), shall be deemed to have made an election under section 338(g) with respect to such noncontrolled corporation.

5. *See* chapter 6, note 8.

ified as an acquisitive reorganization but for the failure to satisfy the continuity of interest requirement. This recognition rule applies whether or not the continuity of interest requirement is satisfied.

Proposed Section 368(a)(5)(I) is illustrated in chapter 9, p. 135.

Demonstration of Neutrality of the Mandatory Section 338 Election

The adoption of the proposal contained in this chapter together with the proposals contained in chapters 5 and 6 would promote neutrality between taxable stock and asset acquisitions. This neutrality results because of the interrelationships among (1) the carryover basis provisions of Proposed Section 368(a)(5)(A), (2) the taxable election provisions of Proposed Section 368(a)(5)(E)(i), (3) the exception for goodwill in both taxable elections under Proposed Section 368(a)(5)(E)(ii) and Section 338 elections under Proposed Section 368(a)(5)(F), and (4) the mandatory Section 338 election of Proposed Section 368(a)(5)(I). This neutrality is illustrated in the examples in chapter 9 and is demonstrated in the chart in appendix A.

In row [D] on the horizontal axis of the chart, the acquisition fails the substantially all test and either fails or does not fail the continuity of interest test. Consequently, as indicated on the vertical axis, in an asset acquisition the carryover basis rule of Proposed Section 368(a)(5)(A) (see chapter 5) does not apply because of the failure to satisfy the substantially all requirement. Consequently, such asset acquisitions are fully taxable to the to target. In a stock acquisition, the mandatory Section 338 election of Proposed Section 368(a)(5)(F) applies because of the failure to satisfy the substantially all requirement. Further, the exception for goodwill proposed in chapter 6 does not apply because of the failure to satisfy the substantially all test. Consequently, there is full recognition at the target corporation level in both an asset acquisition and a stock acquisition. The treatment to the parties to the transaction (*e.g.*, the target corporation, the target's shareholders, and the acquiring corporation), is the same for all forms of stock and asset acquisitions.

Appendix A is further discussed in the *Conclusion*, chapter 16.

. . . .

Proposed Curtailment of Misallocation of Purchase Price in Both Acquisitive Reorganizations and Taxable Acquisitions

As indicated in chapter 2, in many corporate acquisitions the parties are mischaracterizing a portion of the purchase price as a payment in respect of a covenant not to compete or other deductible payment ("deductible payment"). Because the 28 percent rate on long-term capital gains is only three points lower than the maximum 31 percent rate on ordinary income of individuals, there is little reason for the selling shareholders to object to an allocation of purchase price to a deductible item. Acquiring corporations, on the other hand, have a large incentive for allocating as much of the purchase price as possible to deductible payments.

This problem exists also in the context of reorganizations. The acquiring corporation in an acquisitive reorganization may make bona fide payments for covenants not to compete and similar deductible items to the target's shareholders without affecting the availability of nonrecognition treatment for the target's shareholders upon receipt of stock of the acquiring corporation. The parties may, however, attempt to abuse this general rule by misallocating a portion of the purchase price of the target's stock to deductible payments, such as payments for covenants not to compete. In an effort to guard against such misallocations in reorganizations, the Service requires that ruling requests on reorganization transactions contain a standard representation that the fair market value of the stock of the acquiring corporation and other consideration received by each target shareholder will be approximately equal to the fair market value of the target's stock surrendered in the transaction.[1]

---

1. Rev. Proc. 86–42, 1986–2 C.B. 722.

Curtailment of Misallocation Proposal

Proposed Section 368(a)(4)(P),[2] which applies to acquisitive reorganizations, and Proposed Section 368(a)(5)(H),[3] which applies to taxable acquisitions, are designed to prevent a misallocation of purchase price in both acquisitive reorganizations and taxable acquisitions. Under these sections, a portion of a deductible payment received by a shareholder may be treated as additional purchase price. The nondeductible portion is equal to the excess of (1) the present value of the deductible payments, over (2) the average annual salary compensation received by the shareholder during the five most recent taxable years before the date of the acquisition.

For example, if the present value of purported deductible payments is $900K and the shareholder-employee's average annual compensation is $100K, $800K of the deductible payment is treated as additional purchase price paid in the transaction. Thus, there is an absolute barrier against allocating more than the shareholder's average annual compensation to deductible payments. This provision does not establish any presumption with

---

2. Proposed Section 368(a)(4)(P).
PREVENTION OF MISALLOCATION OF PURCHASE PRICE IN ACQUISITIVE REORGANIZATIONS—In the case of any payment, pursuant to a transaction intended to qualify under paragraph (1)(A), (1)(B) or (1)(C), to a shareholder of the target corporation made (or to be made) by or on behalf of the acquiring corporation, which payment is treated (or intended to be treated) by the payor as a deductible payment under section 162 as compensation for a covenant not to compete or similar arrangement (hereinafter referred to as a "deductible payment"), then the non-deductible amount, as determined in the next sentence, shall be treated as part of the consideration paid for the target corporation stock and not as a deductible payment under section 162. The "non-deductible amount" is an amount equal to the excess of (i) the present value, determined under the principles of section 1274(b)(2), of the deductible payments, over (ii) the average annual salary compensation received by such shareholder from the target corporation (or any subsidiary corporation in the same affiliated group, determined under section 1504, as the target corporation) during the most recent 5 taxable years before the date of the reorganization. This provision shall not give rise to the presumption that any payments that are not non-deductible amounts are deductible under section 162.

3. Proposed Section 368(a)(5)(H).
PREVENTION OF MISALLOCATION OF PURCHASE PRICE IN TAXABLE ACQUISITIONS—Rules similar to the rules of paragraph (4)(P) regarding prevention of misallocation of purchase price in acquisitive reorganizations, shall, pursuant to regulations, apply in the case of the acquisition by any person or persons of (i) control as defined in section 304(c) of a corporation or (ii) a major portion of a corporation's assets.

respect to purported deductible payments that are below the average compensation threshold. Such payments would have to satisfy the facts and circumstances test of current law to be deductible.

This provision is modeled after the golden parachute provision in Section 280G, but operates independently of that provision. This provision is not intended to affect reasonable salaries paid for services actually rendered by former shareholders of the target after the acquisition. Any such salaries should, however, be closely scrutinized.

Demonstration of Neutrality of Allocation Provision

This provision applies to all forms of reorganization and nonreorganization acquisitions and, therefore, satisfies the neutrality principle. This neutrality is illustrated in the examples in chapter 9 and is demonstrated in footnote 4 in appendix A.

CHAPTER 9

Illustration of the Proposed Rules Regarding Mergers and Acquisitions

The proposed rules relating to acquisitive reorganizations and taxable acquisitions are illustrated in this section by reference to the following basic fact pattern:

Acquiring parent ("AP"), a large publicly held corporation, owns all of the stock of acquiring corporation ("AC"), a corporation formed to acquire the stock or assets of target corporation ("TC"). AP has only one class of voting common stock outstanding. TC has one class of voting common stock outstanding and one class of nonvoting preferred. Eighty-five percent of the voting common stock of TC is held by the public, and fifteen percent is held by the president ("Pres") of TC. One hundred percent of TC's preferred stock is held by an insurance company ("IC"). There have been no redemptions of TC stock pursuant to a plan or arrangement with AC or AP and, therefore, TC's present shareholders are its only historic shareholders within the meaning of Proposed Section 368(a)(4)(F). (*See* chapter 4, p. 74.) TC's common stock has a value of $90 million, and the value of the preferred stock is $10 million. TC operates two separate divisions (Division 1 and Division 2) each of which conducts an active trade or business within the meaning of Section 355(b)(2), except that only Division 1 has been conducted for the required five year period. The assets of both divisions are substantially appreciated and both have substantial amounts of goodwill. TC also owns all of the common stock, which is the only outstanding stock, of a subsidiary corporation ("TS"), which conducts an active trade or business within the meaning of Section 355(b)(2). TC formed TS 10 years ago and TS has been in business for that entire period. TS's business is also sub-

Figure 3. Structure of Acquiring and Target Corporations

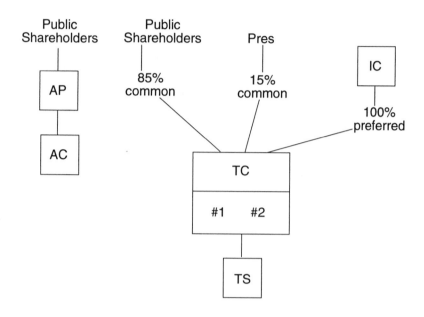

stantially appreciated and has substantial goodwill. The fair market values of Division 1, Division 2, and TS are approximately the same.

This structure can be diagramed in figure 3, with boxes indicating corporations.

The proposed rules are illustrated in the following transactions:

1. The acquisition of TC in an acquisitive reorganization in which neither AP nor AC has a prior stock ownership interest in TC. (*See* p. 127.)
2. The acquisition of TC in an acquisitive reorganization in which AP has a prior stock ownership in TC (*i.e.*, a creeping acquisition of TC). (*See* p. 129.)
3. The acquisition of TS or a newly formed subsidiary of TC combined with a Section 355 distribution. (*See* p. 132.)

4. The acquisition of TC in a nonreorganization carryover basis asset acquisition. (*See* p. 133.)
5. The acquisition of TC in a nonreorganization asset acquisition for which the taxable election is filed. (*See* p. 134.)
6. The purchase of the stock of TC in a mandatory and non-mandatory Section 338 transaction. (*See* p. 135.)

Assume that the business purpose and continuity of business enterprise doctrines (*see* chapter 4, p. 53.) are satisfied in each form of reorganization.

Acquisitive Reorganization for an Independent Stand-Alone Target

AP proposes to acquire TC in a tax-free acquisitive reorganization by issuing voting common stock of AP. The amount of stock to be issued by AP will not cause the shareholders of TC to own at least 50 percent of the stock of AP. Consequently, the transaction will not constitute a reverse acquisition within the meaning of Proposed Section 368(a)(4)(D). (*See* chapter 4, p. 83.) The continuity of interest requirement of Proposed Section 368(a)(4)(E) is satisfied as long as AP issues its voting common stock for at least 80 percent of TC's outstanding common stock and 80 percent of TC's outstanding preferred stock. (*See* chapter 4, p. 76.)

Pursuant to regulations, however, AP may issue its preferred stock (or any type of its common stock) for 80 percent of TC's outstanding preferred stock. Further, pursuant to regulations, AP could purchase TC's preferred stock for cash as long as AP established that AP acquired TC common stock in exchange for AP common stock that had a fair market value at least equal to 80 percent of the total fair market value of TC's common and preferred stock. Thus, in order for this exception to apply, AP would have to issue its voting common stock in exchange for approximately 90 percent of the outstanding common stock of TC (*i.e.*, 90 percent of $90 million fair market value equals $81 million), which is 81 percent of the total fair market value of TC's common and preferred stock.

Pursuant to the definition of historic shareholders in Proposed Section 368(a)(4)(F), all of the shareholders of TC constitute historic shareholders as long as such shareholders did not acquire their shares pursuant to a plan or arrangement with AP or AC or a related party. (*See* chapter 4, p. 76.) Thus, historic shareholders include those who purchase shares of TC in anticipation of the reorganization, such as arbitrageurs, as long as such purchases are not arranged by AP or AC. Further, to satisfy the continuity of interest requirement of Section 368(a)(4)(E), the historic shareholders who receive stock that satisfies the continuity of interest requirement must have unrestricted rights with respect to such stock and must not have any plan or intention to dispose of such stock. (*See* chapter 4, p. 76.)

Any amounts paid to Pres for covenants not to compete or similar arrangements in excess of the amounts determined under Proposed Section 368(a)(4)(P) are treated as additional purchase price for Pres' stock. (*See* chapter 8, p. 122.)

In order to satisfy the substantially all requirement of Proposed Sections 368(a)(4)(G) and (H), TC cannot, as part of the transaction, dispose of the assets of either of its divisions or of the stock of TS in a taxable sale or distribution. (*See* chapter 4, p. 87.) Under the definition of historic assets in Proposed Section 368(a)(4)(H), TC could, however, dispose of its divisions or of the stock of TS in a Section 355 distribution. (*See* chapter 4, p. 88.) This type of transaction is illustrated later in this chapter.

As long as the continuity of interest and the substantially all requirements are satisfied, the acquisition of TC under any of the following structures qualifies as an acquisitive reorganization under the proposed rules (*see* chapter 4, p. 68):

1. *Direct Merger.* A merger, under Proposed Section 368(a)(1)(A), of TC into AP with AP acquiring substantially all of TC's assets and the shareholders of TC receiving stock of AP that satisfies the 80 percent continuity of interest requirement (*i.e.*, a direct (A) merger).

2. *Forward Triangular Merger.* A merger, under Proposed Section 368(a)(1)(A), of TC into AC with AC holding substantially all of TC's assets and the shareholders of TC receiving stock of AP that satisfies the 80 percent continuity of interest requirement (*i.e.*, a forward triangular (A) merger).

3. *Reverse Triangular Merger.* A merger, under Proposed Section 368(a)(1)(A), of AC into TC with (a) AP having control, within the meaning of Section 368(c), of TC (that is, except as provided in regulations, with AP owning at least 80 percent of the common stock of TC and at least 80 percent of the preferred stock of TC); (b) TC holding substantially all of its assets; and (c) the shareholders of TC receiving stock of AP that satisfies the 80 percent continuity of interest requirement (*i.e.*, a reverse triangular (A) merger).

4. *Direct Stock for Stock.* An acquisition, under Proposed Section 368(a)(1)(B), by AP of control, within the meaning of Section 368(c), of TC with (a) TC holding substantially all of its assets, and (b) the shareholders of TC receiving stock of AP that satisfies the 80 percent continuity of interest requirement (*i.e.*, a direct (B)).

5. *Triangular Stock for Stock.* An acquisition, under Proposed Section 368(a)(1)(B), by AC of control, within the meaning of Section 368(c), of TC with (a) TC holding substantially all of its assets, and (b) the share-

holders of TC receiving stock of AP that satisfies the 80 percent continuity of interest requirement (*i.e.*, a triangular (B)).

6. *Direct Stock for Assets.* An acquisition, under Proposed Section 368(a)(1)(C), by AP of substantially all of TC's assets followed by a liquidation of TC, with the shareholders of TC receiving stock of AP that satisfies the 80 percent continuity of interest requirement (*i.e.*, a direct (C)).

7. *Triangular Stock for Assets.* An acquisition, under Proposed Section 368(a)(1)(C), by AC of substantially all of TC's assets followed by a liquidation of TC, with the shareholders of TC receiving stock of AP that satisfies the 80 percent continuity of interest requirement (*i.e.*, a triangular (C)).

These seven forms of reorganization follow the pattern of the seven forms of acquisitive reorganizations under current law specified in chapter 4. Under the proposed rules, however, a uniform continuity of interest and uniform substantially all requirement apply to each form of reorganization.

Because of the definition of acquiring parent in Proposed Section 368(a)(4)(C), the results above would be the same if AC were an indirect 80 percent subsidiary of AP. (*See* chapter 4, p. 80.) Pursuant to the proposed amendment to Section 368(a)(2)(C), after the transaction, AC could, without violating the continuity of interest or the substantially all requirements, push the stock or assets acquired down to a direct or indirect 80 percent subsidiary or up to AP, and AP could push the stock or assets acquired down to AC or to an 80 percent direct or indirect subsidiary of AC. (*See* chapter 4, pp. 82 and p. 90.)

The parties could not use Section 351 to give Pres tax-free treatment while the other shareholders of TC receive nonstock consideration for their shares. Under Proposed Section 368(a)(4)(N), any such transaction would be tested under the reorganization provisions, and the continuity of interest requirement would not be satisfied. (*See* chapter 4, p. 85.)

If within a year before the acquisition, AC or AP had purchased (other than in the ordinary course of business) an asset from TC, then pursuant to the consistency rule of Proposed Section 368(a)(4)(L), such asset would be deemed to have been acquired in the reorganization. AC or AP would, therefore, have a carryover basis for such asset. (*See* chapter 4, p. 95.)

Creeping Acquisitive Reorganization of Stand-Alone Target Corporation

The facts are the same as in the principal example, except AP has owned for five years 25 percent of the voting common stock of TC. The public owns 60 percent, and Pres owns 15 percent. AP proposes to acquire TC in a tax-free acquisitive reorganization by issuing voting common stock of AP.

The amount of stock to be issued by AP will not cause the shareholders of TC to own 50 percent of the stock of AP. Consequently, the transaction will not be a reverse acquisition within the meaning of Proposed Section 368(a)(4)(D). (*See* chapter 4, p. 83.)

Since AP has held 25 percent of the common stock of TC for a substantial period of time, AP is a historic shareholder of TC under Proposed Section 368(a)(4)(F). Its stock ownership, therefore, counts for continuity of interest purposes. (*See* chapter 4, pp. 76 and p. 79.) As a consequence, the continuity of interest requirement of Proposed Section 368(a)(4)(E) could be satisfied, for example, by having AP acquire in exchange for AP voting common stock an additional 55 percent of TC's common and 80 percent of TC's preferred.

In order to satisfy the substantially all requirement, TC may not, as part of the plan of reorganization, dispose of the assets of either of its divisions or of the stock of TS in a taxable sale or distribution. (*See* chapter 4, p. 87.) TC could, however, as illustrated in the next section, spin-off its divisions or the stock of TS in a Section 355 transaction. (*See* chapter 4, p. 88.)

The acquisition of TC under any of the following structures qualifies as an acquisitive reorganization under the proposed rules (*see* chapter 4, p. 79):

1. *Direct Merger.* A merger, under Proposed Section 368(a)(1)(A), of TC into AP with (a) AP acquiring substantially all of TC's assets; (b) the common shareholders of TC other than AP receiving voting common stock of AP for at least 55 percent of the outstanding common shares; and (c) except as provided in regulations, the preferred shareholders of TC receiving in exchange for at least 80 percent of such preferred similar preferred of AP or AP common stock (*i.e.*, a direct (A) merger).

2. *Forward Triangular Merger.* A merger, under Proposed Section 368(a)(1)(A), of TC into AC with (a) AC acquiring substantially all of TC's assets; (b) AP's stock interest in TC being canceled; (c) the holders of TC common stock other than AP receiving voting common stock of AP for at least 55 percent of the outstanding common shares; and (d) except as provided in regulations, the preferred shareholders of TC receiving, in exchange for at least 80 percent of such preferred, similar preferred of AP or AP common stock (*i.e.*, a forward triangular (A) merger).

3. *Reverse Triangular Merger.* A merger, under Proposed Section 368(a)(1)(A), of AC into TC with (a) AP having control of TC within the meaning of Section 368(c); (b) TC holding substantially all of its assets, (c) the common shareholders of TC, other than AP, receiving voting common stock of AP for at least 55 percent of the outstanding common shares; and (d) except as provided in regulations, the preferred shareholders of TC receiving, in exchange for at least 80 percent of such preferred, similar preferred of AP or AP common stock[1] (*i.e.*, a reverse triangular (A) merger).

---

1. This type of creeping reverse subsidiary merger would not qualify as a reor-

4. *Direct Stock for Stock.* An acquisition, under Proposed Section 368(a)(1)(B), by AP of control of TC within the meaning of Section 368(c), with (a) TC holding substantially all of its assets; (b) the common shareholders of TC other than AP receiving voting common stock of AP for at least 55 percent of the outstanding common shares; and (c) except as provided in regulations, the preferred shareholders of TC receiving, in exchange for at least 80 percent of such preferred, similar preferred of AP or AP common stock (*i.e.*, a direct (B)).[2]

5. *Triangular Stock for Stock.* An acquisition, under Proposed Section 368(a)(1)(B), by AC of control of TC within the meaning of Section 368(c), with (a) TC holding substantially all of its assets; (b) the common shareholders of TC other than AP receiving voting common stock of AP for at least 55 percent of the outstanding common shares; and (c) except as provided in regulations, the preferred shareholders of TC receiving, in exchange for at least 80 percent of such preferred, similar preferred of AP or AP common stock (*i.e.*, a triangular (B)).

6. *Direct Stock for Asset.* An acquisition, under Proposed Section 368(a)(1)(C), by AP of substantially all of TC's assets followed by a liquidation of TC, with (a) the cancellation of AP's stock interest in TC; (b) the common shareholders of TC other than AP receiving voting common stock of AP for at least 55 percent of the outstanding common shares; and (c) except as provided in regulations, the preferred shareholders of TC receiving, in exchange for at least 80 percent of such preferred, similar preferred of AP or AP common stock (*i.e.*, a direct (C)).[3]

7. *Triangular Stock for Asset.* An acquisition, under Proposed Section 368(a)(1)(C), by AC of substantially all of TC's assets followed by a liquidation of TC, with (a) the cancellation of AP's stock interest in TC; (b) the common shareholders of TC other than AP receiving voting common stock of AP for at least 55 percent of the outstanding common shares; and (c) except as provided in regulations, the preferred shareholders of TC receiving, in exchange for at least 80 percent of such preferred, similar preferred of AP or AP common stock (*i.e.*, a triangular (C)).

---

ganization under the current Section 368(a)(2)(E) because AP does not acquire control of TC in the merger as required by Treas. Reg. § 1.368–2(j)(3)(i) (1985).

2. This transaction is similar to the creeping (B) reorganization under Treas. Reg. 1.368–2(c) (1985), except there is no solely for voting stock requirement.

3. This transaction would not qualify as a (C) reorganization under the current statute because under the *Bausch & Lomb* decision, *supra* chapter 4, note 104, AP is viewed as receiving 25 percent of TC's assets in exchange for AP's 25 percent stock ownership interest in TC, thereby violating the solely for voting stock requirement. The *Bausch & Lomb* decision is overridden by the definition of historic shareholders in Proposed Section 368(a)(4)(F)(v). *See* the discussion of this point in chapter 4, p. 79.

The above discussion illustrates that under the proposed rules, there is uniform treatment of creeping acquisitions under the various forms of acquisitive reorganization. Thus, the non-uniform treatment under the current reorganization provisions is eliminated.

Acquisitive Reorganization for a Pre-Existing or Newly Formed Subsidiary, and Illustration of Section 355 Distribution Rule

AP proposes to acquire TS, the wholly-owned subsidiary of TC, in a tax-free acquisitive reorganization by issuing voting common stock of AP. The amount of stock to be issued by AP will not cause TC, the shareholder of TS, to own at least 50 percent of the stock of AP. Consequently, the transaction will not constitute a reverse acquisition within the meaning of Section 368(a)(4)(D). (*See* chapter 4, p. 83.) The continuity of interest requirement of Proposed Section 368(a)(4)(E) will be satisfied as long as AP issues its voting common stock for at least 80 percent of TS's outstanding common stock, which is its only class of stock. The transaction may be effectuated with either a direct or triangular reorganization under Proposed Sections 368(a)(1)(A), (B), or (C), as illustrated in an earlier section of this chapter.

TS has conducted an active trade or business within the meaning of Section 355(b)(2) for the required five-year period. Therefore, because of the definition of historic assets in Proposed Section 368(a)(4)(H), TC could distribute the stock of TS in a tax-free spinoff under Section 355 and then an acquiring corporation could acquire in any form of an acquisitive reorganization either or both TC and TS. (*See* chapter 4, pp. 59 and p. 88.) Thus, the classic *Morris Trust* type transaction is allowed prior to any type of acquisitive reorganization. Under the current statute, such transactions are allowed only in the direct merger under Section 368(a)(1)(A) and the stock for stock acquisition under Section 368(a)(1)(B).

Also, under Proposed Section 368(a)(4)(I), TC could do directly what it could accomplish indirectly by spinning-off TS and having TS acquired by AP. (*See* chapter 4, p. 93.) That is, AP could acquire TS in an acquisitive reorganization, and TC could then distribute all of the consideration received from AP to the shareholders of TC. Under Proposed Section 368(a)(4)(I), TC would not have any gain recognition on the distribution of the proceeds because Section 361 would apply to such distribution, and the shareholders of TC would receive nonrecognition treatment under Sections 355 and 356. Thus, for example, if all of the consideration paid for the TS stock was stock of AP and TC distributed that stock to its shareholders, there would be (1) nonrecognition treatment under Section 354 to TC upon receipt of the AP stock; (2) nonrecognition treatment under Section 361 to TC upon distribution of the AP stock; and (3) nonrecognition treatment under Section 355 to the shareholders of TC upon receipt of the stock of AP. These results are the same as those that would apply if there were first a distribution by TC of the TS stock to its shareholders, followed by an acquisition by AP of TS in an acquisitive reorganization solely in exchange for the stock of AP.

Under the Section 355 regulations, the maximum amount of boot that can be issued in an acquisitive reorganization following a Section 355 spin off is 20 percent.[4] This rule is implicit in the 80 percent continuity of interest requirement proposed in chapter 4, p. 59.

Pursuant to Proposed Section 368(a)(4)(0) (relating to Section 351 transactions), Proposed Section 368(a)(4)(F)(iii) (relating to definition of historic shareholders), and Proposed Section 368(a)(4)(H)(iii) (relating to the definition of historic assets), TC could transfer the assets of Division 1 or Division 2 to a new subsidiary and have that subsidiary acquired by AP in an acquisitive reorganization. (*See* chapter 4, p. 92.) Since the assets of Division 2 have not been operated for the requisite five-year period, TC could not, pursuant to the rule of Proposed Section 368(a)(4)(I), distribute to the shareholders of TC the proceeds received in an acquisitive reorganization of a newly formed subsidiary that contained the assets of Division 2. (*See* chapter 4, p. 93.) This rule is correct because TC could not distribute the stock of a newly formed subsidiary that held the Division 2 assets to its shareholders in a Section 355 transaction.

Acquisition of a Stand-Alone Target in a Nonreorganization Carryover Basis Acquisition

AC proposes to acquire the assets of TC in either a taxable merger of TC into AC[5] or a taxable purchase by AC of TC's assets. AC will acquire substantially all of TC's historic assets within the meaning of Proposed Section 368(a)(4)(G). The consideration paid will be a combination of cash and notes, and as a consequence, the continuity of interest requirement under Section 368(a)(4)(E) will not be satisfied. (*See* chapter 5, p. 100.) Although the transaction will be taxable to the shareholders of TC, provided the parties do not make a taxable election under Proposed Section 368(a)(5)(D), the transaction is treated as a carryover basis acquisition un-

---

4. *See* Treas. Reg. § 1.355–2(c)(2) (1989).

5. *See, e.g., Westshore Fuel, Inc. v. United States*, 598 F.2d 1236 (2d Cir. 1978). *See* chapter 2.

der Proposed Section 368(a)(5)(A). This is because (1) TC is a noncontrolled corporation; and (2) the transaction would have qualified as an acquisitive reorganization under Proposed Section 368(a)(1)(A) or (a)(1)(C) but for the fact that the continuity of interest requirement is not satisfied. (*See* chapter 5, p. 100.) Consequently, TC has nonrecognition treatment under Section 361 on both the disposition of its assets and the distribution of the proceeds, and AC's basis for TC's assets is a carryover basis under Section 362(b).

Consideration paid to Pres for a covenant not to compete or similar arrangement in an amount in excess of that determined in Proposed Section 368(a)(5)(H) is treated as additional purchase price for the TC assets. (*See* chapter 8, p. 122.) A consistency requirement applies under Proposed Section 368(a)(5)(C). (*See* chapter 5, p. 100.)

For the reasons discussed in chapter 5, it is not possible under the proposed rules for AC to separately acquire TC's divisions or the stock of TS in a nonreorganization carryover basis acquisition. Thus, the ALI's "clean mirror" approach is rejected.

Acquisition of a Stand-Alone Target in a Nonreorganization Asset Acquisition for which a Taxable Election is Filed

The facts are the same as those specified in the section beginning on p. 133, except pursuant to Proposed Section 368(a)(5)(D), an election is made to have the transaction treated as a taxable sale of assets rather than a carryover basis acquisition under Section 368(a)(5)(A). (*See* chapter 6, p. 110.) As a result of making that election, pursuant to Proposed Section 368(a)(5)(E)(i), TC recognizes gain or loss on the sale of its assets and AC takes a cost basis for the assets. Pursuant to Proposed Section 368(a)(5)(E)(ii), TC may, however, avoid gain with respect to the goodwill associated with Divisions 1 and 2, provided the parties enter into an allocation agreement with respect to all the transferred assets and the AC agrees not to deduct any amounts allocated to goodwill or other nonamortizable intangibles.

TC recognizes gain on the sale of the stock of TS. The parties may, however, make a Section 338(h)(10) election to treat that transaction as a sale of the assets of TS. Under Proposed Section 368(a)(5)(F), since Section 338 applies in any event to the stock of TS, TS will not be taxed with respect to its deemed sale of goodwill or similar nonamortizable intangibles, provided AC and TS agree not to deduct any amount with respect to such intangibles.

For the reasons stated in chapter 6, the exception for goodwill applies only in the case of an acquisition of a stand-alone TC.

Purchase of the Stock of a Stand-Alone Target in Mandatory and Non-Mandatory Section 338 Transactions

AC proposes to purchase all of the stock of TC for cash in either a reverse subsidiary merger[6] or a direct stock purchase. AC does not, however, desire to acquire TC's Division 1 and, therefore, pursuant to an arrangement between AC and TC, prior to AC's acquisition of the stock of TC, TC sells Division 1 to an unrelated party and distributes the cash to its shareholders. Immediately thereafter AC purchases all of the stock of TC. Since Division 1 is a historic asset of TC within the meaning of Proposed Section 368(a)(4)(H), at the time of the acquisition of the stock of TC by AC, TC did not hold substantially all of its historic assets within the meaning of Proposed Section 368(a)(4)(G). (*See* chapter 4, p. 87.) Consequently, the acquisition of TC's stock would not have qualified as either a reverse subsidiary merger reorganization under Proposed Section 368(a)(1)(A) or as a stock for stock reorganization under Proposed Section 368(a)(1)(B) because, among other things, the substantially all requirement is not satisfied. Consequently, under Proposed Section 368(a)(5)(I), as a result of the stock acquisition, AC is deemed to have made a Section 338 election with respect to TC. (*See* chapter 7, p. 119.) Therefore, TC and TS are deemed to have sold all of their assets and each takes a fair market value basis for the assets. There is complete recognition in such deemed sale, because the exception for goodwill in Proposed Section 368(a)(5)(F) is not applicable. (*See* chapter 6, p. 110.)

On the other hand, if TC did not dispose of Division 1 prior to the purchase of its stock by AC, the substantially all test would have been satisfied and there would not have been a mandatory Section 338 election. The transaction would have qualified as an acquisitive reorganization but for the failure to satisfy the continuity of interest requirement. Consequently, under Proposed Section 368(a)(5)(F), if AC makes a Section 338 election there is no recognition with respect to the goodwill of either TC or TS, provided there is an agreement not to deduct any amounts allocated to goodwill.

---

6. A reverse subsidiary cash merger is treated as a stock purchase. *See* Rev. Rul. 73–427, 1973–2 C.B. 301. *See* chapter 2, p. 29.

Part 3
LBOs and Related Transactions

CHAPTER 10

Current Treatment of LBOs and Related Transactions

This chapter lays the ground work for the discussion in the balance of this part 3. First, it discusses the structure under current law of LBO transactions involving stand-alone (*i.e.*, nonsubsidiary) target corporations. Next, the impact the proposals contained in part 2, which deal with both taxable and tax-free mergers and acquisitions, would have on LBOs is discussed. The next section discusses the relationship between the rules regarding LBOs contained in parts 2 and 3.

Finally, the use of leverage in LBOs and leveraged recapitalizations is discussed. Both of these transactions involve the conversion of corporate equity to debt and thus, are referred to as equity conversion transactions. A leveraged recapitalization can be used to accomplish the same economic effect as an LBO; therefore, in addressing LBOs it is necessary also to address leveraged recapitalizations. The proposals contained in chapter 12 would curtail the use of excessive leverage in LBOs and similar equity conversion transactions involving publicly held corporations.

Structure of LBOs Under Current Law

LBOs are taxable acquisitions in which a substantial portion of the consideration is raised by the issuance of debt. The corporate mechanism under current law for effectuating an LBO of a stand-alone (nonsubsidiary) target is generally the taxable reverse subsidiary merger, which is discussed in chapter 2, p. 29 and explained on p. 35. This mechanism is used so that the acquisition of the target will be treated as a stock acquisition, thus avoiding a tax at the target level. Also, as a result of the merger of the acquiring sub into the target, the target automatically assumes any debt issued by the acquiring sub for purposes of making the acquisition.[1]

---

1. *See* chapter 2, p. 35.

The principal tax issue under current law is whether the debt will be treated as debt for tax purposes so that the interest is deductible. This issue is generally decided under a facts and circumstances test.[2] Even if debt is treated as debt for federal income tax purposes, the interest may still be nondeductible under Sections 279, 163(i),[3] or 163(j).[4] This facts and circumstances test and Sections 279 and 163(i) are explored further on page 141, which examines in greater detail the use of debt in LBOs and other equity conversion transactions. Section 163(j) is explored in chapter 12, p. 183, which deals with acquisitions by foreign corporations of U.S. corporations.

Structure of LBOs Under the Rules Proposed in Part 2

The rules in part 2, which relate to mergers and acquisitions, would apply to LBOs of stand-alone targets in the following manner. First, an LBO will not qualify as a reorganization because under the definition of reorganization proposed in chapter 4 at least 80 percent of the consideration paid by the acquiring corporation would have to constitute its stock. Therefore, the maximum debt that could be used in a reorganization would be 20 percent. An acquisition with 80 percent equity and 20 percent debt would not fall within the general meaning of an LBO.

Second, the carryover basis rule proposed in chapter 5, the goodwill exception rule proposed in chapter 6, the mandatory Section 338 election proposed in chapter 7, and the prohibition on misallocation of purchase price proposed in chapter 8 would apply to any LBO of a stand-alone target corporation. Each of these rules applies to taxable acquisitions, and since an LBO is a taxable acquisition, the rules apply to LBOs. Thus, under the carryover basis rule proposed in chapter 5, an acquiring corporation could acquire a target's assets in an LBO transaction without triggering a taxable gain to the target on the sale of its assets. Under the carryover basis rule, the target has nonrecognition, and the acquiring corporation takes the target's assets with a carryover basis.

If the parties to an asset acquisition do not choose the carryover basis rule, then the target is taxable on the sale of its assets; however, under the goodwill exception contained in chapter 6, no tax is imposed on the sale of goodwill and other nonamortizable intangibles.

---

2. *See, e.g., Fin Hay Realty Co. v. United States*, 398 F.2d 694 (3d Cir. 1968).

3. *See* chapter 10, p. 141.

4. *See* chapter 12, p. 183.

Under the mandatory Section 338 election rule contained in chapter 7, if, pursuant to an arrangement with the acquiring corporation, the target disposes of a substantial portion of its assets prior to an acquisition of the target's stock by the acquiring corporation and, as a result of such disposition, the target's assets could not be acquired in a carryover basis acquisition, then the acquiring corporation is deemed to have made a Section 338 election after the stock acquisition. As a consequence, the target is deemed to have sold and reacquired its assets in a taxable transaction. The purpose of this rule is to ensure parity of treatment between stock acquisitions and asset acquisitions; the only stock acquisitions in which the target keeps its basis for its assets are situations in which the target's assets could be acquired in a carryover basis acquisition.

Under the rules proposed in chapter 8 relating to allocation of purchase price, it would be more difficult for the parties to an LBO to allocate what is economically purchase price for stock, to deductible items such as covenants not to compete.

Thus, all of the provisions in part 2 governing taxable acquisitions apply to LBO transactions.

Relationship Between the Rules Regarding LBOs in Parts 2 and 3

Part 3 proposes special rules relating to LBOs and leveraged recapitalizations. These rules are designed to eliminate the use of excessive leverage and to restrict the interest deduction on junk debt in such transactions involving publicly held corporations. The rules in part 3 primarily address the issue of whether interest on debt issued in LBOs and similar transactions is deductible for federal income tax purposes.

Although both the rules in part 2 and the rules in part 3 apply to LBOs, the rules in part 3 apply also to leveraged recapitalizations.

Use of Leverage in LBOs and Leveraged Recapitalizations Under Current Law[5]

In developing an appropriate tax policy for dealing with the issuance of debt in LBOs and other equity conversion transactions, a basic understand-

---

5. Portions of this section are based on and extensions of Samuel C. Thompson, Jr., *A Suggested Approach to Debt/Equity Issues and Leveraged Acquisitions*, 42 Tax Notes 483 (January 23, 1989) [hereinafter cited as "Thompson, *Suggested Approach to Debt/Equity*"]. This book does not address the general debt/equity characterization issue, which was addressed in the Tax Notes article.

ing of the use of leverage in such transactions is necessary. This section discusses two basic forms of equity conversion transactions: the LBO and the debt (leveraged) recapitalization.

The LBO is illustrated by a discussion of the RJR Nabisco, Inc. transaction. The debt recapitalization is illustrated by a discussion of Unocal's redemption transaction, a defensive response to Mesa Petroleum's attempt to takeover Unocal in an LBO transaction. In a debt recapitalization, the equity base of a stand-alone corporation is shrunk by the issuance of debt either in redemption of part of the stock or as a dividend in respect of the stock. A debt recapitalization can have the same economic effect as an LBO.

The equity conversion feature in an LBO is starkly illustrated by the takeover of RJR Nabisco, Inc. by KKR.[6] Prior to the transaction, RJR had approximately $4.8 billion in debt, and the purchase price for the stock was approximately $25 billion. Thus, the implicit debt/equity ratio before the transaction was approximately one part debt to five parts equity. After the transaction, which was effectuated with a taxable reverse subsidiary merger,[7] this debt to equity ratio was essentially reversed; there was approximately $25.4 billion in debt and $5.6 billion in equity, for a debt/equity ratio of approximately five parts debt to one part equity. Consequently, upon completion of the transaction, approximately $20 billion of equity was converted to $20 billion of debt. The interest payments on the $20 billion of debt are deductible in computing RJR's tax liability, whereas prior to the transaction, any dividends paid on the $20 billion of stock were nondeductible.

The equity conversion feature in a debt recapitalization is illustrated in the 1985 transaction in which Boone Pickens through Mesa Petroleum attempted to take over Unocal Corporation in an LBO transaction. Unocal successfully fended off Mesa by doing a leveraged recapitalization in which debt was issued in exchange for stock.[8] In this transaction, Mesa purchased 13 percent of the stock of Unocal on the open market and then made a tender offer for 37 percent of Unocal's shares for $54 per share. Mesa planned to do a freeze-out merger after the tender offer by issuing junk bonds, purportedly worth $54 per share, in exchange for the nontendered Unocal shares. Unocal responded by making a self tender for 49 percent of its shares (except those held by Unocal) in exchange for debt instruments of Unocal purportedly worth $70 per share. Unocal succeeded in its defensive

---

6. See Deborah A. DeMott, *The Biggest Deal Ever*, 1989 Duke L.J. 1 (1989); Comment, *Federal Income Tax Law: Who Really Bought RJR Nabisco?* 25 Wake Forest L. Rev. 141 (1990); Bryan Burrough and John Helyar, *Barbarians at the Gate* (1990).

7. See chapter 2, p. 29.

8. See, e.g., *Unocal Corporation v. Mesa Petroleum Co.*, 493 A.2d 946 (S.C. Del., 1985).

recapitalization and after the transaction Unocal had approximately $6 billion of additional debt; its equity base was shrunk by $6 billion.

A significant conversion of corporate equity to corporate debt occurred both in the RJR Nabisco LBO and in the Unocal debt recapitalization.[9] These transactions and any variants thereof are hereafter referred to as equity conversion transactions (ECTs).

Notwithstanding the massive substitutions of debt for equity that can occur in ECTs, under the current tax law such debt is likely to be treated as debt for tax purposes, and, therefore, the interest will likely be deductible. The current law, in essence, applies a facts and circumstances test for determining whether debt will be treated as debt for federal income tax purposes.[10]

If the purported debt looks too much like corporate stock (equity), the Internal Revenue Service may successfully treat such debt as equity. As a consequence, the purported interest payments would be treated as non-deductible dividends. One of the many factors to be considered is "the 'thinness' of the capital structure in relation to debt."[11] In many LBOs the capital structures are, indeed, thin; however, other factors generally cause the debt to be treated as debt. The principal factor favoring debt treatment is generally the arms-length nature of the transaction. As long as the principal holders of the debt are not also shareholders of the corporate debtor, the debt generally will be treated as debt under an "economic reality" test.[12] As the court in *Fin Hay* said:

> Under an objective test of economic reality it is useful to compare the form which a similar transaction would have taken had it been between the corporation and an outside lender. . . . [13]

Thus, if the lenders do not have a substantial equity stake in the corporation, which will generally be the case in an LBO, the debt will generally be treated as debt for federal income tax purposes.

Even if the debt is treated as debt, there are two provisions under current law that can cause the interest to be nondeductible. The first provision, Section 279, applies to corporate acquisition indebtedness, that is, debt issued

---

9. *See, e.g., Joint Committee LBO Study, supra* chapter 1, note 18; Congressional Research Serv., 98th Cong., 2d Sess., *Leveraged Buyouts: Sound Corporate Restructuring or Wall Street Alchemy?* (1984); Patricia L. Bryan, *Leverage Buyouts and Tax Policy,* 65 N.C. L. Rev. 1039 (1987).

10. *See, e.g., Fin Hay Realty Co. v. United States,* 398 F.2d 694 (3d Cir. 1968). *See, generally, Federal Taxation of Business Enterprises, supra* chapter 1, note 20, at § 4:03.

11. *Id.,* at 696.

12. *Id.,* at 697.

13. *Id.*

for the purpose of acquiring the stock or assets of a corporation.[14] This provision applies, however, only if the debt is, among other things, (1) subordinated, and (2) convertible into equity. Several conditions must be satisfied in order for the provision to apply, and it is generally possible to plan around the provision. Thus, Section 279 is in reality a toothless tiger; it has no practical bite. The proposals in chapter 12 would amend Section 279 to make it a meaningful provision.

Another provision that can cause interest to be non-deductible is Section 163(i), which applies to applicable high yield discount obligations.[15] This section applies in certain limited cases to a portion of the interest that accrues on debt instruments that are issued with substantial original issue discount (OID). OID arises if the debt instrument does not pay all of the interest on a current basis. This provision applies whether or not the debt instrument is issued in an acquisition. As will be seen in chapter 12, the proposal here for the treatment of OID instruments issued in acquisition transactions is consistent with the underlying theory behind Section 163(i).

---

14. *See, generally, Federal Taxation of Business Enterprises, supra* chapter 1, note 20, at § 35:05.

15. *See Federal Taxation of Business Enterprises, supra* chapter 1, note 20, at § 4:28.

CHAPTER 11

. . . .

Survey of Proposals for Dealing with LBOs and other Equity Conversion Transactions

This chapter first outlines the concerns that have been expressed about LBOs and other equity conversion transactions (ECTs) and then discusses various proposals for dealing with such transactions. It details the concerns, and briefly surveys the numerous proposals for addressing these concerns.

The American Law Institute's (ALI's) proposal for (1) a minimum tax on distributions (MTD), and (2) an interest disallowance rule which can apply in lieu of the MTD are examined. The ALI's proposals are set out in the ALI 1989 Study.[1] That study also contains proposals for reforming the tax treatment of mergers and acquisitions generally. The ALI's merger and acquisition proposals are discussed in chapter 3. The ALI 1989 Study is the most comprehensive study to date of the tax treatment of mergers, acquisitions, and LBOs.

Next, this chapter discusses Professor Yin's extension of the ALI's MTD. Finally, the provisions of the 1987 House Bill[2] relating to LBOs and hostile acquisitions are explored. An analysis of these provisions, which were not enacted, can be helpful in evaluating the proposals made here.

Another proposal for dealing with LBOs and related transactions is the integration of the corporate and individual taxes by eliminating or substantially reducing the tax on corporations. Under complete integration there would be a single shareholder level tax on corporate income. The Treasury 1992 Integration Study, which was released in January 1992, and the ALI Reporter's 1992 Integration Draft, which was released in March 1992, offer

---

1. *ALI 1989 Study, supra* chapter 1, note 2.
2. Budget Reconciliation Bill of 1987, H.R. 3545, 100th Cong., 1st Sess. (1987).

four different prototypes of an integrated system.[3] These studies are examined in chapter 15. The concern with LBOs and other ETCs was the driving force behind these integration studies. The basic conclusions reached in chapter 15, are that (1) only one of these prototypes (*i.e.*, the Treasury's CBIT prototype) would clearly eliminate the benefit of the over-leveraged transaction, and (2) the proposals contained in chapter 12 would have continuing vitality under the Treasury's preferred prototype (*i.e.*, the dividend exclusion prototype).

Concerns with Equity Conversion Transactions

A review of the recent literature reveals four common concerns expressed about ECTs. One of these concerns focuses on the impact of these transactions on the corporate tax structure, and three focus on the broad economic effects of these tax driven transactions.

The principal motivation behind LBOs and other ECTs is the reduction or elimination of the corporate tax through increased interest deductions, and the first concern with these transactions is that they lead to the erosion of the corporate tax base.[4] Thus, ECTs can be used as a way of achieving *de facto* integration of the corporate and personal taxes. Since many of the holders of stock and debt instruments are tax-exempt entities that pay no taxes on capital gains or interest, ECTs can effectively eliminate all taxes with respect to the ownership interests of such entities.

In documenting the macro effects of ECTs, the staff of the Joint Committee reports that from 1983 to 1987, nonfinancial corporations retired $313 billion of net equity while increasing indebtedness by $613 billion.[5] The staff also reports that the corporate interest deduction in 1985 shielded almost half of corporate income, whereas in 1976 this shield was merely a quarter.[6]

The staff points out that the revenue effects of ECTs are uncertain:

> Care must be exercised in analyzing the net revenue effect of the growth in corporate debt finance because the revenue loss attributable

---

3. See *Treasury 1992 Integration Study*, *supra* chapter 1, note 31, and *ALI Reporter's 1992 Integration Draft*, *supra* chapter 1, note 30. See also, chapter 15.

4. See the report of Kaufman's speech in *Daily Tax Report* (January 11, 1989) at G-6 [hereinafter cited as "*Kaufman*"]. See also, Henry Kaufman, *Bush's First Priority: Stopping the Buy Out Mania*, Washington Post, Jan. 1, 1989, at B1 [hereinafter cited as "*Kaufman, Bush's First Priority*"].

5. *Joint Committee LBO Study*, *supra* chapter 1, note 25, at 80.

6. *Id.*

to [corporate] interest deductions must be balanced against the revenue gain associated with interest and capital gains income.[7]

One empirical study purports to show, however, that LBOs actually increase tax revenues.[8] Even though the revenue effect may be uncertain, it would be a backward thinking application of tax policy to sanction an otherwise unwarranted tax abuse on the grounds that, looked at in a larger context, the abuse creates other tax effects that result in revenue neutrality. Such an approach would violate the ability to pay principle of tax policy.[9]

The second commonly expressed concern with ECTs is that there is an enhanced possibility of future financial collapse because businesses that engage in ECTs will not be able to service the debt in times of recession. This could lead to bailouts by the government of major businesses acquired in ECTs.[10] This increased risk of bankruptcy is best illustrated by the recent bankruptcy of several firms which were acquired in LBO transactions, such as Federated Department Stores Inc., which was acquired by Campeau Corporation.

The Federated acquisition was particularly susceptible to bankruptcy because the transaction was financed with 97 percent debt.[11] Campeau's tender offer for Federated required $6.71 billion, which was raised as follows: (1) $3.22 billion in bank loans, (2) $2.09 billion in bridge loans, and (3) nominally $1.4 billion in equity. The $1.4 billion in equity included, however, $1.21 billion of equity loans. Thus, Campeau's actual, real, at-risk equity was only $193 million. If the equity loans are considered debt (which is the effect of the proposals made in chapter 12), Campeau financed more than 97 percent of the $6.7 billion acquisition price with debt.[12] The debt markets failed in this acquisition; the bankruptcy price is being paid now. The proposals contained in chapter 12 would have denied the interest deduction on a significant part of the debt incurred in the acquisition of Federated, thus forcing Campeau to put up more real equity.

---

7. *Id.*

8. Michael C. Jensen et al., *Effects of LBOs on Tax Revenues of the U.S. Treasury*, 42 Tax Notes 727 (1989), also included as chapter 21 in Altman, *The High Yield Debt Market*, *infra* note 112, at 285 [hereinafter cited as "Jensen, et al., *Tax Revenues*"]. *But see*, Kaufman, *Bush's First Priority*, *supra* note 4 (to the contrary).

9. Musgrave and Musgrave, *Public Finance*, *supra* chapter 1, note 56, at 223.

10. *See Kaufman*, *supra* note 4 and Kaufman, *Bush's First Priority*, *supra* note 4. *But see*, Merton H. Miller, *Leverage*, 46 J. Fin. 479 (1991) [hereinafter cited as "Miller, *Leverage*"] (arguing that the cost of bankruptcy is small).

11. Steven N. Kaplan, *Campeau's Acquisition of Federated Value Destroyed or Value Added*, 25 J. Fin. Econ. 191 (1989) [hereinafter cited as "Kaplan, *Campeau's Acquisition of Federated*"].

12. *Id.*, at 196.

In addition to the direct effects of bankruptcy, the secondary effect has been a major erosion in the junk bond market. This has contributed to the S&L debacle and led to the bankruptcy of Executive Life, a major insurance company that overinvested in junk bonds. Thus, excessive debt significantly increases the risk of both primary and secondary business failure.

The third concern is that ECTs automatically lead to reduced R & D and other investment expenditures because of a lack of adequate cash flow after interest payments.[13] This element is illustrated in the defensive recapitalization by USG Corp. After this recapitalization, which prevented a hostile acquisition, USG Corp. cut in half both its R & D expenditures and its capital expenditures.[14] USG is now near bankruptcy.[15]

On a more generalized basis, several studies have found that the R & D expenditures are lower after an LBO.[16] For example, one study found that R & D of LBO firms is lower in the three years after an LBO than in the three years before.[17] The study also points out that targets of LBOs tend not to be R & D intensive.[18] This same study finds that total factor productivity (TFP) in the first three years after an LBO is greater than in any of the prior eight years;[19] in the fourth and fifth years after an LBO, however, the TFP differences are not significant and in some cases are negative.[20] As one possible explanation of this phenomenon, the authors say that "it is possible that after an LBO, resources that were previously allocated to producing long-term intangible investment goods such as R & D, capital, and customer goodwill are shifted to producing current output.[21] Thus, it is possible that cutbacks in R & D and the pursuit of short-term strategies may explain some of the perceived efficiencies associated with LBOs.

Even though R & D and investment expenditures of corporations that are the subject of ECTs may be curtailed, some of the proponents of the present system argue that this is of no concern because part of the cash in the hands of the shareholders of such corporations is ultimately reinvested

---

13. See, e.g., Daily Tax Report Special Report (December 16, 1988) at J-1.

14. Farrell, The Bills Are Coming Due, Bus. Wk. (Sept. 11, 1989) at 84.

15. Wall Street Journal, April 25, 1991, at C8, col. 5.

16. Frank R. Lichtenberg and Donald Siegel, The Effects of Leveraged Buyouts on Productivity and Related Aspects of Firm Behavior, 27 J. Fin. Econ. 165, 193 (1990) [hereinafter cited as "Lichtenberg and Siegel, The Effects of LBOs on Productivity"]; Steven Kaplan, The Effects of Management Buyouts on Operating Performance and Value, 24 J. Fin. Econ. 217 (1989).

17. Lichtenberg and Siegel, The Effects of LBOs on Productivity, supra note 16, at 195.

18. Id., at 188.

19. Id., at 191.

20. Id., at 191.

21. Id., at 181.

in other firms that engage in additional R & D and investment. While this is true to a degree, it seems logically compelling that the primary effect of the immediate loss in R & D and other investment spending of the corporation that is the subject of the ECT is not completely offset by the increased spending on R & D and investment by those firms that ultimately receive the cash the target's shareholders reinvest.

The fourth commonly expressed concern is that ECTs lead to a decrease in overall efficiency because corporations that are presently leveraged at a prudent level for long-term growth likely will be taken over in ECT transactions by parties who are seeking to realize potential short-term gains.[22] This element is illustrated clearly in Unocal. Prior to the proposed takeover by Boone Pickens, Unocal was apparently leveraged at a level that its board of directors thought was prudent. Boone saw an opportunity and proposed a higher level of leverage. The board's response was to out leverage Boone. Who would argue that Unocal is better off after the leveraged recapitalization than before? Who would argue that Boone Pickens, who runs Mesa Limited Partnership, a relatively small natural gas company that has performed poorly,[23] would be a more effective manager for Unocal, one of the largest integrated oil firms, than the management he sought to unseat? The point is that while an LBO may lead to more efficient operations, particularly LBOs that involve divisions and subsidiaries,[24] it may also lead to less efficient management, which was apparently the case with Campeau's takeover of Federated. The less efficient the managers and the greater the leverage, the greater the risk of bankruptcy.

General Survey of Proposals

There are a full range of proposals for dealing with ECTs. On one end of the spectrum, a proposal has been made to completely eliminate the deduction by corporations for interest expense above a minimum level, such as $100,000.[25] On the other end of the spectrum, the former Deputy Assistant Secretary of the Treasury, Michael Graetz, together with many others, has proposed a complete deduction for dividends.[26] His proposal is for *de jure* integration, and the Treasury 1992 Integration Study,[27] which is examined in chapter 15, offers several different models for an integrated system.

---

22. See Harold Bierman, Jr., "*Debt Stock and Junk Bonds*," 41 Tax Notes 1237 (1988) [hereinafter cited as "Bierman"].

23. *See, e.g.*, Vineeta Anand, *It's Just Not Easy Being T. Boone Pickens These Days*, Investor's Daily, July 17, 1991, at col. 1.

24. *See* Ravenscraft and Scherer, *Economic Efficiency, infra* chapter 12, note 13.

25. *See Bierman, supra* note 22.

26. Graetz, *Tax Aspects of LBOs, supra* note 21.

27. *Treasury 1992 Integration Study, supra* chapter 1, note 31.

Further, there are those, such as Professor Netter, who argue that there is no need for any restrictions on deductibility of interest.[28] Professor Netter has set out an elaborate defense of the present system and a strong condemnation of the provisions contained in the House Ways and Means Committee's 1987 House Bill.[29] Since the proposals contained in chapter 12 would modify the current law, chapter 14 analyzes whether these proposals can withstand Professor Netter's arguments in favor of the status quo.

At least one official has suggested that the Treasury attack the problem through its regulatory authority under Section 385, which authorizes the promulgation of regulations distinguishing between debt and equity.[30] Pursuant to its authority under Section 385, the Service previously issued several sets of regulations. Each set was withdrawn because of either heavy criticism from the Tax Bar or creative use of the regulations to have instruments that were most likely equity under the prior case law treated as debt under the regulations.[31]

Congressman Downey and Senator Moynihan have expressed concern that any limitations placed on the deductibility of interest in LBOs will give foreign acquiring corporations an advantage over U.S. acquiring corporations.[32] In a statement on the Senate floor, Senator Moynihan argued:

> The limitation on interest deductions for debt used in a corporate acquisition—though seemingly designed to stem the tide of debt-financed acquisitions of American corporations—would instead close off corporate acquisitions by domestic interests—leaving the field free for foreign purchasers who would still be able to deduct interest against their home country's taxes.[33]

The concern expressed by Congressman Downey and Senator Moynihan is particularly acute if the foreign acquiror can arrange the capital structure

---

28. *See, e.g.*, Jeffrey Netter, *Ending the Interest Deductibility of Debt Used to Finance Takeovers is Still a Bad Idea: The Empirical Evidence on Takeovers, Restrictions on Takeovers, and Restrictions on the Deductibility of Interest*, 15 J. Corp. L. 219 (1990) [hereinafter cited as "Netter, *Continue Interest Deductibility*"].

29. *Id.*

30. *See* Pat Jones, *Congress, Treasury Thinking Over Approaches To Corporate Takeovers*, 42 Tax Notes 144, 145 (1989).

31. *See, e.g.*, Rev. Rul. 83–98, 1983–2 C.B. 40 (dealing with the ARCN controversy, which led to the death of the proposed regulations under Section 385).

32. *See* Pat Jones, *Congress, Treasury Thinking Over Approaches To Corporate Takeovers* 42 Tax Notes 144 (1989); 133 Cong. Rec. S15364 (daily ed., Oct. 25, 1987) (statement of Sen. Moynihan).

33. 133 Cong. Rec. S15364 (daily ed., Oct. 28, 1987) (statement of Sen. Moynihan).

of the acquired U.S. firm in such a way as to cause the U.S. firm to pay to the foreign acquiror amounts that are deductible in computing the target's U.S. taxable income. If this cannot be done, the foreign acquiror will not be able to service its foreign debt with pretax U.S. income. In such case, the transaction is inherently not a leveraged acquisition because the pretax income of the target is not being used to service the debt.

The proposal contained in chapter 12 would prevent the use of the pretax income of a U.S. acquired corporation from servicing foreign debt. Thus, this proposal should eliminate most of any advantage foreign acquiring corporations might have over U.S. acquiring corporations if the rules proposed in chapter 12 for limiting the deduction for interest on debt issued in ECTs are adopted.[34]

In an extensive report, the staff of the Joint Committee has described in detail many of the proposals for dealing with ECTs, including (1) various integration proposals;[35] (2) various proposals for limiting the deductions for interest;[36] (3) a proposal for a combination of an interest limitation and dividend relief;[37] (4) a proposal for corporate recognition of gain on borrowing above basis;[38] (5) a proposal for an excise tax on acquisition indebtedness;[39] (6) the proposal for having more objective standards for distinguishing between debt and equity under Section 385;[40] (7) the imposition of an unrelated business income tax on certain transactions;[41] and (8) the ALI's proposal for either a minimum tax on distributions or a disallowance of interest on debt issued in an ECT. The ALI proposal, which is quite far reaching and comprehensive, is discussed in the next section.

The ALI's Approach to Equity Conversion Transactions

The ALI 1989 Study would get at the problem of LBOs and other equity conversion transactions by imposing a corporate minimum tax on all nondividend distributions ("Covered Distributions"). Covered Distributions are defined broadly to include (1) redemptions, (2) liquidations, and (3)

---

34. Under the rules proposed here a foreign corporation could still deduct its foreign interest expense against its foreign income without limitation.

35. *Joint Committee's LBO Study, supra* chapter 1 note 25, at 82–103.

36. *Id.,* at 103–17.

37. *Id.,* at 116–17.

38. *Id.,* at 118.

39. *Id.,* at 119.

40. *Id.,* at 120.

41. *Id.,* at 123.

acquisitions of shares of another corporation.[42] The tax is referred to as the minimum tax on distributions (MTD) and the rate of the tax is proposed to be 28 percent. A nonrefundable shareholder credit is allowed for the MTD.[43] Also, the tax does not apply to the extent the distribution is out of contributed capital.[44]

The MTD does not apply if debt is issued in connection with a Covered Distribution; in such case, the interest deduction is disallowed on such debt.[45] Thus, under the ALI approach, to the extent debt is issued in connection with an acquisition of shares in an LBO transaction or in connection with a redemption of shares in a leveraged recapitalization, the interest disallowance rule applies, and to the extent the funds used in such transactions are not traced to debt, the MTD applies. The interest disallowance rule is a surrogate for the MTD.

The purpose of MTD seems to be to impose a tax at the time of distribution of cash that no longer will be used to generate taxable earnings at the corporate level. Thus, the MTD might be viewed as a present tax on the taxable income that is foregone as a result of the distribution.[46]

Although it is not the purpose of this book to assess the merits of a general MTD, the justification for the MTD does not seem to be compelling. Further, the MTD would not be sound policy in the acquisition context. This can be seen by a simple example.

Assume that acquiring corporation (AC) that has no outstanding debt uses $100 of its retained earnings to purchase all the stock of target corporation (TC) from its sole shareholder, individual B. The transaction is a Covered Distribution. Since AC has not financed the acquisition with debt, the MTD of 28 percent applies to the distribution. Therefore, AC must pay a tax of $28 at the time of the acquisition. B would receive a credit for the tax to the extent of B's tax on the gain. Thus, the credit is not refundable; it is limited to the actual tax paid by B. If B's tax is less than 28 percent of

---

42. *ALI 1989 Study, supra* chapter 1, note 2, at Proposal 1(a), pp. 54–56. For an even more sweeping form of this proposal, which would impose a corporate level tax on all distributions, *see* George K. Yin, *A Proposed Tax On Corporate Distributions,* 67 Taxes 962 (Dec. 1989) and George K. Yin, *A Different Approach to the Taxation of Corporate Distributions: Theory and Implementation of a Uniform Corporate-Level Distributions Tax,* 78 Geo. L. J. 1837 (1990) [hereinafter cited as "Yin, *Uniform Corporate Level Distributions Tax*"].

43. *ALI 1989 Study, supra* chapter 1, note 2, at Proposal 1(c), p. 56.

44. *Id.,* at 55.

45. *ALI 1989 Study, supra* chapter 1, note 2, at Proposal 2, pp. 80, 84. The disallowance rule applies to any debt outstanding at the time of the Covered Distribution, which debt has not previously been targeted for disallowance.

46. *Id.,* at 6–7, 31, 58. *See also,* Yin, *Uniform Corporate Level Distributions Tax, supra* note 42, at 1858–59.

the amount of the distribution, the excess credit is wasted. For many tax-payers, the tax on the distribution will be less than 28 percent of the amount of the distribution because taxpayers will first recover basis for their shares before computing tax. For example, if a shareholder receives a $100 Covered Distribution in exchange for stock for which the shareholder has a basis of $50, the shareholder's gain is $50. And, assuming a 28 percent tax rate on the gain (which generally applies to individuals today),[47] the share-holder has a $14 tax, which is 14 percent of the Covered Distribution. Thus, in this case, there would be no credit for $14 of the MTD. Also, the MTD on Covered Distributions made to shareholders that are tax-exempt would be completely lost. It is likely that in order to avoid the MTD, AC would borrow the $100 needed for the acquisition and thereby be subject to the interest disallowance rule.

The ALI's proposal would have two perverse effects. First, the proposal would penalize, and thereby discourage, equity financed acquisitions. Second, the proposal would encourage the use of debt in acquisitions. Debt would be used for the purpose of avoiding the MTD rather than for the purpose, as under present law, of securing the maximum interest deduction. The MTD would force firms into the interest disallowance rule; this would be bad tax policy and, therefore, should be rejected.

Although the ALI's disallowance of interest rule (standing alone without the MTD) goes in the right direction, particularly in denying the deduction for interest on debt issued in redemption transactions, the rule is much too broad. The rule disallows the deduction of interest on any debt issued for the purpose of acquiring stock of a target corporation without regard to whether the target is Mom and Pop Grocery, Inc., or publicly held RJR Na-bisco, Inc. Under the ALI approach, there would be no interest deduction in a debt-financed acquisition of the stock or assets of a stand-alone cor-poration without respect to the size of the target corporation, without re-spect to the portion of acquisition price that is debt financed, and without respect to the character of the debt.

Although the approach taken in chapter 12 would limit the deduction for interest in certain acquisitions of stand-alone targets, this approach is tar-geted at the current problem with LBOs and other equity conversion transactions.

Professor Yin's Approach

Building on the ALI's minimum tax proposal, Professor Yin has sug-gested the adoption of a "uniform corporate-level tax on any and all distri-

---

47. See § 1 (h) which applies a maximum 28 percent rate to capital gains of individuals.

butions of earnings out of corporate solution, dividend and nondividend distributions alike, as well as on liquidating and acquisitive transactions that have a distributive effect."[48] Professor Yin refers to his tax as the corporate distributions tax (CDT). The CDT would apply to taxable acquisitions of a target's stock and to liquidating distributions occurring after a taxable acquisition of a target's assets. The tax would not apply to the extent the distribution was made out of contributed capital.[49] The distributee shareholders would not be subject to tax upon receipt of the dividend, nondividend, or liquidating distribution or upon sale of their shares in an acquisition transaction.

Similar to the ALI 1989 Study, Professor Yin's proposal treats the taxable acquisition of stock by an acquiring corporation from a noncorporate shareholder as a distribution by the acquiring corporation that is subject to the CDT.[50] In comparing his proposal to the ALI proposal, Professor Yin says the ALI's "recommendation moves in the same direction as the proposals described in [the Yin] article, although not as far, and with important differences in detail. One could view [the Yin] article's proposal as a purer model of a corporate distribution tax."[51]

As is the case with the ALI's MTD, there do not appear to be compelling reasons for the adoption of a CDT, particularly in the case of acquisition transactions. Under the present system, the selling shareholders in a taxable acquisition are required to pay tax on their gains. There is no sound reason for switching that obligation to the acquiring corporation as would be the case with the CDT.

The 1987 House Bill

The House version of the Budget Reconciliation Bill of 1987 (1987 House Bill)[52] contained provisions designed first to remove tax incentives for corporate merger and acquisitions generally and second to create disincentives for hostile acquisitions. These provisions have already been considered and rejected by Congress. Therefore, before proceeding with the formulation of the proposals made here, it is instructive to analyze these provisions and determine whether Congress was correct in rejecting them.

---

48. Yin, *Uniform Corporate Level Distributions Tax, supra* note 42, at 1840.
49. *Id.*, at 1878–79.
50. *Id.*, at 1861.
51. *Id.*, at 1840, note 7.
52. H.R. 3545, Budget Reconciliation Bill of 1987, 100th Cong., 1st Sess. (1987), [hereinafter cited as "1987 House Bill"], reported in H.R. Rep. No. 391, 100th Cong., 1st Sess. (1987) [hereinafter cited as "1987 House Report"].

In removing the tax incentives for corporate mergers and acquisitions, the 1987 House Bill would have added to the Code Section 279A,[53] which would have disallowed the interest deduction for debt incurred in certain major stock acquisitions. In providing a tax disincentive for hostile acquisitions, the bill would have (1) amended Section 338(i)[54] to provide for a deemed Section 338 election, thus triggering taxable gain at the target level, in a hostile qualified stock purchase, and (2) added Section 280H,[55] which would have disallowed the deduction for interest incurred to acquire stock or assets of a target corporation in a hostile acquisition. Although these provisions were not enacted, in 1987 Congress enacted an excise tax on greenmail[56] and eliminated the use of the mirror subsidiary technique.[57] These two provisions originated in the 1987 House Bill.

Apparently, the principal reason Congress did not enact Sections 279A, 338(i), and 280H was concern that the stock market crash of October 19, 1987 may have been caused at least in part by the announcement on Wednesday, October 14, 1987 that "members of the House Ways and Means Committee were filing legislation to eliminate tax benefits associated with [the] financing of corporate takeovers."[58] The Brady Report on the 1987 market crash indicates that as the risk arbitrageurs became aware of the potential effects of the House action they began to liquidate their positions in

---

53. Section 279A is contained in § 10138 of the 1987 House Bill, *supra* note 52.

54. Section 338(i) is contained in § 10143 of the 1987 House Bill, *supra* note 52.

55. Section 280H is contained in § 10144 of the 1987 House Bill, *supra* note 52.

56. Section 5881 was added by § 10142 of the 1987 House Bill, *supra* note 52. Under Section 5881, an excise tax of 50 percent applies to any gain realized by a person on receipt of a greenmail payment, which is any amount received in redemption of the shareholder's stock in a situation where the shareholder has held the stock for less than two years and has made or threatened to make a tender offer for the stock of the corporation. For a more detailed discussion of Section 5881 *see Federal Taxation of Business Enterprises, supra* chapter 1, note 20, at § 11:17.

57. *See* § 10139 of 1987 House Bill, *supra* note 52. Under the mirror subsidiary technique, an acquiring parent corporation, which had acquired the stock of a target through controlled (mirror) subsidiaries, could dispose of part of the assets of the target without incurring a tax liability. In order to accomplish this the target first liquidated into the mirror subsidiaries by distributing unwanted assets to one subsidiary and wanted assets to another. The acquiring parent then disposed of the stock of the subsidiary with the unwanted assets. The parent would not be taxed on the sale because the parent's basis for the stock of the subsidiaries was equal to the value of the subsidiaries. The mirror transaction is beyond the scope of this book. *See, e.g., Federal Taxation of Business Enterprises, supra* chapter 1, note 20, at § 14:17. For an assessment of the mirror legislation and other related developments, *see* Thompson, *Suggested Alternative Approach, supra* chapter 1, note 3.

58. Report of the Presidential Task Force on Market Mechanisms 15 (January 8, 1988) [hereinafter cited as "*The Brady Report*"].

takeover stocks, which had held the market up. As a consequence of the liquidations, such stocks began to lead the market down.[59] Also, one study has found that there is "strong evidence" that the 1987 House Bill was a major cause of the crash.[60] The SEC Staff Report on the crash has a more balanced evaluation of the effect of the 1987 House Bill on the market. That report says that the 1987 House Bill "may have had an effect on stock prices."[61]

It is not the purpose of this book to attempt to determine the market effect of the 1987 House Bill. It can be expected, however, that any curtailment of the tax benefits associated with acquisitions will result in a reduction in the prices paid in acquisitions. And, it is reasonable to expect that the 1987 House Bill had some negative effect on the stocks of corporations that were perceived to be takeover targets.

Although it may be appropriate to take account of market effects in designing a tax rule, the driving force in the formulation of a rule should be an analysis of whether the rule is a sensible tax policy. In any event, as demonstrated in chapter 14, it is unlikely that the adoption of the proposals contained in chapter 12 would have a significant adverse impact on the market for shares.

Analysis of Proposed Sections 338(i) and 280H Relating to Hostile Acquisitions

For the reasons set out below, proposed Sections 279A, 338(i), and 280H were not sound from a tax policy perspective. Apart from any potential adverse market effect, Congress was correct in not enacting these provisions.

The proposals contained in the 1987 House Bill relating to hostile acquisitions were designed to discourage such takeovers. As explained in the House Report:

> The Committee believes that corporate acquisitions that lack the consent of the acquired corporation are detrimental to the general economy as well as to the welfare of the acquired corporation's employees and community. The committee therefore believes it is appropriate not only to remove tax incentives for corporate acquisitions, but to create tax disincentives for such acquisitions.[62]

---

59. *Id.*

60. Netter, *Continue the Interest Deductibility, supra* note 28, and Mark L. Mitchell and Jeffrey M. Netter, *Triggering the 1987 Stock Market Crash: Antitakeover Provisions in the Proposed House Ways and Means Tax Bill?* 24 J. Fin. Econ. 37 (1989). This is discussed further in chapter 14.

61. SEC Staff Report, The October 1987 Market Break 3–10 (Feb. 1988) ["*SEC Staff Report*"].

62. 1987 House Report, *supra* note 52, at 1086.

In implementing this committee judgment the 1987 House Bill would have amended Section 338(i) and Section 280H. If enacted, Section 338(i) would have applied if (1) an acquiring corporation (including certain related parties and parties acting in concert) purchased at least 80 percent of the stock of a target corporation, and (2) any "significant portion" of such stock was acquired pursuant to an offer to the target's shareholders which offer was not approved by a majority of the target's independent directors (*i.e.*, a hostile offer). If these conditions were satisfied, the acquiring corporation would have been deemed to have made a Section 338 election with respect to the target corporation.

As a consequence of this deemed Section 338 election, the target corporation would have been treated as if it had sold and then repurchased its assets for fair market value. In view of the repeal of the *General Utilities* doctrine by the Tax Reform Act of 1986, the deemed Section 338 election would have resulted in full taxation of the gain inherent in the target's assets. Unless the target had net operating or other losses to offset the gain, the deemed Section 338 election would have made most hostile acquisitions prohibitively expensive. Consequently, few hostile takeovers would have occurred if Section 338(i) had been enacted.

If enacted, Section 280H would have provided that if an acquiring corporation (including certain related parties and parties acting in concert) purchased at least 20 percent of the stock of a target corporation in a hostile offer, then no deduction would have been allowed on indebtedness incurred (1) to purchase or carry such stock, or (2) to purchase or carry any assets held by the target corporation. Thus, this provision would have denied the interest deduction on debt financed (1) hostile acquisitions of at least 20 percent of a target's stock, and (2) asset acquisitions occurring after such a hostile stock acquisition.

Both Sections 338(i) and 280H as proposed in the 1987 House Bill are predicated on the assumption that hostile takeovers are necessarily bad. Although there are many associated with the free market school, such as Professor Netter,[63] who argue that the empirical evidence is to the contrary (that is, that hostile takeovers are definitely good for society), a dispassionate look at the empirical evidence would lead one to the same conclusion which Professor Roll has reached in his analysis of the empirical evidence. Professor Roll summarizes his conclusions as follows:

> From the policy perspective, there is no empirical justification for limiting takeover activity because of potential damage to target firm

---

63. *See, e.g.*, Netter, *Continue the Interest Deductibility, supra* note 28; Jensen, *The Takeover Controversy: Analysis and Evidence*, in John Coffee, Louis Lowenstein, and Susan Rose-Ackerman, *Knights, Raiders & Targets, the Impact of the Hostile Takeover* (1988) [the book is hereinafter cited as "*Knights, Raiders & Targets*"].

shareholders. There is no empirical justification for restricting the activities of bidding firms, even for the paternalistic prevention of self-inflicted economic loss. Finally, the empirical evidence on private takeover activity is inconclusive. At present, it could support no particular social policy.[64]

Without respect to the market reaction to the 1987 House Bill, Professor Roll's conclusion that the empirical evidence could support no particular social policy clearly argues against the enactment of Sections 338(i) and 280H. Those provisions are designed to penalize hostile acquisition, and it is not at all clear that hostile acquisitions are bad for society. Congress was correct in rejecting these provisions; they were built on a faulty premise and are not sound tax policy. In contrast, the proposals contained in chapter 12 are not designed to discourage hostile acquisitions; the purpose of these proposals is to ensure that there is an adequate level of equity capital in all acquisitions of publicly held firms whether hostile or friendly.

Analysis of Proposed Section 279A, Relating to Interest Disallowance in Major Stock Acquisitions

In explaining the reasons for proposing Section 279A, the Committee Report to the 1987 House Bill says that there are "unwarranted tax incentives for corporate mergers and acquisitions" and that the "interest deduction encourages the replacement of corporate equity with debt."[65] The Committee Report also says that present Section 279 is an "ineffective deterrent to such acquisitions." Further, the Committee Report says:

> The committee is concerned that the excessive leveraging that has manifested itself in recent years reduces the corporate income tax base by replacing corporate equity with debt, particularly in circumstances where no corporate-level tax has been paid on appreciated assets and the earning derived from those assets are sheltered by post-acquisition interest deductions. The committee is also concerned that such leveraging may be particularly likely to occur in the context of an acquisition or significant redemption and may threaten the health of the corporate sector and the economy in general.[66]

Here the Committee Report has set out valid reasons for concern. It is clear that the interest deduction encourages the replacement of corporate

---

64. Richard Roll, *Empirical Evidence on Takeover Activity and Shareholder Wealth,* in *Knights, Raiders & Targets, supra* note 63, at 241 [hereinafter cited as "Roll, *Empirical Evidence on Takeovers*"].

65. 1987 House Report, *supra* note 52, at 1085.

66. *Id.,* at 1085.

equity with debt and thereby reduces the corporate income tax base. As long as there is a corporate income tax (and the case for eliminating it has not yet been made),[67] it is sound tax policy to protect the corporate base. On the other hand, any provision that is designed to protect the corporate base should not impose an unnecessary impediment to acquisition transactions.

The corporate tax base has been eroded by overly leveraged acquisitions, which usually involve the issuance of junk bonds. The proposals contained in chapter 12 are directed at the prevention of both the overly leveraged acquisition and the curtailment of the use of junk bonds in acquisition type transactions. Thus, the proposals here are specifically tailored to deal with the types of transactions that are likely to result in the unwarranted erosion of the corporate tax base without imposing an unjustified damper on reasonably structured debt financed acquisitions. On the other hand, Section 279A is both overinclusive and underinclusive in protecting the corporate tax base. It would penalize certain nonabusive transactions and not reach certain abusive transactions.

Under Section 279A, as proposed in the 1987 House Bill, no deduction is allowed for any stock acquisition interest paid or incurred by a C corporation during any taxable year to the extent such interest exceeds $5,000,000. The provision does not apply if a Section 338 election is made after the stock acquisition. Stock acquisition interest means any interest paid on indebtedness incurred in connection with a major stock acquisition. A major stock acquisition is a transaction in which the stock in a target corporation is acquired pursuant to a plan of the acquiring corporation (or certain related parties and other parties acting in concert) to acquire 50 percent or more of such stock during a three-year period. Also, a major stock acquisition includes a redemption of 50 percent or more of the stock of a corporation.

Assume an acquiring corporation purchases 60 percent of the stock of a target corporation for $160 million and the transaction is financed with $80 million of nonjunk debt that pays 10 percent interest and $80 million of equity. The annual interest payment is $8 million. Since this is a major stock acquisition, the $8 million of interest is stock acquisition interest, and therefore, $3 million of the interest (*i.e.*, $8 million minus $5 million) is disallowed. This interest disallowance applies even though this acquisition is not overly leveraged (because 50 percent of the purchase price is equity) and the debt is not junk debt. There are no good tax policy reasons for disallowing the interest in this situation; therefore, Section 279A is overinclusive.

---

67. *See, e.g.*, Kwall, *The Uncertain Case*, *supra* chapter 1, note 33 and chapter 15.

On the other hand, assume that an acquiring corporation purchases 60 percent of the stock of a target corporation for $25 million in a transaction that is fully financed with junk debt that pays interest of 20 percent or $5 million annually. Although there is a major stock acquisition and the $5 million of interest is stock acquisition interest, there is no disallowance of interest under Section 279A because of the $5 million floor. This acquisition is an overly leveraged junk bond acquisition of the most egregious type but Section 279A would not disallow any of the interest. Thus, Section 279A is underinclusive.

Other problems exist with Section 279A as proposed in the 1987 House Bill. First, it applies across the board to stock acquisitions of publicly held corporations, to privately held corporations, and to subsidiaries. As explained in chapter 12, there are strong reasons for excepting both privately held corporations and subsidiaries from any interest disallowance rule. Second, Section 279A does not apply to asset acquisitions and, therefore, it would not apply, for example, to the acquisition of a publicly held target corporation in an asset acquisition. This type of transaction has an equity conversion feature and should be addressed by any interest limitation rule. Finally, Section 279A does not apply if after an acquisition a Section 338 election is made. There is no good reason for exempting from an interest disallowance rule an overly leveraged stock acquisition merely because a Section 338 election is filed. Such an election is likely to be filed only when the target has substantial net operating losses which shelter the gain realized on the election.

Although the 1987 House Bill was going in the right direction with Section 279A, the provision was not narrowly focused and Congress was correct in rejecting it.

On the other hand, the proposals set forth in chapter 12 are focused at the real problem with overly leveraged acquisitions.

POSTSCRIPT: Most of the studies that have been generally supportive of ECTs have focused on microeconomic effects. It seems clear, however, that the LBO binge of the 1980s contributed significantly to the macroeconomic problems of the 1990s. In his July 22, 1992 testimony before the House Banking Committee, Alan Greenspan, Chairman of the Federal Reserve Board, said that the "economy still is recuperating from past excesses involving a generalized over-reliance on debt." He further said that the "sharp increase in debt and the unprecedented liquidation of corporate equity" has led to a "period of adjustment." Adoption of the proposals in chapter 12 should prevent a return to a period of "over-reliance on debt."

CHAPTER 12

· ·

Proposal for Denial of Deductibility of Interest in Certain Equity Conversion Transactions

This chapter discusses the proposals for the denial of deductibility of interest in LBOs and related transactions. First, it lays out the rationale for these proposals, and it sketches the broad scope of the rules. Then, it addresses the definition of the publicly held corporations to which the proposals apply and discusses the interest limitation rules that apply to leveraged redemptions, dividends, and recapitalizations. Finally, it examines the application of such rules in stock and asset acquisitions and addresses the treatment of acquisitions by foreign corporations of the stock of U.S. corporations. The application of these rules is illustrated in chapter 13. Chapter 14 examines the case against interest limitation rules, and chapter 15 examines whether these rules and the rules relating to mergers and acquisitions in part 2 would be needed in an integrated system.

The Rationale for the Proposed Rules

The interest disallowance rules proposed below apply only to equity conversion transactions of publicly held corporations. It is this type of transaction that has led to the concerns discussed in chapter 11.

Thus, the disallowance rules proposed here do not apply to (1) acquisitions of stock or assets of closely held corporations, or (2) acquisitions of less than substantially all the assets of a publicly held corporation, such as the acquisition of the assets of a division or of the stock of a subsidiary of a publicly held corporation. The rules proposed here do not eliminate the deduction for interest on any and all indebtedness incurred on the acquisition of corporate stock, which is the effect of the ALI 1989 Study.[1]

Under the proposal here, the interest deduction for debt issued to buy plant and equipment continues to be allowed. Even the ALI 1989 Study acknowledges that disallowance of the interest deduction on debt issued to finance real investment would be unwise.[2] Thus, there would continue to be a built-in tax incentive for the issuance of debt for the acquisition of bricks and mortar which add to the overall GNP.

The balance of this section explores, among other things, the reasons these proposed rules are directed only at publicly held corporations. It lays out the basic case for focusing on publicly held corporations and puts forth the reasons for excluding acquisitions of closely held firms and of divisions and subsidiaries of publicly held firms. These acquisitions are referred to here as private type acquisitions. It discusses the credit market failure that has characterized the market for the acquisition of publicly held firms and discusses the impact an interest limitation provision will have on takeover premiums.

Some readers may wonder why the limitations proposed here are needed now since the wave of LBOs that swept the country in the mid-1980s has abated. Although LBOs and other equity conversion transactions are now in a state of quiescence, a new wave could return, and if the proposals suggested here are enacted into law, it would be more likely that there would be a prudent level of equity in such transactions. Further, leveraged acquisitions have been a part of the business landscape for many years, and such activity will continue. It is sensible to adopt rationale rules for dealing with these transactions without respect to the level of activity.

Focus on Equity Conversion Transactions of Publicly Held Corporations

Equity conversion transactions involving publicly held corporations led to the present concern with the use of corporate debt, and it is, therefore, appropriate to focus on these transactions. For instance, the staff of the SEC in its 1990 Report on Recent Developments in the High Yield Market (that is, the junk bond market) says that "[m]ost registered original issue offerings of high yield bonds are acquisition financing, refinancing of acquisitions debt or issued in recapitalizations."[3] Although this statement re-

---

1. *ALI 1989 Study, supra* chapter 1, note 2, at 42.

2. *Id.*, at 42.

3. SEC Staff Report, *Recent Developments in the High Yield Market* 20 (1990) [hereinafter cited as "*SEC Staff Report on Junk Bonds*"]. *See also,* General Accounting Office, *Financial Markets, Issuers, Purchasers, and Purposes of High Yield, Non-Investment Grade Bonds* (Feb. 1988).

lates only to public offerings it would appear that the same is true for private offerings of junk debt. In this regard the SEC Staff Report says that although there is little hard information available, "[b]ased on information obtained from industry sources, it appears that both the original issue and secondary private markets generally parallel the equivalent public market."[4]

Also, the SEC Staff Report points out that (1) Drexel Burnham found that acquisition related financing represented 79 percent of the junk bond market in 1987 and 83 percent in 1988,[5] and (2) First Boston reports that acquisition related financing represented 75.9 percent of the junk bond market in 1989.[6]

Further, it appears that most junk bond financing is in connection with acquisitions of publicly held corporations as opposed to acquisitions of closely held corporations, divisions, or subsidiaries. In the words of Merton Miller, one of the winners of the 1990 Nobel Prize in economics: "The LBO's of the 1980's differed only in scale [from prior period LBOs] in that they involved publicly held rather than privately held corporations and that the takeovers were often hostile."[7]

It is logical that junk debt would principally be issued in equity conversion transactions because corporations that are not overly leveraged (which is the case for most corporations) could issue nonjunk debt with lower interest rates for normal operating purposes. The Conference Report to the Revenue Reconciliation Act of 1989 points out that most corporations are not overly leveraged. In discussing Section 163(j), the earnings stripping provision (which is discussed further below), the Conference Report points out that "the median debt-equity ratio for U.S. corporations is generally measured at less than 1.5 to 1."[8] The Conference Report further says that "many corporations with what can fairly be called typical capital structures have debt-equity ratios below [1.5 to 1]."[9]

A debt-equity ratio of 1.5 to 1 does not even approach the range where the Service would be concerned that the corporation might be overly leveraged and, therefore, the debt might be equity. This is demonstrated by the

---

4. *Id.*, at 13.

5. *Id.*, citing Drexel Burnham Lambert, *1989 High Yield Market Report: Financing America's Future* (1989).

6. *Id.*, citing First Boston, *High Yield Research* (2d Quarter Review (1989)).

7. Miller, *Leverage, supra* chapter 11, note 10, at 479. *See also*, C. Bruck, *The Predators Ball* (1989), which discusses many of the transactions (most of which involved publicly held corporations) in which junk bonds were issued through Drexel Burnham.

8. H.R. Conf. Rep. No. 386, 101st Cong., 1st Sess., 67 (1989) [hereinafter cited as "1989 Conf. Rep."].

9. *Id.*

safe harbor for characterizing straight debt as debt (and not equity) under the Treasury's previously proposed but withdrawn regulations under Section 385.[10] These regulations provided that straight debt would be treated as debt if the corporation's outside debt to equity ratio did not exceed 10 to 1 and its inside ratio did not exceed 3 to 1. The outside ratio included all debt, whereas the inside ratio included only debt held by shareholders. The inside safe harbor provided for twice as much debt as the 1.5 to 1 ratio, which the Conference Report says is more than such ratio in the "typical capital structure."[11]

The point is that junk debt and excessive leverage do not generally arise in the context of the conduct by a corporation of its normal operating functions. Rather, junk debt and excessive leverage is likely to arise in an equity conversion transaction, in particular those involving publicly held corporations. Consequently, this proposal does not prohibit the issuance of junk debt for the purpose of expanding a business, such as the junk debt issued by MCI[12] for the purpose of expanding its long-distance telephone operations and thereby making it better able to compete with AT&T. Further, as indicated in the next section, there are sound reasons for applying the rules here only to acquisitions of publicly held corporations.

Justification of Exception for Equity Conversion Transactions Involving Closely Held Corporations, Divisions, and Subsidiaries

Acquisitions of closely held corporations and acquisitions of divisions and subsidiaries of publicly held corporations are not subject to the interest limitation rules suggested here. The motives for such transactions are likely to be closer to the strategic business purposes that drive the acquisition of bricks and mortar than to the speculative purposes that drive many debt financed acquisitions of publicly held corporations.

There is clear evidence that LBO transactions involving the acquisitions of divisions and subsidiaries of publicly held corporations tend to be efficiency enhancing. As pointed out in a study of such transactions by Professors Ravenscraft and Scherer:

> The behavioral effects of moving from conglomerate ownership to this high-risk, high-potential-gain environment were striking. Cost-cutting opportunities that had previously gone unexploited were seized. Austere offices were substituted for lavish ones. Staffs were cut back sharply. New and more cost-effective field sales organizations

---

10. Former Prop. Treas. Reg. § 1.385–6(g)(3) (1981).

11. 1989 Conf. Rep., *supra* note 8, at 63.

12. MCI Prospectus (dated April 8, 1986).

were adopted. Inexpensive computer services were found to substitute for expensive in-house operations. Make versus buy decisions were reevaluated, and lower-cost alternatives were embraced. Efforts were made to improve labor-management relations. . . . Tight inventory controls were implemented. . . . [13]

Another study of management led LBOs of divisions found that such transactions "1) represent an efficient reallocation of corporate resources to higher valued uses and 2) allow parent company stockholders to share in the expected benefits from this ownership change."[14]

Acquisitions of closely held firms in LBOs are likely to promote efficiency for some of the same reasons that apply to acquisitions of divisions and subsidiaries.

The imposition of limits on the deductibility of interest in LBO transactions involving the acquisition of closely held corporations would (at least to a degree) deter the alienability of such firms. It is economically important for the owners of closely held corporations to have an avenue to sell their shares because the possibility of a future sale is oftentimes one of the driving forces behind the entrepreneurial spirit. On the other hand, a shareholder of a publicly held corporation can generally sell his or her shares in the market.

Further, as pointed out by Professor Miller, LBO acquisitions of closely held firms have for a long time been a popular way of disposing of such firms.[15] The same is true of LBOs involving the acquisition of divisions and subsidiaries.

If it were not for the wave of LBO takeovers of publicly held firms in the 1980s, it is likely that there would be no serious concern today about LBOs involving closely held corporations, divisions, and subsidiaries. It appears that the reason no discernible problems have arisen with such LBOs is that

---

13. David J. Ravenscraft and F. M. Scherer, *Mergers, Self-Offs, and Economic Efficiency* 154 (The Brookings Institution, 1987) [hereinafter cited as "Ravenscraft and Scherer, *Economic Efficiency*"].

14. Gailen L. Hite and Michael R. Vetsuypens, *Management Buyouts of Divisions and Shareholders Wealth*, 44 J. Fin. 953, 969 (1989).

15. Miller, *Leverage, supra* chapter 11, note 10, at 479. Such transactions may also present policy concerns, but any such concerns are not of the same magnitude as the concerns presented by transactions like the takeover of RJR Nabisco. Also, this book does not address the general questions of the proper rules for distinguishing between debt and equity. For a suggestion in this regard, *see* Thompson, *Suggested Approach to the Debt/Equity, supra* chapter 10, note 5. Although the appropriate role of debt generally in the corporate tax structure presents significant policy questions, this book is limited to the appropriate treatment of debt used in equity conversion transactions of publicly held corporations.

the providers of credit for such acquisitions (*e.g.*, banks, insurance companies, and the sellers) have an economic incentive to ensure that the transactions are not overly leveraged. Thus, notwithstanding the tax deduction for interest the lenders have a clear incentive to insist upon an adequate amount of equity. As discussed below, this does not appear to have been the case with the junk bond market.

Credit Market Failure in Acquisitions of Publicly Held Firms

LBOs involving the acquisition of publicly held firms may also be efficiency enhancing.[16] Many such transactions are, however, excessively leveraged. This excessive leverage seems to have resulted from a failure of the purchasers of junk bonds (particularly thrifts and insurance companies) to insist upon adequate levels of equity. Thus, there has been a failure in the credit markets.

Klarman and Lowenstein make the following assertion concerning this market failure:

> Thrifts and insurance companies are attracted to junk bonds by the prospect of high current returns. Federal insurance of thrift deposits had tended to foster a 'heads I win, tails you lose' attitude in thrift executives vis-à-vis the U.S. government. If they buy junk bonds, they currently earn fat spreads and fat salaries. If the bonds don't default, they earn high returns and become rich. If the junk bonds eventually default, the government bears virtually all of the losses.
>
> . . . . .
>
> Many insurance companies invest policyholders' funds in junk bonds. Policyholders assume that insurers are investing their money prudently, and have virtually no knowledge of the insurer's assets un-

---

16. *See, e.g.*, Lichtenberg and Siegel, *The Effects of Leveraged Buyouts on Productivity*, *supra* chapter 11, note 16, at 191 (finding that total factor productivity is significantly higher in the first three years after an LBO than in any of the prior eight years). *See also*, Michael C. Jensen, *Eclipse of the Public Corporation*, 67 Harv. Bus. Rev. 61 (Sept.–Oct. 1989) [hereinafter cited as "Jensen, *Eclipse of the Public Corporation*"]. Jensen says that private corporations "resolve[] the weakness of the public corporation—the conflict between owners and managers over the control and use of the corporate resources. These organizations are making remarkable gains in operating efficiencies, employee productivity and shareholder value." *Id.*, at 61–62. *But see*, David J. Ravenscraft and F. M. Scherer, *Life After Takeover*, XXXVI J. Ind. Econ. 147 (1987) [hereinafter cited as "Ravenscraft and Scherer, *Life After Takeover*"] (finding that nine years after takeover by tender offer, targets "performed appreciably less well" than before the takeover. *Id.*, at 154).

derlying their policy. The lure of high current returns and a low historical default rate is hard for many insurance companies to resist.[17]

The same point is made by Professor Markowitz, one of the winners of the 1990 Nobel Prize in economics:

> The S&L structure encouraged gambling by S&L managements with S&L funds. The risks they took were in real estate and junk bonds. The game was structured so that if bets were won on average, then the S&L and its management gained; if they lost, then the U.S. taxpayer lost.
> A similar game was available to some insurance companies. A good example is Fred Carr's First Executive Corp. As Ms. Bruck tells us in 'The Predators' Ball,' Mr. Carr was one of Mr. Milken's best customers. The money with which Mr. Carr bought junk bonds was mostly the reserves of insurance policyholders. As with S&Ls, Fred Carr bore little of the risk of the junk bonds. The risk was principally borne by the policyholders, who were not warned of the risk.[18]

First Executive, which Professor Markowitz refers to, is now in bankruptcy because of overinvestments in junk bonds and the same is true of many S&Ls. It has been reported that one-fifth of Executive Life's junk bonds will default in 1991 and 15 percent in 1992.[19]

This absence of risk has also been noted by the well-known mergers and acquisitions lawyer, Martin Lipton, who points out that "the relative ease of obtaining acquisition financing and leveraged buyout fund capital allowed acquirors to make risky acquisitions with little of their own money invested, and thus little downside risk to themselves."[20]

Adoption of the proposals here could help prevent the future bankruptcy of insurance companies like First Executive and other potential investors in junk bonds by making it less likely that the issuers of acquisition indebted-

---

17. Seth A. Klarman and Louis Lowenstein, *Junk Bonds: It's Too Soon to Tell*, ch. 18 in Edward I. Altman, *The High Yield Debt Market* 223, 236 (Dow Jones-Irwin, 1990) [the book is hereinafter cited as "Altman, *The High Yield Debt Market*"].

18. Harry M. Markowitz, *Markets and Morality*, The Wall Street Journal, May 14, 1991, at A22, col. 3. *But see*, Miller, *Leverage, supra* chapter 11, note 10, at 487–88 (generally extolling the virtues of junk bond financing).

19. Frederick Rose, *Executive Life Had a Deficit at Year End*, Wall Street Journal, A3 June 7, 1991, at A3, col. 1.

20. Martin Lipton and Steven A. Rosenblum, *A New System of Corporate Governance: The Quinquennial Election of Directors*, 58 U. Chi. L. Rev. 187, 200 (1991) [hereinafter cited as "Lipton and Rosenblum, *A New System of Corporate Governance*"].

ness will become excessively leveraged and, therefore, particularly susceptible to bankruptcy.[21] Thus, the rules proposed here may be viewed as statutorily mandated prudent lender rules for LBOs and related transactions
involving public corporations. These rules would make it more likely that
acquiring corporations will have a sufficient amount of equity at risk in
transactions. Consequently, it can be expected that acquirors would only
pursue transactions that make economic sense.

In the words of one of the preeminent financial economists and defenders
of LBOs, Professor Jensen of the Harvard Business School, junk bonds "reflect more of the risk borne by shareholders in the typical public company."[22] Professor Miller, the Nobel Laureate, makes the same point: "The
high nominal yields [on junk bonds], in short, were essentially risk premiums."[23] Professor Miller illustrates the point by an example in which 40
percent of a corporation's shareholders convert their shares to subordinated
junk debt.[24] The return on this junk debt is greater than the return on the
firm's nonjunk debt and less than the expected returns on the equity. He
says that the results would be the same if preferred stock had been issued
instead of the junk debt. He then goes on to say: "Preferred stocks, in fact,
were effectively the junk bonds of finance . . . prior to the 1930's when the
steep rise in corporate tax rates made them less attractive than tax-deduct-
ible, interest-bearing securities of equivalent priority."[25]

This economic analysis leads to the conclusion that junk debt is the economic equivalent of equity. Although this reasoning could support a rule
that denied the deduction for interest on all junk debt, the proposal here
only disallows the interest on junk debt issued in acquisitions of publicly
held corporations. This is the kind of debt that led to the present concerns
with LBOs.

Curtailment of Interest Deduction as a Source of Takeover Premiums

It can be expected that the adoption of these proposals will take some of
the premium out of many transactions in corporate control. But this is not
bad.

Professor Kaplan has studied management led LBOs occurring during
the period 1980 to 1985 in which publicly held firms were taken private. He

---

21. S&Ls are now prohibited from investing in junk bonds. *See, e.g.,* Soh-Yung
M. Kim Note, *Evaluation of FIRREA's Impact on Thrift Investment in Junk Bonds* 10
Ann. Rev. Banking L. 547, 569 (1991) [hereinafter cited as "Evaluation of
FIRREA"].

22. Jensen, *Eclipse of the Public Corporation, supra* note 16, at 69.

23. Miller, *Leverage, supra* chapter 11, note 10, at 481–82.

24. *Id.,* at 483.

25. *Id.,* at 483, note 2.

found that in these transactions the interest deduction accounted for 129 percent of the premiums paid assuming (1) the 46 percent corporate tax rate that was then in effect, and (2) the increase in debt was permanent.[26] If the debt was assumed to be repaid in 8 years, the interest deduction accounted for 40 percent of the premium.[27] With an assumed 30 percent tax rate and permanent debt, the interest deduction accounted for 84.5 percent of the premium, and with a 30 percent rate and an assumed 8-year repayment period, the interest deduction accounted for 26 percent of the premium. These findings are summarized in the following table:

The Corporate Tax Rate

Debt Maturity	46%	30%
	Interest Shield as percentage of Premium	
Permanent Debt	129%	84.5%
Eight Years	40%	26%

As Professor Kaplan acknowledges,[28] the interest deduction is an "important source of wealth gains,"[29] that is, the premiums paid, in the transactions. When the depreciation benefit from the step-up in basis of assets (which could be accomplished prior to the repeal of the *General Utilities* doctrine by the Tax Reform Act of 1986) was added to the interest deduction, tax benefits accounted for 142.6 percent of the premiums paid assuming a 46 percent rate and permanent debt.[30]

A large part of the premiums received by the shareholders in LBO transactions is attributable to the abusive use of the tax subsidy for interest. This abusive use arises from the excessive use of debt in LBO transactions, which has unreasonably eroded the corporate tax base. If a more rationale rule governed the deductibility of interest, the target's shareholders would not

---

26. Steven Kaplan, *Management Buyouts: Evidence on Taxes as a Source of Value*, 44 J. Fin. 611, 617 (1989) [hereinafter cited as "Kaplan, *MBOs and Taxes*"].

27. *Id.*

28. *Id.*, at 630.

29. *Id.* Professor Miller says, however, that "taxes savings alone cannot plausibly account for the observed LBO premiums." Miller, *Leverage, supra* chapter 11, note 10, at 480.

30. *Id.*, at 623.

receive tax driven premiums, and the transactions would make much more economic sense.

Outline of the General Rules

Dividend and redemption transactions can be used to accomplish the same purpose as a stock acquisition. For that reason, in structuring a rule to deal with equity conversion transactions, it is necessary to consider both (1) transactions in which debt is issued to effect a dividend or redemption of a stand-alone public corporation,[31] and (2) transactions in which debt is issued to acquire the stock or assets of a stand-alone public corporation.

Under the proposal regarding dividends and redemptions, no deduction is allowed for interest on debt that is directly or indirectly issued in (or in facilitation of) an extraordinary redemption or extraordinary dividend of a stand-alone, publicly traded corporation. This proposal is implemented by amendments to Section 163, which are contained in appendix C. These rules are explored below.

Under the proposal regarding stock and asset acquisitions, no deduction is allowed for interest paid on excessive debt or on junk debt issued directly or indirectly for the purpose of making (1) a stock acquisition of a stand-alone, publicly traded target corporation, or (2) an acquisition of substantially all the assets of a stand-alone, publicly traded target corporation.

Acquisition debt is excessive if the debt exceeds 75 percent of the acquisition price of the stock or assets. No interest deduction is allowed on debt in excess of the 75 percent threshold. The purpose of this excessive debt rule is to make it more likely that a significant amount of equity will be at risk in every acquisition of a publicly held target corporation. The presence of a substantial equity cushion reduces the risk of bankruptcy and likely would be required by any prudent lender.

This 75 percent debt limitation or 25 percent equity requirement is consistent with Federal Reserve guidelines which classify a loan as "highly leveraged" if the loan is issued in an LBO, acquisition, or recapitalization and as a result the subject corporation has a capitalization of 75 percent debt or a doubling of liabilities to an amount equal to at least 50 percent of its capitalization.[32] Although these guidelines were discontinued after June 30, 1992,[33] the bank supervisory agencies continue to use this definition of

31. A stand-alone corporation is a nonsubsidiary corporation. However, a stand-alone corporation may own the stock of subsidiaries.

32. *SEC Staff Report on Junk Bonds, supra* note 3, at 29, footnote 34 citing American Banker, Nov. 9, 1989, at 23.

33. Department of the Treasury, Office of Comptroller of the Currency, Federal

highly leveraged transactions "for assessing individual credits that finance corporate restructuring and for evaluating internal processes for initiating and reviewing these credits."[34]

Junk debt as defined in these proposals is debt with (1) an unusually long maturity period, (2) a large amount of deferred interest due to original issue discount, (3) a large portion of its value attributable to a convertibility feature, (4) an exceedingly high interest rate, (5) a contingent interest feature, or (6) a payment-in-kind feature. For the first three types of debt the entire instrument is treated as junk debt, and therefore, all the interest with respect to such instruments is disallowed. For the last three types, only the portion of the principal that is attributable to the excessive interest, contingent interest, or payment-in-kind amount is treated as junk debt. Thus, the instrument is divided between the junk debt and nonjunk debt, and only the interest with respect to the junk debt portion (*i.e.*, the excessive, contingent, and payment-in-kind interest) is nondeductible.

These rules do not prevent an acquiring corporation from issuing in an acquisition either debt in excess of the 75 percent limit or junk debt. As a practical matter, however, the acquiring corporation can be expected to attempt to keep its debt below the limit and to avoid the use of junk debt; the acquiring corporation will not want to be obligated to make interest payments for which no deduction is allowed.

These rules would replace the present Section 279, which disallows the interest deduction on certain corporate acquisition indebtedness. The Proposed Section 279 is contained in appendix D. These rules are explored later in this chapter.

Definition of Publicly Held Corporations to Which the Provisions Apply

Before fashioning the rules for dividends, redemptions, and acquisitions, it is first necessary to draw a line between publicly traded and privately traded corporations. This line could be drawn in many different places.

One approach would be to adopt the 35 shareholder limit that applies to S corporations.[35] As long as a corporation has no more than 35 shareholders and certain other conditions are satisfied, an election may be made to treat the corporation as an S corporation. If this election is made, the cor-

---

Deposit Insurance Corporation, Federal Reserve System, Notice Concerning *The Supervisory Definition of Highly Leveraged Transactions*, 57 F.R. 5040, (Feb 11, 1992).

34. *Id.*

35. *See* I.R.C. § 1361(b)(1)(A) (1991).

porate level tax generally does not apply, and the shareholders are taxable on their pro rata shares of the corporation's taxable income.

A similar 35 shareholder approach applies under Regulation D,[36] which provides a safe harbor for determining whether an issuance of securities qualifies as a private offering under the Securities Act of 1933. If the issuance qualifies as a private offering, the securities do not have to be registered with the SEC. Under Section 506 of Regulation D, which provides the private offering safe harbor, an issuer can sell securities to as many as 35 nonaccredited investors (*i.e.*, 35 small investors).

Another approach would be to follow the line drawn under the Securities Exchange Act of 1934 (Exchange Act) for determining corporations subject to the reporting requirements of that Act. Section 12(g) of the Exchange Act provides that any issuer that has both (1) 500 holders of its securities, and (2) assets of $1 million dollars, is subject to the reporting requirements, including the Williams Act[37] provisions, of the Act. This definition picks up all exchange traded corporations and a large number of corporations that have stock traded over the counter.

A similar approach would be to adopt the principle in Code Section 7704, which treats publicly traded partnerships as corporations, thus denying the benefit of pass-through of income and loss to the partners. Under Section 7704(b), a publicly traded partnership "means a partnership if (1) interest in such partnership are traded on an established securities market, or (2) interest in such partnership are readily tradeable on a secondary market (or the substantial equivalent thereof)." Under this approach, a publicly held corporation would be defined as a corporation the stock of which is traded on an established securities market or readily tradeable on a secondary market.

The 35 shareholder approach followed by the SEC in Regulation D and by the Code in defining an S corporation is a logical place to draw the line between publicly held and privately held firms. The manner of counting the number of shareholders should follow the shareholder counting rules in Regulation D. These rules are designed to treat a single economic unit as one shareholder.

This definition of publicly held corporation will ensure that the alienability of most small privately held corporations is not adversely affected by the adoption of the limitations proposed here. Also, this definition implicitly excludes from the applicability of the proposed limitation those C corporations that could probably satisfy (or could restructure to satisfy) the 35

---

36. Regulation D, Securities Act of 1933.

37. The Williams Act, 15 U.S.C. §§ 78m, 78n (West 1981), added Sections 13(d) and (e), and 14(d), (e), and (f) to the Exchange Act. These provisions regulate open market purchases and tender offers.

shareholder limit that applies to S corporations. Since the corporate level tax does not generally apply to S corporations, the S election is made for most corporations that can qualify as S corporations. Thus, as a practical matter, the proposals here would apply mostly to those C corporations that do not satisfy the 35 shareholder limitation that applies to S corporations.

Further, there is no demonstrated need to apply the rules proposed here to S corporations. Since S corporations are generally not subject to tax, it appears that leverage has not been used to erode the corporate tax base of such corporations.

This 35 shareholder rule may be too stringent in certain cases, and for that reason the Treasury should have the regulatory authority to relax the rule in appropriate circumstances.

If substantial abuses develop with this 35 shareholder rule, then the line should be redrawn. In the absence of clear evidence of abuse, however, it is not prudent to adopt broad-based rules that could adversely affect (1) the alienability of private corporations, and (2) the ability of entrepreneurs to participate in the market for control of such corporations.

The definition of publicly held corporation is set forth in Proposed Section 163(m), which is contained in appendix C and also as a note.[38]

Redemptions, Dividends, and Leveraged Recapitalizations

The rationale for the disallowance rule for extraordinary leveraged redemptions and extraordinary leveraged dividend transactions is overwhelming. For publicly held corporations, there appears to be no conceivable purpose for such a transaction other than either to defeat a hostile bid or to shift control to a group of insiders who do not tender their shares. Probably the only reason the management of Unocal would issue $6 billion of debt to its shareholders in redemption of their stock would be to thwart a takeover attempt.

Also, under the proposals here, interest is not allowed on debt issued as a dividend. There would rarely be a compelling business purpose for issuing a debt instrument as a dividend. Good business purposes exist, how-

---

38. Proposed Section 163(m). Definition of Publicly Held Corporation. A publicly held corporation means a corporation with more than 35 shareholders determined under the principles of Regulation D under the Securities Act of 1933. The Treasury is authorized to promulgate regulations (1) dealing with the determination of the number of shareholders, and (2) relaxing the 35 shareholder limitation in appropriate circumstances.

ever, for issuing debt to purchase a retiring or deceased shareholder's shares or to purchase shares pursuant to a buy sell agreement. Therefore, these transactions are not affected by this proposal. Also, debt issued to raise funds to pay regular or ordinary (as distinguished from extraordinary) dividends is not affected. Further, the proposals here do not change the treatment of non-debt financed redemptions and extraordinary dividends.[39]

More specifically, the proposal here is to eliminate completely the deduction for interest paid on debt issued directly or indirectly, for the purpose of making a distribution as a dividend on stock or as a redemption of stock, except for debt issued (1) to effectuate an ordinary redemption transaction (as specified in regulations), or (2) to pay in cash an ordinary dividend (as specified in regulations). This proposal is implemented by Proposed Sections 163(k) and 163(l). These sections are set out in appendix C (with commentary) and also in the notes.

Under Proposed Section 163(k),[40] a publicly held corporation is not allowed a deduction for interest paid or accrued on debt issued with respect to the corporation's stock (whether by way of dividend, redemption, or otherwise) unless such debt is issued in an ordinary redemption transaction. Thus, Proposed Section 163(k) deals with the direct issuance by a corporation of debt instruments to its shareholders in respect of their stock. An ordinary redemption is to be defined in regulations to encompass the types of redemption transactions that corporations have traditionally used to redeem the interest of retiring or deceased shareholders. Under this proposal, Unocal would not be allowed a deduction for the interest on the debt issued in its recapitalization.

Under Proposed Section 163(l),[41] a publicly held corporation is not allowed a deduction for the interest on debt instruments issued directly or

---

39. Such transactions would, however, be subject to the ALI's minimum tax on distributions. *See* chapter 11, at 151.

40. Proposed Section 163(k). Extraordinary Dividends and Redemptions. In the case of a publicly held corporation, as defined in subsection (m), no deduction shall be allowed to such corporation (or to any member of such corporation's affiliated group within the meaning of section 1504(a)) for interest paid or accrued on a debt instrument that is issued with respect to stock in such corporation, except for debt that is issued for the purpose of making an ordinary redemption of the stock of the corporation. The Treasury shall promulgate regulations delineating the meaning of ordinary redemption.

41. Proposed Section 163(l). Ordinary Dividends and Redemptions. In the case of a publicly held corporation as defined in subsection (m), no deduction shall be allowed to such corporation (or to any member of such corporation's affiliated group within the meaning of section 1504(a)) for interest paid or accrued on a debt instrument that is directly or indirectly issued for the purpose of raising funds in order to make a distribution (whether by way of redemption, dividend, or other-

indirectly, to make extraordinary redemptions or to pay extraordinary dividends. Thus, Proposed Section 163(l) deals with situations in which a corporation issues debt to raise cash to make a distribution in respect of its stock.

Ordinary redemptions are to be defined in the regulations the same as such term is defined in Proposed Section 163(k), that is, as standard-type redemptions of the stock of retiring or deceased shareholders. An ordinary dividend is, also, to be defined in regulations; the definition should limit the use of debt financed dividends to those that are standard and ordinary for the particular corporation. The regulations are to address the question of whether debt is issued "directly or indirectly" for the proscribed purpose.

Under Proposed Section 163(l), Unocal could not avoid the effect of Proposed Section 163(k) by issuing debt for cash and using the cash to redeem its stock; the interest on the debt would be nondeductible. Also, Unocal could not have issued debt for cash and then used the cash to pay a $6 billion dividend; again, the interest on the debt would not be deductible. Unocal could, however, issue debt in order to make a regular quarterly dividend payment without giving rise to a limitation on the deductibility of the interest on such debt.

Stock and Asset Acquisitions

Two rules are proposed here to apply to stock and asset acquisitions of publicly held corporations as defined in Proposed Section 163(m): (1) the excessive debt rule, and (2) the junk debt rule.

The excessive debt rule denies the deduction for interest on any acquisition debt to the extent such debt exceeds 75 percent of the acquisition price of (1) control stock of a publicly held corporation, or (2) substantially all the assets of a publicly held corporation. The junk debt rule denies the deduction for interest on such debt issued, directly or indirectly, to acquire control stock or substantially all the assets of a publicly held corporation.

These rules are implemented by Proposed Section 279, which is proposed to replace the current Section 279. This provision is set out in the

---

wise) with respect to the stock in such corporation, except for debt that is issued for the purpose of (1) making in cash an ordinary redemption of the stock of the corporation, or (2) paying in cash an ordinary dividend in respect of the stock of the corporation. The Treasury shall promulgate regulations delineating the meaning of the terms ordinary dividend and ordinary redemption and setting forth rules for determining whether debt is issued "directly or indirectly" for the proscribed purpose.

notes and in appendix D. The present Section 279 is both a toothless tiger[42] and a trap for the unwary; it should, therefore, be replaced.

As is the case with the present Section 279, the interest disallowance rule of Proposed Section 279 does not treat debt that is subject to its provisions as equity; only the interest deduction is disallowed. The disallowed interest is not treated as a dividend and does not qualify for the dividends received deduction.[43] This should be an additional incentive for taxpayers to structure acquisitions with sufficient equity in order to avoid the impact of Proposed Section 279.

The disallowance of deduction rule is set forth in Proposed Section 279(a).[44] Proposed Section 279(b)[45] deals with the definition of "corporate acquisition indebtedness" and the related concepts of control stock, substantially all, and publicly held corporation. The definition of "excessive debt" is set forth in Proposed Section 279(c),[46] and "junk debt" is defined in Proposed Section 279(d).[47] General regulatory authority is contained in Proposed Section 279(e).[48]

---

42. 1987 House Bill, *supra* chapter 11, note 52, at 1085.

43. Corporate owners of shares qualify for a 70 percent, 80 percent, or 100 percent dividend received deduction under Section 243. *See Federal Taxation of Business Enterprises, supra* chapter 1, note 20, at §§ 9:10, 9:11.

44. Proposed Section 279. (a) General Rule. No deduction shall be allowed for interest paid or accrued with respect to the principal of corporate acquisition indebtedness that is treated as excessive debt or junk debt.

45. Proposed Section 279. (b) Corporate Acquisition Indebtedness. Corporate acquisition indebtedness is indebtedness issued directly or indirectly by a corporation or any members of such corporation's affiliated group (as defined in Section 1504(a)) for the purpose of acquiring (1) more than 5 percent of any class of stock of a publicly held corporation, as defined in section 163(m), or (2) substantially all (applying the 90 percent/70 percent test set out in section 368(a)(4)(G)) of the assets of a publicly held corporation, as defined in section 163(m). The Treasury shall promulgate regulations setting forth rules for determining whether debt is issued "directly or indirectly" for the proscribed purpose. The Treasury may by regulations exempt from this section acquisitions of stock made solely for investment purposes.

46. Proposed Section 279. (c) Excessive Debt. Excessive debt is that portion of the principal on any corporate acquisition indebtedness that exceeds 75 percent of the purchase price of either the stock or assets purchased with such corporate acquisition indebtedness. In determining the amount of excessive debt, the principal amount of any debt that is treated as junk debt under subsection (d) shall be treated as equity.

47. Proposed Section 279. (d) Junk Debt. Junk debt is the portion of the principal of any corporate acquisition indebtedness specified in the following paragraphs:

(1) Excessive Maturity. If the average weighted life (determined under regulations) at the time of issuance of corporate acquisition indebtedness exceeds 10 years,

In stock acquisitions, the excessive debt and junk debt rules apply to any acquisition by one person (or group of related persons) of more than 5 percent of the outstanding stock of a publicly held corporation. Such a transaction is considered an acquisition of control stock. (*See* Proposed section 279(b).)[49] This 5 percent threshold is the same as the one that applies under Section 13(d) of the Williams Act amendments to the Exchange Act. Under Section 13(d), any person (or group) that acquires more than 5 percent of the stock of certain publicly held corporations is required to file a

---

then the entire principal of such corporate acquisition indebtedness shall be treated as junk debt.

(2) Minimum Interest Paid Currently. If the interest on corporate acquisition indebtedness that is contractually payable currently (as determined under regulations) is at any time during the term of such instrument less than the applicable federal rate (determined under section 1274) at the time such instrument is issued, then the entire principal of such instrument shall be treated as junk debt.

(3) Convertible Instruments. In the case of corporate acquisition indebtedness that is directly or indirectly convertible into stock of the issuer (or of another member of the issuer's affiliated group as defined in Section 1504(a)), if the interest that is contractually payable currently (as determined under regulations) is at any time during the term of such instrument less than 90 percent of the applicable federal rate (determined under section 1274) at the time such instrument is issued, then the entire principal amount of such corporate acquisition indebtedness shall be treated as junk debt.

(4) High Yield. If, at the time of issuance, the yield to maturity (determined under section 1274) of any corporate acquisition indebtedness exceeds an amount equal to the average yield to maturity on bonds with an equivalent maturity that are rated Baa by Moody's Investor Service (or are similarly rated by a rating agency of equivalent standing), then the portion of the principal that is under regulations attributable to the excess interest shall be treated as junk debt. The Secretary shall determine monthly the average yield to maturity on bonds rated Baa for various maturity periods. Such determinations shall be consistent with the provisions governing the determination of the applicable federal rate under section 1274(d).

(5) Contingent Interest. If the payment of interest on any corporate acquisition indebtedness is in any way contingent on earnings, performance, or any similar factor, then the portion of the principal that is under regulations attributable to the contingent interest shall be treated as junk debt.

(6) Payments in Kind. If the interest on any corporate acquisition indebtedness is paid or possibly payable in stock or securities of the issuer, then the portion of the principal of such corporate acquisition indebtedness that is under regulations attributable to the stock or securities shall be treated as junk debt.

48. Proposed Section 279. (e) Regulatory Authority. The Secretary shall promulgate such regulations as may be necessary to carry out the purposes of this section, including regulations to ensure that foreign corporations do not directly or indirectly avoid the purposes embodied in this section.

49. *See* Proposed Section 279(b), *supra* note 45, and appendix D.

statement with the SEC and the corporation explaining, among other things, the purpose of the acquisition. The 5 percent threshold in the Williams Act was chosen because Congress believed that an acquisition of more than 5 percent of a public corporation's stock could signal a change in control.

This 5 percent threshold seems appropriate for determining when the excessive debt rule applies. The acquisition of more than 5 percent of the stock of a publicly held corporation is likely not to be purely for investment motives and is likely to have some change of control purpose or effect. Consequently, it is appropriate to apply the excessive debt rule to such acquisitions. The same is true of the junk debt rule.

Pursuant to regulations, an exception applies to this 5 percent rule for acquisitions that are purely for investment purposes, such as most acquisitions by investment companies and trust departments of banks.

For asset acquisitions, the excessive debt and junk debt rules apply only to an acquisition by an acquiring corporation (or related persons) of substantially all of the assets of a publicly held corporation. (*See* Proposed Section 279(b).)[50] Substantially all is to be interpreted the same as it is interpreted for the current (C) reorganization under Section 368(a)(1)(C), that is, 90 percent of the target's net assets and 70 percent of its gross assets, taking into account all assets held by the target at the time the transaction was first contemplated.[51] Thus, the excessive debt and junk debt rules do not apply to acquisitions of only part (*i.e.*, less than substantially all) of the assets of a publicly held corporation.

Since corporate acquisition indebtedness includes debt issued "directly or indirectly" for the purpose of making a covered stock or asset acquisition, the term encompasses (1) debt issued by an acquiring corporation to raise part of the equity for an acquisition (*i.e.*, equity loans),[52] (2) debt issued to refinance previously issued corporate acquisition indebtedness and to replace equity that was previously used to effectuate such an acquisition, and (3) any assumed debt that was incurred in anticipation of the acquisition. The Treasury is authorized to issue regulations dealing with the scope of the "directly and indirectly" concepts.

Junk debt is defined in such a way as to deny all or part of the interest deductions for acquisition debt that has (1) substantial equity features, (2) a substantial deferral of the payment of interest, (3) an unusually long ma-

---

50. *Id.*

51. *See* Rev. Proc. 77–37, 1977–2 C.B. 568 and Proposed Section 368(a)(4)(G), appendix B. The historic asset concept in Proposed Section 368(a)(4)(G) has no applicability here.

52. For an illustration of equity loans see the discussion of the Campeau acquisition of Federated, *supra* chapter 11 text accompanying notes 11 and 12.

turity period, or (4) an unusually high rate of interest. (*See* Proposed Section 279(d).)[53] The rules are designed to be bright line rules that can be clearly understood.

More specifically, junk debt is corporate debt that (1) is issued, directly or indirectly, for the purpose of acquiring either control stock or substantially all the assets of a publicly held corporation (acquisition debt) (*see* Proposed Section 279(b)),[54] *and* (2) is described in any of the following paragraphs. (*See* Proposed Section 279(d).)[55]

The first three paragraphs treat the entire acquisition debt as junk debt, thereby denying the deduction for all the interest paid with respect to such debt. The last three paragraphs treat only a part of the acquisition debt as junk debt, thereby denying the deductions for only a part of the interest.

Debt with Average Weighted Life in Excess of 10 Years

Under Proposed Section 279(d)(1),[56] acquisition debt that has an average weighted life of greater than 10 years is treated as junk debt. Acquisition debt includes any loan (or replacement loan) that, pursuant to regulations, is treated as acquisition debt.

The theory of this rule is that the average third-party creditor is not going to provide acquisition debt with an excessively long maturity period. Any such debt takes on the form of preferred stock and, therefore, should be treated as equity.

One reason for the ten-year cutoff period for determining whether corporate acquisition indebtedness is subject to the interest disallowance rule is that standard preferred stock that has an average weighted life of at least 10 years is generally treated as preferred stock for federal incomes tax purposes.[57] It is appropriate, therefore, to treat corporate acquisition indebtedness with a term of at least 10 years as the economic equivalent of preferred stock.

---

53. *See* Proposed Section 279(d), *supra* note 47 and appendix D.
54. *See* Proposed Section 279(b), *supra* note 45 and appendix D.
55. *See* Proposed Section 279(d), *supra* note 47 and appendix D.
56. Proposed Section 279(d)(1).
(1) Excessive Maturity. If the average weighted life (determined under regulations) at the time of issuance of corporate acquisition indebtedness exceeds 10 years, then the entire principal of such corporate acquisition indebtedness shall be treated as junk debt.
57. *See, e.g.*, previously issued and withdrawn Prop. Treas. Reg. § 1.385–10(a) (1980) (treating a standard preferred with at least a ten-year average weighted life as preferred); *Ragland Investment Co v. Commissioner*, 52 T.C. 867 (1969) (preferred with a sinking fund of 5 percent a year commencing in fifth year treated as preferred notwithstanding preferred redeemed after only a couple of years).

Minimum Amount of Interest Paid Currently

Under Proposed Section 279(d)(2),[58] acquisition debt is treated as junk debt unless at the time of issuance interest in an amount equal to the applicable federal rate (AFR) is contractually payable annually over the life of the debt. This test is based on the issue price of the debt instrument. Thus, this rule treats, for example, zero coupon bonds that are acquisition debt as equity. Also, acquisition debt with a substantial amount of original issue discount (OID) would be treated as equity.

This rule is based on the theory that if the payment of a significant amount of interest is put off for a substantial period, the instrument automatically takes on the character of equity. Thus, for example, under this rule, acquisition debt is treated as equity if the AFR is 10 percent and the debt is issued with (1) an issue price of $80, (2) a stated redemption price at maturity (SRPM) of $100, and (3) a current interest payment of $5 annually. The annual interest payment of $5 is not at least equal to the AFR times the issue price of $80 (*i.e.*, 10 percent of $80 is $8).

This rule applies independently of Sections 163(e)(5) and (i), which disallow the interest on applicable high yield discount obligations.[59] These are obligations with a large amount of original issue discount.

Treatment of Convertible Instruments

Under Proposed Section 279(d)(3),[60] any acquisition debt instrument that is directly or indirectly[61] convertible into stock of the issuer or related

---

58. Proposed Section 279(d)(2).

(2) Minimum Interest Paid Currently. If the interest on corporate acquisition indebtedness that is contractually payable currently (as determined under regulations) is at any time during the term of such instrument less than the applicable federal rate (determined under section 1274) at the time such instrument is issued, then the entire principal of such instrument shall be treated as junk debt.

59. For a discussion of applicable high yield discount obligations, *see Federal Taxation of Business Enterprises, supra* chapter 1, note 20, at § 4:38.

60. Proposed Section 279(d)(3).

(3) Convertible Instruments. In the case of corporate acquisition indebtedness that is, directly or indirectly, convertible into stock of the issuer (or of another member of the issuer's affiliated group as defined in section 1504(a)), if the interest that is contractually payable currently (as determined under regulations) is at any time during the term of such instrument less than 90 percent of the applicable federal rate (determined under section 1274) at the time such instrument is issued, then the entire principal amount of such corporate acquisition indebtedness shall be treated as junk debt.

61. This "indirectly" concept is to be dealt with in the regulations. For example, in appropriate cases, debt instruments issued with warrants may be treated as indirectly convertible.

party and that provides for interest to be paid annually at a rate less than at least 90 percent of the AFR is treated as equity. Thus, for example, if the AFR is 10 percent, and a convertible acquisition debt instrument with an issue price and an SRPM of $100 is issued with an interest rate of 7.5 percent, the instrument is treated as equity. On the other hand, if the instrument has an interest rate of at least 9 percent, it is treated as debt, unless the instrument is treated as junk debt under one of the other rules.

The rationale for this rule is that once the convertibility factor becomes a significant part of the value of the instrument, the instrument should be treated as equity.[62]

Excessively High Interest

Under Proposed Section 279(d)(4),[63] if at the time of issuance of acquisition debt, the yield to maturity on such debt exceeds the average yield on bonds with an equivalent maturity that are rated Baa by Moody's Investor Service (or are similarly rated by an agency of equivalent standing), then the excess interest is treated as a payment in respect of junk debt and is, therefore, not deductible. This rule does not treat all the interest as nondeductible; the disallowed amount is only the portion of the total interest that exceeds the average yield to maturity on bonds with an equivalent maturity that are rated Baa.

As explained by one of the leading texts on corporate finance, bonds below Baa are noninvestment grade and are considered junk bonds.[64] Thus,

---

62. Under this rule, the ARCNs which were classified as equity in Rev. Rul. 83–98, 1983–2 C.B. 40, and which led to the withdrawal of the Section 385 regulations, would automatically be classified as equity, if they were corporate acquisition indebtedness.

63. Proposed Section 279(d)(4).

(4) High Yield. If, at the time of issuance, the yield to maturity (determined under section 1274) of any corporate acquisition indebtedness exceeds an amount equal to the average yield to maturity on bonds with an equivalent maturity that are rated Baa by Moody's Investor Service (or are similarly rated by a rating agency of equivalent standing), then the portion of the principal that is under regulations attributable to the excess interest shall be treated as junk debt. The Secretary shall determine monthly the average yield to maturity on bonds rated Baa for various maturity periods. Such determinations shall be consistent with the provisions governing the determination of the applicable federal rate under section 1274(d).

64. Richard A. Brealey and Stewart C. Myers, *Principles of Corporate Finance* 581 (4th ed. 1991) [hereinafter cited as "Brealey and Myers"]. Also, bonds rated less than BBB by Standard and Poor's are considered junk bonds. *See* Kaplan and Stein, *The Evolution of Buyout Pricing and Financial Structure in the 1980s* 21 (draft, April 22, 1991) [hereinafter cited as "Kaplan and Stein, *Buyout Evolution*"]. For a general discussion of bond ratings *see Evaluation of FIRREA, supra* note 21, at 553–555.

Proposed Section 279(d)(4) disallows the portion of the interest on corporate acquisition debt that causes the debt to be characterized as junk debt. This rule, in essence, treats the excess interest as an equity payment. This treatment is consistent both with (1) Professor Jensen's characterization of junk bonds as "reflect[ing] more of the risk borne by shareholders in the typical public company,"[65] and (2) Professor Miller's observation that the "high nominal yields on [junk bonds]...[are] essentially risk premiums."[66] Thus, the theory of this rule is that interest above a certain level is likely to be a surrogate for an equity return and, therefore, should not be deductible.

The effect of the rule should be to substantially reduce the use of junk debt in acquisition financing; the parties will not want to be subject to the interest disallowance rule. It can be expected that acquisitions will have a sufficient amount of equity so that the debt will not fall below a Baa rating.

This rule applies only if at the time of the initial issuance of the bonds[67] the yield to maturity on such bonds exceeds the average yield on bonds of an equivalent maturity rated Baa. Thus, the rule does not apply to "fallen angels," that is, bonds with an initial rating of Baa or better that have fallen into junk status.

Contingent Interest

Under Proposed Section 279(d)(5),[68] any contingent interest paid with respect to acquisition debt is treated as payable on junk debt and, therefore, is nondeductible. Thus, the only interest on acquisition debt that is deductible is interest that is payable in all events and which gives rise to a standard default upon nonpayment. The theory of this rule is that contingent payments inherently are an equity feature.[69] This provision does not affect the deductibility of interest that is not contingent.

Interest Paid in Stock or Securities of Issuer

Under Proposed Section 279(d)(6),[70] interest on acquisition debt that is paid (or possibly payable) in stock or securities of the issuer is considered

---

65. Jensen, *Eclipse of the Public Corporation, supra* note 16, at 69.

66. Miller, *Leverage, supra* chapter 11, note 10, at 481–82.

67. One study reports that although only one pre-1985 buyout used junk debt, over 54 percent of subsequent buyouts used such debt. *See* Kaplan and Stein, *Buyout Evolution, supra* note 64, at 21.

68. Proposed Section 279(d)(5).

(5) Contingent Interest. If the payment of interest on any corporate acquisition indebtedness is in any way contingent on earnings, performance, or any similar factor, then the portion of the principal that is under regulations attributable to the contingent interest shall be treated as junk debt.

69. *See, e.g., Farley Realty Corp. v. Commissioner*, 279 F.2d 701 (2d Cir. 1960).

70. Proposed Section 279(d)(6).

to be payable on junk debt. Therefore, such interest is nondeductible. Such debt is generally referred to as payment-in-kind or PIK bonds. The theory of this rule is that a prudent third-party lender would rarely agree to payment of interest with stock or securities of the issuer, and therefore, such instruments are inherently equity to the extent of the PIK interest. This rule does not affect the deductibility of any non-PIK interest.

This rule applies independently of the similar rule that applies under current law to applicable high yield discount obligations.[71]

Acquisitions by Foreign Corporations of U.S. Corporations[72]

As indicated in chapter 11, concern has been expressed that any limitation on the deductibility of interest on debt issued in an equity conversion transaction would create an unlevel playing field for foreign acquiring corporations and U.S. acquiring corporations. The unlevel field would exist if the interest limitation rules applied only to U.S. acquiring corporations.[73]

This concern was at least partially addressed by Congress with the enactment of Section 163(j) by the Revenue Reconciliation Act of 1989.[74] This section disallows the deduction for interest paid by a U.S. corporation to a related foreign corporation under the following circumstances: First, the U.S. subsidiary has a debt to equity ratio that exceeds 1.5 to 1.[75] Second, the U.S. subsidiary has substantial interest deductions relative to its taxable income.[76] Third, because of an exemption under a tax treaty, the interest is not subject to the 30 percent withholding tax that generally applies to payments of interest by U.S. persons to foreign persons.[77] Thus, if these conditions are satisfied, the U.S. subsidiary does not receive a deduction for interest payments to the foreign parent.

---

(6) Payments in Kind. If the interest on any corporate acquisition indebtedness is paid or possibly payable in stock or securities of the issuer, then the portion of the principal of such corporate acquisition indebtedness that is under regulations attributable to the stock or securities shall be treated as junk debt.

71. For a discussion of applicable high yield discount obligations *see Federal Taxation of Business Enterprises, supra* chapter 1, note 20, at § 4:38.

72. This section is based on, and an extension of, a concept first developed in Thompson, *A Suggested Approach to Debt/Equity, supra* chapter 11, note 5.

73. *See* chapter 11, at 149.

74. Revenue Reconciliation Act of 1989, Pub. L. No. 101–239, 103 Stat. 2106 (1989). *See, generally, Federal Taxation of Business Enterprises, supra* chapter 1, note 20, vol. 2, ch. 19, at § 19:18.

75. I.R.C. § 163(j)(2)(A)(ii) (1991).

76. I.R.C. § 163(j)(2)(B) (1991).

77. I.R.C. §§ 163(j)(3)(A), 871, 881, 1141, and 1442 (1991).

This provision applies generally and not just in the acquisition context. Although this provision should go a long way in addressing the concerns expressed about foreign acquirors avoiding U.S. interest limitation rules, it is possible that the provision may not be effective in all cases. For that reason a backstop to Section 163(j) is proposed here.

The following situation is one in which a foreign acquiring corporation could be given an advantage over a U.S. acquiring corporation that is subject to the interest limitation rules set out in Proposed Section 279:

An acquisition by a foreign corporation of a U.S. corporation is structured to accomplish the following two results. First, the income stream of the U.S. corporation is used to create deductible interest payments in the U.S., which payments are then used by the foreign acquiring corporation to service the interest on the acquisition indebtedness issued by such corporation in a foreign country. Second, because of the limitation in Proposed Section 279, there would have been no interest deduction on the foreign acquisition indebtedness if such debt had been issued in the United States.

It would appear that this type of situation could arise principally in a stock acquisition, such as is illustrated in the following example:

Foreign acquiring corporation (FAC) operates in country X, which has an effective corporate tax rate of 34 percent. Country X has an income tax treaty with the U.S. that provides for a zero withholding tax on cross border interest payments. FAC decides to make a bid for a U.S. target corporation (USTC) and plans to offer $26 billion cash which tops KKR's offer of $25 billion. The tax laws in country X permit interest deductions on junk bonds (country X junk bonds) which, under Proposed Section 279, would not give rise to an interest deduction if FAC were to issue such bonds in the U.S. FAC sells in country X $20 billion of junk bonds in order to raise part of the cash needed to complete the acquisition of USTC. Thus, FAC has an advantage over KKR because if KKR were to issue similar bonds in the U.S., there would be no interest deduction under Proposed Section 279. The $6 billion balance of the purchase price comes from FAC's retained earnings.

The acquisition is structured as follows. FAC forms a U.S. acquiring subsidiary (USAS), and transfers $26 billion to USAS in exchange for $20 billion in bonds (which constitute debt for U.S. tax purposes) and $6 billion of stock. USAS then acquires USTC for $26 billion. The excessive debt rule in Proposed Section 279(c) does not apply because at least 25 percent of the acquisition price is funded with equity. USAS and USTC constitute an affiliated group and file consolidated returns. Assume that the interest paid by USAS on its bonds is not limited by Section 163(j), which would be the case, *inter alia*, if the net interest expense of the USAS and USTC affiliated group did not exceed 50 percent of the group's adjusted taxable income.[78]

After the dust settles, FAC holds $20 billion of debt issued by USAS, and FAC has outstanding $20 billion in country X junk bonds. The interest paid by USAS on the $20 billion of pure debt bonds is deductible in the U.S. by the USAS and USTC affiliated group. There is no withholding tax on the interest paid by USAS to FAC because of the income tax treaty between the U.S. and country X. FAC has income in country X upon receipt of the interest payments with respect to such bonds, but it receives an offsetting interest deduction in country X on the payment of the interest on the country X junk bonds.

Thus, under this structure, the USAS and USTC affiliated group has deductible interest payments in the United States, which payments are then used by FAC to pay the interest on the country X junk bonds. This scheme provides FAC with an advantage over KKR or any other potential U.S. acquiror.

The above example is probably not the only way in which foreign acquiring corporations could have an advantage over U.S. acquiring corporations if Proposed Section 279 is adopted.[79]

In order to eliminate the use of the above type of transaction or any transaction that has a similar effect, a rule should be adopted that prevents the use of interest on debt issued by a U.S. corporation from funding interest payments (or deductible dividend payments) made by a foreign acquiring corporation with respect to foreign acquisition indebtedness. The limitation should apply only to the extent the foreign acquisition indebtedness would be subject to the interest limitation rules of Proposed Section 279 or would otherwise not be treated as indebtedness if it were issued in the U.S. This rule is referred to here as the look-through deduction rule.

This rule, applies to any transaction in which a foreign acquiring corporation directly or indirectly acquires the stock or assets of a U.S. corporation in a transaction described in Proposed Section 279(b) (*i.e.*, an acquisition of at least 5 percent of the stock or of substantially all the assets of a

---

78. *See* I.R.C. § 163(j)(2)(B) (1991).

79. Indeed, even under the present debt/equity rules and present Section 279, a foreign acquiring corporation could have an advantage over a U.S. acquiring corporation. For example, if in the above example country X permitted a deduction for dividends paid on stock and FAC raised the $26 billion acquisition price through the issuance of stock in country X, the interest paid by USAS on the debt held by FAC would, in essence, be used to pay the deductible dividends on the stock issued by FAC to make the acquisition.

publicly held corporation). The rule allows a deduction for interest paid with respect to debt issued directly or indirectly by a U.S. target corporation to the foreign acquiring corporation only to the extent that the foreign acquiring corporation satisfies one of the following conditions. First, it shows that the interest is neither directly nor indirectly used to pay interest on acquisition indebtedness issued by the foreign acquiring corporation in a foreign country. Second, it shows that the interest is paid on such acquisition indebtedness but such indebtedness is not the kind of debt that is subject to the interest limitation rules of Proposed Section 279.

Thus, in the above example, since FAC issued country X junk bonds to raise the $20 billion of the purchase price and the interest on such bonds would have been nondeductible under Proposed Section 279 if the bonds had been issued in the U.S., then under the look-through deductibility rule, no deduction is allowed for any of the interest payments on the $20 billion in debt that is issued by USAS to FAC.

The look-through deductibility rule also applies to any deductible dividends paid by the foreign corporation with respect to stock issued to raise the acquisition price.

This look-through deductibility rule, and any other rule that may be needed to ensure that foreign acquiring corporations do not have an unfair advantage over U.S. acquiring corporations can be implemented by the adoption of Proposed Section 279(e).[80] This provision will not, however, affect a foreign corporation's ability to deduct interest on foreign junk debt against foreign income. It only affects the deductibility of U.S. interest against U.S. income.

---

80. Proposed Section 279(e).

(e) Regulatory Authority. The Secretary shall promulgate such regulations as may be necessary to carry out the purposes of this section, including regulations to ensure that foreign corporations do not directly or indirectly avoid the purposes embodied in this section.

· ·

CHAPTER 13

Illustration of the Proposed Rules Regarding Equity Conversion Transactions

This chapter illustrates the application of the rules in chapter 12 to LBOs and other equity conversion transactions. It illustrates the applicability of Proposed Section 279 to debt financed acquisitions of publicly held corporations. Also this chapter illustrates the applicability of the debt financed dividend and redemption rules of Proposed Sections 163(k) and (l), which are backstops for the rules of Proposed Section 279. Finally, the complexity issue is addressed.

Effect of Proposed Section 279

The effect of the adoption of Proposed Section 279, which prohibits the use of excessive debt or junk debt in acquisitions, would be to ensure that corporate acquisitions are driven by the economic bona fides of the transactions and not by abusive use of the interest deduction. The adoption of these rules would not eliminate the use of sound debt financing in corporate mergers and acquisitions, but these rules would eliminate the use of clearly abusive techniques. The adoption of the proposed rules would redress the failure of the market place to properly restrict the use of junk bonds in corporate acquisitions by making it nonadvantageous to issue such bonds in acquisitions of publicly held corporations. As indicated above, the capital markets do not appear to have failed in policing the use of debt in acquisitions of closely held corporations, and for that reason, the proposals here do not apply to such corporations.

Acquisition debt that does not vary significantly from traditional types of debt could continue to be used in corporate acquisitions of publicly held corporations. For example, KKR could acquire another RJR Nabisco in an LBO; however:

1. There would have to be 25 percent equity in the deal, otherwise the interest deduction would be disallowed on the pure debt in excess of 75 percent of the acquisition price (*see* Proposed Sections 279(a) and (b));

2. The debt portion of the deal would have to have an average weighted life of no more than 10 years, otherwise the interest deduction would be disallowed on all of the debt (*see* Proposed Sections 279(a) and (d)(1));

3. The acquisition debt would have to pay interest currently at a level of the AFR in the case of nonconvertible debt (*see* Proposed Sections 279(a) and (d)(2)) and 90 percent of the AFR in the case of convertible debt (*see* Proposed Sections 279(a) and (d)(3)) otherwise the interest on such debt would be disallowed;

4. The interest on the debt could not exceed an amount equal to the average yield to maturity on bonds of comparable maturity with a Baa rating, otherwise the excess interest would be disallowed (*see* Proposed Sections 279(a) and (d)(4)); and

5. No deduction would be allowed for any contingent interest (*see* Proposed Sections 279(a) and (d)(5)) or interest that is payable in stock or securities of the issuer or a related party (*see* Proposed Sections 279(a) and (d)(6)).

Also, the excessive debt rule of Proposed Section 279(c) would apply in a transaction like Campeau's acquisition of Federated.[1] Campeau financed the $6.7 billion purchase price with only $193 million of real equity, which amounted to 3 percent of the purchase price. Campeau had $1.4 billion in nominal equity; however, $1.21 billion of this amount was raised through equity loans. These equity loans would be considered corporate acquisition indebtedness under the "indirect" concept in Proposed Section 279(b); consequently, they would not count as equity under the 25 percent equity requirement of Proposed Section 279(c).

Under the 25 percent equity rule, interest on $1.482 billion of Campeau's debt would have been disallowed. Consequently, it could be expected that Campeau would have either abandoned the deal or added at least $1.482 billion of real equity to the transaction, for a total equity of $1.675 billion (*i.e.*, 25 percent of $6.7 billion).

Professor Kaplan has found that if Campeau had used $1.59 billion in equity there would not have been a bankruptcy.[2] Therefore, if the excessive debt rule proposed here, which would have required $1.675 billion in equity, had applied to Campeau's acquisition, the bankruptcy of Federated would likely have been avoided.

---

1. Kaplan, *Campeau's Acquisition of Federated*, *supra* chapter 11, note 11, at 196.
2. *Id.*, at 143.

The adoption of Proposed Section 279 would not add undue complexity to corporate acquisitions of publicly held corporations. Indeed, in replacing the convoluted rules of present Section 279, the proposed changes would both move the Code in the direction of simplicity and replace an ineffective provision with rules that would effectively prevent the abusive use of debt in acquisition transactions. Since the rules do not apply to closely held corporations, the rules would not in any way curtail the flexibility in using debt in the acquisition of such corporations, or in the acquisition of divisions or subsidiaries.

The proposals here provide more rational rules regarding the deductibility of interest and should reduce takeover premiums only to the extent such premiums are attributable to the abusive use of the deduction for interest.

Finally, with respect to acquisitions by foreign corporations, the adoption of Proposed Section 279(e) will give the Treasury the authority to ensure that such corporations do not gain an unfair advantage over U.S. acquiring corporations by avoiding the interest disallowance rules contained in Proposed Section 279.

Effect of Proposed Sections 163(k) and (l)

Proposed Sections 163(k) and (l) provide backstops for Proposed Section 279. These sections disallow the interest deduction on any debt used in any redemption transaction or nonordinary dividend (leveraged recapitalization). Thus, a corporation cannot leverage itself through the use of a redemption or dividend, which in many cases has the same economic effect as a third-party leveraging acquisition.

It could be argued that since under Proposed Section 279 a third party may use debt in acquiring the stock of a target corporation, the target itself ought to be able to issue its own debt in a leveraged recapitalization. There are, however, at least two reasons for rejecting this approach.

First, there does not appear to be any legitimate business reason behind a leveraged recapitalization other than as a control shifting or preservation device. Control is shifted in a leveraged recapitalization in which the managers have their percentage stock ownership in the corporation increased as a result of the recapitalization. Thus, this is tantamount to a takeover by third parties. Control is preserved when there is not a significant change in the percentage ownership of the corporation before and after the recapitalization; in other words, the cash or debt is distributed to the shareholders on a pro rata basis. The principal purpose of a control preservation recapitalization may be to make the corporation less attractive as a takeover target. This was the case in the Unocal recapitalization.

In both the control shifting and control preservation cases, the economic effect of the transaction is that the board of directors, without a shareholder vote, has forced on the shareholders (1) either debt instruments or cash raised from the issuance of debt, and (2) a lower valued equity stake in a highly leveraged corporation. This could give the incumbent managers an unfair advantage over potential third-party acquirors; the flat disallowance of interest deductions in all leveraged recapitalizations levels the playing field.

If the managers of a corporation decide to take over the corporation, they can proceed pursuant to a third-party takeover proposal (*e.g.*, a management led LBO) just as any other third party may use that device.

The second reason for disallowing the interest deduction in a leveraged recapitalization is the protection of the integrity of the at-risk requirement that is embedded in the excessive debt rule of Proposed Section 279. Under the excessive debt rule, in the acquisition of control stock (*i.e.*, more than 5 percent of any class of stock of a publicly held corporation) (*see* Proposed Section 279(b)), the maximum amount of deductible debt that may be used is 75 percent of the purchase price for the stock. Thus, in essence, the purchaser must be at risk to the extent of at least 25 percent of the purchase price of the control stock acquired. This 25 percent at-risk concept could be avoided if debt could be issued in leveraged recapitalizations, which are in effect 100 percent debt financed.

Complexity and Avoidance

The rules proposed here are what the Congressional Research Service (CRS) refers to as "targeted restrictions."[3] The CRS says that the disadvantage of targeted restrictions is that they add complexity to the tax code, [and] [t]hey . . . encourage firms to find ways to avoid them . . . ."[4]

The proposals here should not add significantly to the complexity of the Code, and indeed they may even give rise to a net decrease in complexity. This is because the proposals would (1) eliminate the present convoluted Section 279, and (2) by requiring more equity in acquisition transactions significantly reduce the number of transactions in which it is necessary to determine whether what purports to be debt is in fact equity.

Further, since the proposals here reach both acquisition indebtedness and recapitalization indebtedness, it should not be possible for firms to avoid the effects of these rules.

---

3. Congressional Research Service Report (Jane G. Gravelle), *Tax Aspects of Leveraged Buyouts* 10 (March 2, 1989) (available as Tax Notes Doc. 89–1841).
4. *Id.*

CHAPTER 14

. . . .

Examining the Case for the Status Quo

Professor Netter has set out what appears to be the most comprehensive argument against ending the deduction for interest on debt used in takeovers.[1] It is appropriate to carefully examine whether Professor Netter's objections should lead Congress to reject the proposals contained in chapter 12.

Professor Netter has deduced that the following three claims are made by those who seek to eliminate the deduction for interest paid to finance takeovers:

> First, it is a way to restrict takeovers, especially hostile takeovers, that are allegedly detrimental to the economy. Second, considering that takeovers are motivated by the tax advantages of leveraging, which is supposedly detrimental both to firms and the economy, this restriction would improve efficiency. Third, tax revenues would increase.[2]

Professor Netter goes on to say that the validity of these three claims is based on the following four premises:

> (1) takeovers, especially hostile takeovers, are detrimental, (2) tax considerations motivate takeovers, especially leveraged takeovers, (3) the replacement of equity with debt is harmful, and (4) eliminating the interest deductibility of debt would increase tax revenues.[3]

He then sets out to demonstrate on the basis of "theoretical and empirical evidence recently developed by financial economists,"[4] that "takeovers

---

1. *See* Netter, *Continue the Interest Deductibility, supra* chapter 11, note 28.
2. *Id.*, at 221.
3. *Id.*
4. *Id.*, at 222.

are beneficial, and that restrictions on takeovers are detrimental."[5] He further purports to show that debt plays an important role in preventing management from engaging in nonvalue maximizing strategies.[6] He also argues that there should not be an artificial distinction that restricts the deductibility of interest on debt used in takeovers as contrasted with other debt.[7] Finally, he presents what he says is evidence that the proposals made by the House Ways and Means Committee in the Budget Reconciliation Bill of 1987[8] had a "large negative impact on the stock market and was a major factor triggering the [1987] crash."[9] His position is that this negative market effect "provides strong evidence of the importance and benefits of takeovers to the economy."[10]

This chapter analyzes Professor Netter's argument as follows: it examines his claims that there are potential adverse market effects from the imposition of an interest limitation; it then explores the empirical evidence he cites for the proposition that takeovers are beneficial and any limitations on takeovers would be detrimental; and finally, it assesses his claim that taxes cannot explain takeover activity.

Potential Adverse Market Effect of Adopting an Interest Limitation Provision

Professor Netter argues that the adverse market effect of the 1987 House Bill, which is discussed and analyzed in chapter 11, is a reason for Congress to refrain from legislating in this area. This is a species of the argument often made by lobbyists: "If you change the law on us; we won't survive!" Here it's: "If you modify the deduction for interest in takeovers, the market will crash like it did in October 1987." This is a powerful claim and must be examined carefully.

As pointed out in chapter 11, the SEC's analysis of the 1987 crash does not ascribe to the 1987 House Bill nearly as much of a negative market effect as does Professor Netter. The SEC study says the tax bill "may have had an effect on stock prices,"[11] whereas Professor Netter says the tax bill had a "large and negative impact." This difference in view may be attributable to the fact that the negative effects of the tax bill may have taken effect on October 14 and 16, 1987, after announcement of action by the House Ways and

---

5. *Id.*
6. *Id.*
7. *Id.*
8. 1987 House Bill, *supra* chapter 11, note 52.
9. Netter, *Continue the Interest Deductibility, supra* chapter 11, note 28, at 222.
10. *Id.*, at 222.
11. SEC Staff Report, *supra* chapter 11, note 61, at 3–10.

Means Committee. The most significant market fall, which in the view of the SEC was linked in a major way to certain portfolio selling strategies, occurred on October 19, 1987. Although Professor Netter's thesis on the market effect of the 1987 House Bill may not be completely accepted by others, it is at least on an intuitive level believable that the 1987 House Bill had some adverse effect on the market price of shares.

Professor Netter does not attempt to attribute any portion of the stock price decline to particular provisions of the Bill. It would appear, however, that a large part of the decline was attributable to those provisions that imposed a prohibitively high tax cost on hostile takeovers, that is, the mandatory Section 338 election and the disallowance of interest in hostile takeovers. To the extent this is so, Professor Netter's market effect argument loses much of its weight when it comes to analyzing interest limitation provisions like those proposed in chapter 12. These proposals are unlikely to produce as significant a negative market effect as that ascribed to the 1987 House Bill by Professor Netter. Furthermore, as pointed out in chapter 11, the provisions of the 1987 House Bill dealing with hostile takeovers were bad policy, and Congress was correct in rejecting them, without respect to their market effect.

In any event, it is reasonable to expect that there would be at least some negative market effect from the interest limitation provisions proposed in chapter 12. This leads to the question of whether Professor Netter is correct when he says that the importance of his findings of a negative market effect is that it "illustrates the harmful impact of such a proposal." As support for this proposition Professor Netter cites the following quote from the *Wall Street Journal*:

> It is not clear how many members [of Congress] are eager to risk another panic on Wall Street, but it is no secret that many Congressmen are itching to 'do something.' The [Mitchell and Netter] study should at least remind them that there is hard evidence of what happens when Congress, in the name of stopping takeovers and restructurings, threatens to convert the tax code into a giant poison pill.[12]

This is a very weak justification for continuing the deductibility of interest on debt issued in takeovers. A negative market effect could result from a sound or unsound policy change. Indeed, it can be expected that market changes will result from most significant tax changes. This does not mean, however, that a tax change should be rejected because of a resulting market change. Rather, the question is this: What is the correct tax policy?

---

12. *The Market's Maginot Line*, Wall St. J., May 10, 1989, at A18, col. 1.

Professor Netter's logic could lead one to conclude that even if the market is artificially propped up because of a flawed policy, the policy should not be changed because of the anticipated large negative market reaction.

The judgment here is that the current policy on the deductibility of interest is flawed; the policy should be changed for excessively leveraged and junk bond finance acquisitions of publicly held corporations. Any adverse market effect from the adoption of these proposals is acceptable because any such effect eliminates from the market the portion of the price that is attributable to the flawed tax policy.

In any event, Congress need not be concerned that the adoption of the proposals in chapter 12 would have a "large and negative" market effect or cause a "panic on Wall Street." This is particularly so if Congress acts now, during a time when there are not a large number of overly leveraged acquisitions.

Restrictions on Takeovers are Detrimental

This section examines Professor Netter's argument that "takeovers are beneficial and restrictions on takeovers are detrimental."[13] The discussion proceeds as follows: First, it examines his claims regarding large premiums. Second, it examines his claim that takeovers solve agency problems by disciplining inefficient managers, and then examines the related theory that LBOs force inefficient managers to pay out free cash flow. Next, it discusses his mutual gain theory. The final two sections explore the potential sources of net gains, if any, from takeovers. The impact of each theory on the proposals made here is examined.

Takeovers Produce Large Premiums

Professor Netter begins by pointing out that target shareholders have experienced large gains from takeovers and that during the 1980s the premiums paid in tender offers averaged approximately 30 percent.[14] He concludes that this is necessarily good for society.

Although target shareholders realize large premiums, the interest deduction, as pointed out by Professor Kaplan, is an "important source" of the premiums.[15] The purpose of the interest deduction, however, is not to ensure that target shareholders receive large premiums. Consequently, Congress should not reject the proposals here because of the potential reduction in takeover premiums.

---

13. Netter, *Continue Interest Deductibility, supra* chapter 11, note 28, at 222.
14. *Id.*, at 223.
15. Kaplan, *MBOs and Taxes, supra* chapter 12, note 26, at 630.

Takeovers Discipline Inefficient Managers

In assessing the motivations for takeovers, Professor Netter first points out that a major benefit of takeovers is that they can help to mitigate the agency problem between managers and shareholders, by forcing the managers to act more in the interest of shareholders.[16] As he acknowledges, this argument was first developed by Professor Manne in a 1965 article[17] and has been strenuously pressed by Judge Easterbrook and Professor Fischel who have argued that a target's board should remain passive in the face of a hostile acquisition.[18] Professor Netter also points out that the development of the junk bond market, which he says is the most important factor motivating mergers in the 1980s, made even very large corporations susceptible to takeover. Therefore, the junk bond market helps to mitigate the agency problem in such corporations.

Takeovers may solve some agency problems by forcing some managers to operate more efficiently. On the other hand, takeovers may create agency problems by causing some managers to spend more time attempting to make their firms takeover-proof by pursuing short-term strategies and by implementing anti-takeover devices. Martin Lipton has forcefully made this point. He has argued that hostile acquisitions contribute significantly to an emphasis on the short run and do not effectively discipline inefficient managers:[19]

> The academic literature has vastly overstated the benefits of the hostile takeover. Even if one accepts the priority of disciplining managers, the hostile takeover has proven a particularly destructive and inefficient means of such discipline. Hostile takeovers have not led managers to manage more effectively or to create more successful business enterprises. Instead, together with the increasing dominance of institutional stockholders, hostile takeover activity has led to an inordinate focus on short-term results and a dangerous overleveraging of the American and British economies, the ill effects of which are only beginning to emerge.[20]

Professors Ravenscraft and Scherer indicate this position cannot be casually disregarded:

16. Netter, *Continue Interest Deductibility, supra* chapter 11, note 28, at 224.

17. Henry G. Manne, *Mergers and the Market for Corporate Control*, 73 J. Pol. Econ. 110 (1965).

18. Frank H. Easterbrook and Daniel R. Fischel, *The Proper Role of a Target's Management in Responding to a Tender Offer*, 94 Harv. L. Rev. 1161 (1981).

19. Lipton and Rosenblum, *A New System of Corporate Governance, supra* chapter 12, note 20, at 188.

20. *Id.*

[T]here remain unsettled but burning questions as to whether pervasive takeover threats induce managers to become more short-sighted in their pricing and investment decisions and to employ defensive tactics that increase operating cost and risk.[21]

Further, one theoretical study has found that this managerial myopia theory cannot be rejected in favor of the market discipline theory pressed by Professor Manne and others.[22] Also, Professor Brown argues that the "central theme propounded by proponents of an unfettered market for corporate control—that takeovers lead to profit-maximizing behavior—appears to be wrong."[23] Professor Brown argues that rather than maximizing profits potential targets may follow a hiding strategy, that is, "attempt to make the search difficult by denying bidders an objective, easily identifiable source of gain."[24] He says that a hiding strategy requires the pursuit of average earnings and risk aversion, rather than profit maximization.[25] Thus, a hiding strategy inherently requires a focus on the short run.

Although Professor Netter and others state that takeovers help solve agency problems, apparently no direct empirical evidence supports the bold assertion. Moreover, if the hypothesis is correct it would seem that one would find empirical evidence that during periods of heightened takeover activity, such as occurred in the 1980s, managers of potential targets are particularly diligent and effective and as a result, the stock prices of such firms is high and takeovers less likely.

There is both empirical and anecdotal evidence that refutes the inefficient-management proposition. In their study of mergers and sell offs, Professors Ravenscraft and Scherer conclude that there is no "strong support for the efficiency-through-management-displacement merger motive."[26] To the contrary, they found that "acquirers sought well-managed companies and tried, not always successfully, to retain their managers."[27]

Further, one leading merger and acquisition investment banker at Soloman Brothers has said that from his experience in searching for potential

21. Ravenscraft and Scherer, *Economic Efficiency, supra* chapter 12, note 13, at 226.

22. Jeremy C. Stein, *Takeover Threats and Managerial Myopia*, 96 J. Pol. Econ. 61 (1988) [hereinafter cited as "Stein, *Managerial Myopia*"].

23. Robert J. Brown, Jr., *In Defense of Management Buyouts*, 65 Tul. L. Rev. 57 (1990). *See also*, Ravenscraft and Scherer, *Life After Takeover, supra* chapter 12, note 16.

24. *Id.*, at 72.

25. *Id.*

26. Ravenscraft and Scherer, *Economic Efficiency, supra* chapter 12, note 13, at 212.

27. *Id.*

targets, acquiring corporations look for well-managed firms.[28] Also, Martin Lipton has cited anecdotal evidence indicating that well-managed corporations are just as likely as poorly managed corporations to become targets of hostile takeovers.[29]

Given the current state of the empirical evidence, it is impossible to resolve the debate between the market discipline and the market myopia theories. Indeed, one study, which finds that there is no evidence that LBOs have a significant negative effect, summarizes the battle lines as follows:

> Proponents of LBOs argue that the associated organizational changes improve managers' incentives to maximize value and therefore lead to better operating and investment decisions. An opposing view is that the increased financial leverage associated with LBOs makes firms short-term-oriented and vulnerable to financial distress, leading to a decline in their competitiveness.[30]

A resolution of this great debate is not needed in evaluating the proposals here because the purpose of the interest deduction is not to mitigate the effects of agency problems. Therefore, in determining whether to adopt these proposals, Congress should not be affected by any particular view of the impact of takeovers on agency problems.

Adoption of the proposals here should not, however, substantially curtail LBOs and, therefore, should not substantially curtail any positive effect LBOs may have in solving agency problems. The proposals here would have the definite positive effect of increasing the likelihood that there would be an adequate level of equity in LBOs of publicly held firms, thereby reducing the risk of bankruptcy and better allowing such firms to pursue long-term strategies such as investing in R & D. As explained in chapter 12, there are good reasons for exempting closely held firms from these rules.

Forcing Firms to Pay Out Free Cash Flow

Another motivational reason behind takeovers, according to Professor Netter, is to force firms to pay out excess cash flow.[31] This argument, which was developed by Professor Jensen,[32] holds that many firms have free cash

---

28. Raymond S. Troubh, *Characteristics of Target Corporations*, 32 Bus. Law. 1301 (1977).

29. Lipton and Rosenblum, *A New System of Corporate Governance, supra* chapter 12, note 20, at 201.

30. Krishna G. Palepu, *Consequences of Leveraged Buyouts*, 27 J. Fin. Econ. 247, 248 (1990).

31. Netter, *Continue Interest Deductibility, supra* chapter 11, note 28, at 225.

32. Michael C. Jensen, *Agency Cost of Free Cash Flow, Corporate Finance and Take-*

flow that is in excess of the firm's profitable investment opportunities (*i.e.*, projects with positive net present values).[33] Management may not however, want to pay the free cash flow out to shareholders as dividends and may instead invest the funds in projects with negative net present values, thereby harming the shareholders. Debt resulting from an LBO or similar transaction can, according to this theory, help to control this type of agency cost and promote efficient management by requiring the pay out of the free cash flow to service the debt.

There are several fundamental flaws with this so-called theory, which is not a theory of why mergers occur but rather is an explanation of an effect. Yes, the primary effect of an LBO transaction is a dedication of free cash flows to service the debt. However, there would appear to be at least two possible secondary effects resulting from the debt. First, the firm may not be able to invest in positive net present value projects. Second, the firm may not be able to invest in negative net present value projects. Professors Netter and Jensen assert that LBOs promote efficiency by preventing managers from investing in negative net present value projects. It would appear, however, that it is at least as likely that an LBO could hurt efficiency by preventing managers from investing in projects with positive net present values.

In any event, the purpose of the deduction for interest is not to prevent managers from investing in either positive or negative net present value projects. The limitation on the interest deduction proposed here would not prevent the shareholders of a corporation from saddling the corporation with debt or preferred stock for the purpose of preventing the managers from investing in negative net present value projects. The only consequence is that all or some portion of the interest may not be deductible.

Value Created Through Mutual Gain

Professor Netter says that the "disciplining of inefficient managers is only one motivation behind takeovers and should not be overemphasized."[34] He argues that the "theoretical underpinning" behind the view that takeovers promote efficiency is the neoclassical economic theory that "value is created through mutual gains to voluntary trade" and that "takeovers increase value

---

overs, 76 Am. Econ. Rev. 323 (1986). *See also*, Jensen, *Eclipse of the Public Corporation*, *supra* chapter 12, note 16. (Debt the "sword" is a powerful agent for change. Equity the "pillow" is not. *Id.*, at 67.)

33. Financial Theory teaches that only investments with a positive net present value should be undertaken. Net present value is determined by subtracting from the present value of all expected cash inflows the present value of all expected cash outflows. *See* Brealey and Myers, *supra* chapter 12, note 64, at 73–89, 99–100.

34. Netter, *Continue Interest Deductibility*, *supra* chapter 11, note 28, at 228.

by enabling resources to flow to the highest valued use."[35] He further argues that the theoretical argument that takeovers force management to focus on the short run at the expense of the long run[36] is not supported by the empirical evidence.[37] It cannot be seriously disputed that many mergers, acquisitions, and takeovers promote economic efficiency. On the other hand, it cannot be seriously disputed that many LBO transactions have been excessively leveraged;[38] the recent bankruptcy of LBO companies, such as Federated Department Stores, attests to this excessive leverage. The proposals contained in chapter 12 do not in any way deter or eliminate the efficiency gains from most mergers. The proposals would force a restructuring of some future transactions that may have been excessively leveraged; but to that extent the proposal would promote efficiency and also protect the corporate tax base.

Efficiency: The Source of Net Gains from Takeovers

Professor Netter next turns to an analysis of the empirical evidence. Here he first outlines the scope of event studies which examine the impact of certain events (such as the announcement of a tender offer or a merger) on the price of the relevant company's stock.[39] These studies are based on the efficient capital markets hypothesis which holds that security prices reflect all relevant and ascertainable information. As Professor Netter says, under this theory: "If information about a firm—technically about its future cash flow—is available to investors, they will use this information in their investment decisions, thus incorporating this information into stock prices."[40]

Professor Netter then summarizes the results of several event studies which in general show that (1) the shareholders of target firms in tender offers and going private transactions, including LBOs, receive premiums of approximately 30 percent, (2) the returns to the acquiring firm's shareholders is small and has been declining over time, and (3) when balancing the gains to the target and the losses, if any, to the acquiring corporation's shareholders, there are positive net gains from takeovers. From this he then argues:

---

35. *Id.*, at 226.

36. *See* Stein, *Managerial Myopia, supra* note 22 (arguing that management cannot properly signal to the market the value of its long-term projects and, therefore, in order to insulate itself from takeover will invest in short-term projects), and Ravenscraft and Scherer, *Economic Efficiency, supra* chapter 12, note 13, at 226 (concluding that the short-run theory cannot be rejected).

37. Netter, *Continue Interest Deductibility, supra* chapter 11, note 28, at 230–31.

38. *See* Peter C. Canellos, *The Over-Leveraged Acquisition*, 39 Tax Law 91 (1985).

39. Netter, *Continue Interest Deductibility, supra* chapter 11, note 28, at 227.

40. *Id.*, citing a prior edition of Brealey & Myers, *Principles of Corporate Finance, supra* chapter 12, note 64.

Given the apparent net gains to shareholders in takeovers, the question for policymakers should be: What is the source of the gains in takeovers? There should be a presumption that if bidders offer a thirty percent premium for the shares of the target, the resources of the firm can be used more efficiently and thus, society benefits from the takeovers. Therefore, the burden should be on those who want to restrict takeovers to provide evidence that takeovers are harmful.[41]

Although this efficiency thesis may be correct in many instances,[42] some studies discredit the theory. For example, the study by Professors Ravenscraft and Scherer finds that for mergers occurring in the 1960s and early '70s "on average profitability declines and efficiency losses resulted...."[43] The study concludes that this evidence "cast doubt on the widespread applicability of an efficiency theory of merger motives."[44] Also, another study of mergers and takeovers occurring in the years 1976 to 1981 finds that three years after an acquisition "the acquiring firm's shareholders are significantly worse off... than they would have been had the acquiring firms continued to perform as they had over the three years... prior to the acquisition."[45] The study also finds that there is no significant impact on an acquiring firm's shareholders at the time of the announcement of an acquisition.

There are other possible interpretations of why a target's shareholders gain. First, to some extent the high premiums are merely a reflection of the future tax benefits associated with the interest deductions on the debt issued in these transactions. As noted in chapter 12, Professor Kaplan found that, under certain assumptions, the tax savings from the interest deduction accounts for as much as 129 percent of the premium in management led LBOs.[46]

---

41. *Id.*, at 230–31.

42. The 1985 *Economic Report of the President* 216 (Feb. 1985) concludes that the available evidence indicates that takeovers generate net benefits for the economy.

43. Ravenscraft and Scherer, *Economic Efficiency, supra* chapter 12, note 13, at 211–212. *See also*, Ravenscraft and Scherer, *Life After Takeover, supra* chapter 12, note 16 (finding that nine years after takeover by tender offer targets perform less well than previously).

44. Ravenscraft and Scherer, *Economic Efficiency, supra* chapter 12, note 13, at 212.

45. Magenheim and Mueller, *Are Acquiring-Firm Shareholders Better Off After an Acquisition?* in *Knights, Raiders & Targets, supra* chapter 11 note 63, at 181. The authors also discuss other studies which are generally to the same effect. *Id.*, at 182–88.

46. Kaplan, *MBOs and Taxes, supra* chapter 12, note 26, at 617. *See* chapter 12, p. 168. *But see*, Auerbach and Reishus, *The Effects of Taxation on the Merger Decision*, ch. 6, p. 157 in Auerbach, *Corporate Takeovers: Causes and Consequences* (1988)

Second, Professor Roll has argued that the high premiums are attributable to "hubris" on the part of the managers of acquiring firms, that is, the "overbearing presumption by bidders that their valuations are correct."[47] The hubris hypothesis is based on the assumption that the average increase in the value of targets is offset by the average decrease in the value of acquirors and that takeover expenses produce a net loss. The theory seems to apply in both leveraged and nonleveraged acquisitions.

Professor Roll says that the "evidence about total gains on takeovers must be judged inconclusive,"[48] thus, allowing for the possibility that his hubris hypothesis is correct.[49] The study by Professors Ravenscraft and Scherer supports this hubris hypothesis. They conclude that "merger-makers of the 1960s and 1970s suffered from massive hubris."[50]

Another possible interpretation, which is similar to Professor Roll's hubris theory, is the overpayment hypothesis advanced by Professor Black.[51] He argues that in many takeovers the target shareholders gain partly because of overpayments by bidders. These overpayments do not cause the stock prices of bidders to drop because the shareholders "already expect the bidder to waste money, one way or another."[52]

As can be seen, many questions have been raised about the efficiency argument. But, in any event, the adoption of the proposals made here, which would ensure that there would be more equity in LBOs involving publicly held firms, would make it even more likely that such firms would perform efficiently after LBOs.

Redistribution: Not the Source of Net Gains in Takeovers

Professor Netter next argues that the evidence shows that the alleged net gains in acquisitions do not result from a redistribution from other groups such as from labor or debt holders.[53] From this he concludes:

(concluding that "the potential increase in interest deductions could not have been an important factor influencing merger activity during the period in question"). *Id.*, at 178.

47. Richard Roll, *The Hubris Hypothesis of Corporate Takeovers*, 59 J. Bus. 197, 200 (1986) [hereinafter cited as "Roll, *The Hubris Hypothesis*"].

48. *Id.*, at 205.

49. Another article by Professor Roll, which surveys the empirical evidence on takeover activity, concludes that at present such evidence "could support no particular social policy." Roll, *Empirical Evidence on Takeovers, supra* chapter 11, note 64, at 241.

50. Ravenscraft and Scherer, *Economic Efficiency, supra* chapter 12, note 13, at 212.

51. Bernard S. Black, *Bidder Overpayment in Takeovers*, 41 Stan. L. Rev. 597 (1989).

52. *Id.*, at 599.

53. One recent study has found, contrary to Professor Netter's assertion, that

[T]he large premiums paid in takeovers, combined with the findings that the premiums are not attributable to redistributions or market inefficiencies, strongly suggest that takeovers promote efficiency.[54]

It would be an impossible task to tally the net gains from takeovers because there could be hidden gains and hidden costs. For example, in examining the redistribution theories, Professor Netter does not mention the cost incurred by the indirect holders of junk debt, such as the depositors in the savings and loans that overinvested in junk debt and now are defunct or the policy holders in insurance companies like Executive Life that overinvested in junk debt and now are bankrupt. Nor does he tally the cost to the American taxpayer for the tax dollars that go to bail out those S & Ls that overinvested in junk debt.

Although Professor Netter appears to overstate the case for positive net gains in takeovers, this does not mean that the interest deduction should be taken away in all acquisition transactions. Rather, it means that Congress should not hesitate to modify the tax laws to eliminate the tax incentive for excessive leverage in acquisition. In doing so Congress would, among other things, prevent the infliction of real cost on the indirect holders of debt that is particularly susceptible to default.

Taxes Cannot Explain Takeover Activity

In his final defense of the status quo Professor Netter argues that "taxes cannot explain most takeover activity,"[55] and, consequently, no changes in the tax law are needed. His article here sets out six points in support of this defense of the status quo. His points are taken up as follows. First examined is his observation that corporations would avoid any interest limitation on acquisitions by entering into self-leveraging transactions. Second, his position that leveraged acquisitions are not primarily motivated by the interest deduction is discussed. Then, his assertion that any limit on the deduction of interest on acquisition indebtedness would lead to an unwarranted bias in favor of internal expansion is examined. Next, his position that bankruptcy costs are low and, therefore, should be of no concern is considered. Professor Netter's fifth and sixth points—LBOs do not deplete tax revenues, and the potential adverse market effect of an interest limitation provision—have already been examined and rejected.[56]

---

bondholders suffer large losses in LBOs unless they are adequately protected in covenants. Paul Acquith and Thierry A. Wizman, *Event Risk, Covenants, and Bondholder Returns in Leveraged Buyouts*, 27 J. Fin. Econ. 195, 196 (1990).

54. Netter, *Continue Interest Deductibility*, *supra* chapter 11, note 28, at 238.

55. *Id.*, at 242.

56. *See* p. 192.

Limitation on Takeovers Only is Insufficient

Professor Netter discusses an article by Gilson, Scholes, and Wolfson[57] which makes the point that those who claim that there are tax subsidies for acquisitions ignore the fact that other nonacquisition transactions can have the same effect. For example, a leveraged recapitalization can have the same economic effect as a leveraged acquisition. He draws the following policy conclusion from this observation:

> There is a straightforward implication of the Gilson, Scholes and Wolfson thesis for policymakers considering restrictions on the deductibility of debt used in takeovers. While taxes may be a motivation for a firm to increase leverage, this need not be accomplished through a takeover. To capture this tax benefit, an existing firm can restructure, substituting debt for equity.[58]

There are at least two responses to this observation. First, most firms do not voluntarily over leverage themselves unless the transaction is effectuated for some change of control (or prevention of a change in control) purpose, as was the case with the Unocal leveraged recapitalization. Second, any rational limitation on the deductibility of interest in acquisition transactions would also contain a limitation on the deductibility of interest in leveraged recapitalizations. As stated by Gilson, et al., "[a]ny analysis that singles out for attention only acquisitions and ignores [the] alternatives misses entirely the real issue."[59]

The proposals set out in chapter 12 do not miss the "real issue"; they would limit the deduction for interest in both leveraged acquisitions and leveraged recapitalizations.

Does the Interest Deduction Lead to Leveraged Acquisitions

Professor Netter first acknowledges that by lowering the personal tax rate on interest and eliminating the capital gains rate, the Tax Reform Act of 1986 increased the incentive for corporations to leverage. He then attempts to deflate this concern by saying that there is no evidence that leveraged takeovers are primarily motivated by tax considerations.[60]

---

57. Ronald Gilson, *et al.*, *Taxation and the Dynamics of Corporate Control: The Uncertain Case for Tax Motivated Transactions* in *Knights, Raiders & Targets, supra* chapter 11, note 63, at 271 [hereinafter cited as "Gilson, et al., *Taxation and Corporate Control*"].

58. Netter, *Continue Interest Deductibility, supra* chapter 11, note 28, at 243.

59. Gilson et, al., *Taxation and Corporate Control, supra* note 57, at 273.

60. Netter, *Continue the Interest Deductibility, supra* chapter 11, note 28, at 244–45.

Here Professor Netter's reasoning appears to be flawed for at least two reasons. First, the argument that leveraged takeovers are not primarily motivated by tax reasons could be a justification for a complete elimination of the interest deduction in such transactions. If these transactions are not motivated by taxes, then they would persist notwithstanding the elimination of the interest deduction. This statement, however, cannot be true. There is no credible evidence that companies would over leverage themselves if there were no deduction for interest. Professor Netter's own argument concerning the adverse market effect of the 1987 proposed legislation proves this point. Thus, it seems incontrovertible that there would be significantly fewer leveraged acquisitions if there were no deduction for interest.

The second reason his statement is flawed is that it ignores Professor Kaplan's finding that the interest deduction accounts for a significant portion of premiums paid in management led LBOs.[61]

Bias for Debt for Internal Expansion

Professor Netter argues that if the interest on debt issued for the purpose of internal expansion is deductible, but interest on debt issued in takeovers is not, a reduction in the number of takeovers would result. This is because firms would substitute tax subsidized internal growth for growth through acquisition. He argues:

> A restriction on the deductibility of debt used to finance takeovers would be inefficient and would drive a wedge between takeover growth and growth through the building of new capital.[62]

On the basis of this observation he concludes that a limitation of the deduction of interest on debt issued in acquisitions could lead to an oversupply of plant and equipment because firms will make their build or buy decision on the basis of taxes and not economics. This argument has some appeal when considering an absolute prohibition on the deduction for interest on acquisition debt. The proposals here, however, would not completely eliminate the deduction; rather, they would only disallow the deduction for excessively leveraged transactions involving publicly held firms.

Bankruptcy Costs Are Low

Professor Netter argues that although, as he acknowledges, leveraged acquisitions increase the risk of bankruptcy by substituting debt for equity, in an economic sense there is little difference between debtholders and equi-

---

61. Kaplan, *MBOs and Taxes, supra* chapter 12, note 26, at 630.
62. Netter, *Continue Interest Deductibility, supra* chapter 11, note 28, at 245.

tyholders. They both transfer money to the firm even though only debt-holders can put the firm in bankruptcy. From this observation, he concludes:

> Therefore, the appropriate question for concern is whether bankruptcy costs are high; is it costly to reorganize the assets of a firm in bankruptcy? Until opponents of takeovers provide empirical evidence that there are dangerous levels of debt in the economy caused by takeovers and that bankruptcy costs are high, we should not rely on arguments against takeovers based on the leveraging of America.[63]

As pointed out earlier, Professor Netter does not mention the cost associated with the Federal bailout of the S & L industry or the cost to the holders of insurance policies issued by bankrupt insurance companies. Many of these costs can be directly linked to investments by these institutions in the junk bonds of companies that are now in bankruptcy.

The proposals contained here would reduce the number of future bankruptcies resulting from LBO transactions of publicly held firms by making it more likely that an adequate amount of equity would be present in such transactions.

Summary

The bottom line is that the arguments made in favor of retaining the current deductibility of interest in LBOs and related transactions are not sound reasons for failing to enact the proposals made in chapter 12. The enactment of these proposals should not cause a serious adverse market effect and should not deter efficiency enhancing acquisitions. By ensuring at least 25 percent equity and curtailing the use of junk debt, these proposals should enhance efficiency by making publicly held firms that are acquired in LBOs less susceptible to bankrupcy and more able to engage in post-LBO value maximizing strategies.

---

63. *Id.*, at 247. Professor Miller makes this same argument, *See* Miller, *Leverage*, *supra* chapter 11, note 10, at 483–86.

Part 4
Impact of Integration Proposals and Conclusion

CHAPTER 15

· ·

Impact of the Treasury and ALI Integration Proposals on the Proposals in Parts 2 and 3

On January 6, 1992, the Treasury Department presented to Congress a report dealing with the integration of the individual and corporate tax systems (Treasury 1992 Integration Study).[1] This report was produced in response to a provision in the Tax Reform Act of 1986 that directed the Treasury to study reforms of the taxation of corporate income under Subchapter C.[2] As spelled out more fully in chapter 1, when Congress issued this directive in 1986, it was generally anticipated that the Treasury's study of Subchapter C would focus broadly on issues concerning mergers and acquisitions. In 1988 the Treasury issued an outline of the issues to be addressed in the study,[3] and the focus of the outline was on mergers and acquisitions.

As indicated in the preface, this chapter was prepared shortly after the publication of the Treasury 1992 Integration Study, *supra* chapter 1, note 31, and the ALI Reporter's 1992 Integration Draft, *supra* chapter 1, note 30. I am particularly indebted to the following people for their valuable and timely comments on a draft of this chapter: Anne Alstott, Treasury, Tax Legislation Counsel's Office; Professor Jennifer J. S. Brooks, International Tax Program, Harvard; Professor Daniel I. Halperin, Georgetown Law School; Jeffrey Sheffield, Kirkland and Ellis; Professor Alvin C. Warren, Jr., Harvard Law School; and Diana L. Wolman, Law Clerk to U.S. District Court Judge Kelleher. Helpful assistance was provided by Byron W. Cooper, one of my research assistants at UCLA. Of course, I am fully responsible for any errors and for the views expressed.

1. *Treasury 1992 Integration Study, supra* chapter 1, note 31.

2. *See Gideon Integration Letter, supra* chapter 1, note 32. Subchapter C of the Internal Revenue Code contains the principal provisions affecting corporations.

3. *Treasury Subchapter C Outline, supra* chapter 1, note 16.

The intervening concern of Congress and the Treasury with leveraged buyouts (LBOs),[4] however, deflected the Treasury from a comprehensive look at mergers and acquisitions to a comprehensive look at integration. Many tax professionals, including Yale Law School Professor Michael Graetz, argued that the solution to the LBO problem (that is, the elimination of the tax on corporate income by use of the interest deduction on debt) is the adoption of an integrated system of taxing corporate income.[5] Professor Graetz was later appointed the Deputy Assistant Secretary of Treasury for Tax Policy and was responsible for the supervision of the Treasury 1992 Integration Study.

In its transmittal letter to Congress, the Treasury says that Congress's "mandate" to the Treasury in the Tax Reform Act of 1986 is "quite broad." The Treasury, therefore, concluded that a "comprehensive study of the issues presented by integration of the corporate and individual income tax would address fundamental questions concerning how the corporate income tax might be restructured to reduce tax distortions of important corporate financial decisions and to achieve a more efficient system."[6] The principal distortion, most would agree, is the bias under the current system in favor of the use of debt in structuring the capital of a corporation, particularly the use of debt in LBOs. The Treasury's transmittal letter goes on to say that the Treasury believes an examination of integration issues "should precede consideration of other, less fundamental, approaches to corporate income tax reform."[7]

The issuance of the Treasury 1992 Integration Study was followed on March 2, 1992 with the release of an ALI Reporter's Study on integration (ALI Reporter's 1992 Integration Draft).[8] This ALI draft was discussed at a meeting of the ALI's Tax Advisory Group on March 20, 1992, and both the ALI draft and the Treasury study were discussed at a meeting of the ABA Integration Task Force on March 21, 1992. It can be expected that both studies will be carefully examined by many different interested groups. Further, it is anticipated that Congress will hold hearings on the integration issue in the fall of 1992. Thus, it can be expected that there will be a public debate on the merits of adopting an integrated system.

The purpose of this chapter is to discuss the impact of both the Treasury 1992 Integration Study and the ALI Reporter's 1992 Integration Draft on the proposals contained in this book. Discussed first, in broad outline, are the principal features of the current classical system and the purpose and

---

4. *See* chapter 1, at p. 7.
5. Graetz, *Tax Aspects of LBOs*, *supra* chapter 1, note 28.
6. *Gideon Letter*, *supra* chapter 1, note 32.
7. *Id.*
8. *ALI Reporter's 1992 Integration Draft*, *supra* chapter 1, note 30.

general effect of the various integration prototypes set forth in the Treasury and ALI studies. The next five sections provide general descriptions of the prototypes, and the following section discusses the treatment of retirement plans under each of the prototypes. This is an important topic because, as demonstrated later in the chapter, if in an integrated system, retirement plans (and other tax-exempt organizations) are not taxed on interest income, a tax incentive exists for corporations to engage in LBOs and leveraged recapitalizations.

Finally, the chapter examines the impact of the prototypes on the merger and acquisition proposals contained in part 2, and explores the impact of the prototypes on the LBO and leveraged recapitalization proposals contained in part 3.

The Classical System and the Integration Prototypes

The current system of taxing corporations and shareholders imposes a corporate level tax on income earned by the corporation[9] and a second shareholder level tax on distributions of after-tax proceeds to shareholders as dividends.[10] This double tax results in a tax of 54.28 percent on distributed corporate earnings.[11] Also, on the sale of stock at a capital gain, shareholders are indirectly taxed on their allocable shares of both undistributed earnings and net-unrealized gain in the corporation's assets.

Indeed, a triple level of tax may apply when retained earnings are distributed after a sale of stock. The first tax applies at the corporate level on the earnings. A second indirect tax with respect to the retained earnings applies at the shareholder level on sale of the stock. A third tax applies to the purchasing shareholder upon receipt of a distribution of the retained earnings. This third tax may be offset by a loss when the shareholder sells the stock. The loss would result because the value of the stock is decreased by the amount of the dividend. This system of corporate and shareholder level taxes is referred to as the classical system.

The Treasury 1992 Integration Study says that the "central issue" concerning the "role of the corporate income tax in the federal tax structure . . . [is] . . . whether corporate earnings should be taxed once rather than taxed both when earned and when distributed to shareholders."[12] The Treasury

---

9. I.R.C. § 11 (1991).

10. I.R.C. §§ 301(c)(1), 316 (1991).

11. *See* chapter 2, p. 28. (The individual on dividends is 31%).

12. *Treasury 1992 Integration Study, supra* chapter 1, note 31, at 1.

goes on to say that "[i]ntegration of the individual and corporate income tax refers to the taxation of corporate income once."[13]

The Treasury 1992 Integration Study "presents three prototypes representing a range of integration systems":[14] (1) the dividend exclusion prototype; (2) the shareholder allocation prototype; and (3) the comprehensive business income tax prototype (CBIT). The Treasury indicates that it currently prefers the dividend exclusion prototype,[15] but that the "CBIT prototype represents a very long term, comprehensive option for equalizing the tax treatment of debt and equity."[16] The Treasury recommends further study of the dividend exclusion and CBIT prototypes.[17]

Although the Treasury 1992 Integration Study discusses under the heading "The Roads not Taken" a shareholder credit prototype,[18] the ALI Reporter's 1992 Integration Draft recommends that such a prototype be adopted. The three principal Treasury prototypes and the one ALI prototype are explored here.

Under the Treasury's dividend exclusion prototype, dividends are generally tax-free to the shareholder. Under the Treasury's shareholder allocation prototype, corporate income is deemed to be taxed at the shareholder level; this is similar to the treatment of partnerships and S corporations. Under the Treasury's CBIT prototype, income of all business entities, including corporations, partnerships, and sole proprietorships, is subject to a single level of tax at the entity level without deductions for interest payments on debt. Under the ALI's shareholder credit proposal, upon receipt of dividends shareholders include in gross income both the dividend and the corporate level tax paid with respect to the dividend (*i.e.*, gross-up the dividend) and then credit the corporate tax against the shareholder level tax. Each of these methods imposes one level of tax on corporate income.

The Treasury 1992 Integration Study explains that the Treasury views "integration primarily as a means of reducing the distortions of the classical system and improving economic efficiency."[19] The Treasury study sets forth four goals for enhancing neutrality in the design of an integrated system:

1. "Integration should make more uniform the taxation of investment across sectors of the economy,"[20] thereby eliminating the bias against corporate investment;

---

13. *Id.*
14. *Id.*, at 2.
15. *Id.*, at 15.
16. *Id.*, at 39.
17. *Id.*, at 15.
18. *Id.*, at 95–106.
19. *Id.*, at 13.
20. *Id.*

2. "Integration should make more uniform the taxation of returns earned on alternative financial instruments, particularly debt and equity;"[21]

3. "Integration should distort as little as possible the choice between retaining and distributing earnings;"[22] and

4. "Integration should create a system that taxes capital income once."[23]

In addition to pointing out the above three distortions caused by the classical system, the ALI Reporter's 1992 Integration Draft also says the classical system provides "an incentive to distribute corporate earnings in nondividend transactions, rather than as dividends."[24] Although it is commonly acknowledged that these distortions exist with a classical system, the most important distortion is the bias in favor of debt over equity. This is the distortion that the proposals in part 3 address.

In view of the adverse revenue effect associated with some of the prototypes and the increased taxes on various present untaxed sectors under other prototypes, it does not appear at this time that Congress will soon enact any of these prototypes. In this regard, the preface to the Treasury 1992 Integration Study says that the study is not "a legislative proposal but rather a source document to begin the debate on the desirability of integration."[25]

Basic Description of Each Prototype

This section discusses the basic elements of each of the prototypes. This discussion does not examine in any detail the more esoteric aspects of the prototypes, such as the treatment of foreign income and the treatment of corporate level preference income, such as tax-exempt interest and income sheltered by accelerated depreciation.

Each prototype is illustrated by reference to the following hypothetical, which demonstrates the effect of the double tax under the current classical system:

Example 1: *Classical System.* An individual shareholder (S) owns all of the stock of a subchapter C corporation (C). S initially contributed $100 to C, and, therefore, S's initial basis for her C shares is $100. C issues $900 of bonds. Half of the purchasers of the bonds are taxable individuals and half

---

21. *Id.*

22. *Id.*

23. *Id.*

24. *ALI Reporter's 1992 Integration Draft, supra* chapter 1, note 30, at 19. The Treasury study also addresses nondividend transactions. *Treasury 1992 Integration Study, supra* chapter 1, note 31, at 8–11, and 117.

25. *Treasury 1992 Integration Study, supra* chapter 1, note 31, at ix.

are tax-exempt pension funds. (The Treasury 1992 Integration Study points out that in 1990, 58 percent of corporate debt was held by the tax-exempt sector, which includes foreigners, pension funds, IRA's, Keoghs, and non-profit institutions.[26]) The bonds pay interest at a rate of 11.1 percent per year, which is $100 of interest per year. C uses all of its capital in its business, and its initial basis for its assets is $1,000. In its first year of operating, C has $100 of taxable income after deducting the $100 of interest on its bonds. C has no preference income. C is subject to a 34 percent tax rate[27] and, therefore, incurs a tax of $34. C has $66 after tax, and since C has no preference income, C has earnings and profits (*i.e.*, after-tax earnings) of $66.[28] If C distributes its after-tax income, S has a dividend of $66[29] and incurs a shareholder level tax at a 31 percent rate,[30] which results in a tax of $20.46. The dividend does not change S's basis for her shares in C. If C distributes all of its after-tax income, a combined double tax of $54.46 applies to the $100 of corporate income (*i.e.*, a $34 corporate level tax plus a $20.46 shareholder level tax). On the other hand, if C retains the after-tax earnings, the shareholder level tax is deferred until (1) the after-tax earnings are distributed, or (2) S sells her shares.

Of the $100 of interest paid on the bonds, $50 is subject to tax to the individual bondholders; the $50 received by the pension fund is not subject to tax. Thus, none of the interest is subject to a corporate level tax because the interest is deductible in computing taxable income, and only $50 of the $100 of interest is taxable at the bondholder level because half of the bonds are held by tax-exempt entities. The beneficiaries of the pension fund will, however, be taxed on the interest income upon receipt of a distribution of the interest from the fund.[31]

The above example demonstrates three of the distortions in the classical system.[32] First, there is a bias in favor of debt financing over equity financing because of the deductibility of interest payments. Since interest is deductible in computing taxable income at the corporate level, there is only one possible level of tax on the interest and that is a tax on the holder of the

----

26. *Id.*, at 68.

27. I.R.C. § 11 (1991).

28. I.R.C. § 312 (1991).

29. I.R.C. §§ 301(c) and 316 (1991).

30. I.R.C. § 1 (1991).

31. I.R.C. § 402 (1992). The Treasury study points out that the benefits received from the deductibility of contributions to a pension fund and the deferral of employee tax is "equivalent to simply exempting from income tax the pension fund's investment income." *Treasury 1992 Integration Study, supra* chapter 1, note 31, at 67.

32. *Treasury 1992 Integration Study, supra* chapter 1, note 31, at 13.

debt instrument upon receipt of the interest. If the debt instrument is held by a pension plan, the tax on the interest is deferred until distribution to the beneficiaries. If the debt instrument is held by tax-exempt charities or foreigners, there may be no U.S. tax on the interest. Thus, the use of debt certainly eliminates the corporate level tax, and depending on the status of the holder of the debt instrument, all U.S. tax on the interest income may be completely eliminated. If, on the other hand, the $900 of debt were equity there would be a corporate level tax on the income stream that produced the dividend, and there may also be a tax on the receipt of the dividend.

Second, with the tax rates in this example, there is a bias in favor of retaining after-tax earnings in corporate solution in order to avoid the shareholder level tax. If the earnings are retained, there is just a 34 percent immediate tax at the corporate level on the earnings, and the shareholder level tax is deferred until distribution or sale of the shares.[33]

Third, the double tax is biased against investment in the corporate sector, thereby giving a benefit to investment in partnerships and S corporations that have a single level of tax at the partner or shareholder level.[34]

Treasury's Dividend Exclusion Prototype[35]

Under the Treasury's dividend exclusion prototype, a corporation's taxable income, which is determined under current law, is subject to a 34 percent tax. The after-tax income is added to an Excludable Distributions Account (EDA), and dividends paid out of the EDA are not subject to shareholder level tax.[36] Thus, dividends are subject to a single corporate level tax. A corporation's tax preference income is not added to the EDA[37]; therefore, dividends paid out of preference income are taxable to shareholders. Dividends are considered as first being paid out of the EDA and then, only after the EDA has been reduced to zero, from preference income.

An indirect second level shareholder tax on retained earnings can arise upon the sale of stock by a shareholder. This second level tax can be avoided, however, if the corporation elects a dividend reinvestment plan (DRIP), which treats the shareholders as if they receive a distribution of

---

33. A Congressional Research Service Report estimates that the effective rate of tax on corporate equity is 48 percent, and the effective rate of tax on corporate debt is 20 percent. Jane G. Gravelle, *Corporate Tax Integration: Issues and Options*, Congressional Research Service, Washington, D.C. (1991). *See also, Treasury 1992 Integration Study, supra* chapter 1, note 31, at 3 and 6.

34. *See, generally, Federal Taxation of Business Enterprises, supra* chapter 1, note 20, at chapters 15–18.

35. *Treasury 1992 Integration Study, supra* chapter 1, note 31, at 17–25.

36. *Id.*, at 17.

37. *Id.*

the retained earnings as an excludable cash dividend and then reinvest the cash in the corporation.[38] The DRIP is limited to the balance in the EDA. The reinvestment results in an increase in the basis of the shareholders' shares, and therefore, upon sale of the stock, the shareholder is not subject to a second level of tax on the retained earnings.[39] Subsequent distributions of income deemed distributed and reinvested pursuant to a DRIP election are tax-free.[40] The shareholder reduces the basis of her shares by the amount of such a tax-free distribution.[41]

The dividend exclusion prototype is demonstrated in Example (2) below, by references to the facts illustrating the present classical system in Example (1) above:

Example 2: *Dividend Exclusion Prototype.* S has an initial basis for her shares in C corporation of $100. C Corporation determines its taxable income under current law, and therefore, C has taxable income of $100 after payment of all expenses, including the $100 of interest on its bonds. C incurs a $34 tax on its taxable income. The $66 after-tax income is added to C's EDA. C has no preference income. If C pays a $66 dividend, S excludes from her gross income the $66 dividend, and C reduces its EDA by $66. If C does not pay S a dividend, C will probably elect a DRIP in which case (1) S is deemed to have received a cash distribution of $66, (2) S excludes the deemed dividend from income, (3) S is deemed to have reinvested the $66 so that S's basis for her C stock increases by $66 to $166, and (4) C reduces its EDA by $66. As a result of the DRIP election, the $66 of retained earnings does not result in a capital gain to S upon the sale of her shares. S has, however, a capital gain on the sale of her shares to the extent of the net unrealized gain in C's assets. If C distributes the $66 of retained earnings after making a DRIP election, S does not have income on receipt of the distribution and reduces the basis of her shares by the amount of the distribution. The interest paid by C on its bonds is taxable to the taxable holder and tax-free to the pension fund. On the final distribution by the fund of the interest, the beneficiaries are taxed.

The dividend exclusion prototype eliminates the shareholder level tax on dividends out of non-preference income, thereby imposing only a 34 percent tax on corporate income. Since this prototype provides an exclusion from gross income, tax-exempt shareholders and foreigners (*i.e.*, the tax-

---

38. *Id.*, at 24.
39. *Id.*
40. *Id.*, at 88.
41. *Id.*

exempt sector), which in 1990 owned in the aggregate 43 percent of corporate equity,[42] do not benefit from this prototype.

The Treasury recommends that "foreign shareholders not be granted integration benefits by statute, but instead that this issue be addressed on a bilateral basis through treaty negotiations."[43] Consequently, foreign shareholders (*i.e.*, foreign corporations and nonresident aliens) continue to be subject to the 30 percent withholding tax on dividends that applies under Sections 871 and 881, except to the extent the withholding tax is reduced or eliminated by tax treaty.

The principal beneficiaries of the tax cut associated with the dividend exclusion prototype are individual holders of corporate equity.[44]

In evaluating the dividend exclusion method the Treasury considers the impact of this prototype on the three distortions of the current classical system that integration seeks to address: (1) the bias in favor of corporate debt over equity; (2) the bias in favor of corporate retentions over distributions; and (3) the bias in favor of the noncorporate form over the corporate form.[45]

The Treasury concludes that the dividend exclusion prototype, which is the Treasury's preferred prototype,[46] "would narrow (but not eliminate) the rate differential between distributed corporate and noncorporate equity income and between corporate equity income and interest."[47] The Treasury goes on to say that these "reductions in differentials would help reduce the debt-over-corporate-equity-finance and noncorporate-over-corporate form distortions."[48] Under this dividend exclusion prototype, a tax incentive for entering into an LBO or leveraged recapitalization still exists, as demonstrated on page 238.

With respect to the retention distortion, the Treasury points out that unless a DRIP election is made, the rate of tax on undistributed earnings would be higher than the rate on distributions because of the capital gains tax. Thus, the Treasury concludes that the "tax bias against corporate distributions would likely be reversed, in absence of a DRIP."[49]

The Treasury estimates that adoption of the dividend exclusion prototype would result in a revenue loss of "$13.1 billion annually at 1991 levels

---

42. *Id.*, at 68.

43. *Id.*, at 79.

44. This assumes that the incidence of the present dividends tax is on shareholders and not customers or others. *See Treasury 1992 Integration Study, supra* chapter 1, note 31, at 146.

45. *Id.*, at 18.

46. *Id.*, at 15.

47. *Id.*, at 18.

48. *Id.*

49. *Id.*

of income."[50] The estimated revenue loss is based on the assumption that "tax provisions other than those included in the proposals remain the same as under current law."[51]

On the positive side the study says:

> Overall the prototypes improve economic welfare in all calculations, and the improvement ranges from an annual equivalent of 0.07 percent of annual consumption (actual consumer spending on goods and services) to an amount equivalent to 0.73 percent of consumption, or from approximately $2.5 billion to $25 billion per year.[52]

This welfare estimate was computed under the assumption that government revenues remain "constant after introduction of the integration prototypes."[53] The computations were made using "two types of replacement taxes: (1) lump sum taxes; and (2) adjustments to statutory rates on capital income."[54]

Treasury's Shareholder Allocation Prototype[55]

Under the Treasury's shareholder allocation prototype, corporations are subject to a 34 percent tax rate on taxable income, determined under current law. The corporation's taxable income is allocated to the shareholders, and the shareholders include this income in gross income. The shareholders compute tax on the taxable income at the rate that applies to shareholders (*i.e.*, 15 percent, 28 percent, or 31 percent). The shareholders then credit the corporate tax against their tax liability. If the corporate tax rate is 34 percent and the maximum individual rate is 31 percent, an adjustment would be made to the "amount of tax passed through to shareholders to allow shareholders a tax credit no greater than the maximum 31 percent individual rate."[56] If the corporate tax exceeds the shareholder's tax on the allocated income, the excess can be used to offset the shareholder's tax liability on other income. Excess credits cannot, however, be utilized to generate a refund (*i.e.*, the credit is nonrefundable).[57] Corporate level preferences are generally extended to shareholders under this prototype.[58]

---

50. *Id.*, at 151.
51. *Id.*, at 150.
52. *Id.*, at 111.
53. *Id.*, at 119.
54. *Id.*
55. *Id.*, at chapter 3, pp. 27–37.
56. *Id.*, at chapter 3, note 5, p. 198.
57. *Id.*, at 28.
58. *Id.*, at 27, 30–31.

The shareholder's basis for her shares is increased by the amount of the allocated after-tax income, that is, the basis increases in an amount equal to the allocated taxable income minus the allocated taxes paid by the corporation. Also, if the corporation has preference income, such as tax-exempt interest, the shareholder's basis is increased by an allocable share of the preference income. The shareholder does not have income upon the distribution by the corporation of the after-tax or preference income, and the basis of the shareholder's shares is reduced by the amount of the distribution. Any distribution in excess of basis would produce gain. Corporate tax credits are passed through to shareholders;[59] however, corporate losses do not pass through.[60]

This system is similar to the current treatment of S corporations, except the tax is paid at the corporate level and the character of the various items of corporate income and deduction generally do not pass through to the shareholders.

The Treasury does not recommend adoption of the shareholder allocation prototype because of the "policy results and administrative complexities it produces."[61] For example, various administrative problems would result from any attempted allocation of the income by corporations with complex capital structures. Allocations by S corporations are rather simple because S corporations can have only one class of stock.[62]

The shareholder allocation prototype is demonstrated in Example 3 below, by reference to the facts illustrating the present classical system in Example 1 above:

Example 3: *Shareholder Allocation Prototype.* S has an initial $100 basis for her C corporation shares. C has taxable income of $100 after payment of all expenses including interest of $100 on its bonds. C incurs a $34 tax on its taxable income. The full amount of C's taxable income is allocated to S. S has a tax liability of $31 on the $100 of attributed income, and S credits $31 of the $34 corporate tax against the $31. The $3 of excess corporate tax cannot be used by S to reduce her tax liability on other taxable income.[63] S increases the basis of her C shares by $66, which is the amount of the after-tax income. Consequently, she is not taxed on the retained earnings in the form of a capital gain when she sells her shares. If C later distributes the $66 of after-tax income, S does not have income upon receipt of the distribution and reduces the basis of her shares by $66. The interest paid by C

---

59. *Id.*, at 27.
60. *Id.*, at 28.
61. *Id.*, at 27.
62. I.R.C. § 1361.
63. *Treasury 1992 Integration Study, supra* chapter 1, note 31, at chapter 3, note 5, p. 198.

on its bonds is taxable to the taxable holder and tax-free to the pension fund. On the final distribution by the fund of the interest the beneficiaries are taxed.

———

The shareholder allocation prototype not only eliminates the shareholder level tax on corporate income, but also allows the shareholder to utilize any excess corporate tax credits against the shareholder's tax liability on other taxable income. Tax-exempt shareholders, such as pension funds, get no benefit from the credit.[64] Thus, the principal beneficiaries of the tax cut resulting from the shareholder allocation prototype are individual holders of corporate equity.

The Treasury concludes that the "[e]qualization of the tax rate across all sources of income for individuals means that shareholder allocation reduces all three current law distortions,"[65] that is, the prototype reduces the bias against equity financing, the bias in favor of retentions, and the bias in favor of the noncorporate form. As demonstrated on p. 241, however, this prototype does not eliminate the tax incentive for engaging in LBOs and leveraged recapitalizations.

The Treasury estimates that the shareholder allocation prototype would result in a revenue loss of $36.8 billion annually at 1991 levels of income.[66] As previously indicated, the revenue neutral estimate of the improvement in general welfare from the prototypes ranges from $2.5 billion to $25 billion annually.[67]

Treasury's Comprehensive Business Income Tax (CBIT) Prototype[68]

Under the Treasury's CBIT prototype, all businesses including corporations, partnerships, and sole proprietorships, would be subject to a single level of tax. An exception would apply, however, for small businesses with gross receipts of less than $100,000.[69] In computing taxable income, no deduction would be allowed for interest on funded indebtedness, like bonds.[70] CBIT entities would be subject to tax on taxable income at a 31 percent rate.[71] Dividends and interest would be excluded from income of

———

64. *Id.*, at 28.
65. *Id.*, at 29.
66. *Id.*, at 152.
67. *Id.*, at 111.
68. *Id.*, at chapter 4, pp. 39–60.
69. *Id.*, at 42.
70. *Id.*, at 40.
71. *Id.*

shareholders and debtholders,[72] and under certain circumstances, investors would not be taxed on capital gains on the equity and debt of CBIT entities.[73]

This exclusion applies both to taxable and tax-exempt holders of debt and equity. The effect of the corporate level tax on the interest is to impose a tax on the interest received by tax-exempt entities. Such entities currently bear the burden of the corporate level tax on dividends but bear no tax on interest income.[74] The beneficiaries of a pension plan, IRA, or Keogh, each of which is tax-exempt, exclude from income distributions by such entities of CBIT interest and dividends.[75]

Losses do not pass through to shareholders.[76] A CBIT entity adds its after-tax income to an Excludable Distributions Account (EDA). The EDA is reduced by all dividend and interest payments.[77] A CBIT entity could make a DRIP election to treat all undistributed equity income as distributed and then recontributed by the shareholders.[78] The deemed distribution is limited to the amount of the EDA and is excluded from the shareholder's income. The shareholder increases the basis of her shares by the amount of the deemed distribution.

To prevent the pass through of tax preferences, a flat nonrefundable tax of 31 percent could be imposed at the entity level on dividends and interest paid out of preference income.[79] This tax is referred to as a "compensatory tax." Alternatively, the recipients of preference income could be required to include such dividends and interest in income.[80]

The Treasury concludes that the "CBIT prototype represents a very long-term, comprehensive option for equalizing the tax treatment of debt and equity." [81]

The CBIT prototype is demonstrated in Example 4 below by reference to the facts illustrating the present classical system in Example 1 above:

---

72. *Id.*, at 39.

73. If a compensatory tax on preference income applies at the CBIT entity level, an exemption for investor level capital gains (and nonrecognition of capital losses) would be "consistent" with CBIT principles. *Id.*, at 83.

74. If a corporation pays dividends to a tax-exempt entity out of preference income, such as tax-exempt interest, no corporate level tax and no shareholder level tax apply.

75. *Treasury 1992 Integration Study, supra* chapter 1, note 31, at 55.

76. *Id.*, at 40.

77. *Id.*, at 44.

78. *Id.*, at 56.

79. *Id.*, at 40.

80. *Id.*

81. *Id.*, at 39.

Example 4: *CBIT Prototype.* S has an initial basis of $100 for her shares in C corporation, a CBIT entity. In computing its taxable income, C does not deduct the $100 of interest paid on its bonds. Therefore, C's taxable income is $200, rather than $100, which it has under both the dividend exclusion and shareholder allocation prototypes. C's tax liability is 31 percent of that amount, or $62. C has after-tax income of $138 (*i.e.*, $200 less $62) and adds this amount to its EDA. C pays to the bondholders $69, which is the required interest of $100 less the $31 tax on the interest paid by C. The bondholders are not subject to tax on receipt of the $69, and C reduces its EDA by $69 to reflect this distribution. C retains the $69 balance of its after-tax earnings and makes a DRIP election. Therefore, S is deemed to have received a $69 excludable dividend and to have reinvested the $69 in C. S's basis in her C shares is increased by $69. S will, therefore, not be subject to tax on the $69 of retained earnings upon sale of the stock of C. Also, S is not subject to tax upon the later distribution of the after-tax income. C reduces its EDA by $69 to reflect the deemed DRIP distribution to S. As an alternative to making a DRIP election, C could distribute the $69 to S. S would exclude the full amount, and C would reduce its EDA by $69.

The CBIT has several effects. First, it imposes one level of tax on corporate income at a 31 percent rate, thereby eliminating the double tax on dividend distributions to taxable shareholders. (The 31 percent tax rate is a 3 percentage point reduction from the 34 percent rate that currently applies to such income). Second, CBIT in effect imposes a 31 percent tax on interest payments, including interest payments to tax-exempt entities.[82] Although, this tax on interest should not significantly affect most taxable holders of debt, this tax results in a significant tax increase on the current tax-exempt holders of debt, such as pension plans.

For example, in Example (4), 50 percent of C's debt is held by a pension plan, which is currently not subject to tax on the interest received from C. Under CBIT, the pension plan is in effect subject to a 31 percent tax on interest paid by a CBIT entity. Thus, the corporation has available for payment to the pension plan only $34.5 of interest. The $15.5 balance is the tax paid by C with respect to the interest.

Interest on Treasury bonds and on tax-exempt state and local bonds would not be subject to this tax.[83] Therefore, it could be expected that tax-exempt entities would reduce their holdings of corporate debt and increase their holdings of Treasury debt.

---

82. *Id.*, at 41.
83. *Id.*, at 54.

At the time the pension plan distributes to its beneficiaries the earnings on CBIT debt and equity, the beneficiaries exclude such earnings from income.[84] Thus, under CBIT, the beneficiaries, like other shareholders, receive a tax reduction with respect to dividends received by pension plans because they are not subject to tax upon the receipt of a distribution of the dividends from the pension plan.

On the other hand, the beneficiaries receive a tax increase, in the form of a loss of the deferral that applies under current law, with respect to interest on CBIT debt received by pension plans. The interest is paid out of after-tax corporate income, as contrasted to pre-tax corporate income, as under current law. Although the beneficiary is not taxed on such interest at the time of distribution, the loss of the deferral benefit (*i.e.*, under current law the interest is not taxed until distributed) is a substantial economic loss to beneficiaries. The Treasury study does not say whether the loss by beneficiaries of the benefit of deferral on interest will be offset by the gain to beneficiaries from the exclusion for dividends. The treatment of interest and dividends earned by retirement plans (*i.e.*, pensions, IRAs, and Keoghs) is discussed further below.

The Treasury explains that the "CBIT is very successful in achieving the goals of integration because it removes most differentials in the tax rates on alternative income sources for domestic and foreign investors and tax-exempt entities."[85] Under CBIT, there is (1) no bias in favor of debt financing because interest is taxed like dividends, (2) no bias in favor of retentions, and (3) no bias in favor of the noncorporate form.

The Treasury says that under CBIT "[t]hin capitalization will no longer be a tax concern" and that, therefore, numerous provisions of the Code dealing with (1) the distinction between debt and equity (*see* Section 385), and (2) the disallowance of interest deductions (*see, e.g.*, Sections 163 (e)(5), (i), (j), and 279) could be repealed.[86] As demonstrated later in this chapter, CBIT would eliminate the tax incentive for engaging in an LBO or leveraged recapitalization.

The Treasury estimates that without taxation of capital gains the CBIT prototype would result in an annual increase in revenue of $3.2 billion, and that with current law treatment of capital gains CBIT produces a revenue increase of $41.5 billion.[87] The Treasury points out, however, that under CBIT, "individual tax payments would be substantially reduced because dividends, noncorporate business income, most interest, and some capital gains would no longer be taxable to individual recipients."[88]

---

84. *Id.*, at 55.
85. *Id.*, at 41.
86. *Id.*, at 52.
87. *Id.*, at 151.
88. *Id.*

The ALI's Shareholder Credit Prototype[89]

Under the ALI's shareholder credit prototype, a withholding tax is levied on dividend distributions.[90] This is referred to as the Dividend Withholding Tax (DWT). The DWT is imposed at the highest individual shareholder rate, which is presently 31 percent.[91] Shareholders are required to include in income both the actual dividend and the associated DWT, and receive a refundable tax credit for the DWT.[92]

Corporations are, however, still subject to the corporate tax, which is fully creditable against the DWT.[93] The corporate tax rate is the highest individual tax rate.[94] The corporation maintains a taxes paid account (TPA) which is increased by corporate taxes paid and decreased in the amount of the DWT due on payment of dividends.[95] Thus, as a practical matter, if a corporation does not have any preference income, the amount in the TPA will equal the DWT. In such case, no additional DWT will be due upon payment of dividends.

If, however, the corporation has preference income and pays dividends out of the preference income at a time when there is no balance in the corporation's TPA, then the DWT applies upon the payment of such dividends.[96] Such DWT is, however, creditable against future corporate tax liability.[97] The DWT that applies upon the distribution of preference income acts as a "compensatory tax." The ALI Reporter's 1992 Integration Draft explains: "Income that was tax-preferred to the corporation is thus generally taxable when distributed to shareholders to prevent superintegration."[98]

Although the ALI would generally impose a DWT on the payment of dividends out of preference income, the proposals contain a mechanism, referred to as the exempt income account (EIA), that would allow certain preferences (to be determined later) to be passed through to shareholders.[99]

---

89. *ALI Reporter's 1992 Integration Draft, supra* chapter 1, note 30.

90. *Id.*, at 4.

91. *Id.*, at 10, Proposal 1(a).

92. *Id.*, at 4 and 11, Proposal 2(a).

93. *Id.*

94. *Id.*, at 10, Proposal 1(a).

95. *Id.*, at 11, Proposal 1(c) and (d).

96. *Id.*, at 10, Proposal 1(a) and 83.

97. *Id.*, at 10, Proposal 1(e) and 83.

98. *Id.*, at 83. Under "superintegration" corporate level preferences, such as tax-exempt interest, are passed through on a tax-free basis to shareholders.

99. *Id.*, at 91, Proposed 3 and 92–94.

A withholding tax is also levied on payments of corporate interest.[100] This is referred to as the Interest Withholding Tax (IWT), and this tax is fully creditable and refundable by the recipient of the interest. The IWT applies to interest paid to both taxable and tax-exempt debtholders. A new tax is to be levied on the investment income, including interest, dividends, and capital gains, of tax-exempt investors such as pension funds.[101] The DWT and IWT are fully creditable against the tax on tax-exempts (TTE).[102] The TTE on foreign investors is referred to as the foreign investors tax (FIT).[103]

The ALI Reporter's 1992 Integration Draft does not make a recommendation for the rate of the TTE. Thus, the ALI draft says that the rate of TTE could be set at different levels for different categories of tax-exempt entities.[104] Thus, for example, the TTE on charities might be higher or lower than the TTE on retirement plans.

The stated purpose of the TTE is to eliminate the distortion in the treatment of debt and equity held by tax-exempts. The ALI Reporter's 1992 Integration Draft explains:

In a classical system, a charitable organization or pension fund that invests in corporate equities is not taxed on dividend receipts, but the income streams that produced the dividends may be taxable at the corporate level. Corporate taxable income distributed as dividends to exempt shareholders thus bears a single, corporate-level tax, while exempt recipients of corporate interest payments receive a corporate income flow that is not taxed under current law at either the investor or the corporate level.[105]

The ALI draft then goes on to say:

As a result of the current differential between debt and equity, it would not be possible to achieve equivalent treatment of debt and equity under shareholder credit integration without either increasing or decreasing the tax burdens of exempt organizations on interest or dividends.[106]

---

100. *Id.*
101. *Id.*, at 136, Proposal 9.
102. *Id.*
103. *Id.*, at 158, Proposal 10 and 159–64.
104. *Id.*
105. *Id.*, at 133.
106. *Id.*

Although the ALI draft does not recommend a rate of TTE, as demonstrated on p. 242, if the top individual rate is 31 percent, the only rate of TTE that will completely eliminate the bias in favor of debt financing is the 31 percent rate. If the TTE is zero, then there is a tax incentive under the ALI's shareholder credit prototype (as there is under the Treasury's dividend exclusion prototype) for engaging in LBOs and leveraged recapitalizations. The more closely the rate of TTE approaches the maximum individual rate, the less the incentive for entering such transactions.

In discussing the ALI's shareholder credit prototype below, it is assumed that the rate of the TTE on all tax-exempts is 31 percent. This is, in effect, the rate of tax that applies to the dividend and interest income of tax-exempts under the Treasury CBIT prototype.[107] The ALI draft, as indicated, does not suggest a rate of TTE.[108]

Unlike the CBIT prototype, the ALI's shareholder credit prototype does not pass through interest and dividends to the beneficiaries of retirement plans on a tax-free basis. Thus, although the ALI draft imposes a TTE on the interest and dividends received by retirement plans, the draft still imposes a tax on the beneficiaries of such plans upon receipt of the distribution.

Corporations could make credits available to shareholders by declaring constructive dividends and reinvestments.[109] This procedure, which prevents the double taxation of retained earnings, is similar to the DRIP election that applies under the Treasury's proposals. Distributions of previously taxed retained earnings would be tax-free to the shareholders and would reduce the basis of the shareholder's shares.

The ALI draft concludes that this method of integration eliminates the "tax-induced distortions of the classical system,"[110] including such distortions as (1) the "tax disincentive for individuals to invest in new corporate equity," and (2) "the tax incentive for corporations to finance their investments by retained earnings or debt rather than the issuance of new shares."[111] The ALI draft goes on to say:

> These distortions are undesirable if they influence corporate financial policy in a detrimental manner, encouraging, for example, the substitution of debt for equity, thus increasing the risk of bankruptcy.[112]

---

107. *See* p. 220.

108. Presumably, a 7.6 percent rate of TTE would not alter the current tax burden of tax-exempts resulting from the corporate tax on the dividend streams received by tax-exempt entities.

109. *ALI Reporter's 1992 Integration Draft, supra* chapter 1, note 30, at 5.

110. *Id.*, at 40

111. *Id.*, at 34–35

112. *Id.*, at 35

The ALI says that it rejects the Treasury's dividend exclusion prototype because that method "would preclude the application of graduated rates to investors."[113]

The ALI's shareholder credit prototype is demonstrated in Example 5 below, by reference to the facts illustrating the present classical system in Example 1 above (*see* p. 213):

Example 5: *ALI's Shareholder Credit Prototype.* S has an initial basis of $100 for her shares in C corporation. C has taxable income of $100, computed under current law, and C incurs a $31 tax liability on the $100 of income, leaving C with $69 after tax. C's TPA has a balance of $31. If C pays a dividend of $69, the dividend is subject to the DWT; however, since the TPA has a balance of $31 no additional DWT is paid. S includes in gross income $100 (*i.e.*, $69 dividend plus $31 DWT) and receives a refundable credit of $31. Since S is in the 31 percent bracket, the credit equals S's tax liability on the dividend. If C does not pay a dividend it can elect to constructively pay the dividend of $69 and to have that amount deemed reinvested by S. The treatment to S under the constructive dividend is the same as the receipt of an actual dividend plus a $69 increase in the basis of her shares. A later distribution of the $69 is tax-free to S and reduces S's basis in that amount.

Although C deducts the interest paid on the bonds in computing taxable income, the IWT applies upon the payment by C of the interest. Therefore, the interest paid to both the taxable holder and to the tax-exempt pension plan is subject to an IWT, at a rate of 31 percent. Both the taxable holders and the pension plan (1) include the actual interest received plus the IWT in gross income, (2) compute their tax liability on the grossed-up amount, and (3) receive a refundable credit for the IWT. They each would have after-tax interest of $34.5 computed as follows. They would each (1) have a grossed-up dividend of $50 (*i.e.*, actual dividend of $34.5 plus gross-up of IWT of $15.5), (2) be subject to a 31 percent tax of $15.5, and (3) receive a credit of $15.5 for the tax.

For individual shareholders, this shareholder credit system produces similar results to the Treasury's dividend exclusion method and shareholder allocation method. Under all three prototypes, individual shareholders get the benefit of a substantial tax reduction. Tax-exempt shareholders, such a pension funds, however, are subject to tax on corporate interest income, which is presently exempt. Also, the interest income is again subject to tax upon distribution to the beneficiaries. The treatment of retirement plans under current law and each of the prototypes is discussed further below.

---

113. *Id.*, at 42.

The ALI draft does not have a revenue estimate for its shareholder credit prototype. The Treasury estimates that its shareholder credit prototype, which is not recommended by the Treasury, would result in a revenue loss of $14.6 billion a year.[114] Significant differences exist, however, between the Treasury's shareholder credit prototype and the ALI's prototype.

Treatment of Retirement Plans Under Each of the Proposals

As will be seen later in this chapter, the treatment of retirement plans (*i.e.*, pension plans, IRAs, and Keoghs) is of crucial importance in structuring LBOs and recapitalizations. For this reason, this section considers the impact of the various prototypes on stock and debt held by retirement plans.

Both the Treasury's CBIT prototype and the ALI's shareholder credit prototype would effectively impose a uniform tax on both dividend and corporate interest income of tax-exempt entities, including retirement plans. The reason for this uniformity is to eliminate one of the major differences in the treatment of debt and equity: tax-exempts bear no tax on interest.

The tax-exempt sector holds 58 percent of the corporate debt and 43 percent of corporate equity,[115] and retirement plans hold 45 percent of corporate debt and 32 percent of corporate equity. Thus, the treatment of retirement plans under these prototypes can have a significant impact.

The Treasury's dividend exclusion and shareholder allocation prototypes do not change the current law treatment of the taxation of exempt taxpayers. Thus, as under current law, in both a dividend exclusion or shareholder allocation system a retirement plan that holds stock bears indirectly the corporate tax imposed on the income stream from which the dividends are paid. On the other hand, if a retirement plan holds corporate debt, there is no tax on the interest payments at the corporate[116] or retirement plan levels. The beneficiaries are, however, subject to tax at the time the interest and dividend income is ultimately distributed.[117] This is the same treatment as under current law.

Thus, although no tax is imposed on retirement plans, a tax on dividend and interest income applies at the beneficiary level upon distribution.[118] Re-

---

114. *Treasury 1992 Integration Study, supra* chapter 1, note 31, at 152.

115. *Id.*, at 68.

116. I.R.C. § 163 (1991).

117. I.R.C. § 402 (1991).

118. I.R.C. § 402 (1991).

tirement plans, thus, provide a deferral in the taxation of income earned by the plan.

Retirement plans also provide a deduction for the beneficiary upon a contribution to the plan.[119] The beneficiary is, however, taxed at the time the amount contributed is later distributed.[120] Thus, retirement plans also provide a deferral in the taxation of contributed amounts.

These deferral benefits under current law, the dividend exclusion prototype, and the shareholder allocation prototype are illustrated by the following example:

Example 6: *Treatment of Retirement Plans Under Current Law and the Dividend Exclusion and Shareholder Allocation Prototypes.* Assume that at the beginning of year 1 a $2,000 deductible contribution is made to a pension plan (PP) for the benefit of employee E. PP invests $1,000 in stock of X corporation and $1,000 in bonds of X. At the end of the first taxable year, X corporation, which is subject to a 34 percent tax rate, pays $100 of interest on the bonds held by PP, and $66 of dividends on the stock held by PP. The $66 is X's after-tax earnings that are attributable to the X stock held by PP. Thus, X's pre-tax earnings attributable to the stock held by PP was $100, and X incurred $34 of tax with respect to that amount.

At the end of year 1, PP has $166 of income from interest ($100) and dividends ($66). At this point, PP has incurred no tax on the interest, but has indirectly borne the burden of the $34 corporate tax on the dividend.[121]

On the first day of year 2, PP sells the bonds for $1,000 and the stock for $1,000 and distributes to E all of its assets, which consist of $2,166. E is subject to tax on the full distribution at a 31 percent rate. Therefore, E incurs a tax of $641.46. This tax on E is imposed on the following three elements:

1. The $2,000 of wages that was excluded from E's income in year 1.
2. The $100 of interest received by PP.
3. The $66 of dividends received by PP.

Thus, one level of tax applies to the $100 of interest and a second level tax applies to the $66 of dividends. After tax, E has $1,494.54.[122]

Under the Treasury's CBIT prototype, the following results obtain under the facts in Example (6) above:

---

119. I.R.C. § 404 (1991).

120. I.R.C. § 402 (1991).

121. This assumes that the incidence of the corporate tax falls on shareholders and not customers or others. *See, generally, Treasury 1992 Integration Study, supra* chapter 1, note 31, at 146.

122. As pointed out by the Treasury, the effect of this tax treatment is "equivalent

Example 7: *Treatment of Retirement Plans Under CBIT.* The basic facts are the same as in Example 6 above, except X is subject to CBIT. First, X does not receive a deduction for interest and, therefore, its taxable income is larger by the amount of the interest payments. This means that there is a corporate level tax on the income stream out of which interest is paid. The corporate tax rate is 31 percent and, therefore, PP receives a $69 dividend (*i.e.*, net of the $31 tax) and a $69 interest payment (*i.e.*, net of the $31 tax). PP excludes both of these amounts from income. At the beginning of year 2, PP sells the X stock and bonds for $1,000 each and then distributes the $2,138 (*i.e.*, $2,000 from the sale of the stock and bonds plus $69 of interest and $69 of dividends).

E receives $138 tax-free, but pays a tax of $620 on the $2,000 of deferred salary income. Therefore, after-tax E has $1,518.

With respect to the dividend income, E is much better off than under current law because (1) the corporate level tax is reduced from 34 percent to 31 percent and the distribution is nontaxable. E is, however, worse off than under current law with regard to the interest because the interest is subject to tax at the corporate level, and, therefore, less interest will grow tax-free in PP. In effect, CBIT front-loads the tax on interest earned by retirement plans but relieves the beneficiary from tax on distributions of CBIT dividends and interest income.

Under the ALI's shareholder credit prototype, the following results arise under the basic facts in Example 6.

Example 8: *Treatment of Retirement Plans Under the ALI's Shareholder Credit Prototype.* The basic facts are the same as in Example 6, except the shareholder credit system applies. The tax on tax exempts (TTE) is assumed to be 31 percent,[123] and PP is subject to both a DWT and an IWT at a 31 percent rate. Consequently, PP receives $69 of dividends and $69 of interest. PP grosses up each of these amounts to $100, and credits the DWT and IWT against the TTE. After the sale of the X stock and bond, PP has $2,138 to distribute to E, which is the same amount as under CBIT. E is taxed on this full amount at a 31 percent rate, which is a tax of $662.79. Thus, E has $1,475.21 after-tax.

---

to simply exempting from income tax the pension fund's investment income." *Treasury 1992 Integration Study, supra* chapter 1, note 31, at 67.

123. As indicated, the ALI study does not specify a rate of TTE. *See* p. 224.

The following chart summarizes the above results under current law and the four prototypes.

	Current Law	Treasury's Dividend Exclusion Prototype	Treasury's Shareholder Allocation Prototype	Treasury's CBIT Prototype	ALI's Shareholder Credit Prototype
(1) Contribution of $2,000 in Year 1	$2,000 Deductible Contribution	$2,000 Deductible Contribution	$2,000 Deductible Contribution	$2,000 Deductible Contribution	$2,000 Deductible Contribution
(2) Dividend out of $100 of Corporate Earnings in Year 1	$66 34% Rate	$66 34% Rate	$66 34% Rate	$69 31% Rate of CBIT	$69 31% Rate of DWT and TTE
(3) Interest out of $100 of Corporate Earnings in Year 1	$100 Deductible	$100 Deductible	$100 Deductible	$69 31% Rate of CBIT	$69 31% Rate of IWT and TTE
(4) Distribution in Year 2 Initial Contribution plus Earnings	$2,166	$2,166	$2,166	$2,138	$2,138
(5) Beneficiary Tax	$671.46 31% of $2,166	$671.46 31% of $2,166	$671.46 31% of $2,166	$620 31% of $2,000 No Tax on the $138 of CBIT Dividends and Interest	$662.79 $31% of $2,138 Tax on the Dividends and Interest
(6) Beneficiary's After Tax Income	$1,494.54	$1,494.54	$1,494.54	$1,518	$1,475.21

As the above chart demonstrates, the Treasury's dividend exclusion and shareholder allocation prototypes do not change the current treatment of retirement plans.

The Treasury's CBIT prototype produces a larger distribution to the beneficiary in this hypothetical than the distribution under current law. This is because of (1) the lower tax rate (31 percent) that applies to the dividend income, and (2) the exclusion from the beneficiary's income of the dividend and interest income. In the long run, however, CBIT will not accumulate as much income in the retirement plan as under current law because of the corporate level tax that applies to the interest. This can be seen on line 4, which shows that after year one there is less cash in the retirement plan under CBIT than under current law.

With a 31 percent rate of TTE, the ALI's shareholder credit prototype produces the worst results for the beneficiary.[124] First, as shown on line 4, there are fewer assets in the retirement plan because of the IWT and TTE that applies to the interest. (The DWT and TTE on dividends is, however, actually less than under current law because the rate of tax is 31 percent rather than 34 percent.) Second, as shown on line 5, the beneficiary is subject to a tax on the interest and dividends upon receipt of the distribution. Under CBIT, the beneficiaries are not taxed on receipt of such interest and dividends.

This chart demonstrates that adoption of the Treasury's CBIT or the ALI's shareholder credit prototypes would change the present benefits provided by retirement plans. This would seem to be the case under the ALI approach without regard to the rate of TTE.

It is not the purpose of this chapter to determine the correct treatment of retirement plans under any of these prototypes. Before adopting any of these prototypes, however, it would be prudent to ascertain the effect of the particular prototype on retirement savings. In any event, the chart demonstrates that if the TTE is set at 31 percent, which is the rate of tax imposed on tax-exempts under CBIT, the ALI and CBIT prototypes produce radically different results for plan beneficiaries.

Impact on the Merger and Acquisition Proposals in Part 2

The proposals in part 2 principally address the appropriate treatment of taxable and tax-free acquisitions. Chapter 4 contains proposed revisions to the reorganization definition to provide for uniform treatment of the various forms of reorganizations. To qualify as a reorganization under the proposals in chapter 4, the acquisition must, without respect to form, satisfy a uniform continuity of interest requirement and a uniform substantially all the historic assets requirement. Chapter 5 suggests the adoption of a carryover basis regime for certain taxable asset acquisitions, and chapter 6 sets

---

124. Of course, the ALI study does not recommend a rate. This 31 percent rate is chosen because that is the only rate that completely eliminates the tax incentive for engaging in an LBO or leveraged recapitalization. See p. 242.

forth a proposed exception to recognition treatment for certain taxable dispositions of goodwill and going concern value. The exceptions apply only if the substantially all the historic assets requirement that applies to reorganizations is satisfied.

The purpose of the proposals in chapter 6 is to eliminate or reduce the tax barrier that presently prevents parties from structuring taxable asset acquisitions. Under current law, taxable acquisitions of stand-alone target corporations are almost always structured as stock acquisitions without a Section 338 election.[125] A taxable asset acquisition of a stand-alone target generally will not be made unless the target has substantial net operating losses that can offset the corporate taxable gain that results from the repeal of the *General Utilities* doctrine.[126]

Chapter 7 contains a proposal for mandatory Section 338 treatment on certain purchases of stock of a stand-alone target. This rule, which treats the target as if it sold and then repurchased its assets, applies if the target does not hold substantially all of its historic assets and, therefore, could not be acquired in a carryover basis asset acquisition. The purpose of this provision is to ensure parity in the treatment of stock and asset acquisitions.

Finally, chapter 8 of part 2 sets out a proposal to prevent the misallocation of purchase price in both taxable and tax-free acquisitions.

Part 2, thus, deals with the structure of the merger and acquisition provisions, including tax-free stock and asset reorganizations, and taxable stock and asset acquisitions.

Since there would continue to be acquisitions under an integrated system, there would be a continuing need for rules governing taxable and tax-free acquisitions under such a system. This point is made both by the Treasury in its discussion of the dividend exclusion and CBIT prototypes and by the ALI in its discussion of the shareholder credit prototype.

The Treasury says that the dividend exclusion prototype "retains the basic rules governing the treatment of taxable and tax-free corporate asset and stock acquisitions."[127] The Treasury further says that this prototype "retains current law rules that treat a qualifying reorganization as tax-free at the corporate level (with the target's tax attributes, including asset bases, carrying over to the acquiror) and at the shareholder level."[128]

Taxable asset acquisitions could be made under the dividend exclusion prototype with only a single level of tax.[129] The corporate tax paid on a liquidating sale of assets "would be treated like any other corporate level tax

---

125. *See* chapter 2, at p. 28.
126. *Id.*
127. *Treasury 1992 Integration Study, supra* chapter 1, note 31, at 23.
128. *Id.*
129. *Id.*

payment and would support a corresponding addition to the EDA . . . "[130] Thus, on liquidation, the proceeds generally could be distributed to the shareholders tax-free.[131] The Treasury study points out that although "upon liquidation shareholders would, as under current law, generally recognize gain to the extent liquidation proceeds exceed share basis . . . [the] shareholder's gain would be excludable . . . to the extent of a proportionate share of the liquidating corporation's EDA."[132]

In discussing its CBIT prototype the Treasury says: "As in the dividend exclusion prototype, the CBIT prototype retains the basic rules of Subchapter C governing the treatment of taxable and tax-free corporate asset and stock acquisitions."[133] Liquidating sales of assets by a CBIT entity would "give rise to additions to the EDA, thereby permitting distribution of the after-tax proceeds of such asset sales to investors without further tax."[134]

Although the Treasury does not discuss mergers and acquisitions in the section dealing with the shareholder allocation prototype, the same point also applies to that system. The shareholder allocation prototype is similar to the treatment of S corporations, and since the basic rules of Subchapter C dealing with taxable and tax-free acquisitions apply to S corporations, it can be expected that similar rules could apply under a shareholder allocation approach.

Although the ALI Reporter's 1992 Integration Draft does not "generally address the changes in the merger and acquisition provisions of the Internal Revenue Code that might be possible under integration," the study says that the shareholder credit prototype "would be consistent" with either the current reorganization provisions or the proposals contained in the ALI 1989 Study.[135] Thus, the ALI Reporter's 1992 Integration Draft acknowledges that the decision to enact its shareholder credit system is independent of the decision to enact the merger and acquisition proposals contained in the ALI 1989 Study.[136]

The ALI draft points out that on liquidation the shareholders are deemed to receive a ratable share of the TPA.[137] This treatment gives similar results to liquidations under the Treasury's dividend exclusion, shareholder

---

130. *Id.*

131. *Id.*

132. *Id.*

133. *Id.*, at 55.

134. *Id.*

135. *ALI 1992 Integration Study, supra* chapter 1, note 31, at 85.

136. *ALI 1989 Study, supra* chapter 1, note 2.

137. *ALI Reporter's 1992 Integration Draft, supra* chapter 1, note 30, at 121, Proposal 7(d), and 123.

allocation, and CBIT prototypes. The ALI study also contains a rule providing that if more than 80 percent of the stock of a target is acquired from noncorporate shareholders by another corporation in a taxable acquisition, the target is entitled to a refund of its TPA balance allocable to the purchased shares.[138] This refund of the target's TPA should redound to the benefit of the selling shareholders in the form of additional purchase price for their shares.

Since the current reorganization provisions could continue to apply under each of these integration prototypes, the reasons for the proposed revisions to the reorganization definition in chapter 4, which would merely rationalize the treatment of reorganizations would apply with equal force under any of the prototypes.

On the other hand, the proposed carryover basis treatment for taxable asset acquisitions contained in chapter 5 would not have much significance in an integrated system. In an integrated system, the taxable asset acquisition would be preferable to a taxable stock acquisition[139] because the acquiring corporation would take a cost basis for the target's assets and the shareholders would generally not be taxed on receipt of the liquidating distribution. Since there would be no double tax, there would be no significant reason for having a carryover basis rule.

For similar reasons, it would not be necessary to adopt either the goodwill exception for taxable asset acquisitions set forth in chapter 6, or the mandatory Section 338 election for certain stock acquisitions contained in chapter 7. Thus, the proposals in chapters 5, 6, and 7 only have significance under a classical system. The same would appear to be true with respect to the proposal in the ALI's 1989 Study for elective carryover basis treatment and for a goodwill exception.[140]

The proposals contained in chapter 8, which are designed to prevent a misallocation of purchase price, would have continuing vitality in an integrated system.

In summary, the suggested modifications to the reorganization definition in chapter 4 and the provision preventing misallocation of purchase price in chapter 8 have significance in both the present classical system and under any of the prototypes. The carryover basis proposal in chapter 5, the goodwill exception in chapter 6, and the mandatory Section 338 election in chapter 7 only have significance in a classical system.

No sound reasons exist for delaying the enactment of any of the proposals contained in part 2. These proposals would substantially improve the cur-

---

138. *Id.*, at 120–21, Proposal 7(c), and 122–23.

139. A Section 338 election would, however, presumably be available after a stock acquisition.

140. *See* chapter 3, p. 41.

rent treatment of mergers and acquisitions. If an integrated prototype is enacted at some point in the future, appropriate adjustments in the merger and acquisition provisions could be made at that time.

Impact on the Interest Disallowance Rules Contained in Chapter 12 of Part 3

This section illustrates the effect of an LBO and a leveraged recapitalization under current law and under each of the four integration prototypes, with a view to determining whether any of the integration prototypes would make the interest limitation rules proposed in chapter 12 of part 3 superfluous.

The rules in chapter 12 apply to LBOs and leveraged recapitalizations, involving publicly held firms. There are three general effects of these rules. First, the interest deduction on the portion of debt used in an LBO of a publicly held firm that exceeds 75 percent of the purchase price is disallowed. Thus, any acquisition of a publicly held firm would, in effect, have to be made with at least 25 percent equity. Second, interest on certain junk debt issued in the acquisition of a publicly held corporation would be disallowed in whole or in part. Third, interest on debt issued in a leveraged recapitalization of a publicly held corporation would be disallowed.

LBOs and Leveraged Recapitalizations Under Current Law

The benefits of a standard LBO under current law are illustrated in Example 9 below, by reference to the facts in illustrating the present classical system in Example 1 (*see* p. 213):

Example 9: *LBO Under Current Law.* C corporation has developed a valuable process. Consequently, C's assets which originally cost $1,000 now have a value of $1,900, and the C stock, which S purchased for $100, now has a value of $1,000. Thus, the value of the C stock is equal to the net value of C's assets, that is, $1,900 value minus C's outstanding $900 of bonds. S has a basis of $100 for her shares.

An acquiring corporation (AC) acquires C in an LBO as follows. AC contributes $100 of equity to a newly formed wholly-owned subsidiary (AC-S). AC-S issues $1,800 of bonds, all of which are purchased by pension plans. AC-S, which now has $1,900 in cash, then merges into C in a reverse subsidiary merger (*see* chapter 2, p. 29) with the following results:

1. C's $900 of outstanding bonds are paid off;
2. S receives $1,000 for her C shares,
3. AC's shares in AC-S are converted into shares of C and, therefore, AC owns all of the C shares after the merger, and

4. C assumes liability for the $1,800 of new debt.
The transaction is treated as a taxable purchase of S's shares, so there is no tax at the C level.[141] Also, there is no step-up in the basis of C's assets. S has a $900 capital gain on the transaction and incures a 28 percent tax of $252. The annual interest on the bonds is $200. C's taxable income before interest remains at $200 and, therefore, after its interest deductions it has no taxable income.

The LBO in Example 9 has wiped out C's taxable income. Therefore, the tax liability that C would have incurred in the absence of the LBO can be utilized to service the debt incurred in the LBO. Since all of the debt is held by pension plans, there is no immediate tax on the interest income. This income will not be taxed until finally distributed to the beneficiaries. Thus, in addition to eliminating C's taxable income, the transaction avoids immediate tax on the interest income. Although C has a high debt to equity ratio (*i.e.*, 18 to 1) after the transaction, the debt likely will be treated as debt for federal income tax purposes because it is not held by shareholders of C.

The proposals contained in chapter 12 would limit the deductibility of interest in the above transaction if C were a publicly held corporation. Under the excessive debt rule proposed in chapter 12, no deduction would be allowed on debt that exceeded 75 percent of the purchase price of C's stock, and under the junk debt rule, which operates independently of the excessive debt rule, all or a portion of the interest on the debt might be disallowed, depending on the structure of the bonds.

A standard type leveraged recapitalization under current law is demonstrated in Example 10 below, by reference to the facts illustrating the LBO in Example 9.

Example 10: *Leveraged Recapitalization Under Current Law.* The facts are the same as in Example 9, except that rather than going through with the LBO, C corporation does a leveraged recapitalization by issuing $900 of bonds to its shareholder S. Assume that the bonds are treated as debt for federal income tax purposes, which under current law is not an unreasonable assumption.[142] S has part dividend, part recovery of capital, and part capital gain on receipt of the $900 of bonds.[143] In any event, S will have $800 of income most of which will be capital gain. S's shares, which had a

---

141. *See* chapter 2, p. 29.
142. *See, generally, Federal Taxation of Business Enterprises, supra* chapter 1 note 20, at §§ 4:02–4:17.
143. I.R.C. § 301(c) (1991).

value of $1,000 before the transaction, have a value of $100 after the transaction. S has a zero basis for her shares.[144]

S immediately sells the bonds to pension plans. C also refunds its old bonds by issuing $900 of new bonds to pension funds and using the proceeds to pay off its old bonds. (This step is not part of the recapitalization). After both of these transactions, C has $1,800 of bonds outstanding, all of which are held by pension plans. After these transactions, C continues to have taxable income before interest of $200. The interest deductions on the bonds is $200, and therefore, as a result of the recapitalization, C's tax liability is reduced by $34.

The above transaction demonstrates that under the current classical system, a leveraged recapitalization can accomplish the same result as an LBO. In both transactions the corporate tax is eliminated by the extra interest deduction and there is no immediate tax on the interest income because the bonds are held by pension funds.

The proposals contained in chapter 12 would deny the deduction for the interest on the bonds issued in the recapitalization if C were a publicly held corporation.

LBOs and Leveraged Recapitalizations Under the Treasury's Dividend Exclusion Prototype

The following two examples illustrate that it would be possible to enter into a standard type LBO and leveraged recapitalization under the Treasury's dividend exclusion prototype. Example 11 below illustrates a standard type LBO under the Treasury's dividend exclusion prototype by reference to the facts illustrating the operation of this prototype in Example 2 (*see* p. 216) and the facts illustrating a standard type LBO under the classical system in Example 9 (*see* p. 236). Although the transaction in Example 9 is structured as a stock acquisition, for the reasons discussed below, the transaction in Example 11 is structured as an asset acquisition:

Example 11: *LBO Under Treasury's Dividend Exclusion Prototype.* The facts are the same as in Example 2, which illustrates the basic features of the dividend exclusion prototype. Assume that C has not made an actual distribution to S but has made a DRIP election. Consequently, S's basis for her C shares is increased from $100 to $166. Because of the development of the valuable process, C's assets are now valued at $1,900, and its shares are now valued at $1,000, which is the net value of C's assets (*i.e.*, $1,900 value minus $900 of bonds). AC proposes to acquire C in an LBO. Since there is just one level of tax under the dividend exclusion prototype, AC decides to

---

144. I.R.C. § 301 (d).

purchase C's assets, which have a basis of $1,066 (*i.e.*, $1,000 original basis plus $66 retained earnings). AC forms AC-S and contributes $100 to AC-S. AC-S issues $1,800 of bonds to pension plans. AC-S then purchases C's assets for $1,900 in cash.[145] AC-S, thus, has a $1,900 basis for C's assets. C has an amount realized of $1,900 on the sale and has a taxable gain of $834 (*i.e.*, $1,900 minus $1,066). C incurs a tax liability of $283.5 (*i.e.*, 34 percent of $834). C's after-tax proceeds are $1,616.5 (*i.e.*, $1,900 cash received, minus $283.5 taxes paid). C adds $550.5 to its Excludable Distributions Account (EDA) (*i.e.*, $834 gain minus $283.5 tax). The EDA previously had a zero balance because of the DRIP election. C pays off its $900 of outstanding bonds and has $716.5 remaining cash. C now liquidates, distributing $716.5 to S. S first computes her gain on the liquidation by substracting her basis for the stock of $166 from the $716.5 liquidation proceeds. This gives S a gain of $550.5, all of which is excluded from income because of the $550.5 balance in the EDA. After the liquidation, S has $716.5 in after-tax proceeds.

AC-S now has C's assets with a basis of $1,900, which is $834 more than the basis of the assets to C. C's assets still produce $200 of taxable income before interest deductions and before the additional depreciation and amortization deductions attributable to the $834 increase in basis of the assets. After the $200 interest deductions on the new bonds, AC-S has zero taxable income. After the additional depreciation and amortization deductions, AC-S has a taxable loss.

The above example illustrates two main points. The Treasury's dividend exclusion prototype does not eliminate the benefit of using debt in an LBO transaction.[146] The use of debt in the above example accomplishes the same results as the use of debt in Example 9, which illustrates an LBO under the current classical system. In both situations, the interest deduction eliminates the corporate tax liability, thereby freeing more corporate assets to service debt. Also, in both cases, no immediate tax is imposed on the interest because the bonds are held by pension funds. Thus, under a dividend exclusion system, there will still be a need for provisions such as Section 385, which authorizes the Treasury to issue regulations dealing with the distinction between debt and equity, Section 279, which disallows the deduction for interest on certain corporate acquisition indebtedness, or some

---

145. Alternatively, C could merge into AC-S in a taxable forward triangular merger, which would be treated as a purchase of C's assets followed by a liquidation of C. *See* chapter 2, at p. 29.

146. The Treasury acknowledges that the dividend exclusion prototype would "narrow (but not eliminate)" the difference between debt and equity. *Treasury 1992 Integration Study, supra* chapter 1, note 31, at 18.

240 Reform of the Taxation of Mergers, Acquisitions, and LBOs

other interest limitation provisions, such as those proposed in chapter 12. The point is: *Under the Treasury dividend exclusion model, which the Treasury favors over all other models, the proposals in chapter 12 would still have vitality.*

The second point is that under the Treasury's dividend exclusion prototype, the preferred acquisition form is the taxable asset acquisition because only one level of tax applies and the basis of the target's assets is stepped-up. This step-up in basis gives additional tax benefits in acquisitions, and this could be an extra incentive under this prototype for corporations to enter such transactions.

Also, it would appear that under the dividend exclusion prototype if a Section 338 election is made after a purchase of a target's stock, the target's corporate level tax liability resulting from the deemed sale should result in a reduction in the tax liabilities of the target's shareholders. This might be accomplished by treating a stock purchase followed by a Section 338 election as giving rise to a liquidation of the target similar to the treatment under Section 338(h)(10).[147] Under this approach, the selling shareholders would be taxed as if the target had sold its assets and then liquidated. The sale of stock would not be taxable but the liquidation would. This form would give the selling shareholders the same treatment that would occur in a taxable asset acquisition followed by liquidation. If this approach is adopted, it could be expected that Section 338 elections would generally be made after taxable stock acquisitions.

Thus, the preferred form of taxable acquisition under the dividend exclusion prototype is the opposite of the preferred form under current law. Under current law, virtually every taxable acquisition of a stand-alone target is effectuated as a stock acquisition without a Section 338 election. This type of stock transaction avoids the corporate level tax that would apply in an asset acquisition as a result of repeal of the *General Utilities* doctrine. (*See* chapter 2, at 28).

As illustrated in Example 12 below, significant tax benefits could arise from a leveraged recapitalization under the Treasury's dividend exclusion prototype.

Example 12: *Leveraged Recapitalization Under the Treasury Dividend Exclusion Prototype.* The facts are the same as in Example 11, except C does a leveraged recapitalization by issuing $900 of junk bonds to S. S has a capital gain of $734 on the transaction (*i.e.*, $900 distribution minus $166 basis for her shares).[148] S immediately sells the bonds to a pension plan. C also refunds its outstanding bonds by issuing $900 of new bonds to pension funds and uses the proceeds to pay off the old bonds. Apparently, there is

---

147. *See* chapter 2, p. 33.
148. I.R.C. § 301(c) (1991).

no increase in C's basis for its assets on the distribution, which is the result under current law. After the transaction C still has $200 of taxable income before deduction of interest. After deduction of the $200 of interest on the new bonds, C has zero taxable income.

The above leveraged recapitalization under the Treasury's dividend exclusion prototype produces essentially the same results as the leveraged recapitalization under the current classical system illustrated in Example 10. In both transactions (1) C's corporate tax liability is eliminated, thereby freeing additional cash to service debt, and (2) the interest is not subject to immediate taxation.

Although the LBO and leveraged recapitalization under current law can produce the same results, under the dividend exclusion prototype, the LBO provides more tax benefits than the leveraged recapitalization because of the step-up in the basis of the target's assets in the LBO.

The proposals in chapter 12 would eliminate the deduction for the interest on the bonds issued in the recapitalization of C if C were a publicly held corporation. This proposal, thus, would have vitality under the Treasury's dividend exclusion prototype.

LBOs and Leveraged Recapitalizations Under the Treasury's Shareholder Allocation Prototype

A standard type LBO or leveraged recapitalization could occur under the Treasury's shareholder allocation prototype with results similar to those under the dividend exclusion prototype discussed above. This is because interest is fully deductible in computing the corporation's taxable income, and the interest is not subject to immediate tax if the debt is held by pension plans. Also, there would be a preference for taxable asset acquisitions to benefit from the higher basis for the target's assets.

Thus, the Treasury's shareholder allocation prototype has the same incentive as under present law for substituting debt for equity and also has the additional incentive of a step-up in basis of the target's assets in an LBO.

LBOs and Leveraged Recapitalizations Under the Treasury's CBIT Prototype

Under the CBIT prototype, interest is not deductible at the corporate level, and both dividends and interest paid to pension plans and other tax-exempt investors bear the same corporate tax. Therefore, there is no tax incentive for engaging in an LBO or leveraged recapitalization. As compared to current law, which has a bias against asset acquisitions because of the double tax,[149] an incentive exists under the CBIT prototype for engaging in taxable asset acquisitions (whether or not leveraged) to get the benefit of a step-up in basis of the target's assets.

In planning the acquisition of C, AC would essentially be indifferent between the use of debt and equity because neither interest nor dividends are deductible. Also there is a 31 percent tax on the income out of which dividends and interests are paid. Consequently, the proposals contained in chapter 12 would not have any vitality under the CBIT prototype.

The Treasury indicates, however, that the CBIT prototype is a long-term solution and would have to be phased in over a 10 year period.[150] During the phase in period, the proposals in chapter 12 might be needed.

LBOs and Leveraged Recaptilizations Under the ALI's Shareholder Credit Prototype

Under the ALI's shareholder credit prototype interest is deductible in computing taxable income of the corporation, but a withholding tax of 31 percent applies to interest payments (IWT). Also a withholding tax of 31 percent applies to dividends (DWT). The DWT can be satisfied by previous payments of the corporate tax (TPA).

Both taxable and tax-exempt entities are taxed on interest received and receive a refundable credit for the IWT, and both are taxed on dividends received and receive a refundable credit for the DWT.

Although the ALI draft does not specify the rate of tax on tax-exempt entities (TTE), in order to eliminate the tax incentive for engaging in LBOs and leveraged recapitalizations, the rate of the TTE would have to be the same as the maximum 31 percent rate of tax that applies to individuals. This is the result under the Treasury's CBIT prototype.[151]

If the rate of TTE on pension plans were set at zero, an LBO or leveraged recapitalization under the ALI's shareholder credit system would produce essentially the same results as an LBO or leveraged recapitalization under the Treasury's dividend exclusion and shareholder allocation prototypes. Under all three prototypes:

1. Interest would be deductible at the corporate level,

2. Interest would not be immediately taxable if paid to a pension plan,

3. An asset acquisition would give rise to a step-up in basis of the target's assets at the cost of only one level of tax, and

---

149. *See* chapter 2, at p. 28.

150. *Treasury 1992 Integration Study, supra* chapter 1, note 31, at 39.

151. Also, in view of the second level of tax that would apply upon distributions from pension plans under the ALI's shareholder credit prototype (*see* p. 228), there would be a disincentive for a pension plan to hold corporate debt or equity.

4. Upon receipt of the liquidation proceeds, the target's shareholders would not be subject to tax.

The closer the rate of TTE is to the maximum individual rate, the less the incentive to engage in LBOs and leveraged recapitalizations.

Summary

The proposals contained in chapter 12 for curtailing the use of debt in LBOs and leveraged recapitalizations have continuing vitality under both the Treasury's dividend exclusion prototype, which the Treasury prefers over all others, and its shareholder allocation prototype. These two prototypes do not eliminate the tax incentive for engaging in debt financed acquisitions and recapitalizations.

If the Treasury's dividend exclusion prototype were adopted without also adopting rules similar to those contained in chapter 12, there would be no barrier against over-leveraged transactions.

The Treasury's CBIT prototype eliminates the present deduction for corporate interest and, therefore, eliminates the bias in favor of debt financed acquisitions and recapitalizations. If this system were fully implemented, there would be no need for the proposals contained in chapter 12.

Depending on the rate of the TTE, the ALI's shareholder credit prototype may or may not eliminate the bias in favor of debt financed acquisitions and recapitalizations.

The proposals contained in chapter 12 move in the direction of the Treasury's CBIT and the ALI's shareholder credit prototypes in that the proposals would restrict the deductibility of corporate interest. The proposals in chapter 12 are, however, much more focused at the problems with over-leveraged transactions and would not require the radical departure from current law that would be required by either the Treasury's CBIT or the ALI's shareholder credit prototypes.

The bottom line is that in view of the failure of the Treasury's preferred dividend exclusion prototype to eliminate the overly leveraged transaction and the admitted long-term nature of a CBIT or shareholder credit prototype, it would be wise for Congress to act now on the proposals contained in chapter 12.

CHAPTER 16

. . . .

Conclusion

This book proposes a new regime for the taxation of mergers, acquisitions, and LBOs. The proposals fall into two broad categories: (1) rules for determining whether the parties to a merger or acquisition receive taxable or tax-free treatment; and (2) rules governing the taxation of LBOs and other equity conversion transactions.

Part 2 contains the proposed rules governing mergers and acquisitions, and part 3 sets out the rules covering LBOs and related transactions. The proposals in part 2 could be adopted by enacting the amendments of the Code proposed in appendix B, and the proposals in part 3 could be adopted by enacting the amendments contained in appendices C and D. The neutrality of these proposals is demonstrated below.

Chapter 15, which together with this chapter constitutes part 4, addresses the impact the adoption of an integrated tax system would have on the proposals contained in parts 2 and 3.

Part 2

The enactment of the rules in part 2 would take a large step in the direction of rationalizing the federal income tax law of mergers and acquisitions. Under these proposals, there would be uniform treatment of the various forms of acquisitive reorganizations. Thus, tax-free treatment would be available in mergers, stock acquisitions, and asset acquisitions only if both the uniform "continuity of interest" requirement and the uniform "substantially all of the assets" requirement are satisfied. (*See* chapter 4).

The adoption of the proposed uniform 80 percent continuity of interest requirement for acquisitive reorganizations, with the focus on the underlying voting stock of the acquiring corporation, would provide nonrecognition treatment only if the target shareholders as a group have a real continuing interest in the assets transferred.

The adoption of the "substantially all" requirement for each of the forms of acquisitive reorganization would ensure the integrity of the reorganization concept by preventing break-up transactions that are partially taxable and partially tax-free. On the other hand, the exception from the substantially all requirement for tax-free spin-offs prior to an acquisitive reorganization would eliminate the nonsensical prohibition under current law of such transactions for certain types of reorganizations.

Two provisions provide relief from the repeal, by the Tax Reform Act of 1986, of the *General Utilities* doctrine. Under the *General Utilites* doctrine, a stand-alone target corporation could sell its assets in a liquidating transaction without being subject to tax, except for certain recapture items. Thus, prior to 1986, there generally was only a shareholder level tax on a liquidating sale or distribution. Now there is both a corporate level and a shareholder level tax that can go as high as 52.48 percent. This double tax has made it practically impossible for a target to sell its assests in a taxable acquisition. Consequently, taxable acquisitions of stand-alone targets are almost always done as stock acquisitions, without a Section 338 election.

Thus, the repeal of the *General Utilities* doctrine has led to the practical repeal of the taxable asset acquisition transaction. This type of transaction can serve a good business purpose and should not be effectively eliminated by an overly harsh tax rule. The carryover basis rule in chapter 5 and the goodwill exception rule in chapter 6 would provide relief from the repeal of the *General Utilities* doctrine. Under the carryover basis rule, a stand-alone target corporation that sells "substantially all" of its assets to an acquiring corporation and then liquidates would have nonrecognition treatment on the sale, and the acquiring corporation would take the target's assets with a carryover basis (*i.e.*, the target's basis for those assets). (*See* chapter 5.) The target's shareholders would, of course, be fully taxable on receipt of the liquidating proceeds. This carryover basis rule would allow taxpayers to again use the taxable asset transaction form of acquisition.

The parties may, however, elect out of carryover basis treatment. If this election out is made, the transaction would be taxable to the target, subject to the goodwill exception noted below, and the acquiring corporation would take the target's assets with a cost basis. Under the goodwill exception, if a target corporation makes a liquidating sale of substantially all of its assets to an acquiring corporation and the parties elect to have the transaction treated as a taxable acquisition, the target would not recognize taxable gain on the disposition of its goodwill and other nonamortizable intangibles. (*See* chapter 6.) This rule is based on the theory that it is inappropriate to impose a double level of tax with respect to the goodwill and other nonamortizable intangibles because the acquiring corporation will not receive any deductions for the portion of the purchase price allocated to such items.

If Congress enacts a provision like Section 197 (contained in the Tax Fairness and Economic Growth Bill of 1992)[1] that makes goodwill and going concern value, along with other intangibles, amortizable, then the target could still qualify for the nonrecognition treatment on the sale of its goodwill and going concern value as long as the acquiring corporation agreed not to take an amortization deduction for such items.

The carryover basis rule for taxable asset acquisitions and the exception for goodwill for elective, taxable asset acquisitions only apply to transactions that would have qualified as acquisitive reorganizations were it not for a failure to satisfy the continuity of interest requirement. Thus, the carryover basis and the goodwill exceptions to *General Utilities* repeal apply to taxable acquisitions that parallel the acquisitive asset reorganization. Since the "substantially all" the assets test must be satisfied in these types of taxable acquisitions, if the continuity of interest test were satisfied, the transaction would constitute a tax-free asset reorganization. This parallelism is a sensible policy because both the carryover basis regime and the exception for goodwill are departures from the general recognition rule and should be construed narrowly.

Either the carryover basis rule or the nonrecognition for goodwill rule should apply in most taxable asset acquisitions. These rules should be particularly helpful in allowing corporations to again enter into taxable asset acquisitions.

Parity in the treatment of stock and asset acquisitions is ensured by the rule requiring a mandatory Section 338 election for stock purchases in which a target corporation, pursuant to an arrangement with an acquiring corporation, sells a significant portion of its assets to a third party prior to the acquisition by the acquiring corporation of the target's stock. (*See* chapter 7.) Under this mandatory Section 338 election, after the stock purchase, the target is deemed to have sold and repurchased its assets in a fully taxable acquisition. This mandatory taxation at the target level for stock purchases only applies under the following conditions: (1) the acquiring corporation purchases at least 80 percent of target's stock, and (2) at the time of the stock purchase the target does not hold "substantially all" of its pre-acquisition assets. Thus, this mandatory tax treatment only applies if the acquiring corporation could not acquire the target's assets in either a tax-free asset reorganization or in a carryover basis taxable asset acquisition because the "substantially all the assets" test could not be met.

The parties to acquisitions have been misallocating the purchase price of stock to covenants not to compete and similar items that are deductible to the acquiring corporation. Since there is presently no substantial difference between the rate of tax on capital gain and the rate on ordinary income,

1. *See* 1992 House Bill, *supra* chapter 6, note 3.

selling shareholders may be essentially indifferent between receiving additional purchase price (and increased capital gain) and having such additional amounts paid for covenants not to compete or similar items that produce ordinary income. Since the acquiror has a great incentive to allocate purchase price to deductible items, and the selling shareholders are essentially indifferent, there have been substantial misallocations. The proposals contained in chapter 8 are designed to prevent such misallocations.

The adoption of the rules in part 2 would promote neutrality between the different forms of acquisitive reorganizations and in the treatment of stock and asset acquisitions. Transactions that have the same economic effect would be taxed the same. This adherence to the neutrality principle of tax policy[2] is demonstrated below.

Part 3

Part 3 proposes that the deduction for interest in acquisitions of the stock or assets of publicly held corporations be disallowed to the extent the transaction is excessively leveraged or financed with junk debt. This limitation would be implemented by the enactment of Proposed Section 279, which is set forth in appendix D. Also, part 3 proposes that the deduction for interest be disallowed in leveraged recapitalizations of publicly held corporations. This proposal would be implemented by enactment of the amendments to Section 163 contained in appendix C.

Acquisitions of closely held corporations and acquisitions of divisions and subsidiaries of publicly held firms are not affected by these rules. There does not appear to have been a significant problem with such transactions.

The principal purpose of the acquisition rule is to ensure that transactions subject to the rule have a significant equity base. Thus, the rule would ensure that in any taxable acquisition of a publicly held corporation at least 25 percent of the acquisition proceeds would have to be financed by equity contributions. This type of equity base will reduce the risk of bankruptcy and permit firms to engage in future value maximizing investments. (*See* chapter 12.)

The principal purpose of the leveraged recapitalization rule is to protect the integrity of the acquisition rule by preventing the use of a leveraged recapitalization to accomplish the economic equivalent of a debt financed acquisition. Both of these rules would curtail the erosion of the corporate tax base that occurs upon the conversion of equity to debt. (*See* chapter 12.)

The adoption of the rules contained in part 3 would not significantly intrude on the operation of the market for corporate control; they would only

---

2. *See* Musgrave and Musgrave, *Public Finance, supra* chapter 1, note 56.

eliminate overly leveraged transactions involving public corporations. The rules should make it less likely that acquisitions of questionable economic efficiency will occur.

None of the arguments in favor of the present interest deduction should lead Congress to reject the proposals in part 3. (*See* chapter 14.) In particular, it is highly unlikely that the adoption of these proposals would cause an adverse market reaction of the kind that arguably resulted in response to the proposed tax changes contained in the 1987 House Bill. This is particularly so at this time because overly leveraged transactions have not been as prevalent as in past years. Congress can avoid a return to such harmful transactions by acting now.

Demonstration of Neutrality

Appendix A contains a chart that demonstrates that the proposals in part 2 comply with the neutrality principle by taxing the three forms of acquisitions (merger, stock acquisition, and asset acquisition) on a uniform basis. Footnotes 10 and 11 to appendix A demonstrate the neutrality of the proposals in part 3 relating to LBOs.

The vertical axis of the chart is divided into two sections. Section I, which is labeled *All Forms of Stock Acquisitions*, encompasses the acquisition of at least 80 percent of the target's stock either directly or in a reverse subsidiary merger. Section II, which is labeled *All Forms of Asset Acquisitions*, encompasses the acquisition of the target's assets either directly or in a forward subsidiary merger with the target liquidating and distributing the proceeds to its shareholders.

Sections I and II are each further subdivided into the following subsections: (1) *Treatment of Target Shareholders*, (2) *Treatment of Target Corporation*, (3) *Treatment of Acquiring Corporation*, and (4) *Treatment of the Acquiring Sub* (in a triangular or grandparent type reorganization or taxable acquisition). Thus, the vertical axis sets out the parties to both stock and asset acquisitions.

The horizontal rows consist of various combinations of (1) either satisfying or not satisfying the uniform continuity of interest requirement (*see* chapter 4) and the uniform substantially all requirement (*see* chapter 4), and (2) either making or not making the taxable asset election (*see* chapter 5) and the Section 338 election (*see* chapter 5).

In row [A], both the continuity of interest test and the substantially all test are satisfied. As a consequence, for each form of stock and asset acquisition indicated on the vertical axis, the transaction is treated as a reorganization with the following results. First, the target's shareholders have nonrecognition treatment on receipt of stock. Second, the target corporation has nonrecognition. Third, the target's assets have a carryover basis in its hands in a stock acquisition and in the acquiring corporation's hands an asset acquisition. Fourth, the acquiring corporation takes a net basis for the target's stock in a stock acquisition and a net basis for the stock of the acquiring sub in a triangular or grandparent type reorganization.

In row [B], the continuity of interest test is not satisfied (*see* chapter 4) (*e.g.*, there is a purchase for cash of the target's stock or assets), but the substantially all test is satisfied (*see* chapter 4) (*i.e.*, the target retains substantially all of its assets in a stock acquisition or has substantially all of its assets acquired in an asset acquisition). Thus, the transaction would have qualified as a reorganization but for the failure to satisfy the continuity of interest test. In a stock acquisition, the Section 338 election is not made, and in an asset acquisition, the taxable asset election is not made (*see* chapter 5). As indicated in the chart, (1) the target's shareholders have taxable treatment, (2) the target corporation has nonrecognition treatment, (3) the target's assets have a carryover basis in its hands in a stock acquisition and in the acquiring corporation's hands in an asset acquisition, and (4) the acquiring corporation takes a cost basis for the target's stock in a stock acquisition and for the stock of the acquiring sub in a triangular or grandparent type acquisition. Although in a stock acquisition the acquiring corporation has a cost basis for the target's stock, the target's assets still have a carryover basis.[3]

In row [C], the transaction fails the continuity of interest requirement but satisfies the substantially all test, and the taxable asset election is made in an asset acquisition (*see* chapter 5) and a Section 338 election is made in a stock acquisition. As a consequence, in each form of acquisition indicated on the vertical axis (1) the target's shareholders are taxable, (2) the target corporation is taxed except with respect to goodwill (*see* chapters 5 and 6), (3) the target's assets have a cost basis in its hands in a stock acquisition and in the acquiring corporation's hands in an asset acquisition, and (4) the acquiring corporation takes a cost basis for the target's stock in a stock acqui-

---

3. It may appear that there is a discontinuity between (1) a stock acquisition in which the acquiring corporation takes a cost basis for the target's stock and the target has a carryover basis for its assets (*see* appendix A, vertical I.3 and horizontal [B]), and (2) an asset acquisition in which the acquiring corporation takes a carryover basis for the target's assets (*see* appendix A, vertical II.3., horizontal [B]). Because of the cost basis for the target's stock, the stock could be resold by the acquiring corporation without further tax, whereas the carryover basis for the target's assets in an asset acquisition gives rise to a potential tax on the resale of the assets. However, this apparent discontinuity is eliminated if either (1) the asset acquisition is made by a subsidiary of the acquiror so that the substance of the transaction is the same as a stock acquisition, or (2) after a stock acquisition the target is liquidated so that the substance of the transaction is the same as an asset acquisition.

sition and for the stock of the acquiring sub in a triangular or grandparent type acquisition.

Finally, in row [D], the transaction fails the substantially all test and either fails or does not fail the continuity of interest test. As a consequence, in each form of acquisition indicated on the vertical axis (1) the target's shareholders are taxable, (2) the target corporation is taxable without an exception for goodwill both in a stock acquisition because of the mandatory Section 338 election (*see* chapter 7) and in an asset acquisition because the goodwill exception does not apply (*see* chapter 6), (3) the target's assets have a cost basis in the target's hands in a stock acquisition and in the hands of the acquiring corporation in an asset acquisition, and (4) the acquiring corporation takes a cost basis for the target's stock in a stock acquisition and for the stock of the acquiring sub in a triangular or grandparent type acquisition. The transaction does not qualify for carryover basis treatment at the target level because of the failure of the transaction to satisfy the substantially all test. Carryover basis treatment should not be available where only a portion of the target's assets are either acquired in an asset acquisition or held by the target at the time of a stock acquisition. (*See* chapter 5.)

As indicated by footnote 4 to the chart, a misallocation of purchase price to deductible payments is prohibited in each form of acquisition (*see* chapter 8).

Thus, this chart demonstrates that under the rules proposed in part 2, the tax treatment to the parties to an acquisition is not governed by the form of the transaction but rather by the substance; if the substance is the same, the tax consequences are the same.

Part 4, Chapter 15

Under the current classical tax system, corporate income is taxed twice: first, when earned by the corporation, and second, when distributed to shareholders. The Treasury 1992 Integration Study and the ALI Reporter's 1992 Integration Draft together set out four possible prototypes for integrating the corporate and individual taxes by taxing corporate income once. Chapter 15 examines the impact these prototypes would have on the proposals contained in parts 2 and 3.

Chapter 15 demonstrates that the proposed revision of the reorganization provision contained in chapter 4 would have vitality under each of the four integration prototypes. This is also true for the rules in chapter 8, which are designed to prevent a misallocation of purchase price. On the other hand, the carryover basis rule contained in chapter 5, the goodwill exception rule contained in chapter 6, and the mandatory Section 338 election contained in chapter 7 would not be needed under any of the prototypes.

Chapter 15 illustrates that the interest disallowance provisions contained in chapter 12 would continue to have vitality under both the Treasury's dividend exclusion prototype, which is the Treasury's preferred option, and its shareholder allocation prototype. The interest limitation rules might have vitality under the ALI's shareholder credit prototype, depending upon the manner in which tax-exempt entities are treated. The interest proposals, however, would not be needed under the Treasury's comprehensive business income tax (CBIT) prototype, which the Treasury says is a long-term option.

It is unlikely that an integrated system will be adopted in the near future, and in any event, many of the proposals contained here are consistent with an integrated system. Therefore, the prospect of a future integrated system is not a reason for delaying action on the proposals contained in parts 2 and 3.

Appendixes

APPENDIX A
Demonstration of Neutrality

	[A]	[B]	[C]	[D]
	Continuity of Interest and Substantially All Tests Met.[10] See chapter 4[3]	No Continuity of Interest, But Substantially All Tests Met. No Taxable Asset Election or § 338 Election.[11] See Chapter 5	No Continuity of Interest, But Substantially All Tests Met. Taxable Asset Election or § 338 Election Made.[11] See Chapters 5 and 6	Fail or Not Fail Continuity of Interest Continuity of Interest Fail Substantially All Tests.[11] See Chapters 5, 6 and 7
I. All Forms of Stock Acquisitions[1]				
1) Treatment of Target Shareholders[4]	Reorganization: Nonrecognition on receipt of stock. See Chapter 4[4]	Taxable See Chapter 4[4]	Taxable See Chapter 4[4]	Taxable See Chapter 4[4]
2) Treatment of Target Corporation	Reorganization: Nonrecognition; Carryover basis. See Chapter 4	Nonrecognition[5] See Chapter 5	Taxable with Nonrecognition for Goodwill. See Chapters 5 and 6	Mandatory § 338 Election: Taxable No exception for Goodwill See chapters 5, 6 and 7
3) Treatment of Acquiring Corporation	Reorganization: Net Basis for Target's Stock.[8] See Chapter 4	Cost Basis for Target's Stock; Carryover Basis for Target's Assets.[5] See Chapter 5	Cost basis for Target's Stock; Cost Basis for Target's Assets. See Chapter 5	Cost Basis for Target's Stock and Assets. See chapter 7
4) Treatment of Acquiring Sub[9]	Same as (3) and Net Basis for Sub's Stock[8]	Same as (3) and Cost Basis for Sub's Stock[7]	Same as (3) and Cost Basis for Sub's Stock[7]	Same as (3) and Cost Basis for Sub's Stock[7]
II. All Forms of Asset Acquisitions[2]				
1) Treatment of Target Shareholders[4]	Reorganization:	Taxable	Taxable	Taxable

254

	Reorganization (See Chapter 4)	(See Chapter 5)	(See Chapters 5 and 6)	(See Chapters 6 and 7)
Receipt of Stock. See Chapter 4[4]				
2) Treatment of Target Corporation	Reorganization: Nonrecognition. See Chapter 4	Nonrecognition[6] See Chapter 5	Taxable with Nonrecognition for Goodwill. See Chapters 5 and 6	Taxable No Exception for Goodwill. See Chapters 6 and 7
3) Treatment of Acquiring Corporation	Reorganization: Carryover Basis for Target's Assets. See Chapter 4	Carryover Basis for Target's Assets.[6] See Chapter 5	Cost Basis for Target's Assets. See Chapters 5 and 6	Cost Basis for Target's Assets. See Chapter 5
4) Treatment of Acquiring Sub[9]	Same as (3) and Net Basis for Sub's Stock[8]	Same as (3) and Cost Basis for Sub's Stock[7]	Same as (3) and Cost Basis for Sub's Stock[7]	Same as (3) and Cost Basis for Sub's Stock[7]

1. Acquisition of at least 80% of the target's stock either directly or in a reverse subsidiary merger.

2. Acquisition of the target's assets either directly or in a forward subsidiary merger with the target liquidating and distributing the proceeds to its shareholders.

3. Since the uniform continuity of interest requirement (see Chapter 4, p. 59) and substantially all tests (see Chapter 4, p. 62) are satisfied, these transactions qualify as acquisitive reorganizations. Assume that the business purpose requirement and the continuity of business enterprise requirement are also satisfied. Each form of reorganization may (1) be completed as a creeping reorganization (see Chapter 4, p. 79), (2) be preceded by a spin-off type transaction (see Chapter 4, p. 63), (3) involve the acquisition of a newly incorporated active business (see Chapter 4, p. 92.), (4) involve the acquisition of a subsidiary which could have been spun off (see Chapter 4, p. 93), or (5) be followed by a redeployment of assets within the acquiring parent's group (see Chapter 4, p. 90).

4. A misallocation of purchase price to deductible payments is curtailed in all transactions. See Chapter 8.

5. Assuming no § 338 election.

6. Assuming no Taxable Asset Election. See Chapter 5.

7. If acquiring corporation (acquiring parent) forms a subsidiary (acquiring sub) to which it transfers the considerations to be paid in the acquisition (i.e., cash) and acquiring sub acquires the target's assets, then the acquiring parent will take a cost basis for the stock of acquiring sub. The acquiring sub will have either a carryover basis or a cost basis for the assets of target.

8. In a stock for stock reorganization under Proposed Section 368(a)(1)(B), the acquiring corporation takes a net basis for the target's stock under principles similar to those in Prop. Treas. Reg. § 1.358-6. Thus, the carryover basis rule of Section 362 does not apply in the case of a (B) reorganization. See Chapter 4, p. 69. The net basis rule of Prop. Treas. Reg. § 1.358-6 also applies to all forms of triangular and grandparent type reorganizations. See Chapter 4, p. 69. Also, in each form of triangular or grandparent type reorganization the acquiring subsidiary does not have recognition upon issuance of the acquiring parent's stock under principles similar to those in Prop. Treas. Reg. § 1.1032. See Chapter 4, p. 69.

9. In a triangular or grandparent type reorganization or taxable acquisition.

10. The proposal in part 3 concerning junk debt applies to reorganizations and taxable acquisitions involving publicly held target corporations, but the proposal concerning excessive debt does not apply to reorganizations. See Chapter 12.

11. The proposals in part 3 relating to LBOs involving publicly held target corporations apply in all forms of taxable acquisition (i.e., non-reorganization acquisitions). See Chapter 12.

* Additions to the current Section 368 are indicated by underlining, and deletions are indicated by lining out.
** The reference to "Chapter _____" in the comments is to the relevant section of the body of the book.

APPENDIX B
Amendments to Section 368

	Comments
SECTION 368. DEFINITIONS RELATING TO CORPORATE REORGANIZATIONS*	
Section 368(a) REORGANIZATION—	
Section 368(a) (1) IN GENERAL—For purposes of parts I and II and this part, the term "reorganization" means—	
(A a statutory merger or consolidation;	
Proposed Section 368(a) (1) (A) . . . [T]he term "reorganization" means . . . a statutory merger or consolidation in which:	*See* Chapter 4, p. 71.** The statutory merger or consolidation requirement is the same as in the present Section 368(a) (1) (A) (the "(A)").
(i) the acquiring corporation (as defined in paragraph (4) (B)) acquires (aa) substantially all (as defined in paragraph (4) (G)) of the historic assets (as defined in paragraph (4) (H)) of the target corporation (as defined in paragraph (4) (A)), or (bb) control (as defined in subsection (c)) of the target corporation (whether or not the acquiring corporation had control immediately before the acquisition) and the target corporation holds substantially all of its historic assets; and	*See* Chapter 4, p. 71. This encompasses the pattern of the current (A) and the current forward and reverse subsidiary mergers under Section 368(a) (2) (D) and (E), with the addition of a substantially all test for the (A). Substantially all the assets do not include assets that are distributed by the target corporation in a Section 355 distribution. *See* the definition of historic assets in Proposed Section 368(a) (4) (H).
(ii) the historic shareholders (as defined in paragraph (4) (F)) of the target corporation receive in exchange for their stock in the target corporation stock of the acquiring corporation (or stock of any acquiring parent (as	*See* Chapter 4, p. 74. In order to satisfy the continuity of interest requirement, at least 80% of the consideration received by the shareholders of the target must in most

256

defined in paragraph (4) (C))) which stock satisfies the continuity of interest requirement (as defined in paragraph (4) (E)).

~~(B) the acquisition by one corporation, in exchange solely for all or part of its voting stock (or in exchange solely for all or a part of the voting stock of a corporation which is in control of the acquiring corporation), of stock of another corporation if, immediately after the acquisition, the acquiring corporation has control of such other corporation (whether or not such acquiring corporation had control immediately before the acquisition);~~

Proposed Section 368 (a) (1) (B) . . . . [T]he term "reorganization" means . . . a stock acquisition in which—

(i) the acquiring corporation acquires control (within the meaning of subsection (c)) of the target corporation (whether or not the acquiring corporation had control immediately before the acquisition);

(ii) after the acquisition the target corporation holds substantially all of its historic assets; and

(iii) the historic shareholders of the target corporation receive in exchange for their stock in the target corporation stock of the acquiring corporation (or stock of any acquiring parent) which stock satisfies the continuity of interest requirement.

~~(C) the acquisition by one corporation, in exchange solely for all or a part of its voting stock (or in exchange solely for all or a part of the voting stock of a corporation which is in control of the acquiring corporation), of substantially all of the properties of another corporation, but in determining whether the exchange is solely for stock the assumption by~~

cases be voting common stock of either the acquiring corporation or the acquiring parent. *See* Proposed Section 368(a) (4) (E). An acquiring parent is any corporation that is a direct or indirect 80% parent of the target.

See Chapter 4, p. 72. This encompasses the current straight and triangular (B).

See Chapter 4, p. 72. The control test is the same 80% requirement that applies under the current statute.

See Chapter 4, p. 87. The substantially all test that presently applies to the (C) and the reverse and forward subsidiary mergers is extended to the Proposed (B). There is an exception, however, for tax-free distributions under Section 355. *See* Proposed Section 368(a) (4) (H).

See Chapter 4, p. 74. In order to satisfy the continuity of interest requirement, 80% of the consideration must be, in essence, voting common stock of either the acquiring corporation or of the acquiring parent. *See* Proposed Section 368(a) (4) (E).

the acquiring corporation of a liability or the other; or the fact that property acquired is subject to a liability, shall be disregarded;

Proposed Section 368(a) (1) (C) . . . . [T]he term "reorganization" means . . . an asset acquisition in which—

(i) the acquiring corporation acquires substantially all of the historic assets of the target corporation;

See Chapter 4, p. 74. This encompasses the current straight and triangular (C).

See Chapter 4, p. 87. The substantially all test is essentially the same as the present test for the (C), except there is an exception that allows a tax-free distribution under Section 355. *See* Proposed Section 368(a) (4) (H).

(ii) the historic shareholders of the target corporation receive in exchange for the stock in the target corporation stock of the acquiring corporation (or stock of any acquiring parent) which stock satisfies the continuity of interest requirement; and

See Chapter 4, p. 74. In order to satisfy the continuity of interest requirement, 80% of the consideration, in essence, must be voting common stock of either the acquiring corporation or the acquiring parent. *See* Proposed Section 368(a) (4) (E).

(iii) the target corporation satisfies the distribution requirement as provided in paragraph (2) (G).

See Chapter 4, p. 74. This is the present liquidation requirement.

Section 368 (a) (1) (D) a transfer by a corporation of all or a part of its assets to another corporation if immediately after the transfer the transferor, or one or more of its shareholders (including persons who were shareholders immediately before the transfer), or any combination thereof, is in control of the corporation to which the assets are transferred; but only if, in pursuance of the plan, stock or securities of the corporation to which the assets are transferred are distributed in a transaction which qualifies under section 354, 355 or 356

Section 368(a) (1) (E) a recapitalization;

Section 368(a) (1) (F) a mere change in identity, form, or place of organization of one corporation, however effected; or

Section 368(a) (1) (G) a transfer by a corporation of all or part of its assets to another corporation in a title 11 or similar case; but only if, in pursuance of the plan, stock or securities of the corporation to which the assets are transferred are distributed in a transaction which qualifies under section 354, 355, or 356

Section 368(a) (2) SPECIAL RULES RELATING TO PARAGRAPH (1)

Section 368(a) (2) (A) REORGANIZATIONS DESCRIBED IN BOTH PARAGRAPH (1) (C) AND PARAGRAPH (1) (D).—If a transaction is described in both paragraph (1) (C) and paragraph (1) (D), then, for purposes of this subchapter (other than for purposes of subparagraph (C), such transaction shall be treated as described only in paragraph (1) (D))).

~~(B) ADDITIONAL CONSIDERATIONS IN CERTAIN PARAGRAPH (1) (C) CASES—IF~~

~~(i) one corporation acquires substantially all of the properties of another corporation;~~

~~(ii) the acquisition would qualify under paragraph (1) (C) but for the fact that the acquiring corporation exchanges money or other property in addition to voting stock; and~~

~~(iii) the acquiring corporation acquires, solely for voting stock described in paragraph (1) (C), property of the other corporation having a fair market value which is at least 80 percent of the fair market value of all of the property of the other corporation;~~

~~then such acquisition shall (subject to subparagraph (A) of this paragraph) be treated as qualifying under paragraph (1) (C). Solely for purposes of determining whether clause (ii) of the preceding sentence applies, the amount of any liability assumed by the acquiring corporation, and the amount of any liability to which any property acquired by the acquiring corporation is subject, shall be treated as money paid for the property.~~

Proposed Section 368(a) (2) (C) TRANSFERS OF ASSETS OR STOCK TO SUBSIDIARIES IN CERTAIN PARAGRAPH (1) (A), (1) (B), (1) (C) and (1) (G) CASES—A transaction otherwise qualifying under paragraph (1) (A), (1) (B) or (1) (C) shall not be disqualified by reason of the fact that part or all of the assets or stock which were acquired in the transaction ~~are transferred to a corporation controlled by the corporation acquiring such assets or stock.,~~ pursuant to regulations, by the acquiring corporation to another corporation that is in the same affiliated group, as defined in section 1504(a), as the acquiring corporation. A similar rule shall apply to a transaction otherwise qualifying under paragraph (1) (G) where the requirements of subparagraphs (A) and (B) of section 354(B) (1) are met with respect to the acquisition of assets.

See Chapter 4, p. 68. The boot relaxation rule for the (C) reorganization is not needed.

See Chapter 4, p. 83 and p. 90. The purpose of this amendment is to allow, pursuant to regulations, a push down or push up of the target's stock or assets to any corporation that is in the same affiliated group as the acquiring corporation.

(D) USE OF STOCK OF CONTROLLING CORPORATION IN PARAGRAPH (1) (A) AND (1) (G) CASES. The acquisition by one corporation, in exchange for stock of a corporation referred to in this subparagraph as "controlling corporation") which is in control of the acquiring corporation, of substantially all of the properties of another corporation shall not disqualify a transaction under paragraph (1) (A) or (1) (G) if—

(i) no stock of the acquiring corporation is used in the transaction, and

(ii) in the case of a transaction under paragraph (1) (A), such transaction would have qualified under paragraph (1) (A) had the merger been into the controlling corporation.

(E) STATUTORY MERGER USING VOTING STOCK OF CORPORATION CONTROLLING MERGED CORPORATION. A transaction otherwise qualifying under paragraph (1) (A) shall not be disqualified by reason of the fact that stock of a corporation (referred to in this subparagraph as the "controlling corporation") which before the merger was in control of the merged corporation is used in the transaction, if—

(i) after the transaction, the corporation surviving the merger holds substantially all of its properties and of the properties of the merged corporation (other than stock of the controlling corporation distributed in the transaction); and

(ii) in the transaction, former shareholders of the surviving corporation exchanged, for an amount of voting stock of the controlling corporation, an amount of stock in the surviving corporation which constitutes control of such corporation.

Section 368(a) (2) (F) CERTAIN TRANSACTIONS INVOLVING 2 OR MORE INVESTMENT COMPANIES—[NO CHANGE]

Section 368(a) (2) (G) DISTRIBUTION REQUIREMENT FOR PARAGRAPH (1) (C).—

(i) IN GENERAL.—A transaction shall fail to meet the requirements of paragraph (1) (C) unless the acquired target corporation distributes the stock, securities, and other properties it receives, as well as its other

See Chapter 4, p. 68. This forward subsidiary merger is encompassed by the Proposed (A) reorganization. There is no prohibition against the use of stock of the acquiring corporation as in the current Section 368(a) (2) (D). Because of the definition of party to a reorganization in Proposed Section 368(b), stock of the acquiring corporation qualifies for nonrecognition treatment under Section 354 and Section 361 even though the continuity of interest requirement is satisfied by stock of the acquiring parent. The reverse is not true. The substantially all test with modifications is retained. *See* Proposed Sections 368(a) (3) (G) and (H).

See Chapter 4, p. 68. This reverse subsidiary merger under Section 368(a) (2) (E) is encompassed by the Proposed (A). The substantially all test is retained; however the requirement under Treas Reg. § 1.368-2(j) (3) (i) that the target's shareholders surrender stock amounting to 80% control of the target in the transaction is eliminated. Thus, a reverse subsidiary merger transaction may qualify under the proposed (A) where the acquiring parent owns more than 20% of the target before the transaction.

The prohibition against reorganization involving certain investment companies is retained.

See Chapter 4, p. 74. This liquidation requirement for the current (C) reorganization applies also for the Proposed (C).

the preceding sentence, if the acquired target corporation is liquidated pursuant to the plan of reorganization, any distribution to its creditors in connection with such liquidation shall be treated as pursuant to the plan of reorganization.

(ii) EXCEPTION—The Secretary may waive the application of clause (i) to any transaction subject to any conditions the Secretary may prescribe.

Proposed Section 368(a) (2) (H). SPECIAL RULE FOR DETERMINING WHETHER CERTAIN TRANSACTIONS ARE QUALIFIED UNDER PARAGRAPH (1) (D)—In the case of any transaction with respect to which the requirements of subparagraphs (A) and (B) of Section 354(B) (1) are met, for purposes of determining whether such transaction qualifies under subparagraph (D) of paragraph (1), the term "control" has the meaning given to such term by section 304(c), and the transaction shall so qualify only if the shareholder or shareholders of the transferor corporation who are in such control of the transferee corporation were also in control, within the meaning of section 304(c), of the transferor corporation immediately before the transaction.

See Chapter 4, p. 86. The purpose of this amendment is to treat a transaction as a nondivisive (D) reorganization only if there is a 50% overlap in the ownership of the stock of the transferor and transferee corporations. This makes the nondivisive (D) consistent with the control requirement of Section 304.

Section 368(a) (3) ADDITIONAL RULES RELATING TO TITLE 11 AND SIMILAR CASES.—[NO CHANGE]

These rules are not changed.

Section 368(a) (4) DEFINITIONS AND SPECIAL REQUIREMENTS RELATING TO ACQUISITIVE REORGANIZATIONS—

Proposed Section 368(a) (4) (A) TARGET CORPORATION—The term "target corporation" means the corporation whose stock or assets are acquired in a transaction described in paragraph (1) (A), (1) (B) or (1) (C).

See Chapter 4, p. 70. This definition encompasses a target corporation that survives in a reverse subsidiary merger under current Section 368(a) (2) (E).

Propose Section 368(a) (4) (B) ACQUIRING CORPORATION—The term "acquiring corporation" means the corporation which as a result of a transaction described in paragraph (1) (A), (1) (B) or (1) (C) acquires either substantially all of the historic assets of the target corporation or

See Chapter 4, p. 70.

controls (as defined in subsection (c)) the target corporation. In the case of a consolidation under paragraph (1) (A), the acquiring corporation is the consolidated corporation whose shareholders own the greatest percentage of the stock of the resulting corporation.

Proposed Section 368(a) (4) (C) ACQUIRING PARENT—The term "acquiring parent" means a corporation that is in direct or indirect control, within the meaning of subsection (c), of the acquiring corporation. In determining whether the indirect control test is met the attribution rule of section 318(a) (2) (C) shall apply (substituting 80% for 50% as used therein).

See Chapter 4, p. 70. This definition of acquiring parent encompasses any upper tier corporation that is in a direct 80% chain that includes the acquiring corporation. Thus, the continuity of interest requirement can be satisfied with (1) stock of the acquiring corporation, (2) stock of the direct 80% parent of the acquiring corporation, or (3) stock of any indirect 80% upper tier parent of the acquiring corporation. Under the definition of party to the reorganization in Section 368(b), if the continuity of interest requirement is satisfied with respect to stock of the acquiring parent, then nonrecognition treatment is accorded under Sections 354 and 361 upon receipt of stock of the acquiring corporation. The reverse is not true.

Proposed Section 368(a) (4) (D) REVERSE ACQUISITION—If as a result of a transaction described in paragraph (1) (A), (1) (B) or (1) (C), the shareholders of the target corporation have control (within the meaning of section 304(c)) of the acquiring corporation or the acquiring parent, then for purposes of determining whether the transaction qualifies under paragraph (1) (A), (1) (B) or (1) (C), the nominal target corporation shall be treated as the acquiring corporation and the nominal acquiring corporation or acquiring parent shall be treated as the target corporation. The Treasury by regulations shall deal with situations in which both the target corporation's shareholders and the acquiring corporation's shareholders are in control of the acquiring corporation.

See Chapter 4, p. 83. This reverse acquisition rule prevents the circumvention of the continuity of interest requirement. The control test is that provided in Section 304(c) which means direct or indirect ownership of 50% of the stock. The Treasury by regulations will address situations in which the shareholders of both corporations are in control.

Proposed Section 368(a) (4) (E) CONTINUITY OF INTEREST REQUIREMENT—

(i) Basic 80% Requirement. The continuity of interest requirement for transactions described in paragraphs (1) (A), (1) (B) or (1) (C) is satisfied if as a result of the transaction the historic shareholders of the target corporation in the aggregate receive (and hold as specified below) in exchange for at least 80% of each class of stock of the target corporation either (1) stock of the acquiring corporation or stock of an acquiring parent, as the case may be, representing the underlying voting common stock of the acquiring corporation or the acquiring parent; or (II) pursuant to regulations, stock of the acquiring corporation or stock of the acquiring parent, as the case may be, with substantially similar terms to, or with greater equity features than, the stock of the target corporation surrendered. Pursuant to regulations, the class of stock requirement may be waived where it is otherwise clear that at least 80% of the consideration paid is the underlying voting stock of the acquiring corporation or of the acquiring parent.

(ii) The Holding Requirement. The historic shareholders are deemed to hold the requisite amount of stock of the acquiring corporation or acquiring parent provided such stock is received with unrestricted rights of ownership and without any preconceived plan or agreement for disposing of such requisite amount of stock.

Proposed Section 368(a) (4) (F) HISTORIC SHAREHOLDERS—

(i) Basic Rule. The term "historic shareholders" means the shareholders of each class of stock of the target corporation who have not acquired their shares pursuant to a plan or arrangement negotiated or agreed upon with the acquiring corporation (or a related party) prior to the transaction intended to qualify under paragraph (1) (A), (1) (B) or (1) (C).

(ii) Redemptions, etc. For purposes of determining the total number of shares held by historic shareholders, any shares redeemed pursuant to a

See Chapter 4, p. 68 and p. 76. This 80% test follows the current reverse subsidiary merger under Section 368(a) (2) (E). Voting common stock must be issued for voting common stock; however, pursuant to regulations preferred stock may be issued for preferred. Since there is a requirement, except as provided in regulations, that at least 80% of each class of the target's stock be exchanged for stock of the acquiring corporation or of the acquiring parent there should be no doubt that at least 80% of the consideration is stock. The unrestricted ownership requirement codifies McDonald's Restaurants of Illinois Inc. v. Comm., 688 F.2d 520 (7th Cir. 1982).

See chapter 4, p. 76, and p. 79. The purpose of Proposed Section 368(a) (4) (F) (i) is to codify the principle of Superior Coach of Florida, Inc. v. Commissioner, 60 TC 895 (1983). The purpose of Proposed Section 368(a) (4) (F) (ii) is to ensure that any shares of the target that are redeemed prior to the transaction, pursuant to an arrangement with the acquiror, are treated as if the historic shareholders continue to hold such shares. Thus, the amounts paid in redemption of such shares are treated as boot paid in the transaction.

plan or arrangement negotiated or agreed upon with the acquiring corporation (or related party) prior to the transaction intended to qualify under paragraph (1) (A), (1) (B) or (1) (C) shall be treated as outstanding and held by historic shareholders.

(iii) Effect of Incorporations. Historic shareholders shall include the owners of any shares received in exchange for the transfer of property to a corporation in a transaction governed by Section 351, provided such property constitutes the historic assets (as defined in subparagraph (H) below) of a trade or business that was actively conducted by such contributing shareholder or shareholders.

(iv) Bausch & Lomb Override. Pursuant to regulations, an acquiring corporation (or related party) that owns stock of a target corporation, which stock was acquired prior to the contemplation of the reorganization, may be considered as a historic shareholder for purposes of determining whether the continuity of interest requirement is satisfied. In such case, the acquiring corporation (or related party) shall for purposes of determining whether an asset reorganization under paragraph (1) (A) or (1) (C) satisfies the continuity of interest requirement of paragraph (4) (E) be treated as receiving in exchange for such stock of the target corporation, stock of the acquiring corporation or the acquiring parent of an equivalent value.

Proposed Section 368(a) (4) (G) SUBSTANTIALLY ALL OF THE HISTORIC ASSETS—The term "substantially all of the historic assets" means at least 90% of the fair market value of the net historic assets and 70% of the fair market value of the gross historic assets.

The purpose of Proposed Section 368(a) (4) (F) (iii) is to allow the continuity of interest requirement to be satisfied where individuals transfer a proprietorship or partnership or a corporation incorporates a division (see Chapter 4, p. 93). The purpose of Proposed Section 368 ((a) (4) (F) (iv) is to allow, pursuant to regulations, an acquiring corporation's (or related party's) stock ownership in the target corporation to be counted in determining whether the continuity of interest requirement is met. (See Chapter 4, p. 79.) Thus if, for example, the acquiring corporation has held for ten years before the acquisition 30% of the outstanding voting common stock of the target, which is the target's only outstanding class, then in order to satisfy the continuity of interest requirement applicable to the Proposed (A), (B) and (C), stock of the acquiring corporation or acquiring parent would only have to be issued for an additional 20% of the target's outstanding stock. The rule in the second sentence is intended to override the decision in Bausch & Lomb v. Commissioner, 267 F.2d 75 (2nd Cir, 1959). Thus, for example, if an acquiring corporation that is the historic shareholder with respect to at least 80% of the target's stock acquires substantially all of the target's assets, the transaction qualifies as a Proposed (C) reorganization without regard to the other consideration paid to the other shareholders. See also I.R.C. § 332.

See Chapter 4, p. 87. This codifies the 90%/70% test of Rev. Proc. 77-37 1977-2, C.B. 568.

Proposed Section 368(a) (4) (H) HISTORIC ASSETS—

(i) General Rule. The term "historic assets" means all assets that were held prior to the contemplation of a transaction described in paragraph (1) (A), (1) (B) or (1) (C).

(ii) Exception for Section 355 Distributions. In the case of a distribution governed by Section 355, the historic assets of the distributing corporation do not include either the stock of any controlled corporation or the assets contributed to such controlled corporation, and the historic assets of the controlled corporation include the assets held by it immediately before the distribution.

(iii) Exception for Section 351 Transfers. Historic assets shall include assets contributed to a target corporation in a transaction qualifying under Section 351, provided such assets constituted an active trade or business, within the meaning of Section 355(b) (2), in the hands of the transferor (or transferors) and such assets were not acquired by such transferor (or transferors) in contemplation of the transaction.

See Chapter 4, p. 87 and p. 92. Proposed Section 368(a) (4) (H) (i) makes clear that historic assets include all of assets held at the time the transaction is first contemplated by the parties. This codifies the rule of Rev Proc 77-37, 1977-2 C.B. 568, regarding pre-reorganization dispositions of property, but rejects the Service's position in Rev Rul 88-48, 1988-1 C.B. 117 which allowed a target, pursuant to a plan, to sell half of its assets for cash and then have the cash and other assets acquired in a (C) reorganization. Proposed Section 368(a) (4) (H) (ii) excludes from historic assets any assets disposed of by a distributing corporation in a transaction governed by Section 355. This overrules the principle of Helvering v. Elkhorn Coal Co., 95 F.2d 732 (4th Cir, 1937), but only with respect to Section 355 distributions that occur before an acquisitive reorganization. Proposed Section 368(a) (4) (H) (iii) allows the historic asset test to be satisfied where prior to an acquisitive reorganization an individual or individuals incorporate a proprietorship or a corporation incorporates a division.

Proposed Section 368(a) (4) (I) SPECIAL DISTRIBUTION RULE FOR SUBSIDIARY REORGANIZATION THAT COULD HAVE QUALIFIED UNDER SECTION 355—If in a reorganization described in paragraph (1) (A), (1) (B) or (1) (C) the target corporation is a controlled subsidiary (as defined in subparagraph (J)) and the parent corporation (as defined in subparagraph (K)) distributes all of the consideration received in the reorganization to one or more of its shareholders and security holders, then Section 361 shall apply to the parent corporation with respect to the distribution and Section 355 or 356 shall apply to the shareholders and security holders of the parent corporation with respect to the receipt of the consideration, provided that the transaction would have qualified under Section 355 and paragraph (1)

See Chapter 4, p. 93. The purpose of this provision is to allow a corporation to dispose of an active trade or business held by a subsidiary in an acquisitive reorganization and to distribute the consideration to the shareholders on a tax-free basis provided the transaction could have been structured first as a tax-free distribution under Section 355 and then as a tax-free acquisitive reorganization

(A), (1) (B) or (1) (C) if the transaction had been structured first as a distribution by the controlling parent of the stock and securities of the controlled subsidiary to one or more of shareholders and security holders of the common parent and after such distribution the acquiring corporation had acquired the stock or assets of the controlled subsidiary, pursuant to the independent decision of the shareholders of such subsidiary.

Proposed Section 368(a) (4) (J) CONTROLLED SUBSIDIARY—The term "controlled subsidiary" means a corporation, the stock of which is controlled within the meaning of subsection (c) by the parent corporation, as defined in subparagraph (K).

See Chapter 4, p. 93 . This term has significance only for purposes of the special distribution rule in Proposed Section 368(a) (4) (I).

Proposed Section 368(a) (4) (K) PARENT CORPORATION—The term "parent corporation" means a corporation that is in control within the meaning of subsection (c) of a controlled subsidiary.

See Chapter 4, p. 93. This term has significance only for purposes of the special distribution rule in Proposed Section 368(a) (4) (I).

Proposed Section 368(a) (4) (L) CONSISTENCY REQUIREMENT— Pursuant to regulations, any assets acquired by the acquiring corporation, or any member of an affiliated group of corporations, within the meaning of Section 1504, of which the acquiring corporation is a member, from the target corporation within the 12 month period prior to a reorganization described in paragraph (1) (A), (1) (B) or (1) (C) shall be considered to have been acquired in the reorganization.

See Chapter 4, p. 95. The purpose of this rule is to extend the consistency rules that apply in the Section 338 context of the reorganization provisions. As long as consistency is required in the Section 338 context it should also be required in the reorganization context. The Service has recently liberalized the consistency requirement under Section 338. See Prop Reg. § 1-338.

Proposed Section 368(a) (4) (M) CONTINUITY OF BUSINESS ENTERPRISE—In order to qualify as a reorganization under paragraph (1) (A), (1) (B) or (1) (C), the transaction must satisfy the continuity of business enterprise requirement as specified in regulations. Such regulations shall provide when and under what circumstances the continuity of business enterprise doctrine is satisfied in situations in which, pursuant to Section 368(a) (4) (H), historic assets are acquired by a corporation in a transaction governed by Section 351.

See Chapter 4, p. 91. With the application of the substantially all the historic assets test to each form of acquisitive reorganization, there is less need for a continuity of business enterprise doctrine; however, the doctrine serves a useful purpose in distinguishing a liquidation from a reorganization and should be retained. Also, the doctrine will block any attempted circumvention of the substantially all test.

Proposed Section 368(a)(4)(N) PRECEDENCE OF SECTION 368 OVER SECTION 351—Any transaction that, pursuant to regulations, fits the pattern of a reorganization under paragraph (1)(A), (1)(B) and (1)(C) may not qualify under Section 351.

See Chapter 4, p. 85. Section 351 should not apply to acquisitive corporate transactions because the provision can be used to undermine the continuity of interest requirement. This proposed rule returns to the original position taken by the Service in Rev Rul 80-284, 1980-2 C.B. 117 and Rev Rul 80-285, 1980-2 C.B. 117, and rejects the Service's position in Rev Rul 84-71, 1984-1 C.B. 106.

Proposed Section 368(a)(4)(O) SECTION 351 INCORPORATIONS PRIOR TO ACQUISITIVE REORGANIZATIONS—A transaction otherwise qualifying under Section 351 shall not fail to qualify under such section solely because after the transfer the transferee corporation is acquired in an acquisitive reorganization. This provision applies only to the transfer of assets that constitute an active trade or business, within the meaning of Section 355(b)(2), without regard to the five year period provided therein.

See Chapter 4, p. 92. This provision permits a newly incorporated corporation to be acquired in an acquisitive reorganization, provided the incorporated assets constitute an active trade or business. The provision overrides Rev Rul 70-140, 1970-1 C.B. 73.

Proposed Section 368(a)(4)(P) PREVENTION OF MISALLOCATION OF PURCHASE PRICE IN ACQUISITIVE REORGANIZATIONS—In the case of any payment, pursuant to a transaction intended to qualify under paragraph (1)(A), (1)(B) or (1)(C), to a shareholder of the target corporation made (or to be made) by or on behalf of the acquiring corporation, which payment is treated (or intended to be treated) by the payor as a deductible payment under section 162 as compensation for a covenant not to compete or similar arrangement (hereinafter referred to as a "deductible payment"), then the non-deductible amount, as determined in the next sentence, shall be treated as part of the consideration paid for the target corporation stock and not as a deductible payment under section 162. The "non-deductible amount" is an amount equal to the excess of (i) the present value, determined under the principles of section 1274(b)(2), of the deductible payments, over (ii) the average annual salary compensation received by such shareholder from the target

See Chapter 8, p. 122. The purpose of the first two sentences is to erect an absolute barrier to prevent avoidance of the continuity of interest requirement by having cash or other non-stock payments for stock disguised as payments for covenants not to compete or other similar payments. The purpose of the third sentence is to make it clear that even though a payment may not be recharacterized under this provision, such payment may nevertheless be treated as a payment for stock under the facts and circumstances test of current law. This provision is not intended to affect reasonable salaries paid for services actually rendered after an acquisition. A similar provision applies to taxable acquisitions under Proposed Section 368(a)(5)(H).

corporation (or any subsidiary corporation in the same affiliated group, determined under section 1504 as the target corporation) during the most recent 5 taxable years before the date of the reorganization. This provision shall not give rise to the presumption that any payments that are not non-deductible amounts are deductible under section 162.

Section 368(a) (5) SPECIAL RULES RELATING TO CERTAIN TAXABLE ACQUISITIONS THAT FAIL TO QUALIFY AS ACQUISITIVE REORGANIZATIONS BECAUSE OF A LACK OF CONTINUITY OF INTEREST

See Chapters 5, 6 and 7. Section 368(a) (5) contains rules relating to taxable acquisitions that could have qualified as acquisitive reorganizations if the continuity of interest requirement had been met.

Proposed Section 368(a) (5) (A) CARRYOVER BASIS FOR NON-QUALIFIED ASSET REORGANIZATION—If an asset acquisition of a noncontrolled corporation, as defined in paragraph (5) (B), would have qualified as a reorganization under paragraph (1) (A) or (1) (C) but for the fact that the continuity of interest requirement of paragraph (4) (E) is not satisfied, then unless a taxable election is made pursuant to paragraph (5) (D), (i) the noncontrolled corporation shall be deemed to have disposed of its assets in a transaction described in Section 361, and (ii) the acquiring corporation's basis for the assets of the noncontrolled corporation shall be determined under Section 362(b).

See Chapter 5 p. 100. This rule provides that if a merger or an asset acquisition of a noncontrolled target corporation fails to qualify as a reorganization solely because of a failure to satisfy the continuity of interest requirement, the target does not have recognition and the acquiring corporation takes a carryover basis for the target's assets, unless the parties elect taxable treatment. This allows a noncontrolled target to dispose of its assets for cash without recognizing gain, provided the other requirements for a Proposed (A) or (C) reorganization are satisfied. The target's shareholders have recognition because the transaction does not qualify as a reorganization.

Proposed Section 368(a) (5) (B) NONCONTROLLED CORPORATION—The term "noncontrolled corporation" means a corporation that is not a member (other than as a common parent corporation) of an affiliated group within the meaning of section 1504(a). However, pursuant to regulations, such term includes a member of an affiliated group of which a noncontrolled corporation that is the common parent of such group is a party to a transaction described in paragraph (5) (A).

See Chapter 5, p. 100. This definition of a noncontrolled corporation allows the carryover basis acquisition rules to apply only to acquisitions of non-subsidiary corporations. This definition prevents, for example, multiple sales of corporations within a single affiliated group in carryover basis acquisitions. However, pursuant to the second sentence, under regulations, if a parent noncontrolled corporation is a party to a carryover basis transaction described in Proposed

268

Section 368(a) (5) (A), then a contemporaneous asset acquisition of a subsidiary of the parent also qualifies for carryover basis treatment in the transaction.

Proposed Section 368(a) (5) (C) CONSISTENCY REQUIREMENT— Pursuant to regulations, any asset acquired by the acquiring corporation or any member of an affiliated group of corporations, within the meaning of section 1504 (a), of which the acquiring corporation is a member, from the target corporation within the 12 month period prior to the carryover basis transaction described in paragraph (5) (A) shall be considered to have been acquired in such a carryover basis transaction.

See Chapter 5, p. 100. This consistency requirement is similar to the one in Proposed Section 368(a) (4) (L) that applies to reorganizations.

Proposed Section 368(a) (5) (D) TAXABLE ELECTION— Pursuant to regulations, a taxable election for a non-qualified asset acquisition under paragraph (5) (A) is made by the acquiring corporation in a transaction meeting the pattern described in paragraph (1) (A) and by the acquiring corporation and the noncontrolled corporation in a transaction meeting the pattern described in paragraph (1) (C).

See Chapter 5, p. 100 . This election has significance only for the rule governing carryover basis non-qualified asset reorganizations in Proposed Section 368(a) (5) (A). If the taxable election is made the target is subject to tax on the transfer of its assets, except with respect to goodwill as provided in Proposed Section 368(a) (5) (E), and the acquiring corporation takes a cost basis for the target's assets, including goodwill. A special rule applies if an amortization deduction is ever allowed for goodwill. *See* Chapter 6.

Proposed Section 368(a) (5) (E) EFFECT OF A TAXABLE ELECTION: TREATMENT OF GOODWILL—

(i) General Rule. If a taxable election is made, the noncontrolled corporation, as defined in paragraph (5) (B), shall be treated as having sold its assets in a taxable transaction and the acquiring corporation shall be treated as having acquired such assets in a taxable acquisition.

See Chapter 5, p. 100. Proposed Section 368(a) (5) (E) (i) permits the parties to elect taxable treatment rather than carryover basis treatment in nonreorganization asset acquisitions.

(ii) Exception for Goodwill. If the transaction could have qualified for carryover basis treatment under section 368(a) (5) (A) in the absence of a taxable election, the noncontrolled corporation shall not recognize gain with respect to its sale or exchange of goodwill or similar nonamortizable intangibles, provided that, pursuant to regulations, the noncontrolled

See Chapter 6, p. 110. Under Proposed Section 368(a) (5) (E) (ii) a stand-alone target (or pursuant to regulations, its subsidiary) is not taxed on a sale of goodwill or other nonamortizable intangible, provided (i) the transaction would have qualified for

corporation and acquiring corporation enter into an allocation agreement with respect to all transferred assets and the acquiring corporation agrees not to deduct under section 162, or otherwise, any amounts allocated to goodwill or other nonamortizable intangibles. Pursuant to regulations, such nonrecognition treatment for goodwill shall also apply to any corporation that is a member of the noncontrolled corporation's affiliated group of corporations, as defined in section 1504(a).

See Chapter 6, p. 112.

reorganization treatment if the continuity of interest requirement were satisfied, (ii) the parties enter into an appropriate allocation agreement, and (iii) the acquiring corporation agrees not to deduct any amounts allocated to the goodwill or other nonamortizable intangible. A special rule applies if an amortization deduction is ever allowed for goodwill. *See* Chapter 6, p. 112.

Section 368(a) (5) (F) EFFECT ON GOODWILL OF SECTION 338 ELECTION AFTER AN OTHERWISE QUALIFYING STOCK REORGANIZATION—If a stock acquisition of a noncontrolled corporation (as defined in paragraph (5) (B)) would have qualified under paragraph (1) (A) or (1) (B) but for the fact that the continuity of interest requirement is not satisfied, and the acquiring corporation makes a section 338 election with respect to the noncontrolled corporation, the noncontrolled corporation (and, pursuant to regulations, any member of its affiliated group, within the meaning of section 1504(a)) shall not recognize gain with respect to the deemed sale under section 338(a) by it of goodwill or similar nonamortizable intangible provided that, pursuant to regulations, both the acquiring corporation and the noncontrolled corporation agree not to deduct under section 162, or otherwise, any amounts allocable to goodwill or other nonamortizable intangible.

See Chapter 6, p. 110. Under this provision, a target corporation (and pursuant to regulations any subsidiary) does not recognize gain on the constructive sale of goodwill as a result of a Section 338 election provided the transaction would have qualified as a reorganization if the continuity of interest test had been satisfied. A special rule applies if an amortization deduction is ever allowed for goodwill.

Proposed Section 368(a) (5) (G) TREATMENT OF GOODWILL IN CERTAIN LIQUIDATING DISTRIBUTIONS—The Secretary is authorized, pursuant to regulations, to provide for nonrecognition treatment upon the liquidating distribution of goodwill and similar items. Such nonrecognition treatment shall be consistent with the purposes of paragraphs (5) (E) and (5) (F).

See Chapter 6, p. 110. This authorizes the Secretary to override the recognition rule of Section 336 for certain liquidating distributions of goodwill. A special rule applies if an amortization deduction is ever allowed for goodwill. *See* Chapter 6, p. 112.

Proposed Section 368(a) (5) (H) PREVENTION OF MISALLOCATION OF PURCHASE PRICE IN TAXABLE ACQUISITIONS—Rules similar to the rules of paragraph (4) (P) regarding prevention of misallocation of

See Chapter 8, p. 122. This provision is similar to the one in Proposed Section 368(a) (4) (P), which applies to acquisitive reorganizations.

purchase price in acquisitive reorganizations, shall, pursuant to regulations, apply in the case of the acquisition by any person or persons of (i) control as defined in section 304(c) of a corporation, or (ii) a major portion of a corporation's assets.

Proposed Section 368(a) (5) (I) MANDATORY SECTION 338 ELECTION FOR STOCK ACQUISITIONS WHEN TARGET DOES NOT HOLD SUBSTANTIALLY ALL OF ITS ASSETS — If the stock of a noncontrolled corporation, as defined in paragraph (5) (B), is acquired in a qualified stock purchase, as defined in section 338(d), and such purchase did not qualify under paragraph (1) (A) or (1) (B) because the substantially all requirement of paragraph (4) (G) is not satisfied (without regard to whether the continuity of interests requirement of paragraph (4) (E) is satisfied), then the purchasing corporation, as defined in section 338 (d) (1), shall be deemed to have made an election under section 338 (g) with respect to such noncontrolled corporation.

~~Proposed Section 368(b) PARTY TO A REORGANIZATION—For purposes of this part, the term "a party to a reorganization" includes—~~

~~(1) a corporation resulting from a reorganization, and~~

~~(2) both corporations, in the case of a reorganization resulting from the acquisition by one corporation of stock or properties of another.~~

~~In the case of a reorganization qualifying under paragraph (1) (B) or (1) (C) of subsection (a), if the stock exchanged for the stock or properties is stock of a corporation which is in control of the acquiring corporation, the term "a party to a reorganization" includes the corporation so controlling the acquiring corporation. In the case of a reorganization qualifying under paragraph (1) (A), (1) (B), (1) (C) or (1) (C) of subsection (a) by reason of paragraph (2) (C) of subsection (A), the term "a party to a reorganization" includes the corporation controlling the corporation to which the acquired assets or stock are transferred. In the case of a reorganization qualifying under paragraph (1) (A) or (1) (C) of~~

See Chapter 7, p. 119. The purpose of this provision is to prevent the use of stock acquisitions to obtain a carryover basis for a target's assets in a situation where, pursuant to the transaction, the target has disposed of a significant portion of its assets in another transaction. Thus, a carryover basis is available in a taxable stock acquisition only in situations in which the target holds substantially all of its assets.

See Chapter 4, p. 78. Section 368(b) (1) and (2) are retained in the Proposed Section 368(b) set out below; however, the flush language, which deals with various forms of triangular reorganizations, is revised.

subsection (a) by reason of paragraph (2) (D) of that subsection, the term "a party to a reorganization" includes the controlling corporation referred to in such paragraph (2) (D). In the case of a reorganization qualifying under subsection (a) (1) (A) by reason of subsection (a) (2) (E), the term "party to a reorganization" includes the controlling corporation referred to in subsection (a) (2) (E).

Section 368(b) PARTY TO A REORGANIZATION—For purposes of this part, the term "a party to a reorganization" includes:

(1) a corporation resulting from a reorganization, and

(2) both corporations, in the case of a reorganization resulting from the acquisition by one corporation of stock or properties of another.

In the case of a reorganization qualifying under paragraph (1) (A), (1) (B) or (1) (C) of subsection (a), if the stock exchanged for the stock or properties is stock of an acquiring parent (as defined in subsection (a) (4) (C)), and such stock satisfies the continuity of interest requirement, the term "a party to a reorganization" includes the acquiring parent. In the case of a reorganization qualifying under paragraph (1) (A), (1) (B), (1) (C) or (1) (G) of subsection (a) by reason of paragraph (2) (C) of subsection (a), the term "a party to a reorganization" includes the corporation controlling directly or indirectly the corporation to which the acquired assets or stock are transferred.

See Chapter 4, p. 78. This proposed definition of the term "a party to a reorganization" allows tax-free treatment under Section 354 and Section 361(a) upon receipt of stock or securities of an acquiring parent only when the stock of the acquiring parent satisfies the continuity of interest requirement. *See* proposed Section 368(a) (4) (E). If the continuity of interest requirement is satisfied with respect to the stock of an acquiring parent, nonrecognition also applies under Section 354 and Section 361(a) on receipt of stock of the acquiring corporation. The reverse is not true.

Section 368(c) CONTROL DEFINED—For purposes of part I (other than section 304), part II, this part, and part V, the term "control" means the ownership of stock possessing at least 80 percent of the total combined voting power of all classes of stock entitled to vote and at least 80 percent of the total number of shares of all other classes of stock of the corporation. Pursuant to regulations, this requirement may be eliminated or modified to make it consistent with the continuity of interest requirement of section 368(a) (4) (E).

See Chapter 4, p. 73.

Amendments to Section 163

	Comments
Proposed Section 163(k). Extraordinary Dividends and Redemptions. In the case of a publicly held corporation, as defined in subsection (m), no deduction shall be allowed to such corporation (or to any member of such corporation's affiliated group within the meaning of section 1504 (a)) for interest paid or accrued on a debt instrument that is issued with respect to stock in such corporation, except for debt that is issued for the purpose of making an ordinary redemption of the stock of the corporation. The Treasury shall promulgate regulations delineating the meaning of ordinary redemption.	*See* Chapter 12, p. 173. This provision, which applies only to publicly held corporations, disallows the interest on debt issued to the shareholders of a corporation in a dividend or extraordinary redemption. Thus, this provision would apply to disallow the deduction on the debt issued in the Unocal redemption. The regulations implementing this limitation are to exclude ordinary redemptions, such as the purchase by a corporation of the stock of a retiring shareholder.
Proposed Section 163(l). Ordinary Dividends and Redemptions. In the case of a publicly held corporation, as defined in subsection (m), no deduction shall be allowed to such corporation (or any member of such corporation's affiliated group within the meaning of section 1504(a)) for interest paid or accrued on a debt instrument that is directly or indirectly issued for the purpose of raising funds in order to make a distribution (whether by way of redemption or dividend or otherwise) with respect to the stock in such corporation, except for debt that is issued for the purpose of (1) making in cash an ordinary redemption of the stock of the corporation, or (2) paying in cash an ordinary dividend in respect of the stock of the corporation. The Treasury shall promulgate regulations delineating the meaning of the terms ordinary dividend and ordinary redemption and setting forth rules for determining whether debt is issued "directly or indirectly" for the proscribed purpose.	*See* Chapter 12, p. 173. Under this provision, which applies only to publicly held corporations, the limitation on the deductibility of interest does not apply to debt issued to raise cash for the purpose of making an ordinary dividend or ordinary redemption. Thus, although under Proposed Section 163(k), deductible debt cannot be issued in an ordinary dividend, under Proposed Section 163(1), deductible debt may be issued to raise the cash to pay an ordinary dividend.
Proposed Section 163(m). Definition of Publicly Held Corporation. A publicly held corporation means a corporation with more than 35 shareholders determined under the principles of Regulation D under the Securities Act of 1933. The Treasury is authorized to promulgate regulations (1) dealing with the determination of the number of shareholders, and (2) relaxing the 35 shareholder limitation in appropriate circumstances.	*See* Chapter 12, p. 171, which sets forth the rationale of this definition.

APPENDIX D

Amendments to Section 279

	Comments
Proposed Section 279. (a) General Rule. No deduction shall be allowed for interest paid or accrued with respect to the principal of corporate acquisition indebtedness that is treated as excessive debt or as junk debt.	See Chapter 12, p. 175. Under this general rule interest is disallowed on corporate acquisition indebtedness as defined in Proposed § 279(b) that is excessive debt, as defined in Proposed § 279(c), or junk debt, as defined in Proposed § 279(d).
(b) Corporate Acquisition Indebtedness. Corporate acquisition indebtedness is indebtedness issued directly or indirectly by a corporation or any members of such corporation's affiliated group (as defined in Section 1504(a)) for the purpose of acquiring (1) more than 5% of any class of stock of a publicly held corporation, as defined in section 163(m), or (2) substantially all (applying the 90%/70% test of section 368 (a) (4) (G)) of the assets of a publicly held corporation, as defined in Section 163(m). The Treasury shall promulgate regulations setting forth rules for determining whether debt is issued "directly or indirectly" for the proscribed purpose. The Treasury may by regulations exempt from this section acquisitions of stock made solely for investment purposes.	*See* Chapter 12, p. 175. The limitation only applies to corporate acquisition debt which is debt issued for the purpose of acquiring either (1) more than 5% of the stock of a publicly held corporation, or (2) substantially all of the assets of a publicly held corporation. The "indirectly" concept encompasses *inter alia* (1) debt issued to raise equity (*i.e.*, equity loans); (2) debt issued to refinance corporate acquisition indebtedness or to replace equity used in such an acquisition, and (3) any assumed debt that was incurred in anticipation of the transaction.
(c) Excessive Debt. Excessive debt is that portion of the principal on any corporate acquisition indebtedness that exceeds 75% of the purchase price of either the stock or assets purchased with such corporate acquisition indebtedness. In determining the amount of excessive debt, the principal amount of any debt that is treated as junk debt under subsection (d) shall be treated as equity.	*See* Chapter 12, p. 175. Under this paragraph, if nonjunk corporate acquisition indebtedness exceeds 75% of the purchase price of the stock or assets, then the interest on the excess debt is not deductible under Proposed § 279(a). This ensures that there will be a significant amount of equity that is at risk in an acquisition.

(d) Junk Debt. Junk debt is the portion of the principal of any corporate acquisition indebtedness specified in the following paragraphs:

(1) Excessive Maturity. If the average weighted life (determined under regulations) at the time of issuance of corporate acquisition indebtedness exceeds 10 years, then the entire principal of such corporate acquisition indebtedness shall be treated as junk debt.

(2) Minimum Interest Paid Currently. If the interest on corporate acquisition indebtedness that is contractually payable currently (as determined under regulations) is at any time during the term of such instrument less than the applicable federal rate (determined under section 1274) at the time such instrument is issued, then the entire principal of such instrument shall be treated as junk debt.

(3) Convertible Instruments. In the case of corporate acquisition indebtedness that is directly or indirectly convertible into stock of the issuer (or of another member of the issuer's affiliated group as defined in section 1504 (a)), if the interest that is contractually payable currently (as determined under regulations) is at any time during the term of such instrument less than 90% of the applicable federal rate (determined under section 1274) at the time such instrument is issued, then the entire principal amount of such corporate acquisition indebtedness shall be treated as junk debt.

(4) High Yield. If, at the time of issuance, the yield to maturity (determined under section 1274) of any corporate acquisition indebtedness exceeds an amount equal to the average yield to maturity on bonds with an equivalent maturity that are rated Baa by Moody's Investor Service (or are similarly rated by a rating agency of equivalent standing), then the portion of the principal that is under regulations attributable to the excess interest shall be treated as junk debt. The Secretary shall determine monthly the average yield to maturity on bonds rated Baa for various maturity periods. Such determinations shall be consistent with the provisions governing the determination of the applicable federal rate under section 1274 (d).

See Chapter 12, pp. 179–83. Proposed § 279(d) defines junk debt. Under Proposed § 279(d)(1), (2) and (3) the entire principal is treated as junk debt, and, therefore, all the interest on such debt is disallowed under Proposed § 279(a). Under Proposed § 279(d)(4), (5) and (6) only the portion of the principal on the corporate acquisition debt that is attributable to equity like payments is treated as junk debt, and therefore, the interest with respect to such principal is disallowed under Proposed § 279(a).

275

(5) Contingent Interest. If the payment of interest on any corporate acquisition indebtedness is in any way contingent on earnings, performance, or any similar factor, then the portion of the principal that is under regulations attributable to the contingent interest shall be treated as junk debt.

(6) Payments in Kind. If the interest on any corporate acquisition indebtedness is paid or possibly payable in stock or securities of the issuer, then the portion of the principal of such corporate acquisition indebtedness that is under regulations attributable to the stock or securities shall be treated as junk debt.

(e) Regulatory Authority. The Secretary shall promulgate such regulations as may be necessary to carry out the purposes of this section, including regulations to ensure that foreign corporations do not directly or indirectly avoid the purposes embodied in this section.

See Chapter 12, pp. 175 and 186. This provision gives the Treasury broad regulatory authority under this section, including the authority to promulgate regulations that are designed to prevent foreign acquiring corporations from avoiding the interest limitation rules in this Proposed Section 279.

276

Index